Great American Sitcoms
of the 1950s

# Great American Sitcoms of the 1950s

*How Lucy, Bilko, Peepers, Gracie and Others Defined a Television Genre*

Jackson Upperco

McFarland & Company, Inc., Publishers
*Jefferson, North Carolina*

LIBRARY OF CONGRESS CATALOGUING-IN-PUBLICATION DATA

Names: Upperco, Jackson, 1994– author.
Title: Great American sitcoms of the 1950s : how Lucy, Bilko, Peepers, Gracie and others defined a television genre / Jackson Upperco.
Description: Jefferson, North Carolina : McFarland & Company, Inc., Publishers, 2025 | Includes bibliographical references and index.
Identifiers: LCCN 2024059961 | ISBN 9781476691046 (paperback : acid free paper) ∞
ISBN 9781476653945 (ebook)
Subjects: LCSH: Situation comedies (Television programs)—United States—History and criticism | Nineteen fifties.
Classification: LCC PN1992.8.C66 U67 2025 | DDC 791.45/617097309045—dc23/eng/20250118
LC record available at https://lccn.loc.gov/2024059961

**ISBN (print) 978-1-4766-9104-6**
**ISBN (ebook) 978-1-4766-5394-5**

© 2025 Jackson Upperco. All rights reserved

*No part of this book may be reproduced or transmitted in any form or by any means, electronic or mechanical, including photocopying or recording, or by any information storage and retrieval system, without permission in writing from the publisher.*

Front cover images: Phil Silvers as Sergeant Bilko (Milburn McCarty Associates); television set (Adobe Firefly)

Printed in the United States of America

*McFarland & Company, Inc., Publishers*
*Box 611, Jefferson, North Carolina 28640*
*www.mcfarlandpub.com*

# Contents

| | |
|---|---|
| *Introduction* | 1 |
| **Part I: The Sitcom's Evolution from Radio to the Small Screen** | 7 |
| One. From Aristotle to Benny: Defining the Situation Comedy | 9 |
| Two. The Prehistoric Era: The Television Sitcom of the 1940s | 25 |
| **Part II: Top Sitcoms and Episodes** | 35 |
| Three. Somewhere Between Radio and Film: The Best Television Sitcoms of 1950–1951 | 37 |
| Four. TV's First Great Situation Comedy: The Best Television Sitcoms of 1951–1952 | 59 |
| Five. Like Lucy: The Best Television Sitcoms of 1952–1953 | 86 |
| Six. (Still) Like Lucy: The Best Television Sitcoms of 1953–1954 | 116 |
| Seven. The Sitcom Boom: The Best Television Sitcoms of 1954–1955 | 140 |
| Eight. The Golden Age: The Best Television Sitcoms of 1955–1956 | 166 |
| Nine. The End of the Beginning: The Best Television Sitcoms of 1956–1957 | 197 |
| Ten. Where's Lucy? The Best Television Sitcoms of 1957–1958 | 215 |
| Eleven. The Sitcom Drought: The Best Television Sitcoms of 1958–1959 | 234 |
| Twelve. Back to Basics: The Best Television Sitcoms of 1959–1960 | 248 |
| *Conclusion. The Genre That Doesn't Die: Television Sitcoms After the 1950s* | 266 |
| *Appendix A. Writers of Top 50 1950s Sitcom Episodes* | 271 |
| *Appendix B. Shows Officially Released on DVD and/or Streaming* | 275 |
| *Chapter Notes* | 277 |
| *Bibliography* | 285 |
| *Index* | 287 |

v

# Introduction

The situation comedy is an art form. The comedy is the art; the situation is the form. In this book, I will be examining some of the best samples that prove the genre's artistry, focusing on the 1950s, the sitcom's first full decade in the medium where it would thrive: television.

While most histories of the sitcom, and television as a whole, have tended to argue that the worth of its content is confined to its function as a tool for cultural study, I will be taking a different approach, for although, yes, every broadcast is a time capsule that transports its viewer back to a specific time and place, if we derive merit primarily from this external context, then we are inevitably undermining any notion of *intrinsic* value. That is, the idea that the situation comedy is only worthy of study because it reflects society is limiting; it is also worthy of study because, like all art forms, and particularly dramatic forms, it is also a craft that takes considerable talent and skill. The situation comedy deserves to be examined, then, for the same reason, say, Elizabethan drama does: some of these examples are great works of art. And while a basic awareness of the twentieth century's cultural evolution will be seminal to any study of this genre because all comedy is hinged on a shared acceptance of social mores and thus evolves in tandem with its audience, my interest here is always greater: I care about the art form itself.

So, to study situation comedy for this book, we will have to establish a basic definition of it, as it's otherwise a nebulous term with malleable parameters. What exactly is a sitcom? We will discuss this in Chapter One, charting the history of the phrase before settling on an understanding that will inform the rhetorical framework I use in my forthcoming exploration of the genre's trajectory when seeking its finest and most illustrative examples. To define the genre, we will have to break "situation comedy" in half. The situation will come to refer to everything that has been preestablished as fodder for the weekly story and, particularly, the regular characters to whom viewers can attach a sustained identification. Comedy, meanwhile, is the more ethereal element—an intellectual and visceral phenomenon that philosophers are still trying to explain. In fact, there are many theories about what comedy is—and, specifically, why we laugh. This book is not going to go into all of them, but I favor what seems the simplest explanation: the idea that laughs come from a "benign incongruity." We will discuss what that means soon. And once we settle on a definition—with help from old Aristotle—we can work around the inherent subjectivity of comedy by at least recognizing how/if certain works are *trying* to be funny, to understand why the pursuit of humor through narrative is worthy of being called art.

From there, we will pair the two words to crystallize a view of the sitcom— series that use the preestablished elements of a "situation" in episodic narratives for the kind of "benign incongruity" that aims for laughter, the sign of successful comedy. This will then create the focus of our analysis, as we go through the best examples from the 1950s, examining the shows, and the individual episodes in support, that most skillfully live up to our definition of situation comedy, validating the notion that it is an art form. Like many written studies of dramatic, performed works, this will be a largely text-based approach. Although we have elements of production and performance to consider, the situation comedy is, at its core, a type of narrative fiction. And as with all narrative fiction, the elements that most guarantee success begin on the page. So the presentation of a text *has* to be our focus. And with me as your guide, this view makes sense.

Let me introduce myself. My name is Jackson Upperco, and I am a theater nerd whose love of television developed as an extension of this fascination with performed humanity. I cannot tell you exactly when my obsession with classic sitcoms started, but I do know I had a *Gilligan's Island* birthday party at nine (and again at 12), a *Bewitched* party at 10, and a six-hour classic sitcom fest at 19, when I made my friends screen 12 of my favorite episodes from the 1950s to the early 2000s— including gems like *The Mary Tyler Moore Show*'s "Chuckles Bites the Dust" (1975) and *Everybody Loves Raymond*'s "The Angry Family" (2001). I started writing sitcom pilots about my friends for fun when I was in fifth grade and followed this path until I went on to earn a bachelor of science degree in film and television at Boston University. During my time at college, I started a blog about all my entertainment interests, specifically sitcoms. It is called THAT'S ENTERTAINMENT, and you can visit it today at http://jacksonupperco.com.

Eleven years later, I still publish new posts every week on THAT'S ENTERTAINMENT! In fact, by the end of 2024, I had analyzed over 20,000 original sitcom episodes, about 18,000 of which I specifically watched for discussion on the blog, where I have examined over 100 different series, offering season-by-season commentary that also seeks, like this book, to find the best episodes to represent each season. Nobody does this like me, with a critical text-based approach to sitcom analysis that has spawned its own terminology, and a guiding theory that I will delve into more during ensuing chapters: the split between idea-driven sitcoms and character-driven sitcoms. All this work on my blog, and the resulting career opportunities, have also been made possible because of my expansive personal collection of sitcoms, a hobby that began when I was in middle school—eager to get that next season of *I Love Lucy* on DVD—but has now become a life's purpose, with hundreds of shows screened and contemplated.

Additionally, my career has been boosted by the fact that I was fortunate to study writing for screen and television at USC's prestigious cinema school, learning from—and even working with—titans of the industry, with credits on *M\*A\*S\*H, Laverne & Shirley, Cheers, The Golden Girls, Frasier, Will & Grace*, and more. My knowledge of the genre has refined tremendously since my time at USC, aided by these experiences studying it in an esteemed MFA program, and then actually writing it alongside some of the best in the business—folks who have elevated the art form. Their mentorship has been invaluable, and this book is largely a testament to them.

A professor at USC once told me it takes 10,000 hours to become a master at something. Well, I have now spent more than 10,000 hours watching sitcoms and even more time talking about the genre in a constructional, analytical context. At this point, and with all due humility, I am comfortable saying that I am, on these terms, an expert. And if there is any doubt about it now, I think this book, which takes seriously the text of sitcoms the way scholars have long examined great theatrical tragedies, will validate your respect for me and the art form to which I've dedicated my career. If you disagree with my thoughts on the subjective notions of comedy or, even more broadly, about whether shows deserve favorable attention based on our understanding of the genre—and you inevitably *will* disagree with me—my hope is that you can at least be sure that my opinion is well informed, and you can see how I reached my conclusions. As for my definition of situation comedy, it will be the cornerstone for how we determine what is worthy of consideration in this genre, with the simplest tenet being a projected or professed interest in the elements of comedy as opposed to "drama." In this regard, any narrative series that is linked or seeks to link itself primarily to this goal (wanting to be funny) can be considered here.

However, I have to set a few parameters. First, I am only discussing American shows. This is not only for the sake of focus but also because the art form really arose from American culture and deserves this specific affiliation. Additionally, the British understanding of situation comedy is different from ours, largely because there are fewer episodes produced per season, and this changes the burden placed on the "situation" to inspire weekly story in pursuit of comedy. Thus, "Britcoms" are not a completely fair point of textual comparison to American efforts.

Also, as indicated, this book is focusing on the 1950s. That means, specifically, all TV seasons between and including 1950–1951 and 1959–1960. While early chapters will examine the genre's genesis from radio and how it existed on television in the 1940s, in terms of the episodic samples I will be highlighting as proof of the situation comedy's artistic merit, we will begin in Chapter Three by exploring 1950–1951, with each chapter following one whole season's worth of shows. With regard to the calendar demarcations, I am going to be flexible, but generally, every new season starts around late September or early October and ends a whole year later. That means, yes, we will be talking about episodes that aired in 1960 to demonstrate trends from 1959 to 1960.

However, covering the 1950s is a daunting prospect because so much of the television from this era is currently unviewable. So much of its programming was live and not preserved, while many of the shows that were filmed have been locked away in various archives—unavailable even to the experts (let alone casual viewers). For that reason, I am not pretending that this book is going to study or address *every single sitcom* or sitcom episode from the 1950s. That is impossible. And I have not tried to view everything, for I know it is impossible. Heck, factoring in rare, short-lived programs that aired for a few weeks in local markets, it would be foolish for anyone to even pretend he could accurately count and list every single sitcom from the early 1950s. Even encyclopedias—of which there are great ones that I can also recommend—end up with blind spots. So instead, I have used my expertise—which has led me to screen nearly 4,000 individual sitcom episodes from the 1950s alone (significantly more than the average consumer)—to intelligently discern what is important, both for my own viewing and for discussion in this book.

To that point, while I cannot claim to present "*the* best" of the 1950s if not all of the 1950s is available, I am comfortable saying that the best of the 1950s, based on what *I* have seen, is almost comparable, considering my expertise and the strength of the ideas presented here, particularly for my top 50 list, which we will be tracking throughout the course of this book.

Last, while a basic understanding of the 1950s is required to appreciate its entertainments (as they are historical artifacts reflective of the social mores of their era)—and this text assumes a person interested in this subject already has a basic understanding of the period—I hope this book can be useful to readers with all different levels of awareness about the specific shows discussed. My goal is that everyone who reads this is able to seek out if not *every* sitcom that comes up, then at least the majority of the 50 episodes I highlight as great examples of the genre. In fact, the average consumer's ability to buy a show on DVD, stream it, or even locate it on YouTube (uploaded by someone who got the series on the so-called gray market) is a major factor that I kept in the back of my mind throughout this writing process. As best I could, I tried to ensure that you could go out and watch for yourself what I examined. There are only a few exceptions.

Fortunately, though, the most artistically worthwhile shows, and the most influential to the development and trajectory of the genre, have tended to stay more visible because of their popularity and influence. Like *Romeo and Juliet* or *Twelfth Night*, there are situation comedies from the 1950s that human beings will be studying and referencing for centuries to come. In this book, we will look seriously at why these classic shows remain so aesthetically pleasing as works of performed narrative fiction. And, yes, to confirm—this is the most serious book you will ever read about shows that endeavor to be taken unseriously. But unserious is not synonymous with unworthy, and that is precisely why this examination *must* be so studious: we are making up for lost time. With comedy perennially undervalued—treated as a lesser, baser form of the Dramatic—and any "situation" a difficult concept to satisfy regularly in story, there are a lot of bad sitcoms out there that make the genre seem undeserving of being called an art form. Heck, *most* sitcoms are bad. Yet that is not because the genre itself is bad. It's because greatness, by definition, must be rare. So it is about time someone focused on the best of the best—and explained *why* they are the best—to prove, once and for all, that the situation comedy at its most ideal is ridiculously beautiful or beautifully ridiculous. Either way, it's an art form that should be respected.

PART I

# The Sitcom's Evolution from Radio to the Small Screen

CHAPTER ONE

# From Aristotle to Benny

*Defining the Situation Comedy*

There is no universally agreed-on definition of the situation comedy—just a set of conventions to which a collection of television shows have adhered since nearly the medium's inception. Today, we use the term in reference to an entire genre of programming—the situation comedy, or "sitcom," the latter of which was said colloquially throughout the 1950s but didn't find formal acceptance as a dictionary-affirmed word until the early 1960s.[1] The relative newness of that portmanteau should not be surprising. "Situation comedy" itself had only developed into a genre in the early 1940s, when many half-hour radio comedies were combining selected aspects of various types of programming into one specifically new, unique set of principles. The term, though, goes back even further. Prior to "situation comedy" emerging as a radio genre in the 1940s, the words were paired together casually (and sparingly) in reference to a *type* of comedy—exhibited in plays, movies, and eventually programs at the dawn of network radio.

However, before we truly chart the development of the term, we have to start with something more basic, for my thesis is that the situation comedy is an art form—with comedy being the art and the situation defining the form. Discussing terminology will explain the form, but it already takes for granted the belief that comedy is an art. So that's where we have to start—comedy. First of all, what is comedy? Both as a genre and as a principle, humor has long been an elusive subject, yielding centuries of philosophical debate and scientific research. This book is not about exploring the many theories of comedy—it would take thousands of words, and we would never get to talk about sitcoms of the 1950s—but we do need a basic, shared understanding.

Let's go back to the beginning: ancient Greece, from whence the word "comedy" can be traced. In a reverse of how "situation comedy" started as a broad description and developed into a specific genre, comedy in Greece began as a specific genre. To the Greeks, comedy was a type of oral poetry, represented best in Drama—a word I capitalize because, in its initial Greek definition, Drama meant poetry acted out in live performance.[2] Today we basically call that theater. It really has only been within the last several hundred years, when "comedy" itself was stretched beyond just a genre to become a broader descriptive term in its own right, that drama (lowercase *d* now) evolved to refer specifically to comedy's opposing narrative subcategory, essentially replacing the literary and dramatic form the ancient Greeks once knew as tragedy.

Tragedy is the oldest of the Greeks' dramatic forms, and in Aristotle's *Poetics*, written around 335 BCE,[3] the great philosopher examined storytelling, referred to as poetry, and Drama, a type of illustrated or performed poetry, theorizing that tragedy was the purest representation of anything considered poetic.[4] Tragedy offered *mimesis* for the purpose of *catharsis*—or an imitation of life in action that seeks to inspire an emotional release[5] of empathetic self-identification—pity and fear being the two prominent responses ("I am sorry this is happening" and "I am afraid this will happen").[6] According to Aristotle, comedy, another genre within the umbrella of Drama, was similarly built around mimesis and catharsis but for an entirely different emotional release.

Unfortunately, his section of *Poetics* about comedy is currently lost, so we do not know the full extent of his theory. From what remains, though, we know that he considered laughter to be evidence of a comedic release[7]—a physical sign of catharsis. He also argued that the pure mimesis, or imitation of life, in tragedy would not be enough to evoke this laughter—a physically observable, measurable response of cathartic success—and as such, he believed that the mimesis in comedy had to be altered in such a way that its representation of truth could become recognizably ugly, or to use a word more congruent in our language, ridiculous.[8] That is, he saw comedy as the perversion, disruption, or aggrandizement of normalcy to the point that we are so aware that what we are seeing is ridiculous—ugly—that we give a communal, physical, verbal indication of our capacity to perceive something as askew. And the purging of the emotions associated with perceiving this ridiculousness should result in a cathartic response—we laugh.

So, while Greek tragedy was about imitating real life to inspire empathy via pity and fear, comedy to Aristotle was hinged on the recognition that real life was being tweaked—with laughter a physical indication of our awareness of a discrepancy, or incongruity. This is the basis for one of the modern theories about comedy—the *incongruity theory*.[9] I like this theory because it is directly applicable to the subjects we will be discussing in this book. For instance, most people spend money in moderation, but Jack Benny is so frugal that he stores his own cash in a bank vault under his house. That is ridiculous. Most people dream of being more than what they are, but few pursue this desire with Lucy Ricardo's methodical intensity, which finds her infiltrating the dancing ensemble of a nightclub show. That is ridiculous. Heck, most people want to be rich but never with the instinctual hunger of Sgt. Ernie Bilko, who would arrange bets on something so trivial as how many times a fidgety speaker will adjust her girdle during a lecture. That is ridiculous. And our ability to discern this ridiculousness—these incongruities from behavior we would consider "normal"—is why we have a release, we laugh.

I would add one other element to this theory: the notion of *benign incongruity*, or the fundamental belief that despite the ugly, caricatured, ridiculousness that we are socially acknowledging via laughter, the subversion of the "normal" is ultimately okay—the characters are not seriously deplorable or in serious jeopardy. As such, laughter is as much an intellectual display of awareness as it is a release of negative emotion. This definition is commonly called the *benign violation*,[10] but I have paired it with the neighboring *incongruity theory* because I find it simpler and more all-encompassing, especially for a modern understanding of humor outside of Drama. I think Aristotle would give some support to this definition, as he opined that comedy deals with lower people with more common concerns[11]—inherently trivial matters compared to the more serious issues faced by the noble characters in tragedies. In other words, comedy is benign.

Of course, he also posited that the reason comedies have happy endings (versus sad endings in tragedies) is because lesser people end up better than they deserve, while in tragedies, good people end up for the worse.[12] That might seem narrow based on today's examples within the "drama" genre. But what Aristotle was arguing here speaks to a perhaps more important point: characters in comedies must be defined differently compared to those in tragedies—with tweaked objectives, flaws, and personality traits that suggest a *caricatured mimesis* in pursuit of laughter, inspiring such plots. That is, they have to be twisted as ugly, or ridiculous, in order to create the desired response. And yet, at the same time, they have to remain not *so* ugly that we find it wrong or unjust when they probably wind up okay in the end. This is a delicate balance.

I should also note here that sometimes a caricatured mimesis is more literally mimetic: it is *naturally* occurring—a truism in our real life, often related to the social mores that we hold as "normal," even though they can sometimes themselves be ridiculous or ugly. That is, sometimes merely pointing out life's natural absurdities—as Jerry Seinfeld, for instance, does—is enough to suggest the benign incongruity that evokes laughter, for the mimesis is already inherently caricatured, or itself ridiculous. Writing for characters in comedies is similar—the above examples all have personality traits with a relatable basis, but their shows deliberately call attention to the aspects that can be made ridiculous via heightening. Calibrating how much this needs to be manipulated—how much things need to be caricatured beyond reality—is the job of the artist.

That said, I think Aristotle also did the world a disservice by laying the foundations for a bias that we have never fully shaken—a belief that the trivial baseness of characters in comedy, and the genre's intentional ridiculousness, makes it less desirable as a type and phenomenon than tragedy, the purest form of Drama, or performed poetry, with a true mimesis yielding catharsis. But if we notice that Aristotle naturally defines poetry in a way that applies to all kinds of art—an imitation of something in pursuit of an emotional response—than the purposeful manipulation of an imitation for a more nuanced response (like laughter) would seem just as valid, if not more intellectually rigorous. In fact, I think Aristotle already gives us enough to believe that comedy is harder to pull off than tragedy and should therefore be more respected.

After all, the desired catharsis of comedy has a measurable response in laughter that makes it more possible to quantify success—that is, the more comedic a comedy, the stronger the reaction, and the more laughter it will garner. Tears are not the direct counterpoint to laughter here, for they are not the singular sign of tragedy's pity and fear, and that genre has no metric. Perhaps in part because of this distinction, tragedies tend not to be held to the same rigid standards as comedies, and thus, the great examples of that genre (in all forms) do not have to be *as* great as the comedies we hold in similar esteem, simply because it is so much easier to critique and call out anything that is imperfect in comedies when we have laughter as a measurable sign of triumph.

Additionally, the idea that humor is subjective is often used as a way to devalue the genre, for of course, with laughter as a barometer of success, there are more perceived failures because nothing will strike every single human being the same. Even if we can all agree on the same set of standards about what *makes for* comedy (a benign incongruity), we are not all going to have exactly the same response with exactly the same emotional power at each moment. And yet, if every earned catharsis is valuable and if we can agree that performed poetry, or Drama, is an art *because* of these catharses, then that inherently extends to comedy as well, with its lower success rate making it something to be even more cherished. That is, if the beautiful release of laughter is harder to deliver, then when we find it, it's all the more precious. And as we will see with the sitcoms studied in this book, evoking laughter is a difficult feat: both the benignity and incongruity of a caricatured mimesis must both be calibrated to our selective liking—we don't want shows/characters that are *too* benign (not ridiculous enough) or *too* incongruous (too ridiculous), as neither would be funny. Like all art, it's delicate, personal, subjective. Beautiful.

Speaking of the situation comedy, now that we know what comedy is and why it should be considered an art, let's move on to the situation. Or, more specifically, the development of what that means in this word pairing. As noted, "situation comedy" did not start in reference to a genre but as a casually deployed description of a *type* of humor being offered in plays and short films of the 1910s and 1920s. The first citation I have found in print of "situation comedy" in reference to a performed work is in a 1908 review from *Variety* that describes a 20-minute sketch from a vaudeville act,[13] and the two words are paired to convey that the humor arose from a precise situation—a story. Indeed, "comedy of situation" soon became a common way to describe plays and movies that were expressly seeking humor from their storytelling—the scenarios created within the text—as opposed to inherently amusing slapstick gags that may provoke laughter but have little to do with elements of dramatic circumstance. Eventually, "comedy of situation" got tightened into "situational comedy" and then "situation comedy," and it spoke not just to the counterpoint of works that were primarily built around broad, physical yuks but also to a certain type of humor in narrative. Here are some of the ways in which "situation comedy" was described in the late 1910s and early 1920s:

> "the comedy of true satire, of penetrating insight into life" [*Fresno Morning Republican*, November 1916][14]
>
> "subjects in which the characters are dressed as they would be in real life, and in which their actions are plausible based upon human motives" [Palmer Photoplay Corporation, 1920][15]
>
> "a refined type [of d]omestic drama with a humorous touch and amusing, but not too broad situations" [*San Francisco Chronicle*, May 1921][16]

All of the above quotes are in reference to films, and they all make a deliberate point to contrast "situation comedy" (or "comedy of situation") against slapstick or gag-driven works—a notion that the early 1920s would soon reconcile by insisting, in essence, that "gags are all right. But they must grow out of the situation naturally" (said Bebe Daniels to the *Los Angeles Times* in December 1925).[17] This reconciliation allowed a blending of these different styles while still keeping the evolution tilted *toward* "situation comedy" and, most particularly, story.

However, the term was not only being used for comedy that came from story. As you can see, the words were being linked to indicate a funny subset of narrative fiction that validated the Aristotelian idea of Drama: with a shift toward a more faithful mimesis ("true satire" and "real life ... based upon human motives") in which the humor would arise, more directly and exclusively, *from* said mimesis—the manipulation of a situation imitating real life. In this regard, "situation comedy" was advocating for a purer, dramatic kind of comedy. *That* means, first and foremost, comedy from the actual imitated elements of human life: the characters.

So, while the term "situation comedy" was only vaguely and sporadically applied in the late 1910s and 1920s, without any strict guidelines yet established by a genre, we can already see the beginnings of our basic definition forming. Creating a genre out of this "situation comedy" term, with its own specific rules and conventions, would require a medium that demanded adherence *to* rules and conventions, with more rigidity than even film or theater or vaudeville.

Enter radio. Although radio as a means for communication initially seemed as free and open as the Wild West when the first commercially licensed station began operating in November 1920,[18] the development of networks NBC and CBS (in 1926 and 1927, respectively)[19] quickly ushered in standards to which all aired material had to obey, both in terms of the various entertainments offered (thereby creating genres) and in the mere programmatic nature of scheduling, with blocks of content—*programs*—planned for certain periods of the day and/or week. This imposed time limits—creating a structure to which producers would have to adhere—while also providing them the newfound blessing and curse of repetition. That is, programs would be on at the same time every day (or every week)—with the same basic entertainments offered every airing; listeners knew what they were basically getting when they tuned in to a broadcast—that was part of the draw. But, of course, each broadcast of a sustaining program also had to be a little bit different to keep listeners engaged, creating a new style of performed entertainment, blending unchanging elemental necessities *with* constant variations.

It took a little while to get there, though. In the 1920s and especially prior to the creation of several big networks, when local stations were still setting their own schedules, the dominant form of entertainment offered on radio matched the dominant form of entertainment in the first few decades of the twentieth century: vaudeville. Most 1920s radio programming, aside from news and sports, consisted of musical programs hosted by local talents who offered a parade of acts. When tuning in to one of these shows, the listener expected a true variety—different performers—but often with the same master of ceremonies and the same basic length and structure. It was only a matter of time, then, before radio began to exploit the uniqueness of the medium's programmatic nature through another one of America's important entertainment traditions—Drama. This came to yield the radio serial—an ongoing dramatic story told in daily increments (usually 15 minutes), with the same set of characters heard in every broadcast and an unfolding narrative that listeners could easily follow from day to day. The serial arose in contrast to another type of dramatic programming—something we would eventually call an anthology series, where every broadcast constituted a different, nonconnected play with a different (or repertory) cast playing a totally different set of characters.

The most famous early serial—the one that started the trend—began locally in 1926 at Chicago's WGN: *Sam 'n' Henry*.[20] It starred and was written by two up-and-coming comics named Freeman Gosden and Charles Correll, who were initially approached about doing a program based on the comic strip *The Gumps*.[21] That idea was quickly dropped, for the pair decided that if they were going to launch their own show, they wanted to create their own characters. The result was Sam and Henry, two Black men who had recently migrated away from the Jim Crow South to Chicago, where there was theoretically more opportunity for guys who looked like them. If this sounds familiar, it should, for Gosden and Correll left WGN in 1928, moved to a rival local station, and started another new but very similar 15-minute serial that year: *Amos 'n Andy*.[22]

A legendary part of American culture, *Amos 'n Andy*—the TV version of which we'll be discussing in a few chapters—has a reputation that precedes it today, and much of the conversation is dominated by its racial origins: namely, the fact that Gosden and Correll were white, but in performance and via their text, the duo gleefully adopted the vocal affects long associated with minstrel shows, a foundational part of nineteenth-century American entertainment—from which vaudeville developed. Many of the tropes and stereotypes from the minstrel tradition understandably make enjoying their radio show difficult for listeners today. However, its importance cannot be denied—it's an early popular program that began, like so much of radio, with a traceable link to vaudeville, which had been the country's dominant form of performed entertainment.

In sitcom histories, *Amos 'n Andy*, and on some occasions its very similar predecessor *Sam 'n' Henry*, is often pointed to as the first situation comedy. But the truth is a lot more complicated, for they both were structurally and tonally not aligned with the genre that would later emerge. This is because, quite simply, Gosden and Correll created a *serial* radio program, and understating its fidelity to that specific genre recognizes the cultural moment that gave rise to their efforts in the first place. The emergence of radio in the 1920s and the natural progression to a serialized form of entertainment coincided with trends in other mediums beyond vaudeville. For instance, the rise of motion pictures, the expansion of newspapers, and the increasing popularity of magazines all contributed to the boom of fiction that could be serialized—parsed out in regular installments, following the same character (or set of characters) over a long period, either in a self-contained story, like the novellas published in literary magazines (a tradition that surged in the 1800s),[23] or a vague continuance of format, like the nationally syndicated newspaper comic strips, which were daily snapshots of a select group of cartoon figures, absent of much plot.

However, the most notable example of serialization appeared in short films of the 1910s—the most well known being *The Perils of Pauline* (beginning in 1914). This tradition of 20-minute movies featuring either an ongoing narrative (like chapters in a book) or a collection of self-contained stories nevertheless united by the continuity of a certain group of characters and the associated particulars of their circumstances made it possible for viewers to meet each film with an initial expectation about who and what the evening's entertainment would be following, even as the details changed each time as a result of the plot's trajectory or the individual elements of the selected narrative. What's more, the ascendance of film as a mass media created our modern-day notion of celebrity—public figures whose work was so visible that audiences formed an emotional attachment. While there were certain stage stars and vaudeville acts who had reputational associations within their own industry, motion pictures quickly achieved a wide, national reach, vaulting select human beings into a limelight never before achieved. And the cultivation of these national celebrities, by an industry that made them famous, largely involved the maintenance of basic public personas; no matter the "characters" they were playing in film, there was an elemental similarity in every work with, say, Charlie Chaplin or Theda Bara. That is, viewers knew what they were getting every time they saw one of their favorite stars in a new picture—and if they did not, disappointment followed. Both the stars and the studios had to account for this fact.

Accordingly, even if the stories that Mary Pickford played onscreen were not dramatically serialized like *Pauline*, there was at least a character-based continuity forming by which the spectator could ascribe certain traits to a star and expect that they be reinforced through every narrative fiction in which that person appeared. For the first time, then, characters, represented by their human players, were emerging beyond story as a through line for audiences, and as celebrity became a phenomenon from the introduction of this mass media, this became an expectation.

I note all this to help give some context to radio's innate understanding of the benefit of serialization with character, particularly at a moment in American culture where this was becoming standard—especially in the motion pictures, as Laurel and Hardy and Our Gang and the Three Stooges were giving continuity to their series of short comic films, creating a sort of parallel to the situation comedy as it was being created on radio, which not only adopted this wave of character-led intertextuality, but also helped further the trend, creating an even more *personal* form of connection via the simple fact that this was a medium bringing these stories—and the human voices performing these stories—literally *into* American homes: their most private, confidential spaces. This intimacy only accelerated the rate of familiarity that audiences felt with the stars on radio, or rather, the "characters" who were emerging at this crucial time in the medium. Perhaps that can explain why *Amos 'n Andy*, which was picked up nationally by the NBC network in 1929,[24] become such a popular phenomenon in such a relatively short time. Every night for 15 minutes, U.S. audiences could hear what was happening with their friends Amos and Andy.

Old-time radio scholar Elizabeth McLeod wrote a great book on the genesis and early years of *Amos 'n Andy* that I recommend, for she helps explain what the series was like in this period.[25] In short, it was a serial in the simplest way we could define the form—it offered an ongoing dramatic narrative. And in this case, "dramatic" means, as a burgeoning genre, the opposite of comedic. Now, there is something of a gray area here, for with the ongoing narrative structure and incorporation of some very serious plot points—near-death experiences, lawsuits, natural disasters—*Amos 'n Andy* actually had some nuance. That may be surprising, given what we have come to associate with the show from its use of minstrel stereotypes—and the fact that it was written and performed by two white men. But as McLeod notes, the show was deliberately interested in presenting these two Black characters as human,[26] with a multidimensionality that made the audience sympathize (pity and fear) in their heavier moments and then laugh in acknowledgment of their heightened mimesis in the lighter moments.

As such, while the characters were rooted in minstrelsy and thus retained a certain rhythmic affectation that suggested humor—what they said was, indeed, sometimes funny—the storytelling itself veered in the opposite direction, with its serialized structure informing the material: dramatic in Aristotle's tragic understanding. In this regard, the way that "situation comedy" was previously used, throughout the 1920s, to refer to humorous dramatic works that derived their laughs from situation, or story, would not actually refer to a serial like *Amos 'n Andy*, whose storytelling was not laugh-inducing.

Additionally, 15-minute broadcasts limited the amount of actual story that could be explored daily. In such a brief time, episodes could only consist of several conversations that slowly progressed an overarching narrative, inch by inch. So the plotting within individual episodes did not resemble the plays (or poems) to which Aristotle referred and which audiences of the time would have recognized from the stage and screen, for there wasn't an exact beginning, middle, and end, with a trackable arc for the leads and other conventions of narrative fiction. All of those Dramatic notions were mostly disregarded, aside from the mounting continuity of character, and the accelerating investment as listeners simply spent more time with these imitations of life—however ridiculous or ugly. And since, as we will see, having individual episodic stories is another trait that we associate with the situation comedy genre, this program certainly does not adhere to those standards. Therefore, McLeod does not call *Amos 'n Andy* a sitcom and, based on everything we know so far about what situation comedy means, I would not either. So, if *Amos 'n Andy* isn't the first sitcom, what is? Well, let's keep going…

The serial craze, which reached its zenith in 1930–1931[27]—as millions of viewers listened in when Madame Queen was suing Andy in a breach of promise suit—spawned dozens of other 15-minute programs that also became household names, among them *The Goldbergs*, a long-running series about a Jewish family in the Bronx. It was created in 1929 (as *The Rise of the Goldbergs*) by its star Gertrude Berg, who played the beloved Molly Goldberg and served as its chief creative force, responsible for its production and, most important, scripting. Her dominance in this medium at such a pioneering era has kept her a fascinating figure—the subject of books, musicals, and movies, with her representation of a Jewish family during the Depression (and the surrounding years) a fascinating social document that reflects an America promising to be an ethnic melting pot. As far as comedy is concerned, there is a lot of confusion today about how to classify *The Goldbergs*—particularly in light of its trajectory, which also extended into television. I think it is most important to note that it also ran as a 15-minute daily show for most of its life (beginning in 1931). So, on the most basic level, it's akin to *Amos 'n Andy*.

In terms of content, *The Goldbergs* is sometimes even categorized as a soap opera[28] (a melodramatic "drama")—a genre that emerged during the 1930s. But this is debatable. Yes, the characters are not jokey and vaudeville-based like Amos and Andy, and the series did, for a large part of its life, run in the daytime with soaps. But there's often a lightness, a humor to the central Molly Goldberg character. Today, we might say the radio version of *The Goldbergs* is more like a "dramedy," where, as with *Amos 'n Andy*, the humanity of its leading characters is a guiding priority. Under those terms, while Aristotle would consider putting it in the comedy category, largely because the desired weekly catharsis is somewhat pleasurable, once we start to cover other shows that more overtly pursue laughter by making an obvious contortion of their elemental mimetic properties, the distinction would be too recognizable for even the great Greek to ignore. And with laughter in very short supply here—because the Goldbergs' mimesis of life is only barely tweaked and hardly ridiculous (if at all)—I'm not comfortable labeling *The Goldbergs* a comedy either—at least not on radio—especially based on the standards of the 1930s. In fact, not only would I say it is definitely NOT a good candidate for being called an early situation comedy, but I think it actually continues the serial genre's association with elements that are *not* comedic.

I make this adjudication largely because there actually *were* 15-minute serials that moved the figurative needle in an expressly more humorous direction—among them *Easy Aces* (debuted 1930), *Lum and Abner* (debuted 1931), and *Vic and Sade* (debuted 1932).[29] All of these featured plainly humorous characters, with the pursuit of laughter a clear objective for each broadcast. Again, though, historians also have a reluctance to call these actual situation comedies, for they structurally resemble serials (and at times are *spoofing* that genre), and the limitations of the 15-minute format are still felt within story. Some, like the malaprop-heavy *Easy Aces*, have arcs that span a certain number of broadcasts and therefore directly mimic the serialized form, while others, like *Vic and Sade*, merely offer dialogue-based interactions between two leads—with little plot and few of the dramatic conventions exemplified in Aristotle's understanding of comedic plays and the emerging definition of the situation comedy—comedy *from* situation, or story.

Our takeaway? Even these more decidedly humorous 15-minute daily serials, regardless of their pronounced comedic intent, nevertheless adhered more to the form and conventions of a type of program that kept them from fully satisfying the growing definition of situation comedy, not to mention the genre that would develop by the early 1940s, which combined traits of *other* formats in addition to what's represented by these rudimentary examples.

So much of our discussion about these early serio-comic, or totally comic, serials has been about the form—the notion that, at 15 minutes a broadcast, it is impossible to be mining humor from "situation," even if there are comic characters with jokey dialogue sparking intended laughs. Thus, the introduction of the 30-minute (non-anthology) comedy serial or series would be vital in actually charting the course of the genre's development and labeling, as I think many are curious, the first *true* sitcom. According to Elizabeth McLeod, the first half-hour comedy series debuted on CBS in September 1929.[30] It was *Mr. and Mrs.*, based on a comic strip of the same name by Claire Briggs, following the amusing exploits of a middle-aged, middle-class, married duo who was prone to battling[31]—a sort of prototype for *The Bickersons*. The series starred Jack Smart and Jane Houston and ran for two years. Sadly, no broadcasts are currently known to exist,[32] so it is difficult to truly get a handle on just how much this early show reinforced what we will come to say represents the fully realized situation comedy. What we do know, however, is that this half-hour format encouraged some kind of episodic plot, and with a weekly slot as opposed to the serialized daily structure, most of these plots were self-contained, like in an anthology drama, but with storytelling *inspired by* the preestablished sustaining characters. So *Mr. and Mrs.* stands out as a program that, based on our emerging standards, could have been called a situation comedy, pursuing humor through a serialization, or continuity, of character, but not necessarily of story.

The most peculiar thing about *Mr. and Mrs.* is that, if it seems truly innovative to us, it actually did not spark a throng of imitators in the same way that *Sam 'n' Henry*, or rather, *Amos 'n Andy*, did.[33] For while the airwaves started to hear more half-hour series, many of them were tonally in the comedy-drama style of *The Goldbergs* and lacked the caricatured mimesis in pursuit of laughter as suggested by *Mr. and Mrs.*, which again was based on a known comic strip. Also, the serial craze of the early 1930s eventually gave way to a renaissance of comedy variety, for, with the Depression killing vaudeville and constraining Broadway, a bunch of hoofers came over to the new medium, bringing their theatrical sensibilities with them. In this group came—among others, Eddie Cantor, Ed Wynn, Fred Allen, George Burns and Gracie Allen, Phil Baker, and Jack Benny. Debuting regular programs between 1931 and 1933, these comedians offered 30-minute (or 60-minute) comedy variety series, anchored by themselves and often in front of a live audience, bringing more of vaudeville into the genre and thereby adding, with Ed Wynn being the first,[34] the sound of communal laughter as an audible cue—something that the situation comedy would adopt by the 1940s as a typical convention of the genre (albeit not an *absolute* necessity).

Additionally, most of these shows surrounded their famous hosts with a supporting cast, each player supplying humor based on his/her specific persona—a few serving other functions as well, like singer or bandleader or announcer. In some cases, this would blur the line between comedy variety and situation comedy, because with a regular set of characters—all of them well defined in the clear caricatured crusade for laughs—and a half hour of time, these programs could veer into story territory, even as they were also ostensibly vaudeville-rooted variety shows, with songs, sketches, and guest stars. The most important example of this quasi-variety/quasi-situation comedy is the *Jack Benny Program*, which debuted in 1932 and would grow to become the most prominent radio comedy of the 1930s and 1940s, with a lingering popularity that maintained through a 15-year run on television as well. We will talk a lot more about this important show soon—it's a paragon of terrific character writing that would keep it influential to the burgeoning genre.

But if the *Jack Benny Program* stumbled into situation comedy almost by accident, thanks to strong characters, the developing form finally started to solidify around 1935, when Jim and Marian Jordan premiered a series for NBC Blue: *Fibber McGee and Molly*. The Jordans were a vaudeville couple whose career in radio started in Chicago during the late 1920s. In 1931, they began a local show called *Smackout*, developed by creator Don Quinn out of an earlier program called *Luke and Mirandy* and set in a Chicago general store.[35] It ran six days a week in 15-minute broadcasts, without the structure most conducive to situation comedy. But it was a big step in that direction, with comedic exchanges involving the general store setting and its regular visitors—all of whom were voiced, incidentally, by Jim and Marian Jordan. In this regard, there was a fixed set of people at a fairly stationary location performing scripts that clearly sought comedy as their main objective. *Smackout* moved to NBC Blue in 1933 and eventually caught the eye of the Johnson Wax Company, which wanted to sponsor a series for the Jordans.[36] This became *Fibber McGee and Molly*, a domestic-set husband-and-wife show that debuted in April

1935. *Fibber McGee and Molly*, also created by Quinn, differed significantly from *Smackout* in several ways. For one, it was a weekly 30-minute show. Second, the Jordans pretty much only played the title characters, with an entire ensemble cast now providing the voices for the other recurring members of Wistful Vista, the neighborhood community where the pair lived from September 1935 onward.[37] And third, the show took its cue from the popular variety efforts of the day and added a live studio audience.

These maneuvers all progressed the Jordans' show into the basic format we now know as the sitcom, for the 30-minute structure required some kind of narrative in every script, however slight. And with *Fibber McGee and Molly* running only once a week, these broadcasts were incentivized to remain self-contained, with continuity coming from the characters in their sustaining framework (Wistful Vista) appearing regularly like figures in a serial, even though each script now could stand on its own narratively: beginning, middle, and end. Each broadcast had *a* situation. Additionally, while the show's comic rhythms were rooted in the vaudeville sensibilities of its stars (there were also musical attractions and vestiges of this earlier programming style as well) and its newfound use of story was slim for the genre as it would soon develop, this was a huge improvement, for the incorporation of an ensemble further moved the show away from *Smackout*'s variety-based display of two stars and into a more Dramatic context, with an emphasis on *character* and how each member of this fictional community could be individually and uniquely defined with the kind of caricatured mimesis that seeks to yield laughter. And if there was any doubt that comedy was the objective, a roaring audience was around to reveal the show's intention. In essence, *Fibber McGee and Molly* brought all the pieces together with comedy indisputably the goal—laughter the desired catharsis, revealed audibly throughout every broadcast—and the presence of weekly stories validating the developing definition of "situation comedy."

Now, as noted, there were probably a dozen earlier half-hour comedic series, with *Mr. and Mrs.* from 1929 likely being the first, and they probably offered a lot of these same qualities. But *Fibber McGee and Molly* took the former's combined serialization of character with anthology-esque self-contained storytelling and added in the vaudeville/variety performative aspect that also sought big yuks (from a studio audience). It brought all three of these genres together, and by virtue of both its popularity and its genuine quality—the fact that it was *good* at making people laugh—it became more influential, giving rise sincerely to other shows that we could put in the same pile. Accordingly, while we probably can't call *Fibber McGee and Molly* the first situation comedy, and we probably have to qualify it as a "*modified* situation comedy" (at least early on), which is the term radio historian Jim Cox uses,[38] due to this show's heavier vaudeville-based, variety elements, it *is* fair to call it the baseline for informing what "situation comedy" meant when this descriptive phrase was turning into an actual programming genre: *the* situation comedy, combining elements of the serial, the anthology drama, and the variety show.

Most historians cite 1939 as the watershed for situation comedy on radio, with the premieres of *The Aldrich Family* and *Blondie*, two comedy shows based on movie series that had previously begun as a play and a comic strip, respectively. And, indeed, their influence is profound—*The Aldrich Family* launched a spate of teenage-led comedies in the early 1940s, and *Blondie* was one of the most well-known brands of the era, popularizing the idea of the bumbling husband/father, which would eventually become a trope for the whole sitcom genre. Interestingly, both began without a live studio audience. By 1941, they were broadcasting before one.

That is the year *I* would posit as the turning point: when the situation comedy became officially a type of radio programming, distinct from any other, for 1941 saw the premieres of *Duffy's Tavern*, a pioneer in the workplace subcategory, *The Life of Riley*, the quintessential bumbling patriarch show of the 1940s, and *The Great Gildersleeve*, the first true sitcom spin-off, starring Harold Peary's popular character from *Fibber McGee and Molly*. What's more, another show that had started as a definite variety program, anchored by two vaudevillians, fully hopped aboard the situation comedy bandwagon in 1941, remaking itself as a domestic-set husband-and-wife series: *The George Burns and Gracie Allen Show*,[39] another genre staple.

Eventually, *Amos 'n Andy* would similarly shed its early structure—as a serial—and adopt the conventions of this new genre, also becoming a weekly half-hour program in 1943 with a live studio audience and a decided emphasis on laughs[40]—from character *and* story. Indeed, the situation comedy had become a full-fledged genre by then, and it only grew to become more dominant postwar, with an emergence of all different types of programs, many of them domestic affairs about couples and/or families—just in time for the baby boom—with *The Adventures of Ozzie and Harriet* (debuted 1944), *Ethel and Albert* (1944), and *Father Knows Best* (1949) being some of the best known, while *The Bickersons* (1951) and *The Phil Harris-Alice Faye Show* (1946) emerged as reactionary spoofs. This was exactly the type of programming TV would soon carry over, as the developing medium sought reliable content as it was just figuring out its own identity.

But first, the emergence of the situation comedy as a bona fide genre brought about a slight change in the definition of the term, for it was no longer referring to a kind of laugh-seeking narrative fiction that was deriving its yuks from story. Now, as a genre comprised of all these traits from different types of programs, the term was being used to define itself in contrast to those other types of programs *exclusively*—variety shows, serials, anthologies. That is, as we have started to see, situation comedies weren't variety shows—they had full stories and characters, like a piece of dramatic fiction. However, unlike a serial, the storytelling would essentially be episodic—with each broadcast containing a beginning, middle, and end: a play unto itself, like every episode of an anthology drama. And yet, unlike anthologies, there would be the same characters and the same basic setting every week, sustaining every narrative (with explanations arising if there were any deviations in this formula), so the audience could expect these elements to appear, creating a continuity of character and other assorted elements but not necessarily plot.

In this regard, the definition of "situation" was taking on a double meaning, moving away from the simple descriptive way of addressing story, for now, when paired with "comedy" to constitute a new genre, the word was having to acknowledge these aforementioned recurring elements too—the things an audience could expect every week, unlike in an anthology or variety series, where those details would change. So, in the 1940s, the definition of situation comedy evolved to mean a type of program that was using a fixed, stable situation—elements that the audience could anticipate for every broadcast—while pursuing comedy in stories that were mostly self-contained, linked *because* of those aforementioned elements. The "situation" then could be extrapolated out to refer to every element informing each show's sustained identity, evidenced in narrative—its premise, its setting, its themes, its patterns, and most important, its characters.

Characters are the most important aspect of any situation because, quite simply, the definition of comedy—heck, the definition of *all* types of Drama as Aristotle told us—is hinged on mimesis and catharsis: the imitation of life and its earned emotional response. With comedy, the catharsis is particularly pleasure-based and revealed, at its best, through laughter. But mimesis is the operative word now, as the imitation of life, for human beings, means the imitation *of* human beings. The imitation of human beings is character. This is why every single piece of dramatic fiction is dependent on having characters. And the most vital attribute of a situation in a situation comedy is how it can caricature its mimesis: the way it defines and uses its characters.

Aristotle always professed that character was secondary to plot,[41] but he inherently prized tragedy over comedy and was not working in the bounds of the sitcom, where a situation with characters sustains every week, not a singular story. In this regard, you can see where the genre demands *our* emphasis: less on story than on character. Meanwhile, our ideas of what is funny in a sitcom will always remain subjective, but Aristotle has given us enough of an objective understanding of the phenomenon in all dramatic works—caricatured mimesis (of benign incongruities)—that we now have a foundation to help us as we go find the best examples within this new genre, with a precise standard for what should be deemed successful by way of the "art" part of this particular art form: we should be laughing. We should be having that catharsis.

So, all together, the situation comedy is an art form that consists of episodic stories inspired by the sustaining elements of a "situation," especially a set of regular characters, all designed for laugh-out-loud comedy, which is caused by the benign incongruities of a caricatured mimesis. My standard for judging sitcoms, then, and finding strong individual episodic examples is predicated on how these series reflect the ideal of the situation comedy art form as we have defined it.

So far, we have seen why comedy deserves to be treated as an art, and we have learned how "situation comedy" evolved to refer to a specific form. Therefore, the best examples of the "sitcom"—at its most ideal—are the ones that most validate its identity *as an art form*, and this means, as a starting point, the art: performed narratives that successfully pursue comedy. More than the mere emotional releases sought by dramatic works whose ancestor is Greek tragedy, these works *primarily* want to make an audience find pleasure via laughter—plain and simple. Then consideration is also given to the form: *how* these shows find their laughter—how they use their situation and especially their characters to be funny. The "situation" is the part of this genre that makes the sitcom unique from other comedic entries—lighthearted serials, comedy-variety shows, and anthology programs—and the "situation" therefore has to be directly involved in the procurement of laughs to validate the situation comedy as a *specific* form. And since, as we have noted, the characters in a sitcom are the most important elements constituting a situation, their use will be the guiding determinant of how good a situation comedy is at being a situation comedy. That is why the main criterion for determining success in the sitcom genre, particularly in episodic terms, is its use of character for comedy, as revealed through the form's required weekly story. This is the guiding framework I will employ to examine individual sitcoms.

Now, before we begin our deep dive into the sitcom's first decade on television—where the new visual medium further refined our understanding of the genre—I want to end on a note that further illustrates the paramount importance of character in comedy and, in particular, the sitcom. To do so, I am hopping back to *The Jack Benny Program*, which began in 1932 as a vehicle for a vaudeville comic who was basically an emcee for a variety show, with songs and sketches. His series never fully moved away from this setup, even after 23 years on radio and 15 years (some overlapping) on TV. But with the cultivation of an ensemble—each regular exceptionally well defined, playing a version of a real-life persona, in turn aiding the notion of mimesis as the basis for humor—Benny's program developed the capacity to put its leads in comical situations that emphasized the very characteristics making them funny. And in some cases, those comical situations were actually motivated by their personality-fueled actions.

In essence, this was a "modified" situation comedy like early *Fibber McGee and Molly*, but perhaps at times, it was also the purest, most artistic form of sitcom on radio in the 1940s, for even though the structure remained an acknowledged variety show—and there were still musical numbers and spoofs of movies and plays throughout its run—the episodes that were simply mining humor from leading characters with comedic personas in relation to one another, and then following them through the everyday happenings of "their lives" were indeed the best and most iconic, including probably the most legendary moment in radio sitcom history.

The scene is a March 1948 episode of *The Jack Benny Program* where Jack Benny is held at gunpoint and the mugger says, "Your money or your life." There's a long pause. The audience laughs. The thug repeats the demand. Finally, Jack retorts, "I'm thinking it over!"[42]

Contrary to myth, it was not the longest laugh in radio history or even the longest laugh of the series.[43] But it became an immortal gag because of the immortal character at its center—Jack Benny, who had been so well defined that listeners knew him, and the ridiculous things that made him so funny: he was vain despite not being beautiful, he thought he was a violin virtuoso despite being a lousy player, and he was notoriously cheap despite having plenty of money. The joke in this classic exchange is based on the idea that Jack parting with his cash would be as grave to him as the loss of his life. This is naturally comical—it is ridiculous for someone to value his cash more than his life—but it is *hilarious* when supported by this wonderfully established, well-known characterization. That is why the audience guffaws in advance—they *know* the Jack Benny character to be so tight that he would be loath to give over his money, even in peril. (Well, the kind of peril that is knowingly benign—no one expects the lead in a comedy program to be shot and killed by a mugger; it is okay, then, to laugh at him in this scenario.) They know Jack so well—they've seen his persona reinforced over and over in dozens of individual stories—that they expect this ridiculous man to react in a ridiculous way. And he does.

Only in a situation comedy could such a knowing laugh happen *before* he reacts in addition to after, elevating the memory of this moment into a legendary example of American comedy. It is a testament to this program, Jack's well-defined character and, of course, the very sitcom format that enables this enhanced response. It's a beautiful moment from an especially unique art form.

CHAPTER TWO

# The Prehistoric Era
*The Television Sitcom of the 1940s*

Before we can use our new understanding of the situation comedy to find its best samples from its first full decade in the new visual medium of television, we have to set the scene for the 1950s by examining the 1940s and the state of the American TV sitcom as it existed in its earliest years. I have called this chapter "The Prehistoric Era" because there is little physical record left of the sitcoms from this period, as the majority of programming was broadcast live, and if films were made for future showings, very few of them survive. So our knowledge about the programs of this time—from all genres, not just sitcoms—is limited, largely based on eyewitness accounts and then-contemporary reviews. However, we do have enough intel to get a basic awareness of its trends, and just like with our quick exploration of radio sitcoms in the previous chapter, this brief overview is necessary for placing 1950s sitcoms in their context.

The quick version of this history is that television technology was first publicly demonstrated in the 1920s,[1] developed during the 1930s via a handful of experimental TV stations across the country[2]—mostly in the big entertainment hub of New York City—and then was practically halted in the early 1940s when the United States entered World War II and the country's attentions went elsewhere.[3] During this era, all programming was local, and while there were regularly scheduled series, most of the shows that we would call comedic in nature were, as on radio, either productions of plays in an anthology-like format or variety shows.[4] It is unlikely that there was anything we could call a situation comedy (which requires character continuity) during this experimental period. Additionally, by the time commercial television officially began in July 1941,[5] the few places that had opened for business—including the flagship New York stations for what would become the NBC and CBS networks—were soon restricted, and there was a ban on the manufacturing of TV sets for consumer use during wartime.[6]

Once rules started lifting in the fall of 1945,[7] the medium progressed with lightning speed, picking up where it had left off and then some, as the development of the long-distance coaxial cable made it possible to create TV networks.[8] A network is a connection of stations either owned or affiliated with a broadcasting company that provides its offered programming. As of 1946, most coaxial connections were small and close together, and the initial network hookups for NBC and DuMont consisted of only a few actual stations on the East Coast, emanating from their central New York bases. In fact, the first officially licensed TV station west of the Mississippi River—KTLA—did not debut until January 1947, bringing commercial television to Los Angeles.[9]

It was also in 1947 (November) that the series commonly called America's first television sitcom premiered on DuMont—*Mary Kay and Johnny*, a gentle husband-and-wife show starring real-life marrieds Johnny and Mary Kay Stearns.[10] *Mary Kay and Johnny* was a relatable domestic comedy most known today for the trivia of probably being the first network series to show a couple in a single bed. It was also the first sitcom—if not network show entirely—to acknowledge a pregnant woman on air and incorporate her blessed event into the story (yes, years before *I Love Lucy*).[11] This is because TV was such an infant medium that broadcast standards and practices had yet to be written—in 1948, when Christopher Stearns was born, it was not big news.

Our understanding of *Mary Kay and Johnny* today is similarly defined by the fact that it existed at a time when the medium was in flux—and the series went through a lot of evolutions itself. Broadcast without a studio audience[12] for the duration of its three-season run, the show bounced from DuMont to NBC to CBS and back to NBC, going from a weekly 15-minute program, to a weekly 20-minute program,[13] to a weekly 30-minute program, to a *daily* 15-minute program, and finally to a weekly 30-minute program again.[14] Sadly, it was always broadcast live, and its preservation on kinescope was rare. A kinescope is a film taken of a television set (or monitor) as it is broadcasting a show;[15] kinescopes of live programs were sent to stations affiliated with a network but not physically connected, and they would often be shown weeks after the initial transmission. Only one episode of *Mary Kay and Johnny* is publicly known to exist today, via kinescope.

The episode, which I screened at the Paley Center, comes from June 1949, when the series had moved back to NBC and was being shown—for the first time—in daily 15-minute slots during the evening. How indicative this entry is of the 30-minute iteration is unclear, but what I saw indicated a sweet yet decidedly laugh-seeking program about a naive wife—not stupid but simple—and her wise-guy husband, who usually comes out the fool, living in postwar New York City. If that sounds a bit like *I Love Lucy*, the comparison gets stronger, for the surviving installment uses a story almost identical to the latter's "Sales Resistance" (January 26, 1953), about a wife's inability to turn down a manipulative salesman with a handy new floor-cleaning device. And, yes, the term "sales resistance" is also used in this *Mary Kay and Johnny*.

Now, before we go accusing the *I Love Lucy* scribes of plagiarism, I think it would be fair to point out that the "sales resistance" term predates both series by decades[16] and the story is generally predicated on a domestic cliché—the idea of a housewife sitting at home and being susceptible to door-to-door salesmen while the husband is away—and it therefore might not be unique enough, in itself, to be directly copyable. Indeed, this speaks to a point that we will soon find reiterated through this decade—there really are very few fresh stories and original premises, and the only thing that can make shows unique are their characters, whose individual definitions should supply details that enliven the narratives and make them seem special. In this case, the *I Love Lucy* sample is significantly funnier—not only because its script is bolder and more committed to laughs (evidenced by the show's utilization of a studio audience) but also because it really tailors itself to be a showcase for the Lucy Ricardo character, whom we will discuss at length in Chapter Four. *Mary Kay and Johnny* does not have any figure as well established—both Mary Kay and Johnny are vaguer and less descript, perhaps in the (misguided) hopes of achieving relatability. What's more, their series' take on the story, despite matching the same basic arc of *Lucy*'s, gives the biggest comedic material to Johnny, who does not have the strong comic shape of Lucy or even Ricky. Accordingly, the two shows are not competitive in terms of which is better situation comedy—the strength of the Ricardos, as characters, better supports a generic, uninspired narrative, making the proceedings funnier *and* more directly linked to a "situation."

However, what is remarkable about this sole surviving sample of *Mary Kay and Johnny* is that even in its 15-minute daily format, it is engaging a story that could be and indeed was employed on an unambiguous half-hour sitcom, meaning that doubts we might have about this series' shorter runtimes, and how that maybe disqualifies it from being considered a true situation comedy as we have defined its form, are somewhat allayed. On the other hand, perhaps the daily 15-minute version was merely maintaining the learned sensibilities of its 30-minute format, which it would not yet have known in its original run on DuMont during 1947–1948. That is, we might be calling *Mary Kay and Johnny* the first American television sitcom, even if it had to grow into the term and would not have been a perfect candidate upon its 1947 debut.

The problem with this era in television, especially for a critical study like this, which is dependent on viewing dramatic texts in performance, is that, again, so little of this period's shows exist and are available for direct examination. Based only on what we have of *Mary Kay and Johnny*—one episode from when it was running for 15 minutes daily, a year and a half after its debut—it *is* an abbreviated version of a situation comedy, with humor from a situation of regular characters displayed through episodic story (however slight), in a way that we could not really claim to be true of the 15-minute radio serials from the early 1930s. Also, to its credit, the 1949 episode I screened employed visual gags—meaning, it was consciously aware of the unique opportunities presented to television sitcoms as opposed to those on radio. This makes it unique among the other surviving series of the time, for in general, most of this early programming was still adapting to the fact that a story could now be told outside of dialogue and sound effects.

In other news, 1948 saw the official launch of the CBS and ABC television networks,[17] and several more 15- and 30-minute shows that modern sources cite as sitcoms would follow in the 1948–1949 and 1949–1950 seasons. This book is not recounting all of them—some only lasted a month or two, and with local stations still offering their own programming, it would be a fool's errand to try accounting for *every* single short-lived series with sustaining characters, particularly at this time, where again the physical record barely exists. I would surely be leaving something out, and in this era, shows that were dramatic in tone were also likely half hours, meaning there is already a lot of assumptions about these programs that I do not feel comfortable indulging.

However, a few half-hour series from the 1948–1949 season worth noting here briefly are *The Laytons*, which ran from August to October 1948 on DuMont and included Amanda Randolph as the housekeeper of a middle-class family, making her the first African American regular on a network TV series,[18] and its replacement, *The Growing Paynes*, another family sitcom that briefly counted Elaine Stritch as a cast member.[19] A few episodes of the latter exist at the Paley Center—it appears to be a half-hour tonally ambiguous series (with no studio audience) that employs some classic conventions of comedic plays, like misunderstandings, without much support from well-defined, nuanced characterizations.

*The Laytons* is jokier but comparable, as suggested by a published script for one episode.[20] Along with *Mary Kay and Johnny*, the constrictions of live television at the time demanded both shows employ limited actors and few sets per episode, which in turn restricted the storytelling. So while all three of these early samples look to indeed have a sense of narrative that validates our ideas of the situation comedy, the character work on each sounds similarly rudimentary—a regression from the hilarious efforts concurrently airing on radio. And most of the other live, short-lived sitcoms from New York that premiered during 1949, such as NBC's *The Hartmans* (sort of an urban *Fibber McGee and Molly*), were similarly received.[21]

In this regard, it was almost as if the newness of TV as a still-gestating technology, and the unsurety of how to write for something so unknown and uncommon (it is estimated that only one million TV sets were in operation in the United States at the start of 1949)[22] had set back the conception of the situation comedy. To wit, this is both because of and *the cause* of the medium's early reliance on comedy-variety shows, particularly the *Texaco Star Theater* with Milton Berle, the most popular funnyman on TV in the late 1940s[23] thanks to his heavily visual, vaudeville-inspired work. Indeed, with the sitcom best evidenced on radio, comedy-variety shows had more of a place on television, and some, like Morey Amsterdam's self-titled series, blended elements of vaudeville with the sitcom, à la *The Jack Benny Program* but with less of an emphasis on the situation, due unsurprisingly to a lack of the command or interest in character (with which Benny thrived). We could try to call *The Morey Amsterdam Show*, which ran from December 1948 to October 1950,[24] a sitcom, but I personally would not; its focus was on the weekly floor show—a succession of variety acts, not characters in relation. With this series and several others like it, television looked like it would have to relearn the lessons of radio as far as the sitcom was concerned.

But if this new medium put the situation comedy in an identity crisis, by 1949, TV was already starting to realize that the most assured way of finding fast success was imitation, for this is when the networks began transitioning their radio hits to the small screen. The year 1949 alone saw the television debuts of radio hits *The Goldbergs*, *The Aldrich Family*, *Easy Aces*, and *The Life of Riley*. While *Easy Aces* retained its initial 15-minute format[25]—ignoring several brief stretches on radio as a definitive sitcom in a 30-minute weekly slot—and *The Aldrich Family* came over with the same half-hour comic sensibility only no live audience, *The Goldbergs*, despite also having no audience, took the opportunity to redefine itself, moving from 15 minutes daily to a once-a-week half-hour slot when this expanded version of the series debuted on CBS-TV in January 1949.[26]

Now, this half-hour structure was not unique to comedies. Many programs, including shows more tonally dramatic, were also 30-minute weeklies in that era, and for the most part, the TV version of *The Goldbergs* retained the radio series' ethos, with a serio-comic vibe that not only used mimesis for laughter but for a plethora of human emotions, much like another live (audience-less) half-hour series that also premiered in 1949, based on the play and film *I Remember Mama*. CBS-TV's *Mama* won awards as a dramatic series[27]—boasting regular characters in self-contained somewhat serious stories but with less melodrama than the soaps or anthology dramas visible at the time. Like *The Goldbergs*, *Mama* was also a family show anchored by a folksy matriarch with a unique dialect. There are quite a few kinscopes of *The Goldbergs* available today, starting from August 1949—they are commercially available on DVD from Shout Factory![28]—but not nearly as much of *Mama*, so it is difficult to contrast the two fairly, particularly in their earliest forms.

But from what I have seen, both series use their situations moderately, focusing primarily on their central characters, via heightened portrayals of both matriarchs who thus seem like figures that belong in a comedy (where the players are representative of real life but caricatured in some benignly incongruous way). This is in spite of a narrative pattern and rhythmic sensibility that is more low key and certainly less ridiculous than the funniest fare from the period, where the vaudeville sensibility, live audience, and personalities designed to yield laugh-out-loud jokes all overtake the kind of muted sweetness seen in the human but sentimental *Goldbergs* and *Mama*. Ultimately, at this point—and they both ran, in some form, into the mid–1950s—I put *Mama* more in the figurative gray area of the serio-comic, which is to say, on the chance that it *wants* to be called a sitcom, I must treat it as such and say it's not great, for while it's far away from the tragedies of Aristotle's day, pleasure from the ridiculous does not seem to be its aim, and if it is, its mimesis is not maneuvered to reliably yield the only true barometer of success: laughter.

Thus, although worthwhile in the sense that the projection of humanity is always worthwhile, in terms of *this* art form, it does not validate the sitcom's comedic needs as a prime consideration. It is not reliably funny. And to be fair, it received awards frequently as a "drama,"[29] so I think it was more comfortable being referred to as such. As for TV's *The Goldbergs*, although it's missing the variety show DNA that pushes for big laughs, its story structure and central character do a better job of indicating humor as an objective. So while it's ultimately less rowdy than some contemporaries—like *The Aldrich Family*, a teen show where the central character is decidedly quirky and it's got obvious comic ideas—the sitcom style is more embraced in a way that it never was in *The Goldbergs*'s radio incarnation. And unlike *Mama*, *The Goldbergs* gets funnier as its TV run continues. So we'll follow it.

A similar live series that premiered in 1949 was *The Ruggles*, a bland family comedy starring movie man Charlie Ruggles. It cast him as a gentle and mostly wise father in quiet stories seeking to emulate suburban life. The scripts seem like they want to be funny—they want to give Ruggles things to which he can react—but all the characters are too generic, too benign.

Launching a three-season ABC run in October 1949, *The Ruggles* is most notable today for being produced live on the West Coast, which was a rarity for national programming in 1949.[30] The strongest and biggest network connections were still predominantly rooted out of New York, where there were more viewers and stations. Most network shows therefore came *from* New York (with Chicago catering to the Midwest in second place) because it had the widest immediate reach;[31] and remember, the only way to see a live broadcast after the fact was a kinescope—a film literally taken of a screen while it was playing. As such, kinescopes had a reputation for being lower quality, and sponsors made their preference known.[32] So it was better at the time for a network to air a program live in the New York area, where the greatest number of stations and people could see it immediately and in decent quality than from anywhere else, including movie hub Los Angeles. For that reason—along with the fact that the ABC network had the fewest stations across the country—Hollywood's *The Ruggles* was never a big hit. It made as little an impression on the audience as its quality as a situation comedy would genuinely warrant.

However, these struggles with live programming, location, and quality had a solution, and it was a solution that the medium initially wanted to ignore: film. Television, even as an experimental form in the 1930s, had long relied on motion pictures to fill time, and kinescopes, of course, were themselves film (typically 16 mm). Yet, as a matter of original programming, the high cost of film production—and all it entailed—compared to a simple live broadcast, made sponsors wary of sparing the extra expense.[33] This would eventually come to a head, for as millions of new viewers were popping up all over, the inferior picture quality of shipped kinescopes began to negatively impact the ratings, which negatively impacted sponsor fees, which in turn negatively impacted business.[34] By the early 1950s, if networks wanted to remain competitive, then they would eventually have to encourage rival technology or, more likely, pony up for film.

Several men had the foresight to recognize this trajectory in advance, and using their experiences and resources in Hollywood, they went about advocating for more film-based television productions by, well, simply producing them. One was famed producer Hal Roach, whose studio made many of the shorts that offered the same type of self-contained stories using a continuity of assembled characters (e.g., Our Gang) that would resemble the simultaneously emerging situation comedy on radio during the late 1930s. His studio started getting involved with dramatic TV series on film in 1948, with the first airing in 1949—*Your Show Time*.[35] But even he was beaten to the punch by the precocious Jerry Fairbanks, a producer and director whose importance to the medium—and this genre, in particular—will be better appreciated in a few chapters. In 1947, he produced what is widely believed to be the first dramatic television series shot on film[36]—*Public Prosecutor*, which was supposed to run for twenty-six 20-minute episodes on NBC. But no sponsor wanted to buy a program that would not fit in 15-minute increments, so the series didn't make it to air until 1951, when it was recut as fodder for a panel game show.[37]

In 1949, Fairbanks produced his first filmed television comedy—a half-hour domestic show called *Jackson and Jill*, with the familiar premise of a silly housewife and her beleaguered mate. Thirteen episodes were shot, with the hope of a network pickup. Unfortunately, test broadcasts by NBC failed to arouse sponsor interest, and the series was not run until it was sold—syndicated—to local stations in the 1950s.[38] Most installments currently circulate. They suggest the series to be a broader, more overtly comic offering than most from the 1940s, with manic plots of farce and misunderstanding, and despite no audience or "laugh track," the show clearly wants to make its viewers chuckle from the ridiculousness. Unfortunately, its two leads' basic temperamental distinctions—already clichéd by 1949—do not help inspire original episodic narratives or spark the bulk of the intended yuks, which arise, if at all, from these otherwise loud but uninspired plots. In essence, then, the elements of the situation—specifically, the characters—are not themselves being used with any evident specificity for comedy, and accordingly, *Jackson and Jill* is not a great sample of the genre. (We will see many series like this, with situations that have nothing to rely on *but* character and yet disappoint because they simply cannot rise to this fundamental challenge.)

Although *Jackson and Jill* did not make NBC's schedule, there was another filmed comedy that did—the TV version of radio staple *The Life of Riley*. Or as history will tell us, the *first* TV version of radio staple *The Life of Riley*, for this show would actually return in the mid-1950s for a lengthy, more successful run. We will discuss it more then. In the meantime, this first iteration is notable because it was the first *filmed* sitcom on network television,[39] airing for one season from October 1949 to March 1950. Producer Irving Brecher, also creator of the concurrent radio series, was able to shoot the TV version cheaply with help from Filmtone,[40] which was known for its economy. Although that economy shows up on screen, the important thing is, it shows up. Unlike most 1940s sitcoms, it was filmed—preserved—and all 26 episodes are out there, watchable.

Brecher was aware that television was the wave of the future and he had been trying to get his series to the small screen for nearly two years, creating several pilot presentations before the one that eventually sold in 1949,[41] utilizing a trial film format that circumvented the kinescope issue and allowed him to stay out in Los Angeles with the radio show. He also had an eye for talent. As TV's first Chester A. Riley, the blue-collar riveter and quintessential down-on-his-luck father of a lower-middle class California family, Brecher cast a young comic named Jackie Gleason.

Yes, this series starred *the* Jackie Gleason, eventually the face of a more popular 1950s sitcom that we will examine in a few chapters (*The Honeymooners*). He replaced *the* William Bendix, the concurrent star of the radio series (and the film that had been released earlier in 1949) whose studio contract wouldn't permit any other filmed projects.[42] Fortunately, by 1953, Bendix was able to re-create for TV the role that radio listeners knew so well—a fact that was vital in the series' resurrection. That's right, despite the great technological success of this first *Riley*—which even earned an early Emmy[43]—the show failed to be as creatively successful as its long-running radio predecessor, and the lack of Bendix, who instilled in Riley so much relatable pathos, seemed to be the generally accepted reason as to why.[44]

Having seen both series, I must agree: there *is* a huge difference between the two. While Gleason's comic prowess would become even more legendary later, his take on Chester A. Riley made the character more of a scenery-chewing aggressor than a put-upon loser. That is, simply by Gleason's innate qualities as a performer, the characterization to which audiences had become accustomed changed; the qualities that made Bendix's Riley funny were *different* from those that made Gleason's Riley funny—and this was a breach to the show's understanding of its situation, even if the premise remained the same.

I posit this as an explanation for how the show was viewed at the time. Today, and in the context of this book's pursuit of ideal samples of the situation comedy genre, Gleason is really the only thing worth watching in the 1949 TV version of *Riley*, for although he sticks out as cartoonish, nobody else has as much energy in this otherwise bland domestic structure, where somewhat relatable yet nevertheless familiar and unimaginative stories sit with little support from the particulars of uniquely defined characters. It is yet another example of a situation comedy not using its situation well for comedy because it does not have characters strong enough to uphold the necessary associations. Fortunately, Bendix would bestow the second version of this TV series with the hit radio program's initial narrative disposition, so stories could feel a little more connected to the situation than they do with Gleason, who figuratively flails about, trying to give the audience something beyond the title's basic familiarity. As for performance, a comparison between Gleason's premiere entry, "Tonsils" (October 4, 1949), and Bendix's later take on the same plot in his series' "Riley's Operation" (April 24, 1953) is illustrative—Bendix tugs on the heart; Gleason tugs on the scenery. It's the difference between seeing Chester A. Riley and a proto–Ralph Kramden. And ultimately, this show was written for Chester A. Riley.

In fact, Gleason clearly wishes it was bigger and bolder—like his eventual *Honeymooners*—taking advantage of his natural kinetic energy and the visual nature of this new medium. But the writing doesn't give him much. Throughout its run and with very few exceptions, this 1949 *Riley* instead remains reliant on lighthearted but banal dialogue. Like so many of these early TV comedies, it might as well be on radio—though, of course, its *actual* radio counterpart was superior, boasting both a star more suited for its narrower aims and an encouraging live studio audience that could cue listeners to laughter and inspire scripts to write laugh-worthy jokes. In contrast, there's no live studio audience for the first TV *Riley*, which willingly trades the spontaneity of theater for the improved visual quality of film. This choice means that the series does look better than any kinescope of the time, proving the point that even cheaply produced films like these could be a solution to the growing constraints of liveness. However, the industry's view of filmed TV comedy remained mixed, with many radio stars affirming—via their forthcoming choices—a prevailing belief that comic players still needed the immediacy of liveness, or at least a present audience, to fuel their performances. That was worth more than picture quality.

Eventually, a group of brilliant minds would find a way to make performance and visual quality not mutually exclusive. In the meantime, there were also a few brief but interesting live efforts aired from New York in 1949-1950, like *That Wonderful Guy*, which starred Jack Lemmon as a wannabe actor working as the valet to a crusty critic.[45] But nothing new caught on in the 1940s, as the TV sitcom was still trying to discover itself inside a medium that hadn't discovered itself yet, calling upon radio stalwarts—like *The Goldbergs* and *The Life of Riley*—to represent the genre during this transitional period, demanding adherence to new practicalities that sometimes altered a show's original charms while also relying on them. Accordingly, the television sitcom was not yet able to cultivate a unique definition, for TV was not radio, and if networks were going to model known successes, they first needed successful models from *within* this new medium. Those would not come overnight. For the time being, adapting radio hits with slight tweaks seemed to be the simplest course of action going into 1950-1951, the first season of TV's defining decade.

# Part II

# Top Sitcoms and Episodes

*Top 50 Sitcom Episodes of the 1950s*

Season is denoted by S followed by a number in parentheses

1. I LOVE LUCY (S2): "Job Switching" (1952)
2. I LOVE LUCY (S1): "Lucy Does a TV Commercial" (1952)
3. THE PHIL SILVERS SHOW (S1): "The Court Martial" (1956)
4. THE HONEYMOONERS (S1): "Better Living Through TV" (1955)
5. I LOVE LUCY (S5): "Lucy's Italian Movie" (1956)
6. THE HONEYMOONERS (S1): "The $99,000 Answer" (1956)
7. BURNS AND ALLEN (S8): "Gracie Is Brilliant" (1958)
8. BURNS AND ALLEN (S8): "Hypnotizing Gracie" (1958)
9. I LOVE LUCY (S4): "L.A. at Last!" (1955)
10. I LOVE LUCY (S4): "Mr. and Mrs. TV Show" (1954)
11. I LOVE LUCY (S4): "Lucy Gets Into Pictures" (1955)
12. I LOVE LUCY (S6): "Lucy Does the Tango" (1957)
13. I LOVE LUCY (S3): "Lucy Tells the Truth" (1953)
14. BURNS AND ALLEN (S8): "A Hole in the Carpet" (1957)
15. OUR MISS BROOKS (S1): "Aunt Mattie Boynton" (1953)
16. I LOVE LUCY (S2): "The Handcuffs" (1952)
17. THE PHIL SILVERS SHOW (S2): "Love That Guardhouse" (1957)
18. THE JACK BENNY PROGRAM (S8): "Christmas Shopping Show" (1957)
19. THE HONEYMOONERS (S1): "The Golfer" (1955)
20. I LOVE LUCY (S5): "The Great Train Robbery" (1955)
21. BURNS AND ALLEN (S4): "An Elephant Sits on Gracie's Fender" (1954)
22. TROUBLE WITH FATHER (S1): "TV Comes to the Erwins" (1951)
23. THE MANY LOVES OF DOBIE GILLIS (S1): "Rock-a-Bye Dobie" (1960)
24. I LOVE LUCY (S4): "Ethel's Birthday" (1954)
25. THE PHIL SILVERS SHOW (S1): "Empty Store" (1955)
26. I LOVE LUCY (S3): "The Million Dollar Idea" (1954)
27. I LOVE LUCY (S4): "The Star Upstairs" (1955)
28. THE BOB CUMMINGS SHOW (S3): "Double Date" (1956)
29. THE MANY LOVES OF DOBIE GILLIS: "The Best Dressed Man" (1959)
30. STANLEY (S1): "Celia Goes to a TV Show" (1956)
31. MISTER PEEPERS (S2): "Nervous Wes" [4/19/53] (1953)
32. THE DANNY THOMAS SHOW (S5): "Uncle Tonoose Meets Mr. Daly" (1958)

33. THE PHIL SILVERS SHOW (S2): "A Mess Sergeant Can't Win" (1956)
34. I LOVE LUCY (S2): "The Operetta" (1952)
35. THE PHIL SILVERS SHOW (S1): "Bivouac" (1955)
36. THE AMOS 'N ANDY SHOW (S1): "Rare Coin" (1951)
37. BURNS AND ALLEN (S6): "Mrs. Sohmers Needs a Psychologist" (1956)
38. THE PHIL SILVERS SHOW (S1): "The Twitch" (1955)
39. THE MANY LOVES OF DOBIE GILLIS (S1): "Love Is a Science" (1959)
40. I LOVE LUCY (S1): "The Ballet" (1952)
41. I LOVE LUCY (S4): "Ethel's Home Town" (1955)
42. I LOVE LUCY (S4): "Harpo Marx" (1955)
43. THE DANNY THOMAS SHOW (S7): "Danny and the Little Men" (1959)
44. OUR MISS BROOKS (S2): "Second Hand First Aid" (1954)
45. BURNS AND ALLEN (S3): "Silky Thompson; Gracie Writes 'My Life with George Burns'" (1952)
46. THE PHIL SILVERS SHOW (S2): "Doberman's Sister" (1956)
47. I LOVE LUCY (S2): "Lucy's Show Biz Swan Song" (1952)
48. MISTER PEEPERS (S2): "The Drive-In Movie" [11/30/52] (1952)
49. OZZIE AND HARRIET (S6): "Tutti-Frutti Ice Cream" (1957)
50. THE BOB CUMMINGS SHOW (S3): "Bob Tangles with Ruthie" (1957)

## Top 10 Favorite Sitcoms of the 1950s

1. I LOVE LUCY (CBS)
2. THE PHIL SILVERS SHOW (CBS)
3. THE HONEYMOONERS (CBS)
4. THE GEORGE BURNS AND GRACIE ALLEN SHOW (CBS)
5. THE BOB CUMMINGS SHOW (NBC/CBS/NBC)
6. THE MANY LOVES OF DOBIE GILLIS (CBS)
7. THE DANNY THOMAS SHOW (ABC/CBS)
8. MISTER PEEPERS (NBC)
9. OUR MISS BROOKS (CBS)
10. THE AMOS 'N ANDY SHOW (CBS/Syndication)

CHAPTER THREE

# Somewhere Between Radio and Film
## *The Best Television Sitcoms of 1950–1951*

At the start of 1950, fewer than four million American households had a television set.[1] That was approximately 9 percent of the population.[2] By the start of 1951, those numbers had jumped to over 10.3 million households, or 23.5 percent—the greatest single-year increase in the medium's history.[3] If there was any thought in the 1940s that television was a passing fad—or a technology too rudimentary for discerning consumers—1950 proved that it was here to stay, and viewers were decidedly interested in what it had to offer. In addition to various practical matters, like the emerging number of TV stations and the lowering cost of individual sets, the improving nature of the content being programmed also had something to do with this quick acceleration.

Welcome to the 1950s and the bulk of this book's focus. We will be going year by year in search of the best examples of situation comedy as I have defined the term. As noted previously, I will not be discussing every single sitcom that aired on TV—local, network, syndication, or otherwise—but only the ones that I believe are most essential for a well-rounded study of the genre in this era and in support of my thesis that the situation comedy is an art form.

Let's start where we left off in the last chapter—with the sitcom trying to figure out the best way to exist within this new medium, as the networks were looking for guaranteed successes, adapting radio hits with mixed results. While NBC's version of *The Life of Riley*, the first filmed network sitcom, failed to make it out of spring 1950 and its single season, other radio staples performed solidly, like CBS's *The Goldbergs*, a serio-comedy that, in its new half-hour format, was slowly embracing more of the genre's conventions even though there was still a comparative lack of intentionality with regard to humor as its primary source of catharsis, and *The Aldrich Family*, a more obviously comic endeavor that found itself rising in the ratings on NBC. In fact, *The Aldrich Family*, which was also broadcast live from New York, ended the 1950–1951 season as the only sitcom in the Nielsen top 30.[4] Also in that esteemed group was *Mama*, another genre-muddying series classified more often as a drama than a comedy. As discussed, I don't think it's funny enough—or *wants to be* funny enough—to be considered a sitcom, and it doesn't show any evolution in the comedic direction (like *The Goldbergs*). So, I tend not to put it in this category—and from here on out, this study will not consider it a worthy example.

That means only one actual sitcom was in the top 30. This seeming lack of popularity for the sitcom in 1950–1951 can be attributed to a few things. For one, TV still didn't offer a lot of programming that satisfies our definition of the genre. Additionally, the funniest material on television at the time tended to come from the variety shows—*Texaco Star Theater*, starring Milton Berle; *Your Show of Shows*, starring Sid Caesar, Imogene Coca, and a young Carl Reiner; and *The Colgate Comedy Hour*, with Eddie Cantor, Dean Martin and Jerry Lewis, and Bud Abbott and Lou Costello. Those three were represented in the 1950–1951 TV season's top five most-watched regular programs according to Nielsen.[5] And one thing that united them—aside from the fact that they turned back to vaudeville influences and were performed live in front of audiences—is that they all recognized the vital difference between radio and television. Television, unlike radio, is a *visual* medium. To capitalize on this opportunity, Berle dressed in drag, Caesar and Coca offered extended pantomimes, and Cantor mugged to the rafters—and it was unique hilarity: a theatrical, vaudeville-like experience transmitted *into people's homes* for the first time.

In contrast, the situation comedy, dominated now by radio carryovers, had not quite learned this crucial distinction between the mediums. Or rather, the genre, as a whole, was not yet taking advantage of the unique opportunities presented by television as opposed to radio. Indeed, if there is a central theme about the sitcom as it exists on TV in 1950–1951, it is that it's still trying to figure out its best modes of practice—should it simply be an extension of what already proved to be a hit on radio? Should it be considered even more like vaudeville, with music and spectacle? Or should it adopt some of the qualities of film, a format that was sure to rise in prominence given its visual superiority compared to live telecasts and low-quality kinescopes? That is, if the situation comedy itself already had a definition thanks to radio, how would it best exist in this new medium?

Those questions were all explored in the network's programming choices, and as expected, a lot of what the sitcom had to offer this year would have already been familiar to audiences because they were known titles from radio. Continuing the trend, 1950–1951 saw the TV debuts of many radio staples, including *Meet Corliss Archer*, *The George Burns and Gracie Allen Show*, and *The Jack Benny Program*, all of which were staged live, in a theater before an audience, in hopes of retaining the rhythms and sounds they enjoyed on radio. This, mind you, was unlike the popular and aforementioned *The Aldrich Family*, another radio-to-TV effort now embarking on its second year in the new medium and courting a brief public controversy following NBC's much-discussed firing of Jean Muir, who had been cast as the new Mrs. Aldrich but was blacklisted and banished from the air hours before her intended August 1950 debut.[6]

That series, while more comedic than its serio-comic siblings from 1949, had dropped the live audience it had in radio in favor of a sensibility more reminiscent of the medium's early dramatic anthology shows. Thus, by the others engaging an audience—something, as you'll recall, that the vaudeville performers brought over to the situation comedy format once the two began to merge in the late 1930s—these new TV sitcoms of 1950 were expressing a more explicit desire to make their viewers laugh, using an in-house crowd as the communal indication of intent, and the force to which their scripts would ideally be directing their desired humor, just as in the season's most popular comedy-variety offerings. Laughter was again the goal.

Even the TV version of *Meet Corliss Archer*, a radio sitcom that premiered in 1943 within the wave of *Aldrich Family*–inspired teen-centered programs, delineated itself from its masculine predecessor by coming to television with the live audience it enjoyed on radio.[7] Unfortunately, the series—which, unlike the New York–based *Aldrich*, was produced live in Hollywood[8]—did not get carried weekly in many parts of the country,[9] and though the show returned for a few months in winter 1952, it wasn't until a filmed and recast season produced for syndication in 1954 that the series made a name for itself in television, as it had on radio. Sadly, with zero episodes of this original live run known to exist today, it's hard to know much about its artistic quality. I mention the show here for the trends it suggests—not just the ongoing influx of radio transfers and the increased use of a studio audience for comedies, but also the move of production to Los Angeles, which was obviously going to grow as film became an attractive option for TV. This was also part of the debate that the entire medium was starting to have during 1950–1951.

However, before we get into some of this year's filmed efforts, the time has come to discuss the season's first genuinely laudable sitcom—one of the aforementioned radio transfers whose artistic merit undoubtedly influenced *Meet Corliss Archer*'s production choices: a similarly live, Hollywood-produced, and audience-utilizing classic, *The George Burns and Gracie Allen Show*.

## *Say Hello, Gracie (and Hi, Jack)*

George Burns and Gracie Allen were a husband-and-wife pair of vaudevillians who came to radio in 1932 with the rest of their displaced contemporaries. Originally adhering to a more variety-forward template, the married duo's show refined the personas they had developed on the stage (and screen)—she, the naïf with a literal brand of illogical logic, and he, the sometimes tired but generally amused spectator. This general understanding of their elementary characterizations encouraged the rhythm of their setup, joke, and joke patter (derived, again, from their act), along with memorable gags and stunts, like Gracie's 1932 search for her missing brother and her 1940 campaign for president as a candidate from the fictional "Surprise Party."[10]

In 1941, a landmark year for the situation comedy on radio, Burns and Allen followed the popular tastes and turned their show into a more straightforward sitcom, redefining their characters *as* husband and wife with a step toward a stronger mimesis of their real lives, acknowledging their existence as a showbiz couple but in a largely domestic structure. That is, stories were not about the making of their weekly radio show but about the daily happenings at their home, where the George and Gracie personas continued to solidify as they were now existing within episodic situations that capably displayed them. And, of course, they performed in front of a loud, appreciative studio audience throughout their 18-year radio run. The pair's final season on radio was 1949–1950, their first for CBS, which had scooped the show away from NBC, along with Jack Benny's program and *Amos 'n Andy*, as part of the infamous "Paley raids," when network president Bill Paley saw television on the horizon and had the foresight to recruit top talents just before he knew they would all be making the transition.[11] By then, the series had evolved into the formula that it would adopt for its October 1950 TV debut, with a cast that included George and Gracie; a secondary couple in the Mortons, their neighbors and best pals, played by Bea Benaderet and Hal March; and Bill Goodwin as the bachelor announcer who handled all the commercials.

Since *The George Burns and Gracie Allen Show*—or simply, *Burns and Allen*—was one of the funniest radio sitcoms of the era due to George and Gracie's easily identifiable personas, well reinforced in story by the show's writers—which included a young Paul Henning—CBS wanted to make their transition to television as seamless as possible, maintaining the quality of this already known and viable entity. That's why the radio show's entire main ensemble was picked up. Also, the addition of a theatrical staging now vital for the visual medium required more rehearsal, so the couple was allowed to commit to a biweekly production. Instead of every week, the TV series would air every other week, alternating on the schedule with a half-hour dramatic anthology called *Starlight Theatre*. The cast and crew would receive no hiatus, but this meant they were responsible for only 26 broadcasts in a year—fewer than on radio.

What's more, as vaudeville performers who had helped routinize live audiences as a staple of the radio situation comedy when their own show evolved in that direction, Burns and Allen were determined to continue benefiting from the immediate spectator response. This meant the show had to be broadcast live, and in 1950, maximum success in live television demanded still that the series originate out of New York, where the coaxial connection had the greatest reach, allowing for simultaneous broadcast to the most stations and thus viewers. The problem? Burns and Allen and their entire cast and crew were based out of Hollywood, as so many of the radio comedies of the late 1940s had been, and nobody involved wanted to uproot their lives to the other coast, even if it meant that most of the country would end up seeing their shows in lesser picture quality on kinescope, making Nielsen triumph unlikely. So a compromise was reached.

The show would originate from New York in the fall of 1950 for six episodes, giving East Coast audiences a chance to find the program and become attached to it while they could view it in good quality, and then the company would move to their permanent home in Hollywood—at Columbia Square, a CBS production facility with radio studios that could also accommodate some television production—and that region would now see the show live, while the rest of the country would be treated with kinescopes.[12] Unfortunately, this would guarantee lower national ratings, but everyone expected that eventually technology would improve. Indeed, a coast-to-coast coaxial cable was in the offing and became available for use by the start of the show's following season (we will discuss this more next chapter). In the meantime, this arrangement allowed Burns and Allen to both perform in front of a live audience without permanently moving.

Their return to Los Angeles with the TV series' seventh broadcast also brought the last appearance of Hal March as neighbor Harry Morton, launching an infamous string of replacements in the role that led to two other men pairing opposite Bea Benaderet in the 1950–1951 season alone—first John Brown and later Fred Clark. Initially, Harry Morton was just the clichéd wisecracking put-upon husband, but each actor brought a new twist to the part, informing his depiction. Fred Clark, who stayed with the company until 1953, latched on to the comedic notion of Harry Morton's huge appetite—a trait that then came to define most of his jokes, until he too was replaced by Larry Keating and the part transformed radically again, adopting the cultured pomposity that this actor would later exhibit as a regular on *Mister Ed*, helping to create a more all-encompassing persona for *Burns and Allen*'s secondary husband and in tandem with the show's ascension into a more fully formed television situation comedy. More on that later.

Running for eight seasons on CBS-TV, the series indeed evolved considerably during this time—not just by way of its Harry Mortons. In fact, you can easily divide the series' trajectory into eras, and while we will continue to follow its evolution in later chapters, it is helpful to get a rundown here, starting with the first two years, which were produced live before an audience. They are the *most* like the radio series, with a sense of vaudeville theatricality and a thinness of episodic narrative, as story must compete with musical numbers (dropped early) and integrated commercials typically inserted into the action by announcer Bill Goodwin, later Harry Von Zell, who replaced the former in September 1951. The show then switched to film in 1952, dropping the live audience in favor of an added laugh track (mostly recorded from screenings of fully edited episodes).[13] With this move, the text begins to shed some of its vaudeville origins to become a more typical domestic comedy of the era, enlivened by George's direct address to the audience, which is no longer framed by a stage proscenium but done straight to the camera, in a manner no less theatrical, yet contextualized now within the medium's new aesthetic: film.

In 1956, following the previous year's introduction of Ronnie Burns (the stars' real-life son), the show enters the last two years of its existence—and perhaps its most famous phase—when George Burns reveals his "magic TV," allowing him to watch the action, just as he had done throughout the run, only now through the specific apparatus of the television, which had itself so risen in prominence that it could replace vaudeville, radio, and film as an aesthetic unto itself—a perfect metaphor for how the situation comedy came to embrace a new understanding inside this medium, and how, specifically, *Burns and Allen* is the perfect ambassador for the radio sitcom transferred to TV, slowly adopting more of the traits that made this genre unique. Of course, the show never *totally* abandons the ethos that its performers intrinsically brought before the cameras—their history as hoofers in vaudeville—but as it began to embrace even more elements of the TV situation comedy, the writers also carved out time at the end of every story for the two to step out and offer a quick afterpiece routine, thereby acknowledging what these stars did best without diluting the requirements of weekly plot. It was a cherry on top of the sitcom sundae.

As for the show's use of its situation, its leads—George and Gracie—are always more simplistic than the best characters we will be examining throughout this book, with little nuance or refinement exhibited over their eight-year run. But after decades of entrenchment within American popular culture, their basic personalities, and specifically their relationship with each other, were so immediately recognizable to audiences that the emotional identification was strong. And with writers who knew how to play to those personas—how to play to their formulaic patter within stories that could also showcase "daffy Gracie" and "amused George" in accordance with the audience's expectations—*Burns and Allen* could therefore become a solid example of a sitcom using its characters (okay, primarily Gracie) in episodic narratives for the pursuit of comedy.

Now, the show gets much better about accomplishing all of the above as it progresses; even ideas that were originally performed in the first two live years and then remade during the filmed seasons tend to be better rendered later on, when there's more room for story and, more particularly, more room for these elemental characterizations to be linked with story, for again, these early broadcasts are having to make time *within the action* for commercials.

Additionally, the many casting changes progress the show in a positive direction for character, so early *Burns and Allen*, with its initial ensemble and production setup, is not as rich as what comes ahead. Also, these live shows only exist via kinescope—they are not in syndication—and while 33 of the 52 broadcasts from these first two seasons circulated on YouTube as of a few years ago, they are not in great quality. So the picture we have of the show during this era is inherently limited. In this regard, while I am highlighting the series here in the 1950–1951 chapter as a favorable example of the sitcom from this era—heck, it's this particular season's best sitcom in terms of the art form—keep in mind that by the series' own standards, the best is yet to come, and it is mostly a function of the weaker competition here in *this* TV season that I am even singling it out. That said, there are legitimate reasons to praise the show in the context of 1950–1951 specifically, for though it gets better about using its situation in story later, it is *already* a decided comedy—and a situation comedy to boot, for it is using the continuity of its ridiculous depictions of George and, in particular, Gracie, who are playing themselves in a ridiculous mimesis of their own lives, *for the purposes of making us laugh.*

Not only is the live audience there to fuel the comedic drive of the text and the energy of the performances, removing any (unlikely) doubt as to intent—but also, the writing's inherent understanding of how to emphasize the already jokey Burns and Allen personas, placing them in effortlessly revealing narrative scenarios, helps render this one of the most laugh-filled situation comedies TV had heretofore seen. And that means the most cathartic, most ideal. There are no singular episodes from this season within my official top 50—a list that we will be tracking throughout the book—but if I were picking a highlight from what's available, I would select an entry now referred to as "Happy Hmm Hmm," which first aired on January 4, 1951.

The second segment broadcast from Los Angeles, and the first with John Brown in the role of Harry Morton—George introduces the new actor in an aside to the audience—this episode's story would later be reused in the TV show's fourth year, its second on film. Neither version is notably better, but it's a textbook narrative idea for the series, as it's entirely predicated on Gracie's characterization. That is, while the concept of a circled calendar date with an unknown meaning might be traditional domestic fare with a relatability that most of the shows in this era could employ—with any husband-and-wife sitcom seeking some form of mimesis—when it's coupled with the recognizable and continuity-backed daffiness of Gracie's characterization, it becomes specific and uniquely tailored to her, as now the humor gets something akin to *motivation* for its existence. And while most outings here in the first season of *Burns and Allen* already try to make sure her elemental persona is displayed within their thin weekly stories, the typical template is heavily dependent on external stimuli—a visit from the tax man, from the salesman, from the cop—and how Gracie befuddles and aggravates them by being, well, Gracie. In these, she is driving the comedy, but they are so reliant on obstacles that arise in the plot sans her direct pushing—meaning, she is largely being *placed* in scenarios instead of making individual narrative choices, based on her characterization, that would give rise to them.

You can see the contrast by comparing those segments to "Happy Hmm Hmm," where Gracie's confusion is *the reason* for the story's existence. Again, it's relatively slight, per the series' nature at this point in its life—but it's dependent on her acting in accordance with what we know about her character. To wit, this is one of the closest episodes here in season one to being what we could call "character driven"—meaning, the story and its telling are directly influenced by the characterizations and how they are depicted within this singular half hour (with intellectual support, of course, from the continuity of their sustained personas). So in addition to being merely a good showing for Gracie—as most *Burns and Allen* samples know to be, even here in 1950–1951—and venerating the use of character as the best way of using a situation in story for comedy, this installment's narrative is more prescient than the year's other offerings.

Of course, I also enjoy "Happy Hmm Hmm" because it features a guest cameo by Burns and Allen's real-life friend and colleague Jack Benny, whose own TV career formally began during the 1950–1951 season, following a one-off program for the local Los Angeles area in early 1949.[14] Unlike Burns and Allen, who jumped from one medium to the other, Benny creeped gingerly into television, maintaining his weekly radio series for CBS until 1955. In 1950–1951, he offered only four broadcasts. That number increased to six the following year and then eight the year after until Benny was eventually offering a new TV entry every other week in the latter half of the 1950s. In the fall of 1960, the comic finally resigned himself to the weekly TV grind, which he maintained for CBS-TV until 1964, and then back on NBC (from which he had been "raided" at the end of 1948) for one more season, ending in 1965. With a 15-season run on TV, yielding 261 total episodes, *The Jack Benny Program* went through a lot of changes during its life.

It initially began, here in 1950–1951, as a live show broadcast before an audience from CBS's New York City facilities,[15] converted from former Broadway theaters. By the fall of 1951, the coast-to-coast coaxial cable allowed Benny to stage his television programs in front of an audience in Hollywood,[16] where he remained, save a few on-location endeavors, until 1965. Also, starting in the 1953–1954 season, the company began producing filmed excursions—shot without an audience but laughter added to the soundtrack—and these would be interspersed with the live shows until late 1959, after which the live telecasts became "live to tape," allowing Benny to keep the audience but avoid kinescopes.[17] Today, the series' syndication package includes only 104 episodes,[18] all filmed, and there are still upward of 80 unavailable to even the most ardent Benny collectors, who are lucky to receive access to UCLA's near-complete archive.

However, the problem with *The Jack Benny Program*, as far as this book is concerned, is not just lack of access as a result, largely, of the technological limitations of the time; it is that the TV iteration of this radio series' "modified" situation comedy never progresses in the new medium to reliably become a sitcom comparable with the rest of the genre. While *Burns and Allen* slowly downplayed the elements of vaudeville and variety from which it developed in the 1930s, Benny's program continued to lean into them. On radio, *The Jack Benny Program* was essentially a variety show that was able to offer situation comedy as a result of having a great ensemble of well-defined characters—*the* funniest and best-designed comic characters on radio. And yet, despite this proficiency with character, the central element defining all situation comedies, the series would always stand apart from the rest of TV's sitcoms due to its equal reliance on song and sketch, along with the typical variety show framing—with Jack as master of ceremonies.

But the TV *Jack Benny Program* actually emerges with a disadvantage too— as the radio series' strong ensemble was whittled down to basically just Jack and his faithful announcer Don Wilson, the jovial and rotund but otherwise least-defined member of a cast that had, since 1939, reliably also included snappy sidekick Mary

Livingstone (Benny's real-life wife), naive tenor Dennis Day, incorrigible bandleader Phil Harris, and Jack's long-suffering valet Rochester (played by Eddie Anderson, one of the earliest Black regulars on a radio series).[19] For over a decade—barring Day's stint in the navy during World War II—listeners could expect to hear all of these players every week, but contractual obligations and Livingstone's nervous jitters prohibited seeing them regularly on television. In the four TV shows from 1950–1951, Wilson and Anderson appear twice, Livingstone appears once (her only live episode of the series), and Day and Harris do not appear at all.[20] Benny's show essentially becomes just about Jack with his guests, and removing the central character from his ensemble of other equally well-drawn personalities has the effect of limiting the possibilities for character-driven comedy, especially when the void is filled by celebrities, most of whom just go into their shtick… like in a vaudeville or variety show.

Accordingly, *The Jack Benny Program* on TV—especially at this early juncture, when it was live and out of New York—is *less* of a situation comedy than its best years on radio … even though the strength of Benny's persona alone is like Gracie Allen, one of the richest of this period: most identifiable and utilizable and enough to indeed inspire genuine situation comedy moments, when it so chooses. As far as this TV season is concerned, there is nothing in the sitcom category of note because of how character and story exist, but we will keep one eye on the show—specifically the entries that resemble the genre—as we go forward in this book.

## Black (and White)

Meanwhile, another radio comedy moved over to TV in 1950, and it also originated from New York.[21] But this one was shot on film and less concerned with humor being its paramount objective: *The Beulah Show*. The origins of *Beulah* can be traced back to 1939, when white comic Marlin Hurt introduced the character of a folksy Black domestic worker named Beulah Brown, whom he voiced on the radio series *Hometown Incorporated*, endowing her with all the same minstrel foundations as *Amos 'n Andy*.[22] Hurt and the popular Beulah character then bounced around a few series until landing a recurring role on *Fibber McGee and Molly* in 1944 as the McGee family maid.[23] Beulah quickly became one of that show's most popular attractions (with catchphrases of her own: "Somebody bawl fo' Beulah?" and "Love that man!"), and like Harold Peary's Gildersleeve, Hurt and his beloved characterization soon got their own series. This was *The Marlin Hurt and Beulah Show*, where Hurt played Beulah, her love interest Bill, and a version of himself in a new half-hour sitcom where Beulah was now working as housekeeper and cook for an upper-middle-class white family, the Hendersons.[24] When Hurt died suddenly in 1946, an effort to find a replacement led to a string of on-air auditions before the show finally settled on its pick: another white man, Bob Corley.[25] By this time, the program had been renamed

*The Beulah Show*, but with ratings down and corresponding public outcry from groups like the NAACP, which objected to the grossly stereotypical depiction of a Black housekeeper by a white performer in full "black-voice," something had to be done.[26]

In 1947, something was done. Oscar-winning actress Hattie McDaniel, best known as Mammy from *Gone with the Wind*, made history when she debuted as Beulah—the first Black actor to be the star of a sponsored radio program.[27] The basic format from the Hurt show had remained intact—Beulah was a domestic working for a white family, but she had a best friend named Oriole, the Black cook next door, and a recurring boyfriend in Bill, a charming gadabout who combined a dozen tropes in one, made more glaring by the racial implications associated with the limited depiction of African Americans in media at the time. However, the structure slightly changed, as *The Beulah Show* became a daily 15-minute program instead of the traditional weekly half hour common to this sitcom genre. This did not meaningfully alter the style of the show—it was a definite comedy, with a live audience there to react loudly on command[28]—but the storytelling, as with all 15-minute strips, was naturally influenced by these time limitations.

When the fledgling ABC-TV network—which came late to the television game and thus had fewer stations affiliated with its programming[29]—decided to start moving some of its properties over, *The Beulah Show* was one of its first choices. With the sponsorship of Procter & Gamble, the company and ABC decided—following the technical success of *The Life of Riley*—to film the series. But unlike *Burns and Allen*, which sought a seamless transition between mediums, the powers that be decided not to bring over radio's McDaniel.

Instead, Ethel Waters was cast in the role. Waters was a singer and respected Broadway actress who had some success in the movies, earning an Oscar nod in 1949. Her elevating presence was likely used as a defensive strike against the lingering criticism about the show and its racial stereotyping. A deal was made to shoot the show from New York, where Waters was concurrently starring in a Broadway play, *The Member of the Wedding*, with *Beulah* intending to move west when it closed.[30] But the fundamental premise of the series—a gentle but wise Black woman catering to and solving the benign problems of a white family—were difficult to undersell, and the show was met with anticipated resistance, particularly on the set, where Waters struggled to bring dignity to the role, seeking to emphasize the camaraderie among the other Black cast members, including Percy "Bud" Harris as Bill and the iconic Butterfly McQueen as Oriole. Yet there was only so much they could do, and Harris quit the series after a few months over frustration.[31] He was replaced by Dooley Wilson, who finished the season. However, after 39 episodes, Waters herself had also enough of the noise and bowed out.[32]

The network and sponsor took this opportunity to revamp the show entirely, bringing in a new production company (Roland Reed's), which would continue to film the show for the 1951–1952 season, but out on the West Coast at Hal Roach

Studios.[33] With a whole new cast (including Ruby Dandridge and Ernest Whitman), Hattie McDaniel was finally asked to re-create her radio role on TV, and the visual *Beulah* now better matched the radio program, which had finally earned some NAACP support.[34] Unfortunately, McDaniel was unknowingly battling the cancer that would soon take her life, and after shooting only six episodes, the series was forced into a hiatus[35] as the season's scheduled premiere got pushed back to the spring. Eventually, she would be replaced again by another Black staple in Hollywood, Louise Beavers, who shot the remainder of the next 39 episodes—which eventually aired from April to December 1952 (into the 1952–1953 season), with the six McDaniel episodes tacked on at the end of the summer 1952 run.

Beavers was not as much of a draw as McDaniel, and the show's bad luck, along with some never-subsiding concerns over its origins and premise, led to *Beulah*'s cancellation. The episodes were then sold into syndication but pulled in 1966 amid the civil rights movement.[36] Once off the market, episodes of *The Beulah Show* became collectors' items, and about a dozen now widely circulate. From what *is* accessible, the differences between the three TV Beulahs are clear. Waters is allowed to instill in the role the most individual agency of the three. But with scripts trying hard not to rely on clichés for her comedy, they push off the humor burden to Bill and Oriole, and then make it impossible for the central character to really drive much of anything, including story. The surviving entries from the first season, while not laugh-less, are muted as a result, with Beulah divorced too much from both the situation and the comedy.

The Beavers episodes, meanwhile, offer a more subservient Beulah with the least individualized sensibility—she is there to fulfill the role's function within the premise, and that's it. She is amiable but really makes the discomforting concept—even by the standards of the 1950s—less fun and easy to watch. Although Beavers' time on *Beulah* ran during both the 1951–1952 and 1952–1953 seasons, what is available from her tenure isn't good enough to be fodder for discussion alongside the better examples of situation comedy in the chapters ahead.

And last but certainly not least, I am fortunate to note that four of McDaniel's scant six filmed offerings of *The Beulah Show* are currently available on YouTube. They reveal what is perhaps obvious: the Oscar-winning actress was most able to find a happy medium between the two other women who played the role, for McDaniel's Beulah exists more dominantly in story that satisfies the premise, while also bringing individuality and attitude to the limited characterization. This makes sense—McDaniel *was* Beulah for many years on radio and the star most associated with its concept, so of course she would be the best fit. And yet, even with the best person in the role, the premise remains a problem, as McDaniel's screen persona is very much linked to the aforementioned Mammy of *Gone with the Wind*, a subservient Black woman who can sass at the white folk but only because she is protective of them and has dedicated her whole life to them, with the other Black characters taking more of a metaphorical back seat (something Waters, specifically, hoped to change). This makes for a naturally funnier Beulah, but it is more heavily stereotypical—compared to, say, Waters'—and for as much humanity as McDaniel supplies by the sheer force of her being, even when her show is trying to be explicitly unserious, its mimesis of human life is less capable of instilling pleasure than other shows from this era—there's unspoken tension, and it's not comedic. Too many viewers seemed to agree, both Black and white, for while on radio, this discomfort was easier to hide. Now, the bright, intimate light of humans being projected on a tiny screen into American homes revealed all.

An interesting contrast to *The Beulah Show* was *The Amos 'n Andy Show*, another iconic Black-centered radio comedy that moved to TV during the 1950–1951 season and was shot by the Hal Roach Studios in Los Angeles, where it would be produced and filmed for CBS.

As with *The Beulah Show*, the suits knew some changes would need to be made to transfer the *Amos 'n Andy* radio series, which, as we explored, did not start as a sitcom but adapted to the developed form in 1943, when it went from a daily 15-minute serial, hardened by some serious dramatic moments, to a more exclusively comic affair in the classic 30-minute weekly structure, performed for a studio audience with episodic, self-contained plots that nevertheless used the continuity of its characters. To accommodate this comedic shift, the show's storytelling began moving away from ideas about Amos and Andy, pairing the latter more often with their bumbling but scheming friend the Kingfish (also voiced by Gosden), in plots that followed their weekly get-rich-quick endeavors and the various entanglements into which the Kingfish ensnared Andy.

In the late 1940s, the show was not as big a phenomenon as it had been during the peak of the serial craze, but these characters had become cultural mainstays, the longest running leads of any program on the air. Concerns about the potentially racist tropes that became more prominent when the show grew more interested in courting big laughs in the sitcom form could therefore be somewhat calmed by the emotional affection listeners maintained for the stars, an affinity that stemmed from the serial days and seemed to suggest a valuable type of human connection (as argued by historians like Elizabeth McLeod[37]), despite the fact that the program was still being voiced by white men (who had donned blackface for a film adaptation in the early 1930s).

But television was a visual medium, and as this was starting to become clear when plans were made to bring *Amos 'n Andy* to TV, Gosden and Correll could not feasibly play these characters.[38] If CBS-TV wanted to bring into the new medium its most potent entertainment brand, snagged from NBC in the aforementioned Paley raids, then it would have to cast Black actors—and not just for Amos and Andy but in every main role that audiences knew on the original series. This would thus be a watershed event—the first all–Black cast of a television program—and in a series that, unlike *The Beulah Show*, did not put Black characters on the periphery of a white world, but actually focused on them within an entire community of their own, where they were everything: doctors, lawyers, judges, cops, taxi drivers, singers, good guys, bad guys, and so forth. In the discourse surrounding *The Amos 'n Andy Show* and its regressive stereotypes, the world represented in its text, and the opportunities presented to deserving Black talent, is often overshadowed. This is unfortunate, for with a regular cast that includes Alvin Childress, Spencer Williams, Tim Moore, Johnny Lee, Ernestine Wade, Nick O'Demus, and Amanda Randolph, the TV version of *Amos 'n Andy*, at the time of its debut in June 1951, boasts the strongest collection of performers in any television situation comedy yet.

I make these points to help explain how millions of viewers—still today—can derive genuine enjoyment from a series that, even in the 1950s, made millions of other viewers uncomfortable, just like *Beulah*. In fact, using the social context of the time to discuss artistic merit is necessary since the mimesis of life—and the contortion of it that makes for comedy—is dependent on a shared set of social standards regarding "normalcy." Those standards evolve; normal in the 2020s is certainly different from normal in the 1950s, and because this work was produced to elicit a reaction from 1950s audiences, it is helpful to understand *their* perspective to truly comprehend how well—or even if—the show is successful at being a situation comedy.

Compared simply to *Beulah*, the most attractive thing about TV's *Amos 'n Andy* is that it intends to regularly make its audience laugh out loud. Not only does it offer an added laugh track—which, by 1951, was starting to become more standard for filmed sitcoms—but everything from its punch line–filled dialogue to its chosen comic stories helps the series affirm humor as its priority. What's more, *Amos 'n Andy*, along with *Trouble with Father*, which we will examine later in the chapter, were among the first TV sitcoms to successfully take advantage of the visual benefit of the medium, adding slapstick and physical comedy to the regular roster—laughs that would arise from what audiences were *seeing*, not just what they were hearing. This perhaps makes for the most significant distinction between radio and television comedies.

However, visuality also adds other elements to these dramatic works as well via costumes and makeup, lighting and set design, editing and cinematography. And, of course, via casting—not just based on voice but on look now as well. All of these elements working to achieve the same goals could make for a theoretically stronger product, or conversely, they could make it more difficult for an audience to emotionally invest—to accept what they're seeing as a basic mimesis (however contorted)— for if these elements do not add up, the text could be undermined along with the comedy, a phenomenon dependent on an intellectual compatibility. That is, we must first *notice* a mimesis to recognize the benign incongruities making it funny. Undermining a mimesis too much, and for reasons other than comedic purposes, could very well deflate the humor. And, again, this is a large part of why the TV *Amos 'n Andy* knew to cast Black actors—more than just being socially progressive, it was now necessary for the comedy.

So *Amos 'n Andy* is an intentionally funny series, which makes it easier to like, and the TV version crafted its big decisions around humor—a respectable motivation given that comedy, as we know, is an art. But how does this sitcom stack up given our understanding of the form? Well, the short answer is "very good" by the standards of 1950–1951 but "subpar" by the standards of the 1950s en masse, for we are about to meet some truly clear, well-defined characters, around whom entire series and their storytelling revolve, and when compared to the best of this era, the caricatured personas of figures like the Kingfish feel decidedly thin and sketch-like, drawn in broad, generic strokes, without the kind of details or precision that make future sitcom leads feel more mimetic and, from there, funny. The same is essentially true of many white characters in this period, like Gracie Allen, but the depiction of Black leads—previously played by white actors and still written by white writers—remained affiliated with the tropes of minstrelsy, and it therefore warrants additional scrutiny, for this origin story calls into question these mimetic foundations—how much genuine humanity *can* these characters have as the creations of white men in veritable Black face? And what's more, if we can agree that the heightened depictions of the Kingfish and Andy and Sapphire (Kingfish's wife) et al. make them basically incongruous with "normal," can they also be *benign* given the racial context—meaning, is it socially acceptable to laugh at them?

These questions are not much of a concern for Gracie—she may be a stock type ("the Dumb Dora")—but for many viewers in the 1950s, and certainly for the handful of writers who wrote to satisfy her persona, she is only one degree of separation from their humanity. She's more mimetic. But for the Kingfish and his crew, their blackface origins pushed them one degree further—a mask behind *another* mask—and for the purposes of the sitcom genre, there was more figurative territory to traverse to find a true mimesis. So the benignity of their caricatured, incongruous, laugh-seeking portrayals was up for debate. Naturally, the NAACP was as concerned about *Amos 'n Andy* as *Beulah*,[39] for although this series had finally adopted a Black cast, its more overt pursuit of comedy heightened the characters' ridiculous traits, making figures who already did not feel as human as other shows' seem even less so (especially because, again, it had been a long time since the radio version had moved away from the serial's counterbalancing drama). This created a jarring dichotomy—characters who looked more human than ever before were nevertheless sounding even *less* human than ever before. Or rather, they sounded exactly the same, but in this new medium, where a projected mimesis was more fragile as a result of new visual considerations, that was no longer acceptable. The standards were higher—artistically too.

Thus, despite good ratings,[40] the withdrawal of a nervous sponsor led to the cancellation of the TV show[41] after only two seasons of 52 episodes, with 13 additional segments sold with the rest of the run into syndication, where, a year later, another 13 would be eventually added, creating for CBS one of its most lucrative filmed properties of the decade. Well, until the late 1960s, when, with *Beulah*, the NAACP and other activist groups successfully lobbied to remove *Amos 'n Andy* from the syndication marketplace,[42] cementing its reputation as a racist relic of the pre–civil rights era and unworthy of being seen, despite the complicated qualities that gave it such a fan base, particularly among Black viewers who *did* identify with the characters they saw on their screens—at a time when that was so obviously rare. (This was the subject of a 1983 documentary, *Amos 'n Andy: Anatomy of a Controversy*, in which fans like Redd Foxx and Marla Gibbs championed the series.) Fortunately, this show's popularity—particularly among Black viewers—has kept it more visible than *Beulah* in the years since it was pulled, and the majority of *Amos 'n Andy's* TV run is available online for enjoyment and debate, criticism, and appreciation.

I think this is as it should be, especially because, by our definitions, *Amos 'n Andy* is as good an example of a TV sitcom as we could find in 1951, for although the characters are defined with so many exaggerated traits that the basic mimesis necessary for a comic contortion is below this decade's standards, the leads nevertheless *do* have definition and are capable of propelling story, earning laughs in the process. Oh, yes, there are a lot of circumstantial misunderstandings and weekly plots that engage in clichés removed from the unique qualities of this series' actual situation—so it's not necessarily consistent—but the Kingfish, along with Jack Benny and Gracie Allen, is one of the most comedically reliable sitcom figures in this chapter, and that's evident in all the best segments produced for the TV version of *Amos 'n Andy*. His commitment to bilking others, even his friends, gives him something of a regular objective in story, and the way he plies his charm to counteract the reputation he has for scheming and dishonesty provides him an obvious personality that emphasizes extremes but is more than single faceted. Also, the fact that he can be just as gullible as those whom he's hoping to dupe is an ironic delight—giving comic twists to many stories that otherwise would be straightforward. He's the series' most utilizable figure, while his relationship with Andy is itself well defined and, for this era, well used. So in recognition of the show's relative success at using its characters (namely, Kingfish)—the key aspect of its situation—for comedy in episodic story, there is an entry here that's landed in my top 50.

First, a note: TV's *The Amos 'n Andy Show* premiered in June 1951 and debuted new first-run episodes through December 1951, well into the 1951–1952 season. Although I am hoping to be casual about calendar dates as far as these chapter demarcations are concerned, with the big shows of the following section premiering in late September and early October 1951, this first season of *Amos 'n Andy* is fodder for two different chapters, and consequently, yes, we will be discussing it again (briefly), especially because some of the best episodes from this series' technical first season actually *were* shown during 1951–1952. So I will save them for later in that section and, in the meantime, highlight the first entry that makes it onto our special list.

▶ It's "**Rare Coin**" and comes in at **#36** in my top 50. CBS first broadcast it on **July 19, 1951**. Its script, about the Kingfish trying to cheat Andy out of a valuable

The Kingfish (Tim Moore, left) and Andy (Spencer Williams, Jr.) in *The Amos 'n Andy Show*, "Rare Coin" (1951).

nickel, was written by **Joe Connelly**, **Bob Mosher**, and **Bob Ross**, and it was directed by **Charles Barton**.

"Rare Coin" was produced as the television series' pilot in late 1950,[43] but it was chosen to air fourth. A popular entry called "Kingfish Gets Drafted" (June 28, 1951) was instead used to mark the TV debut. The latter is a less character-driven misunderstanding plot that nevertheless centralizes the Kingfish and is thus worthwhile as an indication of the show's narrative focus, while also introducing us to these new actors playing these now-iconic roles. It is enjoyed by fans for the humor and heart evidenced immediately in Tim Moore's portrayal of the Kingfish. However, I still think the actual pilot is even more beneficial for setting up the series and revealing its strengths. It was adapted, like many of these early TV outings, from an earlier radio script,[44] and it's a perfect display of the series using its comedically-designed Kingfish character, no matter how mimetically strained, to earn big laughs and funny stories that his personality traits can *motivate*.

Additionally, this segment is especially good at exhibiting the dynamic between the Kingfish and Andy (now played by Spencer Williams, Jr.)—the central bond of the series, supplanting Andy's friendship with Amos (Alvin Childress), who became less utilizable upon the radio show's genre switch in 1943. By now, the TV version is more "Andy," who alternates between being the Kingfish's coconspirator and unknowing pigeon. In this entry, he gets to play both, allowing for relationship-based humor that similarly fleshes out *his* characterization and reveals both how he exists within this situation, along with how he can be utilized within story that satisfies their relational rapport, which is a large part of the premise (despite the outdated title).

Another thing worth noting about "Rare Coin" (also known as "The Rare Nickel") is its physical comedy—particularly in the bit with the Kingfish and a phone booth—a gag that could be done on radio with the right dialogue and sound effects but is much funnier here with visuals, and the strong performance by Tim Moore, who plays it to the hilt with his face and body.

Over the course of its run, *Amos 'n Andy* would continue to become bolder with its incorporation of visual humor, so this is just a preview of a key element that would help make the TV show one of the funniest sitcoms from the early 1950s—a show that despite all its controversy, fans still love to watch because of its commitment to humor in all forms. And to answer the questions posed earlier—yes, the show *could* use more humanity, but there's enough humanity here to make laughing at these characters acceptable. And that's exactly what they want us to do.

## *Father Does Slapstick*

Speaking of physical comedy, this brings us to another filmed sitcom from the 1950–1951 season—one also shot and, in this case, produced at Hal Roach Studios with *Beulah*'s Roland Reed. It's the aforementioned *Trouble with Father*, also known as *Life with the Erwins* or *The Stu Erwin Show* in print, but indeed labeled *Trouble with Father* on screen for the majority of its original ABC-TV run. Interestingly, although this series remained on the schedule for five years, from 1950–1951 to 1954–1955, the company ceased production during 1953–1954 while the network played reruns—a luxury it could afford because the show's first season boasted 52 weeks of all new episodes, no summer hiatus. Thus, there are five seasons' worth of *Trouble with Father*, even though it only officially premiered entries in four (out of five) TV seasons.

As a filmed sitcom from the 1950s, you would think that *Trouble with Father* would be a better known title than it is today. But after some life in syndication in the following decades, the series eventually fell into the public domain and faded into obscurity, with only half of its 130-episode run in regular circulation among casual collectors. And because there is no company around who wants to package this public domain title in syndication or release it on home video, *Trouble with Father* does not ring the same bells among sitcom fans as the other shows discussed in this chapter. I think part of this is because it was never very popular—it aired on ABC-TV, which guaranteed a smaller audience as a result of fewer stations and viewers reached. Additionally, unlike the other filmed sitcoms we have discussed so far—*The Life of Riley*, *The Beulah Show*, *The Amos 'n Andy Show*—this is not based on a well-known and preexisting radio property. That is, its premise and characters were designed specifically for TV—a rare example of the medium here in 1950–1951 *not* relying on a prior radio success to help define the sitcom genre on television but actually proffering a new example of what it might be.

These results yield a filmed sitcom—no laugh track (yet)—that stars B-list movie actor Stu Erwin and his real-life wife June Collyer, whose own union brings a foundational mimesis to their roles as dad and mom in an otherwise typical domestic format where he is the principal of a high school, and she is the supportive homemaker, raising their two daughters, one a young girl (played by a pre–*Dobie Gillis* Sheila James), the other a teen (Ann Todd). In this regard, you might consider it a typical family comedy in the vein of *Ozzie and Harriet*, which had premiered on radio in the mid–1940s and would eventually make its own way to television in 1952.

In too many of the sitcoms centered on nuclear families from the late 1940s and throughout the 1950s as well, the simple design and premise made a so-called mimesis of life very possible. A lot of viewers in that era could relate to this domestic structure because they were living a similar existence,[45] or at least recognized it. But these shows tend not to be great. They lead with desired relatability and fail to make any of the characters truly as distinct or comedically contorted enough to stand alongside the best from this era (Gracie Allen, Jack Benny, or even the Kingfish). So in terms of the situation comedy genre, there is often limited success with character in these efforts and, by extension, limited success in pursuing humor, for even if it *is* a series' primary objective, there's seldom as much support from the key elements of the situation as desired. And the use of narrative is often constrained as well, with conventional, overdone episodic notions lacking the one thing that can genuinely make story unique.

From a big-picture view, *Trouble with Father* has this same basic problem—its leads are not as well defined as the best in this genre, even in the context of 1950–1951. But there are a few differences. For starters, Erwin's job as a principal allows this show to engage some school-based stories in addition to the typical household fare, giving *Trouble with Father* a blend of two types of familiar sitcom subcategories instead of one and therefore a little more narrative dexterity than some of the other sitcoms in this domestic mold. Additionally and more important, this show has a very obvious interest in big laughs—like most of the TV sitcoms coming from Hal Roach Studios, which was known for its filmed comedy shorts starring funny people like Laurel and Hardy—and this is displayed in the series' pronounced use of physical comedy.

That's right, in an era where the television sitcom was still largely being written like radio with an emphasis on dialogue, *Trouble with Father* is notable as the first filmed and unimpeachable entry in the genre (before *Amos 'n Andy* premiered the following summer) to recognize the visual nature of the medium and use it to its artistic advantage, delineating it from its radio predecessors and trying to meet the TV audience's tastes where they actually were, for again in 1950, the most popular comedies on TV were variety shows starring comics who often engaged in broad, physical shtick—Milton Berle, Sid Caesar, Martin and Lewis, and so forth. Indeed, the thing that makes this show particularly worth noting in our critical study *is* its use of slapstick: a type of humor initially viewed as antithetical to the "comedy of situation" but now understood as something *not* mutually exclusive—a tool, if attached to the situation or a character, that can aid the genre's needs. Here in *Father*'s long first season, this broader sense of humor sometimes reveals itself in story—for instance, the premiere involves a live goat that the family is trying to hide from a guest[46]—even though about two-thirds of its narrative output is rote and unimaginative.

However, in the other third or so, a recurring pattern emerges, as the show seeks to attach its physical comedy to its situation. The vehicle is Stu himself, who therefore starts to reveal a habit of trying to take care of things around the house, usually with assistance from his live-in handyman Willie, portrayed by Willie Best, a Black actor and staple of Hal Roach Studios. As another African American in an essentially servile and supporting role who lacks any nuance or individualized definition, Willie is nevertheless allowed to act as the second half of a physical comedy duo with the star. And he's therefore crucial. In fact, these "home improvement" scenarios tend to make for the best episodes not only because the series is emphasizing the visual nature of TV, progressing the entire genre beyond radio, but also because they build out a characterization for its star Stu—as the bumbling dad who does *not* "know best" and is actually inept at everyday chores: fixing the pipes, building a barbecue, and so on. That's not only realistic; that's funny.

▶ While some of this incompetent dad energy can be observed in Chester A. Riley from *The Life of Riley*, that series' more blue-collar working man sensibility tends to depict his chronic misfortune as being *as much* a result of a harsh, cruel world as his own personal failings of character. Here, in a more upper-middle-class—suburban—environment, Stu Erwin has no logical excuse to be as humorously clumsy and inept as he is depicted, and this is really accentuated by the slapstick, earned by a few selected stories. Thus, although it is tempting to call *Trouble with Father* the slapstick version of *The Life of Riley*, I think the class distinctions complicate the comparison. Of course, in the wide-angle lens, both of the TV iterations we have seen of these shows otherwise do not boast great character work outside the central "father" stars, among the genre's first put-upon patriarchs, the butt of their series' jokes. It's really all about them—and the perfect episodic representation of these attributes in the slapstick-indulging *Trouble with Father* is **"TV Comes to the Erwins"** and it's ranked at **#22** on my list. Debuting on **July 7, 1951**, this entry's story sees Stu reluctantly buying a new TV set for the family and then trying to install it himself. **Al Martin** is the credited writer, and **James Tinling** directed.

Some may remember the 1962 episode of Lucille Ball's *The Lucy Show* in which Lucy and Viv put up a TV antenna on the roof.[47] It is a stellar display of the famous redhead's physical chops and the strong teamwork between that iconic comedy duo. But it had a long history—even before this funny episode of the otherwise forgotten *Trouble with Father*, where the titular bumbling dad gets into trouble when he and his handyman struggle to properly install the receptor for their new TV set. This bit actually had its roots in Laurel and Hardy, who first struggled to put up a radio antenna in 1930.[48] Eddie Quillan and Wally Vernon then did a version of this sketch in a 1949 short[49]—as would later the Three Stooges in 1953,[50] and Abbott and Costello in 1954.[51]

But if the idea is not terribly original, it works here on *Trouble with Father* because it's attached to premise and character in a way that makes it genuine *situation* comedy—offering big laughs connected to what the show promises to be: a sitcom about a bumbling head of household. In fact, this is a terrific example of how the series is narratively earning its slapstick—by indulging typical "home repair" stories that give the star an opportunity to clown around with some relatable household props, and consequently inspire more of a characterization for himself, as a clumsy nincompoop who mocks the ideals of domesticity without fundamentally challenging them—a benign incongruity. The best part of this rooftop routine is the reaction from the kids below, who are enjoying the guys' clumsy antics, ratcheting up his annoyance and giving proof to the idea that father's depiction is intentionally constructed for laughs. And as this physical comedy indicates the sitcom finally starting to define itself in relation to its new medium, which is different from radio and therefore has additional opportunities and concerns, the depiction of the patriarchal head of the nuclear family in such a silly, ridiculous way will also become more and more commonplace.

Meanwhile, this installment is also fascinating because it literally deals with television—a symbolic indication of how this new technology was slowly but surely coming to dominate American culture, and for our purposes, this use of it within story is also a fitting metaphor for why *Trouble with Father* is worth highlighting here in the 1950–1951 chapter: it's probably the first indication of a *television* situation comedy embracing the possibilities of this new medium and deriving humor from elements unique to it, making it a step forward in self-discovery for the sitcom as it reconciles these corresponding changes with its maintained necessities. And there are a handful of other entries from this series' first season that corroborate this intelligence—like "Stu's Holiday" (November 4, 1950), which is the first in this "home repair" category, and "Barbecue" (July 28, 1951), where efforts to build an outdoor barbecue lead to sparks (literally).

Again, though, the character work in *Trouble with Father* is never great beyond Stu himself, even by the standards of this TV season alone, and this will become more obvious as the genre continues to churn out better characterizations and therefore better sitcoms. So *Father* will never again be fodder for episodic praise. But here in the context of this formative era for the television sitcom, its prescient convergence of several trends to embrace a new frontier—the use of film, the incorporation

## Chapter Three. Somewhere Between Radio and Film 57

**Stu Erwin is an early example of the bumbling patriarch in *Trouble with Father*, "TV Comes to the Erwins" (1951).**

of slapstick, the gentle satire of domesticity via the fallible patriarch—makes it an important subject for our study and a notable sample of the art form at this transition.

Speaking of transition, the blurred distinctions between situation comedy and variety comedy—embodied by formative efforts like *Jack Benny*—was still felt. Some of television's early sitcoms similarly resided in this liminal space, including a series called *The Hank McCune Show*, which is typically only cited as a point of trivia, as it is usually noted as the first network sitcom to employ an added laugh track (i.e., not a response from a live audience watching at the time of production). This is true—it's a filmed series that uses a *prerecorded* laugh track regularly, and it seems to be the first of that description to make it on a network schedule.[52] But its status as a sitcom should be up for debate, for what I have seen indicates a *Jack Benny* show-within-a-show structure but with leads who are not *nearly* as well defined. McCune is sometimes a teacher, but there's an emphasis on skits and fantasies and a heavy use of physical comedy—in the realm of Berle and Caesar but without the continuity of *Trouble with Father*'s domestic format and characters. So in terms of *situation* comedy, it's more like a sketch show.

More fitting for the sitcom label is *The Buster Keaton Show*, which began as a live local LA program[53] before 13 episodes were filmed for syndication and began airing around the country in 1951.[54] From the few episodes available to screen today, the series seems merely an excuse to put the iconic silent film comic in a series of classic slapstick centerpieces. There are scant dramatic circumstances to motivate them—let alone help from well-made characters—beyond the audience's implicit recognition of Keaton's basic celluloid persona and the expectation that he will find himself in such predicaments. In this regard, it is not good situation comedy—it's lazy. But with a basic setup where he is employed behind the counter of a store—as most episodes begin in that location—there *is* some situation there in addition to his physical comedy. The link between the two—via character—is just weak; again, it's sketch-like.

We'll go more into this later, as there are, shall we say, gradations to how well character is applied in everything. In the meantime, *The Buster Keaton Show* is a very basic example of the sitcom, representing the genre's growing interest in film to avoid the technical limitations of its era. Some sitcoms so far have been willing to indulge physical comedy, while others have not. Some believe a live audience improves comedy by forcing the writers and performers to satisfy an actual group of potential laughers, while others do not. Some want to make us laugh hard, while others do not. Heck, some are just radio with costumes; some are just vaudeville but with regulars; some are veritable two-reelers from Hal Roach Studios. Yet all of them, in some way, are trying to define the situation comedy as it should exist on TV—a form that does not yet have one great example to which they can point and say, "Aha! That's it!" Well, it wouldn't be too long now before a special sitcom *would* come along and synthesize all of these elements into the perfect package, creating the first brilliant template for the medium going forward—and one of the purest, most ideal examples we will ever find for why the situation comedy is an art form. Stay tuned….

### JACKSON'S BEST SITCOMS FROM 1950–51
1. THE GEORGE BURNS AND GRACIE ALLEN SHOW (S1)
2. THE AMOS 'N ANDY SHOW (S1)
3. TROUBLE WITH FATHER (S1)

### EPISODES FROM THE 1950–51 SEASON IN JACKSON'S TOP 50 FROM THE '50s
#22. TROUBLE WITH FATHER (S1): "TV Comes to the Erwins" (7/7/51)
#36. THE AMOS 'N ANDY SHOW (S1): "Rare Coin" (7/19/51)

### OTHER NOTABLE EPISODES FROM 1950–51
TROUBLE WITH FATHER (S1): "Stu's Holiday" (11/4/50)
THE GEORGE BURNS AND GRACIE ALLEN SHOW (S1): "Happy Hmm Hmm" (1/4/51)
THE AMOS 'N ANDY SHOW (S1): "Kingfish Gets Drafted" (6/28/51)
TROUBLE WITH FATHER (S1): "Barbecue" (7/28/51)

Chapter Four

# TV's First Great Situation Comedy
## *The Best Television Sitcoms of 1951–1952*

The cornerstone of 1950s television sitcoms—heck, of *all* television sitcoms—is the decade's most popular: the only one that's still regularly the subject of feature films, podcast series, and big-budget documentaries. It is the medium's first home-grown example of what this genre could and should be like on television. And while audiences had seen some decent stuff on the air prior to this—like *Burns and Allen* and *Amos 'n Andy*—those shows were so rooted in the rules of radio that they hadn't yet provided for the industry a model to follow with regard, specifically, to TV. Indeed, this show, as a result of its artistry, created its own visual style that has not only influenced our collective perception of the genre but, since its debut, has also proved technologically durable. There has yet to be a TV season where at least one show does not owe its production aesthetic to the innovations first popularized by this series. Even if you know nothing else about 1950s sitcoms, you know this show. You know *I Love Lucy*.

*I Love Lucy* remains one of the most beloved American institutions—with 1950s-themed merchandise that still regularly sells many decades later.[1] Its sustained popularity is owed, in large part, to its long life in syndication and now both DVD and streaming. But that long life in syndication can be attributed to its quality—both technically and creatively. With regard to the latter, *Lucy*'s character-forward writing satisfies the definition of the situation comedy more perfectly than any other series (on radio or TV) that we have discussed up to this point. However, before we get into our textual appraisal of the show, let's get into the technology. As previous chapters have noted, the sitcom of the early 1950s was slowly embracing the benefits of film, which improved on the picture quality of both live broadcasts and kinescopes (films taken of a screen during broadcast), while also making it possible for every station to run a series at the same time, which was helpful for ratings and therefore more desirable to sponsors.

And yet, film had its drawbacks as well—it was more expensive to produce a television show on film, and for comedic performers used to immediate responses, this format was less ideal because it required jettisoning the live audience that had helped make the sitcom genre on radio, and early comedy-variety shows on TV, so energetically funny and spontaneous. *I Love Lucy*, more than anything else, could boast the distinct honor of traversing the technological barrier so that sitcoms—and all programming—could enjoy the positive effects of shooting on film while also maintaining the positive effects of staging a show as if it was a live broadcast. In fact, *Variety* described it the week before the series' premiere like this: "Referring to their new hybrid technique for 'I Love Lucy,' Lucille Ball and Dezi [sic] Arnaz sum it up with the claim that the show is produced like a play, filmed like a movie, recorded like radio and released as TV."[2]

This is in reference to something we call the "multi-camera" format—a method of television production that was so well utilized on *I Love Lucy* and several other shows throughout the 1950s and 1960s that it would essentially create the dominant sitcom aesthetic during the last three decades of the twentieth century. However, while this series often gets credit for *creating* the multi-camera format outright, the truth, well, is a little more complicated, and it goes back to a name from several chapters ago: Jerry Fairbanks. If you'll recall, Fairbanks was a film producer with the foresight to start producing television shows on film way back in 1947, beginning with *Public Prosecutor*. It was on that show—the first filmed series created for television—that he developed his "multicam system," whereby a show could be staged like a live production before multiple cameras, which were all actually recording on film and united by a synchronized soundtrack.[3] Reserved mostly for dramatic series, this technology was shared by Fairbanks with Al Simon in 1950 for the game show *Truth or Consequences*, which was jumping from radio to TV. Whereas *Public Prosecutor* had been shot on cheaper 16 mm film stock, *Truth or Consequences*, hosted by Ralph Edwards, switched to the premium 35 mm and benefited from Simon's refined intercom system, which made it easier to coordinate shots.[4] Also unique about *Truth or Consequences* was its choice to be filmed in theaters before live audiences.[5,6]

The audience was an important part of Lucille Ball's process. As a B-movie star who had hopped over to radio in 1948 to play in the domestic situation comedy *My Favorite Husband*, about a housewife eager to help her junior bank executive hubby, Ball quickly realized that the key to her success as a comedian was physicality, best appreciated and enhanced by viewers reacting in real time. Taking her cues from Jack Benny, who would play to his studio audience as much as to his listening audience, Ball quickly became a popular radio laugh-maker—exhibiting chops that moviegoers had never seen from her before. Thus, *My Favorite Husband* was one of the first sitcoms that CBS sought to bring over to TV—with Lucille Ball, a movie star, its main attraction. However, the (unnatural) redhead did not want to make the leap into television with her radio husband, Richard Denning, for she was married in real life to Cuban American bandleader Desi Arnaz, whose long tours on the road had proved significantly difficult for their tempestuous marriage.[7] Eager to find a project that would allow the pair to both work together and settle down to start a family, Ball decided that a TV show would be just the right choice for them. And for her to be successful, that meant that she needed a live audience.

As often reported, the network expressed initial resistance to the idea of Desi Arnaz playing Lucille Ball's husband on the grounds that he was Cuban and would not be a believable match for an *all-American* girl like Lucy.[8] However, it soon became clear, via Ball, that if CBS-TV wanted Lucy, they'd be getting Desi too, and that was it.[9] After all, the couple was *indeed* married in real life, and any notions of the audience not buying them as a couple would be allayed by the truth—which aided the textual mimesis and actually made it *easier* to emotionally invest in them. Also, although Arnaz was not *all-American,* his ethnicity did not posit him as the binary opposite of white in 1951, as it would have for the Black actors on *Amos 'n Andy.*

That is, like the Jewish family of *The Goldbergs* or the Italian clan on *Life with Luigi* (which would jump from radio to TV in 1952), Arnaz's Cuban heritage made him subject to the prejudices and stereotypes that all ethnic groups in the 1950s would have faced but structural opposition to him—or the mass public tension undergirding the notion of his civil rights—was not the same. Consider, for instance, that there was none of the formal backlash from advocacy groups that we saw with both *Beulah* and *Amos 'n Andy*. That distinction is relevant because while this book is not a sociopolitical history of the sitcom, a working knowledge of any era's social mores is always crucial in appreciating the pursuit of comedy, which hinges on accepted norms. So it's helpful to note that *I Love Lucy* uses Arnaz's Cuban heritage to create a characterization for Ricky Ricardo that allows for cultural clashes involving ethnicity, but without the controversy of disrespect that unfortunately plagued *Amos 'n Andy* and *Beulah*.

To that point, CBS-TV's initially professed skepticism about Arnaz[10] should also be framed with an understanding that he had little screen success prior to this and there was no indication of his skill range in a husband-and-wife comedy series, especially compared to the actor from the radio show, a proven thing. Most of the reluctance to deviate from *My Favorite Husband*'s formula was because, as shows like *Burns and Allen* and *Jack Benny* illustrated, transferring elements that were already known to work was the best way to mitigate risk. Knowing CBS' hesitation, Arnaz and Ball launched a personal appearance tour over the summer of 1950— their "vaudeville tour"—with material written by the *My Favorite Husband* scribes. They hoped this endeavor would alleviate concerns about the pair's draw as a duo and, specifically, Arnaz's compatibility as the central foil to Ball's comic persona. But again, there was never really another choice: if TV wanted Lucy, it would be getting Desi too. Once Ball started shopping around a pilot idea to other potential networks, CBS immediately acquiesced and accepted the idea of a "Lucy and Desi" pilot—because she was *that* valuable.[11]

With both Lucy and Desi set for TV, the show started to take shape. From the beginning, the pair knew a studio audience, as on the radio show, was a must. Armed with leverage from the fact that NBC was now making overtures, Ball also insisted to CBS that the show be produced in Hollywood,[12] where the couple lived and, as of early 1951, would be starting a family. (Following a miscarriage the year prior, Ball had become pregnant again.) This was not preferable, for remember, having a live audience in 1951 meant being broadcast live, which meant that if it wasn't coming from New York, where there were the most stations, sets, and viewers, the majority of the television audience would be seeing the show via kinescope, which had improved in quality a bit since its inception in the late 1940s but was still of inferior stock and not conducive to major Nielsen success—a fact that mattered a lot to advertisers.

In fact, following the production of a March 1951 pilot, recorded as a high-quality kinescope to match the visual nature of what a live series from Hollywood would look like to New York, the show got a sponsor, who then insisted the show be produced live in New York.[13] By the summer of 1951, with Ball about to give birth to her first baby, a cross-country move was out of the question, and their company turned to the only other alternative: film. The sponsor agreed based on the quality of *Amos 'n Andy* (which was about to premiere in June).[14] But the network was less assured, given its added cost. To ameliorate those concerns, Arnaz came up with the idea of cutting the couple's salary so this extra money could go to production. The network accepted these terms. And as part of the negotiation, Arnaz was also able to make it so, in taking care of this extra cost of producing on film, their company—Desilu—would then get to own the films themselves.[15] At the time, nobody at CBS thought much about this deal, but they soon would.

In the meantime, Ball and Arnaz's show—now called *I Love Lucy* (more on that later)—would be produced on film from Hollywood, like the productions at Hal Roach Studios, such as *Amos 'n Andy* and *Trouble with Father*. But the stars still wanted to perform in front of that live audience. And so, a new central question emerged: how could Desilu film a television sitcom in front of a live audience? For answers, they turned to Al Simon of *Truth or Consequences*, who had been doing this very thing—shooting on 35 mm film in front of an audience. But the system as developed for *Truth or Consequences* would need to be refined for *I Love Lucy,* which demanded a greater degree of flexibility as a result of how it would be staged.

In order to shoot a comedic play in front of an appreciative crowd, Desilu would need to make sure that their production apparatus could guarantee that, like in a theater, the action looked good—particularly on camera—from every angle and at all times. That would require a specific lighting apparatus. Longtime studio cinematographer Karl Freund was able to address this need by creating what we call today a "flat lighting" system[16]—now the standard for multi-camera shows, where everything is lit the way it needs to be at all times, accommodating plenty of movement by the actors (and the cameras) but none from the lights themselves. This ensured that every shot would look professional like a motion picture, but no new setups were required during filming to relight the set. (They'd only stop to reload film or change costumes.)

Freund's sophisticated Hollywood lighting system was made possible by the fact that the show was going to be shot on a genuine Hollywood soundstage. Unlike

*Truth or Consequences* or even other non-filmed live comedy shows performed in front of an audience such as *Burns and Allen*, which was transmitted from a former radio theater that could also accommodate TV production,[17] *I Love Lucy* was going to bring an audience into a motion picture lot.[18] So instead of the film format coming to the theater—the world of live broadcasts—the most important element of live broadcasts, the audience, would be coming to where the film format resided: the movie studio. This decision would prove to be truly innovative, for Desilu now had to work around figurative red tape to make it feasible for bleachers filled with spectators to occupy space on a soundstage in an otherwise closed Hollywood studio.[19] This was a whole new setup.

In addition to the lighting requirements that were aided by the use of a soundstage, other refinements to the "multi-cam" format as used on *Truth or Consequences* were focused on the mobility of the cameras—they needed a greater range of motion to follow the actors in their very physical performances, beyond what would have been expected on a game show. Accordingly, this gave rise to standards of production—for instance, after an initial episode was shot with four cameras, Desilu reduced the number to three, establishing a basic formula for filming: a central camera would take the master shot of the entire action, while two cameras positioned at 90-degree angles on each side would move around and take the two-shots, close-ups, and so forth as needed.[20] And with three cameras instead of four, other developments with regard to the intercom system and editing process followed—specifically, the "Three-Headed Monster," a machine that allowed editor Dann Cahn to run the film from all three cameras into a machine at once.[21] With this, *Lucy* progressively came to establish the best modes of practice for multi-camera-filmed sitcom production, which is still being used today. (Even though most of the multi-camera shows on the air have gone back to four cameras instead of merely three.)

So contrary to the simple narrative about *I Love Lucy* and its technical innovations, it was not the first show shot with multiple cameras, nor the first show shot on film with multiple cameras. Heck, it wasn't even the first show shot on 35 mm film with multiple cameras or even the first show shot on 35 mm film in front of an audience with multiple cameras. But it was the first *sitcom* shot on 35 mm film in front of an audience with multiple cameras. And it was the first show to bring an audience to a movie soundstage as opposed to a theater. And it was the first show to utilize the kind of flat lighting that accommodated these staging requirements, and the first to ensure that—coming from a soundstage—the live audience's reactionary track would sound like it did on radio, as opposed to the distant muffling in an actual theater. In this regard, you can see how the *Variety* quote came to be: *I Love Lucy* was produced like a play (live audience, no stops in the middle of scenes), shot on film (35 mm, with professional movie studio lighting), recorded like radio (on a soundstage with the audience situated in front of microphones), and then shown on television. And this would become—by virtue of *Lucy*'s success and the excellence of the product Desilu delivered—the dominant standard for this programming genre.

But while the show's technical excellence would indeed change the trajectory of the sitcom in this new medium, its creative excellence is really what ended up being persuasive, and with regard to this book's thesis, it actually is the focus of our discussion.

Of course, the maintained popularity of *I Love Lucy* throughout the years has led to so many great books and documentaries that share information and analysis about why it was so successful. In particular, *Lucy* had a brilliant ensemble cast—all of whom would quickly prove adept at handling the broad physical shtick that helped elevate the show's comedy from its competition and reiterate its value as the first great sitcom of this new visual medium, even though their skills might not have been fully obvious when they were first hired. That is, a lot of this series' brilliance—particularly in terms of performance and production—came from the fact that the show was simply blessed to have hired good people who then were able to outperform the expectations initially placed on them. I note this to say, everything that made *Lucy* great was the result of hard work, yes, but not necessarily with the amount of deliberation or forethought that you might expect of a show of its caliber and influence. Rather, smart people made smart choices that were then able to guarantee success and create standards for *future* shows, which would then go back and regard *Lucy* as having an all-knowingness mostly absent during its initial invention.

In terms of the writing and how it set up these great performers for success while supporting the refined multi-camera format, every good decision that was made originated with the creation of its central character—the best-defined and most well-known, fruitful sitcom lead of the decade, and the figure who, more than anyone else in this book, validates the notion of the situation comedy as an art form, by way of our definition: showcasing how the fixed elements of a situation and, most especially, the mimesis that comes from character, can be used to propel regular comedy and sustain a series worth of episodic story. That character is Lucy Ricardo.

Most of the credit for Lucy Ricardo belongs to Jess Oppenheimer, *I Love Lucy*'s producer and head writer, whose affiliation with Ball began in 1948,[22] several weeks into the run of her radio program *My Favorite Husband*, which he helped whip into shape—with assistance from a young pair of scribes, Madelyn Pugh and Bob Carroll, Jr.—by uncovering and then emphasizing the qualities in Ball that she could maximize for laughs. Uncoincidentally, Oppenheimer's most notable prior credit was writing for Fanny Brice on *The Baby Snooks Show*,[23] and many of the attributes that helped fuel Snooks's characterization—like a childishness that allowed for scheming and mercurialness, which then sparked their own running gags, like crying jags—also found their way into Ball's Liz Cooper character on *My Favorite Husband*. But in taking some of the cartoonish facets of Baby Snooks's persona, Oppenheimer also knew how to temper those extremes within *Husband*'s premise, which required fairly routine domestic narratives for a "typical" middle-class pair. Originally, the pair was upper class—a "society couple." Part of Oppenheimer's goal was to make them more relatable, so he bumped their economic standing down, contrasting them against the boss and boss's wife, who represented an even more elite social strata.[24] So as story, and the world surrounding her, kept the Liz character more relatable to a wider swath of the audience, the exacerbated qualities of a Diet Baby Snooks—made fresh by Ball, who juxtaposed this childishness with an inherent sophistication, ensuring that most of these behaviors were *intentional*, and linked to Liz's pursuit of, well, whatever an episode required—also allowed her character, and her comedy, to pop with agency, thus yielding a seemingly character-centric sitcom.

Truthfully, all of this was still fairly banal though, for all *My Favorite Husband* ended up with was a slightly wacky housewife in down-to-earth husband-and-wife plots sans personalization, because although her character pursued weekly goals and Ball's willingness to be silly could provide a source of hilarity, Liz Cooper still lacked individualized continuity. This kept the storytelling from becoming individualized, or unique, as well. And the rest of the cast was the same. Next to Ball, her husband played by Richard Denning was a fairly vanilla "straight man" while the elder secondary couple—his boss played by Gale Gordon and the boss's wife played by Bea Benaderet (both introduced by Oppenheimer during the latter half of the first season)[25]—could only find incidental flourishes in familiar but nondescript comedic banter.

Compare this to *I Love Lucy*. Many of the story ideas used on *My Favorite Husband* would later find their way, in some form, to *Lucy*. But try as I might, I've not found one idea that I could say with sincerity was better employed on the radio show than its TV successor. Oh, yes, because the radio show is very dialogue-dependent, there are some scripts that are jokier. But with less definition in the central Liz Cooper character, nothing plays as better *situation comedy*. This is a testament to the added dimension of the more precise Lucy Ricardo, and specifically, Lucy Ricardo's ability to better support individual episodic stories, of all kinds.

The key decision separating Lucy from Liz was also the invention of Jess Oppenheimer, who signed to write the TV pilot with Carroll and Pugh, once CBS resigned itself to a husband-and-wife show with Lucille Ball and her real-life mate, Cuban bandleader Desi Arnaz. That key decision was the introduction of a central objective for her character—a thing to regularly pursue in episodic story that would not only inspire the majority of the series' plots but also help inform the relationship between the couple, along with their entire characterizations. In other words, it would flesh out the characters and thus create a "situation" beyond the simplistic, colorless domestic design of *My Favorite Husband*. And it was inspired, in large part, by the inclusion of Arnaz over the radio show's bland and stiff Richard Denning—as the differences between the two men meant this couldn't just be the TV version of *Husband*.

In fact, early treatments for the Ball-Arnaz series drew from their real lives and depicted them as a married duo of movie stars,[26] but once CBS had ordered a pilot and Oppenheimer was officially the head writer with support from Pugh and Carroll, they determined that something more relatable would appeal to a broader audience and be better suited to Ball's comic identity as developed on *My Favorite Husband*. So, just as *Burns and Allen* was smart to do with its own pair of married movie stars, and Oppenheimer had instinctively decided when he stepped in to tweak *Husband*, Ball's half-hour TV project got bumped back down into the world of middle-class domesticity, more selectively choosing which of the couple's real-life details to incorporate.

This is how Ricky Ricardo was born—for, like Arnaz, he would also be a Cuban American bandleader, only without the national success of his portrayer. He'd have a regular gig at a New York nightclub, but outside of that realm, he'd pretty much be an unknown—one of those people in show business who punches the clock as if it was any other industry and without the celebrity that would otherwise make his career unrelatable. And in accordance with his job, he'd have a comfortable-but-not-luxurious middle-class residence in a small New York City apartment with his wife Lucy, who unlike her portrayer, wouldn't be a glamorous star but a frustrated young housewife in charge of all the domestic duties. This allowed the show to indulge plots where finances were occasionally an obstacle, and the characters could remain more sympathetic by having common, everyday concerns. In this regard, Oppenheimer was using *more* of the Arnazes' real-life situation to inform their TV show than any of their prior projects, creating an elemental foundation of truth that could then be tweaked and caricatured as needed.

As for Lucy's objective, it was inspired by Ricky's career in show business. Oppenheimer decided that Lucy, the housewife, would yearn to be a part of this world herself—she would want to be, like Ricky, an entertainer. And in deciding that Lucy Ricardo's central objective was to be a performer also, Oppenheimer thereby gave her something to pursue in story: to try getting in show biz, the career of her husband. Relational conflict could then arise between the two from his opposition to her efforts, rooted in his desire for a "normal" middle-class existence at home and his own attitudes about the industry.[27] This character-based premise, again, made all the difference in the world, for stories now not only fleshed out the couple's dramatic relationship, but they also now had a unique engine—motivated by a sustaining character goal that was a vital part of her depiction, and an element of the situation that would allow her to inspire both episodic ideas *and* the comic shtick that everyone also knew was an integral aspect of Ball's persona, with her physicality being a big reason she was courted for TV.

In this regard, Oppenheimer discovered a way to link her character, and to a lesser extent Arnaz's as well, *to* the generation of story (the series' weekly, episodic projection of its own situation) so *she* could be attached to everything that happened, thereby synonymizing Lucille Ball's show with the Lucy Ricardo character. All the plots, all the laughs, all the relationships would be centered on this narrative hook that, more than anything else, allowed the series to become character driven. More than the dull *My Favorite Husband*, where Liz Cooper was a driving force without an engine, this TV show would *be* Lucy Ricardo, and everything that happened within it would be inspired by this strong character and the central goal informing her usage. (Incidentally, Oppenheimer's first two scripts on *My Favorite Husband* were show biz-related, but nothing came from them that stuck with the Liz Cooper character as a *sustaining* want, nor was anything influenced by the situation of her husband, a junior bank executive. It was episodic, unsupported.[28]) And from this design came a natural title: *I Love Lucy*, with Ricky getting informal top billing (to satisfy Arnaz),[29] yet with no doubt about who was the star.

This character centricity all starts from Lucy's objective. But it isn't just the objective alone. It's how this objective touches everything else as well—Ricky included, for while Lucy Ricardo desperately wants to be in show business, this goal is attached to additional details—like the fact that her husband is an entertainer, and so her efforts to be in the same industry as Ricky could also be seen as an attempt to get closer to him (a tangential desire that now has rich, character-rooted support because of this affiliation). And at the same time, his efforts to keep her out of the industry can be read not merely as simple male chauvinism—i.e., he wants a good little housewife, who doesn't compete with him to earn the bacon—but also because he knows this industry and is, in some ways, protecting the person he loves from its harshness, hoping that they can share the "normal" life that, in 1950s America, most people would want.

To that point, there's also an implied cultural distinction about Ricky—he grew up in Cuba and has a more traditional idea of the family, perhaps even more traditional than the popular social mores in 1950s America regarding working women.[30] This is interesting because it provides the character with some dimension and it's another example of *I Love Lucy* using autobiographical details about Desi Arnaz to help inform the Ricky character. Beyond just his career as a bandleader, there's the obvious fact that he's Cuban—and this unique cultural identity, just as with the family on *The Goldbergs* and Luigi of *Life with Luigi*, informs so much of his persona. Some of this is mired in 1950s stereotypes about Hispanics—like his "Latin temper" and the ego that the show associates with his culture—but these *are* continued personality traits that indicate an effort to invoke elements of the actor's real identity (a mimesis) to flesh out a characterization, with jokes and stories stemming from these attributes, along with running gags—like Lucy mocking his accent. It also gives him a history, which would be slowly filled in via details about his childhood, like when the show visits his family in Cuba.[31]

Accordingly, Ricky Ricardo is *as* well defined a character as Lucy; he doesn't have the singular objective that can drive plot—his wants typically suggest an obstacle to hers—but he has so many special qualities that ensure he, unlike the non-starring partner on other domestic shows—the wife on *The Life of Riley*, the wife on *Trouble with Father*, or even Liz's hubby on *My Favorite Husband*—is just as capable of fulfilling the genre's obligations as is the star characterization, whose own depiction is so shaped around his and vice versa. As an example, look at "Be a Pal" (October 22, 1951)—an adaptation of a radio script[32] that changes its structure in the TV version to fit the Ricardos' specific characters, not to mention the medium's visual possibilities, with a centerpiece where Lucy pretends to be Carmen Miranda so Ricky can have the comforts of home. By this example, if Lucy Ricardo is the cause of *I Love Lucy*'s brilliance, then Ricky's immense definition, as her strongest supporting player, is the most persuasive testament to just how great *Lucy* is at using other characterizations to bolster her own.

Because of this, Lucy Ricardo is easily the most well-integrated 1950s sitcom lead in terms of how story and comedy is mined as a result of her depiction, which in turn becomes her series' situation. In being so character-centric and driven by her definition, *I Love Lucy* satisfies, *inherently,* the needs of the situation comedy as we have termed it: a series of episodic stories inspired by the preestablished elements of a situation, and particularly its tweaked but mimetic characters, in evidence of the benign incongruity that creates the comic catharsis of laughter.

Speaking of laughter, *Lucy*'s writers have said that their brainstorming sessions didn't often begin with silly ideas or big slapstick centerpieces, but if they did, they then had to work backward to figure out how the show, and Lucy herself, could get there.[33] This process made sure that *all* comic shtick was motivated by the characters, and particularly Lucy's, such that there was a priority of value: if they couldn't find a way to connect the gag to her character, no matter how funny, it would be rejected. Studying what the show *did* use corroborates this focus.

Let's take a good sample (by this series' own high standards) from its second season: "The Handcuffs" (October 6, 1952)—so chosen because the "handcuffed together" gag is a common comedic trope, enabling so much rich slapstick. Here, when Lucy and Ricky get handcuffed together, look how it's built: landlord Fred Mertz has handcuffs from his old vaudeville days (by then, a well-known aspect of his persona and something that helps aid and abet Lucy's goals), and Lucy puts them on her and Ricky to be playful but also to keep him from going to work (which is an extension of the central conflict and her objective: he's in show biz and she's not, for she's instead trapped at home). And then the finale has her performing with Ricky—which she's always wanted—since he has no choice: *because* of Lucy's actions, they're stuck together.

Unlike *My Favorite Husband*, which employed a similar idea in a December 1949 broadcast,[34] *Lucy*'s version is all motivated by character—all these big comic moments are the result of Lucy Ricardo or those intentionally defined in relation, as her decisions have continuity-backed explanations, and the mere existence of the handcuffs comes from an ensemble character whose own history is thematically appropriate and previously known; we *believe* that he might have handcuffs in his old vaudeville trunk because we know enough about Fred Mertz.

The Mertzes are, of course, a seminal part of *I Love Lucy*'s success—and a bit of the happy accident that the company could never have predicted when they were first cast. Ball had been hoping to carry over the elder couple from *My Favorite Husband*—played by two great performers with their own histories in this genre: Gale Gordon and Bea Benaderet.[35] But by 1951, Benaderet was already the feminine half of the secondary couple on *Burns and Allen*'s TV show, and Gordon was already contracted for the forthcoming television adaptation of the popular radio show *Our Miss Brooks*,[36] with which he was even more associated. So *Lucy* had to make do with others—an old veteran character actor named Bill Frawley and a C-level Broadway actress named Vivian Vance. Both, obviously, were talented and had been involved in big things—he was in *Miracle on 34th Street*, and she had understudied for Ethel Merman in the original *Anything Goes*. But when they were cast, the extent of their skills was not yet known.

For instance, the idea that the Mertzes could even *be* former vaudevillians only came about several weeks into the first season, when it was realized they could, in fact, sing and dance.[37] This was a true miracle—for while I'd like to say that the secondary couple was always designed as a pair of ex-performers whose own dashed dreams helped fuel Lucy's, thereby rendering their inclusion further proof of just how character-centric *I Love Lucy* was designed to be, the truth of the matter is, it wasn't the intention. It just happened, and from there, the show was able to build something that would help *make* their presences even more beneficial to Lucy and the storytelling—so that the ensemble could also help explain her objective and the full characterization suggested by it.

Vivian Vance, in particular, was a phenomenal performer, and while recent appraisals of Ball's career tend to overcredit the Lucy and Ethel bond as *Lucy*'s seminal dynamic despite the husband-and-wife relationship between Lucy and Ricky always being treated in story and design as more central, once the show became more and more comfortable exhibiting its physicality, Ball and Vance really did end up making a terrific comic duo—the first pair of funny ladies on TV doing BIG comedy. Their active, physical routines forged a direct partnership that would grow over the years and then become the primary comedic attraction within the early seasons of Ball's second half-hour TV sitcom, *The Lucy Show*, which premiered in 1962.

To that point, *I Love Lucy*, like *Amos 'n Andy* and *Trouble with Father,* also found success by taking advantage of the fact that TV was a visual medium, at a time in history where the most popular shows were variety programs anchored by physical comics (like Milton Berle, Sid Caesar, and Red Skelton, whose program also debuted in 1951–1952). The fact that Ball proved so adept at physical comedy—which her writers discovered on the radio program and then wrote toward in the couple's 1950 "vaudeville tour"—allowed her TV show to indulge slapstick centerpieces and sight gags. Today, this helps make so many of the episodes memorable; we can recall "the one with the big loaf of bread,"[38] "the one where she gets starched,"[39] "the one with the sunburn."[40] But, again, all of these bits were painstakingly plotted so that they could be motivated by the regulars, and this bigger, broader, vaudeville-like humor—the kind exhibited on those sketch-based comedy-variety shows—was now linked to the strong continuity of the situation, with just as much humor coming from the well-defined leads, who gave the slapstick substance. Again, this is why *Lucy* is such an excellent example of the sitcom: its characters.

Beyond Lucy and Ricky Ricardo, the Mertzes help support this natural character-rooted cohesion—Ethel is a believable pal for Lucy, Fred is a believable pal for Ricky, and both are affiliated with the series' show business veneer that supplies the regulars a form of mimesis, inspiring both Lucy's objective *and* one of her most frequent interpersonal conflicts with Ricky. This is fruitful for story; they can exist in plots as an oppositional force to the Ricardos, or there can be the traditional split along gender lines—"the boys against the girls"—or they can conspire *with* Lucy *against* Ricky (or the reverse). What's more, the Mertzes are similarly, like Ricky, afforded traits of their own—not as many but enough so that we can also form expectations; for example, it quickly becomes an established part of the "situation" that Fred is always crotchety and cheap, and Ethel is always sharp tongued and hungry. And they're consistent.

This collective strength at defining the leads—nobody is vague, as they are on so many inferior sitcoms—allows for an increased reliability. That is, we can trust the general continuity of these characters—and if stories are not serialized, the leads are, as their consistencies help motivate or provide support for the employed comic ideas, predicated on their personalities and histories, with attitudes, objectives, and flaws that are reiterated week to week, displayed in both dialogue and stories that *reveal* and *reinforce* them. And with this continuity exhibited within plot, the leads become even more reliable and thus more believable—with a sense of realism that may not be *totally* in line with the real world's (i.e., there's some suspension of disbelief needed) but consistent within the show and therefore believable as a result of its own internal standards.

I call this *aesthetic realism*—a show's own created sense of logic—versus literal realism, which is what we might collectively accept to be true outside of the bounds of fiction, in our everyday life. *Aesthetic realism* is not a threat to mimesis as long as a show is consistent. *I Love Lucy*, for the most part, is the most consistent show of its era—we know what to expect from these characters, and very few of the laughs from the text, the story ideas they push, or the big slapstick crescendos that make so many of these episodes iconic, breach these expectations. Thus, both in practice and design, this is the strongest sitcom of the 1950s—it makes the most effective use of its characters, whose clear definitions and the consistent reinforcement of said definitions in narrative can be trusted, as can the show's proficiency with comedy—it can make us laugh—for the characters all have the kind of benignly incongruous traits that produce humor, while, Lucy, in particular, has an objective that pushes story and earns the big slapstick climaxes.

However, despite being aesthetically consistent, there was a bit of a learning curve here in the show's first season, as the writers had to get used to these characters and the bounds of the new medium. Specifically, it took a few weeks for Oppenheimer, Pugh, and Carroll to move away from their sensibilities as established on radio. In fact, with a lot of scripts—or at least story ideas—recycled from *My Favorite Husband*, some of the early episodes don't do the best job of getting support,

## Chapter Four. TV's First Great Situation Comedy     71

narratively and comedically, from the TV version's specific situation (that is, the characters). For instance, entries like "Drafted" (December 24, 1951) and "Lucy Plays Cupid" (January 21, 1952) feature comic ideas that have little to do with these leads, let alone Lucy Ricardo's initially story-defining objective. What's more, the addition of visuality as a new source of comedy, along with a way to project and uphold a mimesis, also accompanies different standards of what's believable and not. On radio, which is only aural and requires imagination, there's a more natural suspension of disbelief. A TV mimesis *must* be more literal.

To wit, in the first aired episode of this series, "The Girls Want to Go to a Nightclub" (October 15, 1951), the climax has Lucy and Ethel dressing up in disguise and fooling their husbands for a few minutes—a leap that's harder for the audience to make on TV than on radio, given that we can see the women for ourselves and recognize them as obviously Lucy and Ethel. Therefore, it doesn't make sense for their husbands, who presumably know them better, not to recognize them as well. Eventually, the show will not ask us to make such a leap again—if we can recognize Lucy in disguise, then so can Ricky. By that same token, as visuality forces more adherence to literal realism than on radio, it's implicitly required that the characters be more emotionally real as well, so stories about Lucy falsely believing that Ricky, the man she loves and who loves her, is trying to murder her[41] just don't feel believable, especially without really strong motivation from character (which, in this case, would disprove the worthiness of the whole idea). In essence, it just takes some time for *I Love Lucy* to really get a grip on how to write to its new, specific needs—and this is something that, frankly, is common of most series. Sometimes it takes a few weeks and sometimes a few years to develop the characters enough so that it's easy to write *for* them, using their specifics to shape both the laughs and the stories, as each sitcom requires.

In terms of Lucy, her objective was clear right from the unbroadcast pilot that sold the series, and her impetuous attitude—the mercurial swings in emotion and imprudent scheming that now could be focused specifically on (and a tactic used for) said objective—was also on display, with the same shades of Snooks that were brought along from *My Favorite Husband*, only now more thoughtfully predicated. But what doesn't come into view until episode 13, "The Benefit" (January 7, 1952), is a flaw that helps complicate all of the above: she can't sing, or more simply, she is not a natural talent. This is helpful because it gives her another running source of comedy and also exonerates Ricky for his resistance to her joining him at the club, because not only does it make more sense, but it's also an act of protection—she can't handle this world, and he knows it.

Interestingly, the idea for "The Benefit" was originally used on a March 1949 episode of *My Favorite Husband*.[42] But without Ball's character Liz having a sustaining objective or flaw and the husband not already existing within the entertainment world, it's significantly less motivated—proof, again, of just how much the addition of *Lucy*'s well-defined, unique characters could enhance and better support story. In fact, a January 1950 installment (from which "The Benefit" also cribbed) introduced the "flaw"—the idea that Liz is a terrible singer but only for that one story;[43] it's not regularly attached to her depiction or how she's used in plots thereafter.

As noted, the average delta between an original *My Favorite Husband* and its later *I Love Lucy* iteration, which is always better attached to well-defined characterizations, is sizable throughout the run, even in some of the series' more popular segments, like "Lucy Fakes Illness" (January 28, 1952), which is significantly improved by the Lucy and Ricky characterizations, especially her central objective and how that enhances her emotional credibility. Thus, although *Lucy*'s characters may NOT have *inspired* every story idea—particularly during this first season—the series' understanding, thanks to Oppenheimer, Pugh, and Carroll, of how to tailor its ideas *to* these now better-defined leads naturally improves the humor, *making* the stories character driven via their particular goals and/or the affiliated traits that justify their episodic wants.

So once this additional aspect of the Lucy Ricardo characterization—her lack of talent—is established in January 1952, the last two-thirds of the season are filled with terrific character-driven segments that explore Lucy in pursuit of her goal. The best of these is an all-time classic.

▶ In fact, it comes in at **#2** on my top 50 list for the decade—"**Lucy Does a TV Commercial**," which has Lucy conspiring to star in a commercial during a TV show on which Ricky is appearing. It first aired on **May 5, 1952**, was written by **Jess Oppenheimer, Madelyn Pugh,** and **Bob Carroll, Jr.**, and directed by **Marc Daniels**.

"Lucy Does a TV Commercial" is famous for its centerpiece where Lucy Ricardo gets drunk while rehearsing and then performing a TV commercial for a suspicious health tonic called "Vitameatavegamin," which contains 23 percent alcohol. The routine is a brilliant opportunity for Ball to showcase her facial dexterity and comic inventiveness, as she progressively gets drunker and drunker, muddling the prewritten text of the commercial and eventually causing a ruckus for Ricky during his number on the show. The inebriation routine—a classic set piece that only involves alcohol here in the 1950s, but by the 1970s would come to include other substances as well, especially marijuana—is a common gag for which *I Love Lucy* can't take any credit. (In fact, many critics noted that Red Skelton had a recurring sketch where he too would get progressively drunker while advertising alcohol.[44] But Skelton took the idea from a Fred Allen sketch, and the legend is Allen too lifted it from someone else—and on and on. Such is the case with all vaudeville gags.) But what makes this classic bit unique—beyond Ball's own stellar performance—is that it's supported by the elements of *I Love Lucy*'s situation that render the series itself unique: it's all driven by Lucy Ricardo and what's been established about who she is and what she wants.

Specifically, the first half of the script is all about her discovering that Ricky is going to appear on a television program, and per her established objective of wanting to get in show business, she tries to persuade him to let her be on the show by

Chapter Four. TV's First Great Situation Comedy 73

**Lucille Ball as Lucy Ricardo in *I Love Lucy*, "Lucy Does a TV Commercial" (1952).**

dressing up as the Little Boy in the ads for Philip Morris, the cigarette company that was *I Love Lucy*'s sponsor for the first half of its run. When that fails—as expected, given his resistance to her ambitions—she then takes matters into her own hands and intervenes to ensure that no other girls show up at the audition. It's hers by default. That's exactly the kind of sneaky act a grown-up Snooks might pull—with little regard for the consequences, simply because the impulse to get what she wants is so strong. And then, once she's there, the fun of the Vitameatavegamin kicks in, and she ends up ruining the performance, validating the idea that she wouldn't be very good in show business, even though, in this case, it's not because she can't sing or dance but because she can't handle her health tonic.

Lucy Ricardo drives the action, with support from Ricky as the resistant force who, from being in this show biz world, also invites these narrative trappings to exist—setting the stage for a bit that then feels character based, and thus situationally correct, because of how well supported it's been up to this point. And then the star sells the heck out of it, creating one of the funniest television routines of all time. It's among the most perfect episodes of *I Love Lucy*—if not for the absence of Lucy's usual coconspirator Ethel (Vivian Vance had one of her rare off-weeks), I would have no bones about labeling this *the* quintessential episode of *I Love Lucy*— proof of why it's a great situation comedy.

▶ Now, that is obviously the best of the season. But many others also use her objective in some form—like another entry that I would put at **#40** on my list. It's "The Ballet," from **February 18, 1952**, again written by **Oppenheimer**, **Pugh**, and **Carroll** and directed by **Daniels**. The plot has Lucy desperately trying to get in Ricky's show by studying both ballet and comedy.

"The Ballet" contains some of Ball's finest work on the series, both as a graceless ballerina and also in a classic stage routine, "Slowly, I Turn," which reiterates how *Lucy* uses elements of vaudeville—and comedy-variety shows—to encourage big laughs. As in "Lucy Does a TV Commercial," Lucy's desire to be in Ricky's show motivates all the centerpieces, but the climax has some strained logic; Lucy performing the vaudeville routine when she's really been called down to do ballet is amusing, but once she sees the dancers, the fact that she doesn't immediately recognize the mix-up is a bridge too far, given that the show has already conditioned us to expect a greater degree of logic in Lucy's actions. It's still a great episode because of her performance, but you can see a distinction with this and "TV Commercial" that separates #2 from #40—and "The Ballet" only gets the latter honor because of the strength of Ball's physical performance and the way in which this story, silly climax aside, is otherwise rooted brilliantly inside the series' established situation and the characters who uphold it. Of course, with great characters comes great responsibility to make sure we believe their choices. The show's aesthetic realism allows us to buy that Lucy would take a ballet class and learn a vaudeville routine—that's based on her established objectives, attitudes, and flaws—but it doesn't account for a basic lack of awareness. Again, that's a bridge too far. Usually, *Lucy* is good about not crossing this line, but Season One, remember, is still a bit of a learning curve, even in its latter half—and even in gems like this.

Some of the other first season excursions that wouldn't make a top 50 list but might be squeezable into a top 100 include the aforementioned bread-baking episode, "Pioneer Women" (March 31, 1952), where the foursome gives up twentieth-century technology when the husbands and wives clash over the ease of modern homemaking—a central concern for the show, even when absent the show biz thematics, because it speaks to the basic gender tension at home. That fixation on housekeeping exists under the surface of other popular episodes as well, such as "The Freezer" (April 28, 1952), where Lucy's efforts to streamline her domestic duties by buying a new home freezer and stocking extra meat lead to predictable trouble, and "Lucy's Schedule" (May 26, 1952), where Ricky literally puts Lucy on a time schedule because of her chronic lateness—a conflict totally fomented in the 1950s' attitudes about men and women, exacerbated, on this particular show, by the inherent drama (and comedy) of Lucy's discontent with her role.

To that point, I also want to make it clear that *I Love Lucy* is capable of producing great entries even if they *do not* directly involve her efforts to break into show business. Yes, that objective tends to inspire many of the strongest, most character-driven shows, but once her objective is known as a foundation, with attitudes and flaws built around it, other more traditional domestic stories also gain extra character-based nuance and become both funnier and more situationally specific as well. For instance, her goal to be in show biz—the business of her husband—can also be extrapolated out as a basic desire to break out of the home where she's confined in the societal role of housewife (and soon mother), and to the completely relatable idea that she merely wants to be more than what she's expected to be. Lucy Ricardo is a woman who wants *more* from her life. No, I'm not calling Lucy an early feminist, except that the show's dramatic angst *is* based around her attempts to be and do more than what Ricky wants from her.

In this regard, you can see how her broad objective—to be more than what she's "supposed" to be—then gives emotional support to other, less specific but still-relatable domestic stories. Like when she wants to be more of a friend to Ricky, she's yearning for him to see her as more than merely the housewife.[45] Or when she's trying to help him get along in business, she's asserting her own hope of bringing value to him in the world, beyond just the bounds of the home they've created.[46] Or when she wants to impress the neighbors, she's expressing insecurity about the ordinariness of her day-to-day existence.[47] All of this is emotionally understandable, and it can be tangentially attached to her core, central objective, so even as that objective fades away over time (and is barely used in story in the last few years of the series), these other, simpler episodic goals have a sturdier platform than they would have when employed by other series, which might copy *Lucy*'s plots, and even some of her general traits—like her scheming nature or the swings in emotion—but without truly understanding *why* these actually work here: because of their link to a motivation.

Now, there's some irony in this; Lucille Ball wanted to do a show with her husband because she wanted to settle down, and she appreciated Oppenheimer's domestic format because that's what she, like Ricky Ricardo, yearned to have with her husband. But the drama of the show—the conflict—is always about her attempts to break out. Of course, she always ends up back in the home, for as this genre is soon proving, with a continuity of character but not necessarily plot, the "status quo" must *basically be* reinstated at the end of every episode, so the series' situation can remain intact. Oh, yes, there's room for temporary arcs and surface changes in this genre—like when *Lucy* moves to Hollywood for half a season or goes on a European tour—but the circumstances for the characters must stay close to what's always been premised, or promised, and individual episodes must have their own narrative structure: beginning, middle, and end. The "benign incongruity" proves its benignity when all goes back to normal. Thus, Lucy Ricardo remains a housewife (and mother) despite her best efforts, and we, the audience, have to both be okay with this snap back to "normal" (which we *are* because of the love that she and Ricky have for each other—they are devoted) and we must believe that even if certain episodes are never acknowledged again, like the humans these characters are designed to imitate, she herself has indeed gone through these events and maybe evolved ever so slightly as a result.

Okay, evolution is hardly a concern in the 1950s, even on *Lucy*, whose aesthetic realism is nevertheless more consistent and therefore more believable than most shows. It's still in a broader, more vaudeville-backed ethos that isn't putting as much stock in character *growth* or emotional *maturation*. Those are ideas that will develop in later decades and in shows that take the basic character work applied here but with tweaks and refinements more in line with their eras' own tastes. For instance, future shows that are equally as character driven may divorce themselves from the idea of their main characters *needing* a central goal to drive story. Sometimes—in the same way that Lucy's objective can then be stretched out to apply to other episodic concerns that are tangentially related—future sitcoms will find that it's enough just to have a consistency of personality, reiterated by a high threshold for emotional believability and *even more* literal realism, reinforced by an *even greater* sense of autobiographical mimesis and/or attention to the application of details, for driving and then justifying both story and comedy under the umbrella of a "situation."[48]

However, in the early 1950s, the first great sitcom of this new medium created for itself an identity in Lucy and Ricky Ricardo that was significantly unique from anything before it. The strides made here in the crafting of character, and specifically, giving Lucy an objective that could inform her utilization and define how everyone else exists around her, are remarkably impressive in terms of situation-exploration—beautiful proof of the genre's potential to fulfill the idea of its existence as an art form. And it's the cornerstone for all the great character-driven sitcoms ahead, in the same way that the show's technical advancements, to accommodate its stars' strengths, would also end up highly influential—if not immediately, then in the decades to follow.

Of course, we'll talk more about *Lucy*'s influence in every chapter, for every single year this show is on the air as a half-hour series, it's producing at least a half-dozen great segments worthy of our attention, and indeed, from its excellence, other shows would copy certain aspects to varying degrees of success. So stay tuned for more *Lucy*—there'll be a lot more ahead.

## Well, It Wasn't All "Lucy"

In the meantime, if the premiere of *I Love Lucy* is certainly the headline of the 1951–1952 season, it obviously wasn't the only show on the air. For instance, the three I singled out for praise in the previous chapter—*Burns and Allen*, *Amos 'n Andy*, and *Trouble with Father*—were all back and merit a word or two again. As for the last of that trio, *Trouble with Father*, which stars Stu Erwin as a bumbling patriarch and school principal, returned after a 52-episode first season that concluded in mid–October 1951 for a 26-episode second season the following week, running new entries until April 1952, after which reruns were presented until the fall.

As before, this series remains most notable for its use of slapstick, particularly to evidence the idea of the fallible father, who's the nominal head of the house but a source of much humor because of his ineptitude. Aside from its visual comedy, what's most remarkable about *Trouble with Father*—still—is how it deploys these gags to flesh out a characterization for its lead. In a few years, the sitcom genre is about to move out to the suburbs, where a more idealized and homogenius view of Americana will constrain comedy by forcing its leads to be more conformist than incongruous, and essentially far too benign to yield laugh-out-loud humor. The fact that Stu Erwin is, well, a goofball makes him much more of a character than Jim Anderson and Ward Cleaver will be.

As for the show's value as a situation comedy, *I Love Lucy* has elevated the figurative bar here in 1951–1952, as it's offering the same great physical humor but with excellent genre-affirming character work—the kind of character work that *Trouble with Father* lacks, particularly outside of its lead. So while there are still some fun bits that validate our understanding of the central characterization at the heart of this domestic premise—"Father Does His Homework" (November 23, 1951) being the best of the easily viewable lot—and young Sheila James has a moderately pronounced tomboy persona that takes advantage of her natural talents, it's no longer feasible to pretend that the kind of situation comedy offered by *Lucy* is in any way matched by *Trouble with Father* based on what is available from its sophomore season.

In terms of character usage, both *Burns and Allen* and *Amos 'n Andy* remain superior particularly because of their strong central personas. *The George Burns and Gracie Allen Show* began its second biweekly collection of 26 live episodes (broadcast, still, from a radio theater converted for television usage at Hollywood's Columbia Square) in late September 1951—just days before the regular implementation of the coast-to-coast coaxial cable, which made it possible for shows transmitted on one side of the country to be seen at the same time on the other side.[49] For the industry, this meant specifically that more live TV production could come from Hollywood, and the major stations in New York, where most of the sets and viewers resided, would no longer be forced to see the program weeks later on an inferior kinescope. Now, this technology was not perfect—and there were still limitations. Just because there was a basic connection between the major flagship stations in Los Angeles and New York did not mean that every part of the country could see something all at once. No, kinescopes were still required for live programing, and both they, and even the coaxial connection, were far inferior *visually* to programs that were produced and shipped on film, like *I Love Lucy*. Accordingly, although the coaxial cable seemed to solve a big problem for Hollywood's live TV scene by reducing the concrete necessity of New York, film's superior look remained persuasive, and as more and more shows moved out west, both New York and live programming, on both coasts, would continue to lose their prominence. In just a few years, most production would come from Hollywood, and it would be on film.

As for *Burns and Allen*'s second season, most scripts continue to rate well because they centralize the Gracie characterization, launching misunderstandings that feel motivated because they arise from her elemental persona. Just as before, many of these ideas would be reused in the filmed (syndicatable) run of the show, including the best available entry from this collection, "Gracie Goes to a Psychiatrist" (September 27, 1951), which opened the season.

The idea behind this episode was so good that the show would dust it off twice more in the filmed, syndicatable era—for a 1954 installment[50] and then again, with more tweaks, in 1956.[51] It's another classic story that displays the series' comic storytelling, as inspired by the strong, central characterization, for when Gracie takes Blanche's place at a psychiatrist appointment, by merely being herself, she so confounds the doc that he phones Harry Morton with news that his wife is, well, *not well*. And then the expected shenanigans play out from there—all because of the core Gracie Allen character and her nuttiness, which continues to reliably yield big laughs and is still helping to motivate story—affirming the very traits that make the situation comedy a unique dramatic art form. Now, truthfully, I can't say that this version of the idea is significantly better than its two remakes (in fact, the 1956 version is in my top 50), but in this 1951–1952 chapter, where there is less competition for sitcom greatness, the entry stands out as notable. Of course, the character work, as a whole, is not as strong as *Lucy*'s either—there's a greater sense of vaudeville on *Burns and Allen*, not because there's slapstick (there isn't) but because the central personas of the titular leads are broader and less specifically rendered. They're simpler.

Oh, yes, they're similarly based on the real-world identities of George Burns and Gracie Allen, but the show's storytelling is only concerned with finding ways for, again, the "Dumb Dora" to cause comic confusion, and everyone else is far less defined and utilized, as the specificity and strong aesthetic realism that separates *I Love Lucy* from the rest of its competition is not evident. Now, to be fair, the move to film the following year will help lend *Burns and Allen*'s storytelling more narrative gravitas—further moving it away from its variety-show origins—but the kind of character work we see on *Lucy* will never truly be matched. Instead, what we'll get, at best, is even better examples of what's indicated by "Gracie Goes to a Psychiatrist"—a story fueled and/or exacerbated by the clear Gracie Allen characterization. This, mind you, makes the episode character-centric, which is more than most sitcoms can claim. And that's why, even if it's never quite up to *Lucy*, it's generally always worthwhile, with many truly hilarious excursions that we'll reference and certainly keep highlighting in the many chapters ahead.

*Amos 'n Andy*, meanwhile, didn't premiere until June 1951, so it continued to debut the last half of its 26-episode first season up through December 1951, after which reruns aired until the 26-episode second season began in June 1952[52] (running until June 1953). So, when picking episodes to exemplify this season's best— late September 1951 to mid–September 1952 (as that's when *I Love Lucy*'s second season began)—that requires looking at samples from both the first *and* second "collections" of *Amos 'n Andy*. In doing so, the best entry eligible for inclusion here is probably "Getting Mama Married (I)" (October 18, 1951), the first half of a two-parter.

As with Gracie Allen, the Kingfish on *Amos 'n Andy* is one of the most easily identifiable and therefore best-defined characters from the early part of the 1950s, and although his show, like *Burns and Allen*, lacks the stronger and more consistently realistic characterizations of *I Love Lucy*, he is similarly able to push and inspire story like Gracie and Lucy. And this two-parter—among the best episodes of the entire series—is a great example, for its story starts with his desire to get his mother-in-law (played by the great Amanda Randolph) out of his hair by marrying her off to a rich suitor. The first half of Part I deals with his objective, as he schemes to arrange their date and then literally pushes the lovebirds together until a romance has definitively blossomed. Now, again, this show's brand of aesthetic realism is less literal than *Lucy*'s, with broader characters and story points that require bigger leaps in logic. Also, often there are story beats that are not really motivated by the regulars—they're out of their control. That is, there's a complication that they don't specifically inspire but then must react to and actively deal with to solve the problem. This is less ideal, of course, than a sitcom example where the characters themselves—the fixed and most reliable elements of a situation—are *responsible* for every comic and narrative happening. But this kind of storytelling can still be a showcase for character if they're defined.

And the Kingfish, in particular, *is* comedically defined, so when the second half of Part I pivots with the discovery that Mama has gone off to marry her fella, who turns out to be a con man looking to bilk elderly women, the rascal schemer Kingfish must now spring into action and save his mother-in-law. With help from Andy, who is especially great in a physical bit where he and the Kingfish try to change a tire on the side of the road, this is a lot of fun, utilizing character in a way that evidences *Amos 'n Andy*'s usual storytelling, while also being a superior example of it. In fact, I think, with a story motivated by the Kingfish that then also uses the main characters well—Andy, Sapphire, and her wonderful mother—this is one of the best half-hour samples you can find for this series. As for Part II, once the idea has been established, there's less directly laudable "situation comedy" (and less motivation from character). But there continues to be great slapstick and a lot of jokes that, again, display *Amos 'n Andy* as one of the most laugh-seeking and therefore funniest sitcoms from the early part of the 1950s.

In terms of new sitcoms on the air this season, there wasn't much beyond *Lucy*, although the winter of 1952 saw the TV debuts of two well-liked comedies moving over from radio. In February, Dennis Day, a longtime supporting player on *The Jack Benny Program* who also had his own weekly show from 1946 to 1951,[53] made the transition, playing the same persona established for him in a similar "modified" format. Meanwhile, January had offered the premiere of *My Friend Irma*, which starred Marie Wilson as a scatterbrained blonde stenographer from the Midwest now living in the big city with her sensible brunette roommate. Both series were done live from Los Angeles in front of studio audiences—*The Dennis Day Show* biweekly[54] and *My Friend Irma* weekly.[55] Few episodes circulate today, but they're both examples, similar to *Burns and Allen* and *Amos 'n Andy*, of sitcoms that jumped from radio to TV with one central comic character, around whom all stories revolved. The storytelling wasn't as immersive as *Lucy*'s, though, because no one was as thoroughly defined—even these otherwise strong laugh-yielding leads. But it was a form of sitcommery and more consistently funny than some of the other live, audience-less programming, specifically *The Goldbergs* and *The Ruggles* (the latter in its final season), which employed a lot of sentiment and with less of a pushing desire to make viewers regularly laugh out loud. In contrast, *Dennis Day* and *My Friend Irma* obviously pursued yuks.

Otherwise, most live sitcoms continued to come from New York, and this particular year, the Big Apple offered such titles as *Actors Hotel*, about a Manhattan boarding house; *Young Mr. Bobbin*, about a post–high school teen; and the well-known teen series *A Date with Judy*, which had a brief prime-time run in summer 1952 (after previously having aired in the daytime). *Judy* is the only one to outlast the 1951–1952 season, but no episodes are known to survive from the three.

However, if 1951–1952 didn't initially began as a great season for new sitcoms, the quick success of *I Love Lucy*—which finished the year as the third-most-watched show in the country—immediately led to an increase in development for the genre, beyond just *Dennis Day* and *Irma*. Heck, even DuMont got into the mix—offering a 10-episode New York sitcom that spring called *It's a Business*, about two song publishers in turn-of-the-century Tin Pan Alley. No episodes are known to survive, but music was a key part of its identity, and it was created by future *Lucy* scribe Bob Weiskopf.[56] It's most notable today for being one of the few sitcoms on the ill-fated DuMont.

Everyone wanted in on the sitcom now, and that was definitely evident by the summer of 1952, when the networks sought replacement programming for their usual shows and, eyeing *Lucy*'s popularity, began looking to try out comedies during this usually sleepy period in hopes that if they caught on, they'd be squeezed into the fall schedules. One of the more interesting summer shows came from NBC and aired as a replacement for the anthology drama series *Fireside Theatre*. It was *Boss Lady*, a filmed (single-camera) sitcom starring another B-movie actress, Lynn Bari, who had actually appeared in a brief live 1950 comedy-ish show called *Detective's Wife*.[57] This effort, *Boss Lady*, is best remembered for its unusual premise—wherein Bari played Gwen F. Allen, the chief executive of a construction firm otherwise dominated by men, including her doddering old father who was chairman of the board and whose ineptitude was a regular challenge.

The show was obviously unique because unlike all of the other women-led sitcoms of the era, like *I Love Lucy* and *Burns and Allen* (and even *The Goldbergs*), *Boss Lady* wasn't set in a domestic sphere but in a workplace—and in a workplace where she wasn't either a teacher or secretary but an executive. This made the series more specifically premised—it was about a particular woman in particular circumstances. In terms of its success as a situation comedy, having only seen a few episodes, the scenario definitely informs the action, and while there are a few chuckles in the relationship between father and daughter, this is a show where the characters are otherwise and unfortunately secondary to the premise. We'll see more of these—and talk more about what this means—later. In the meantime, I'll just note that *Boss Lady* may have been atypical, but its fate was not—after its 13-episode summer run, it faded from memory.

More successful was *Mister Peepers*, another NBC sitcom that premiered in the summer of 1952. This one was a replacement for *The James Melton Show* (a musical variety series sponsored by Ford) and it came live from a theater in New York before an audience whose presence gave a vocal signal of the show's comic intent, much more so than live audience-less New York half hours like *The Goldbergs*. *Mister Peepers* had a similarly dramatic pedigree, though—it was produced by one of the kings of the anthology genre, Fred Coe, and created by David Swift, who'd written for several of these series (*Goodyear/Philco* primarily) before crafting this comedy for the amusing Wally Cox, whose career took off just at the birth of live television in New York, leading him to a regular role on an earlier variety-comedy hybrid series on DuMont called *The School House*, where he played a student.[58] That was perfect for his persona—he registered as a young, meek, and often mumbling nerd with a short frame and high-pitched voice. (Later, Cox would become the voice of cartoon character Underdog.) In Swift's *Mister Peepers*, Cox was now playing Robinson J. Peepers, a high school science teacher, but he brought that same basic persona with him, allowing for natural comedy from the juxtaposition of his noncommanding presence, which registered as if he was a high school student himself, with this position of implied authority.

The show premiered in July 1952 for a 10-episode run—the first nine of which exist and have been released on DVD. These early excursions reveal the show to be a workplace sitcom in the school setting, similar to the popular radio series *Our Miss Brooks*, starring Eve Arden as an unmarried English teacher. However, unlike *Our Miss Brooks*, which was about to make its own transition to television in the fall, *Mister Peepers* was a little more exclusively school-set, at least in the beginning. And while *Brooks* tended to push the elements of its school to the background in favor of a focus on several clear, easy-to-understand relationships, early *Peepers* really leans into the trappings of the school and his job as a teacher. Naturally, the genre prefers more support from character, the imitators of life who, when properly developed, are best able to inspire plots and sustain a series over a long time. But by using the setting and the premise, this is a very basic form of situation comedy, and to its credit, *Mister Peepers* has the central Wally Cox characterization, which he brings with him everywhere, anchoring the show as something of a character piece, even if the storytelling is not yet as well motivated *by* him.

Speaking of motivation, early episodes of *Mister Peepers* also indulge a lot of physical, slapstick comedy—perhaps in the New York vaudeville tradition or maybe in evocation of the already hugely successful *Lucy*. But it's not the same. Although it's good fun when Mister Peepers gets stuck in a basketball hoop,[59] or his check gets sucked up by the air-conditioning,[60] or he tries to paint lines on a softball court but the machine goes wild[61]—these gags aren't really earned by his depiction or the active *choices* he makes in evidence of it. What's more, the initial ensemble, though suggesting a true intention to be a workplace sitcom—with a principal, a gym teacher, and a possible love interest among others—there's really a lack of good characters on par with Cox's Peepers … well, until the second episode's introduction of Marion Lorne as Mrs. Gurney, a confused English teacher. You probably know Lorne best as the befuddled, stammering, mistake-prone Aunt Clara on 1964's *Bewitched*. That same basic persona informs her depiction here, only minus the witchcraft. Like Cox, she's a naturally funny performer whose own innate personality allows her to exist both in story and comedy as a unique presence, elevating the show's claim on its character work, even if her function within narrative is not as excellent.

Fortunately, *Peepers* seems to realize its strengths and weaknesses early, and it starts to fade out the blander or less utilizable members of the original ensemble, while moving away from this amusing but unmotivated slapstick. By episode eight, "The School Dance" (September 11, 1952), the show starts to settle into the tonal identity for which it will be associated in the rest of its run (three more seasons), with a quieter, more character-rooted conception of how to find story and derive laughs. This installment is a preview of what lies ahead because it introduces two important new characters: a swinging bachelor history teacher named Harvey Weskit and a sensitive school nurse named Nancy Remington, a potential new love interest for Mister Peepers.

"Wes," especially, is a terrific addition—played by one future half of *The Odd Couple*, Tony Randall. In the beginning of his tenure on *Mister Peepers*, Harvey Weskit's suave demeanor is an obvious contrast to Robinson Peepers, and they're something of their own odd couple—a great predication for a friendship. With Cox and Lorne, Randall's natural charisma inherently guides his usage and further strengthens the show's character-led bona fides. As for Nancy, played by Patricia Benoit, she's relatively duller—the sweet love interest—but she plays the role with appreciated sincerity and helps infuse the text with a palpable humanity, steering it away from gags and back toward people. These four—Peepers, Gurney, Weskit, and Remington—become the core of the show's cast heading into its second season, which debuted in late October 1952, once NBC, impressed with the strong reaction to *Mister Peepers*, eagerly took down a new and well-cast filmed Hollywood sitcom called *Doc Corkle*, about a widower dentist with an eccentric family, after only three scant weeks, just to make room for this potentially burgeoning hit.[62]

From its second season onward, *Peepers* is poised in the direction of character-driven comedy via relationships, anchored by several funny personas and a maintained interest in laughs as a necessity. The show is not always uproarious, but it's always comedic, and the improvement to its character work renders it a fine example of the situation comedy in this era. Now, there are no great episodes in this

Chapter Four. TV's First Great Situation Comedy    83

**Mister Peepers (Wally Cox) falls for school nurse Nancy Remington (Patricia Benoit) in *Mister Peepers*, "The School Dance" (1952).**

batch—"The School Dance" is notable for who it introduces, and the second, third, and fourth entries all have memorable slapstick—but otherwise, the best is yet to come with *Mister Peepers*, including its most famous broadcast: Robinson and Nancy's May 1954 wedding[63]—a testament to the show's ability to make the audience care about its characters and root for developments within their relationships (as Wes would also get a similar arc). So *Mister Peepers* is one of the most charming, lesser known 1950s sitcoms, and considering that it was live and only preserved on kinescope, it might be totally forgotten but for the fact that most episodes survive at the UCLA Film & Television Archive and half of them have been put on DVD. That's how we're able to celebrate it today, as the series has not had a successful syndicated life, like the filmed *Lucy*.

Speaking of syndication, another filmed sitcom that premiered in the summer of 1952 ended up having quite the run in the late 1950s and early 1960s. It was a replacement for *I Love Lucy* (in the same time slot) and already showed some influence, with a bright, leading lady engaging in schemes and participating in slapstick. But the creative comparisons between the two shows do this one no favors, for *My Little Margie* was produced by Roland Reed and Hal Roach, Jr., at Hal Roach Studios—like *Trouble with Father* (which also included Black actor Willie Best, who had a concurrent regular role on *Margie* as well). It's similarly skilled at offering physical gags, only there's barely any link here between its comedy—or its storytelling—*to* the characters themselves: the elements of the situation that *should* inspire everything, in fulfillment of the genre's needs. While *Trouble with Father* at least uses its own slapstick to reveal the persona of its lead (who exists in something of a vacuum), *My Little Margie* starts a little differently: with a core father-and-daughter relationship. Two movie stars anchor the regular cast—veteran Charlie Farrell and the title's eponymous Margie, Gale Storm. Both are attractive, big-eyed performers with a natural affability, and their premised dynamic—a codependency where she is looking out for him now that he's a widower, and he's looking out for her now that she's come of age and is dating—is comedically interesting, suggesting a lot of potential story related to these specific circumstances and how the two leads react against each other.

However, if that relationship is interesting, both characters are vague. Yes, they're mutual schemers, but all the individualization—the objectives, attitudes, and flaws that made Lucy and Ricky so dynamic—are smoothed out in favor of something hazy and generic, totally lacking in the continuity-providing details that helped give *Lucy* such well-defined, believable regulars. Accordingly, without this definition, it's impossible for these leads to inspire plot uniquely, outside of the basic construct that's stated in the opening introduction (where they literally explain their relationship). Essentially, they're too underdeveloped. And even worse, so few stories are actually *about* the premise anyway. Scripts instead focus on wild narrative ideas where the pair schemes and dresses up for a farce, a kind of humor that's dependent on strong characterizations with crystal clear motivations, especially when the maneuverings are so broad and outlandish, far away from literal realism and therefore in need of something more grounding—like character stakes—for the audience to connect to as a basic mimesis.

Unfortunately, the setups and climaxes of most *Margie* stories are ridiculous and not well-supported by actual character stakes. They could occur with any set of undefined fools. This fundamental weakness with character specificity in story is comedically fatal, for without a continuity of well-defined characterizations justifying the action, the big, silly things that occur feel untethered to anything concrete or mimetic, therefore rendering most narrative turns unbelievable, totally lacking *I Love Lucy*'s ability to make us understand *why* silly things happen. So with a strong relationship construct that nevertheless fails to proffer well-defined leads who could then motivate outrageous plots believably, *My Little Margie* is a poor example of the situation comedy. This is a shame because, again, there's potential in the central relationship as premised and even in the cast, which also includes octogenarian Gertrude Hoffmann as the pair's neighbor and Margie's frequent coconspirator. She's inherently quirky and deserved more chances to show it.

Sadly, there is no great episode in all of *Margie*'s four-season run, but the best of this first year is the tenth aired, "Efficiency Expert" (August 18, 1952), which notably guests Alvy Moore (later Hank Kimball of *Green Acres*) as a tightly wound young man whom Margie pretends to be interested in, thinking that in doing so, her father will object and she can go back to her regular beau Freddie (Don Hayden). Only, things don't go as planned and the two are on a course to be married until Margie has a heart-to-heart with her father that's funny, tender, and for once, believable, calling on the premised notion that her mother (his wife) is gone, and their bond is different without her. From this, the two unite against the efficiency expert—which is unusual, because typically they're trying to pull things over on each other—and although the climactic physical comedy sequence itself is goofy, this moment of genuine character connection gives more support to the plot than most of these *My Little Margie* outings can boast. And of course, there's the hilarious Alvy Moore around to increase the laughs. It's not great, but it's the best here.

To be fair, *My Little Margie* will become funnier in its second season, but it's never what we want it to be, especially when compared to *Lucy*. (And these are comparisons that *Margie* willingly invites, like in Gale Storm's trilling vocal affect, which is so similar to Lucille Ball's "Ewww" that it's impossible to ignore.[64]) As we'll see in the next chapter, many forthcoming sitcoms would similarly take aspects of *Lucy*'s identity and try to cash in on success via imitation. But just as *Margie* may have a slapstick leading lady and a narrative structure where schemes drive the action, other shows prove that none of this matters if it's missing the things that made *I Love Lucy* so special: its strong characters. Lucy Ricardo is a foundational example of what makes the situation comedy an art form. And while using her as a model may seem so simple, it was way easier said than done.

## *JACKSON'S BEST SITCOMS FROM 1951-52*

1. I LOVE LUCY (S1)
2. THE GEORGE BURNS AND GRACIE ALLEN SHOW (S2)
3. THE AMOS 'N ANDY SHOW (S1 and S2)

## *EPISODES FROM THE 1951-52 SEASON IN JACKSON'S TOP 50 FROM THE '50s*

#2. I LOVE LUCY (S1): "Lucy Does a TV Commercial" (5/5/52)
#40. I LOVE LUCY (S1): "The Ballet" (2/18/52)

## *OTHER NOTABLE EPISODES FROM 1951-52*

THE GEORGE BURNS AND GRACIE ALLEN SHOW (S2): "Gracie Goes to a Psychiatrist" (9/27/51)
THE AMOS 'N ANDY SHOW (S1): "Getting Mama Married (I)" (10/18/51)
I LOVE LUCY (S1): "Be a Pal" (10/22/51)
TROUBLE WITH FATHER (S2): "Father Does His Homework" (11/23/51)
I LOVE LUCY (S1): "The Benefit" (1/7/52)
I LOVE LUCY (S1): "Pioneer Women" (3/31/52)
I LOVE LUCY (S1): "The Freezer" (4/28/52)
I LOVE LUCY (S1): "Lucy's Schedule" (5/26/52)
MY LITTLE MARGIE (S1): "Efficiency Expert" (8/18/52)
MISTER PEEPERS (S1): "The School Dance" (9/11/52)

CHAPTER FIVE

# Like Lucy

*The Best Television Sitcoms of 1952–1953*

By the end of the 1951–1952 season, *I Love Lucy* had become the most-watched sitcom in the country.[1] Its quick popularity proved to be long lasting—it would retain this status for the duration of its run, emerging as Nielsen's #1 ranked winner (of all programs) in four of its remaining five seasons.[2] This is relevant to our study not because commercial popularity is synonymous with critical merit—it is not— but rather because the intense affection audiences felt toward *Lucy* had a major influence on the development of other sitcoms and therefore the trajectory of the genre. In addition to the technical achievement of Desilu's refined multi-camera format, *I Love Lucy*'s success accelerated the entire medium's shift to filmed programming, more of it naturally emanating from Hollywood. Also and more basically, *I Love Lucy* made the situation comedy even more popular to networks than it had already been. And because it never faltered, other shows specifically looked to *Lucy* for creative aspects that could also be replicated for guaranteed bankability. In this chapter, we will be examining *I Love Lucy*'s immediate influence on the sitcom genre by studying how 1952–1953's new efforts both adhere and do not adhere to the principles that continued to make *Lucy* great. But first, let's stick with *Lucy*.

It's easy to see why viewers adored the show in 1952—it's consistently funny, tying memorable slapstick centerpieces to the Lucy Ricardo characterization via a defined objective that can provide a foundation for extrapolatable motivations, thereby earning its stories through plot points driven *by* Lucy, the central element of the situation. And then the show reinforces her—and her ensemble's—depictions with a continuity of details (some autobiographical) that in turn suggests a consistent mimesis. This makes all the leads *even more* capable of propelling plot, for the audience comes to understand them, and they seem more believable, both validating and receiving validation from episodic ideas that corroborate said understanding. Never do they feel more mimetic, like humans (relative to the rest of this genre), than during *I Love Lucy*'s second season, when Lucille Ball's real-life pregnancy was written into the show and the Ricardos discovered that they too were "'specting" in "Lucy Is Enceinte" (December 8, 1952)—a story arc that culminated miraculously fast on January 19, 1953, with "Lucy Goes to the Hospital," when nearly 72 percent of all homes with TV sets tuned in to see Little Ricky's debut[3]—the exact same day that Ball herself gave birth to the Arnazes' son, Desi Jr.[4]

Now, so many of the regurgitated platitudes about *I Love Lucy* are hinged on this storyline, much of it predicated on the idea that it was controversial. However, some myths have been exaggerated, for remember, in 1948, the series that many historians call the first television sitcom, *Mary Kay and Johnny*, similarly wrote in its starring couple's blessed event. (That series is probably the first sitcom to show a couple in a single bed as well.) As for the use of the "p-word," yes, CBS adhered to a code of broadcasting standards that was derived from radio, and they exercised an abundance of caution in any matters related to the implication of sex, choosing not to possibly offend good taste needlessly on their most popular program by saying "pregnant." To that point, part of the show's marketing involved the very public sanctioning of every pregnancy-related script by a cadre of clergymen.[5] But there really were no vocal critics to which this caution was responding—it was merely part of the blessed event's press.

Similarly overstated is the notion that the sponsor and network were opposed to acknowledging a pregnant woman on the show. Yes, there were discussions and initial worries.[6] But retiring or even temporarily benching the country's most popular series was unlikely, especially when there was an easy solution that might actually *increase* the ratings (which it did). This made the decision far less risky and surprising than it's sometimes framed. In fact, when Louella Parsons got wind of the news in mid–June 1952,[7] well before the network planned to publicly announce anything, she made it sound like a given that their baby would be a part of *I Love Lucy*—a fact confirmed in print just two weeks later.[8] And if there was any doubt, the positive press for the couple should have been encouraging.

Meanwhile, one more myth to clear up is that "Desi Arnaz invented the rerun" when it was decided to intersperse *Lucy*'s second season with repeats from the first, allowing the show to pad its schedule and accommodate Ball's maternity leave. But ever since television started airing filmed programs, the possibility of rerunning shows was self-evident, and even prior to the fall of 1952, sitcoms like *Amos 'n Andy* and *Trouble with Father* not only had select episodes re-aired on their networks—they also had already re-aired them *during* the regular TV season (as opposed to the summer).[9, 10] So while it was a smart move to play repeats to help ease the production burden on the *I Love Lucy* company during Ball's pregnancy—and it was smart to shoot a series of nonpregnancy episodes that could air, with an opening "flashback" scene, in the months while Ball was home postpartum—showing reruns this season was not a revelation; it was a benefit of shooting *Lucy* on film, known to all series that had been produced as such.

As for the arc itself—which only consists of seven actual episodes—it's a valid form of situation comedy in that a temporary and semi-serialized scenario is created inside of a usual situation that grounds the resultingly related but still episodic stories. (Incidentally, story arcs can make for good sitcommery—they can bolster continuity for the characters—as long as each episode plays to the established situation and has an individual narrative structure of its own, existing as more situation than serial.) But this is not *actually* a character-based narrative, for it's not driven by the premised and defining traits of either Lucy or Ricky Ricardo. Sure, it's believable that a young middle-class couple in love would be starting a family, but the arc isn't specific to Lucy and Ricky based on what we know about them uniquely.

In this regard, both characters' individual definitions are sort of immaterial to the joy of the pregnancy discovery and the baby's eventual birth, which means, this isn't the *best* situation comedy that the series has to offer. And frankly, Lucy Ricardo becoming a mother might seem starkly opposed to her otherwise sustaining objective of being in show business—or rather, being more than just the "typical" housewife.

Fortunately, the show smartly keeps its conflict intact, for the Lucy character in Season Two continues to strive for more from her life and in plots that might seem ordinary yet are backed, again, by the continuity established from her guiding objective and what we can extrapolate from it: she wants to be *more*. It's therefore entirely motivated when she takes a break from marriage,[11] studies sculpting,[12] or runs for president of her women's club.[13] And this blessed event is *folded* into her established situation, with entries like "Lucy's Show Biz Swan Song" (December 22, 1952) and the post-baby "The Indian Show" (May 4, 1953) literally addressing what motherhood will do to her show biz ambitions: make them harder to achieve but no less intense. Essentially, then, the baby becomes an extension of her character, as now she strives to be more than an average housewife … *and mother*, another role expected of her.

▶ In fact, this year's commitment to narratively showcasing the Lucy Ricardo character makes *I Love Lucy*'s second season one of the series' finest showings—four of my top 50 episodes come from this collection alone. One of these, at **#47**, is the aforementioned **"Lucy's Show Biz Swan Song" (December 22, 1952)** in which a very pregnant Lucy sneaks into Ricky's 1890s-themed revue, believing it to be her last chance at show biz glory. It was directed by **William Asher** and written by the same crew—**Jess Oppenheimer**; **Madelyn Pugh**; and **Bob Carroll, Jr.**

It's a tightly constructed episode in which Lucy's guiding objective is shaped by her current condition—a temporary aspect of her situation—thereby creating a story that could only exist with these characters during this specific time in the series. Additionally, the ensemble is also used well, with the Mertzes—former vaudevillians, you know—appearing in the revue with Ricky for a climax involving a barbershop quartet where Lucy's rotten singing becomes the comic focal point. It's everything you expect *I Love Lucy* to be, especially here in the 1952–1953 season.

"Lucy's Show Biz Swan Song" is easily the best of the pregnancy shows—and those directly involving the baby here in Season Two. But the kid ends up proving additive also, as Lucy Ricardo is further mired in the joyful trappings of expected femininity, which she enthusiastically embraces, all the while yearning, just as she always had prior to the birth of Little Ricky, for a life more special, evidenced by her pursuits. This makes her goal even tougher now, more emotionally complex. Additionally, the mimetic nature of the events—the fact that most adult viewers watching knew that *both* the Ricardos and Arnazes were expecting and then rearing a child—further solidified the audience's faith in the series' relative emotional realism, which therefore made it easier to invest in them as characters, for now they felt *even more* like real people.

That is, although this was an event that could happen to any young couple on TV, *because* it really happened off-camera as well, the pregnancy arc and its ensuing publicity craze ended up strengthening the show's capacity to delight with its character work, allowing the Ricardos to stand as far more human and thus utilizable within different types of motivated story, where they'd have more emotional leeway than any of their counterparts in the genre, who remained more like caricatures, incapable of such a sincere and genuinely sentimental season.

It's also an incredibly comedic season, with, again, some of the series' best episodes—for example, "The Handcuffs," which I cited in the previous chapter in evidence of *I Love Lucy*'s total emersion in character. It takes a fairly routine story in which two people are handcuffed together and situates it on Lucy's objective, providing a centerpiece directly tied to the show's very conflict, where she is behind the curtain, gleefully performing with her husband.

▶ I won't spend any more space discussing **"The Handcuffs"** here, except to note that it premiered on **October 6, 1952**, and comes in at **#16** on my top 50 list. It was directed by **Marc Daniels**, and written by **Oppenheimer**, **Pugh**, and **Carroll**. (Read more in Chapter Four.)

▶ That same crew delivered a wonderful episode that was initially broadcast a week later, on **October 13, 1952**. It's **"The Operetta,"** and it comes in at **#34** on my list, with a story about Lucy writing, staging, and starring in an original operetta for her women's club.

Obviously, that is a perfect idea for Lucy Ricardo, as it allows her to shine as a performer—exactly like Ricky gets to do every week: the very thing she wants to share. In addition to using her central objective so effortlessly, the episode also makes a lot of comic hay out of Lucy's terrible singing, along with her poor budgeting—two running jokes within her personality that we the audience have come to expect, validating our conception of the character when they're utilized. This is a great example of situation comedy—all the story beats and laughs come *from* Lucy.

▶ However, as great as those episodes are, this season also contains one of the finest episodes of situation comedy *ever* produced. In fact, I think it's *the best* sitcom episode of the 1950s—yes, I put it at **#1** on my list. Casual viewers know it by the iconic image of Lucy and Ethel struggling to properly wrap—and then dispose of—an onslaught of chocolate candies on a conveyer belt. But it's called **"Job Switching"** and aired as the second season's premiere on **September 15, 1952**, with a story about

Lucy and Ethel going out to get jobs while Ricky and Fred attempt to tend the home. **Oppenheimer**, **Pugh**, and **Carroll** wrote the script, while **William Asher** directed.

"Job Switching" takes its basic idea from an earlier *My Favorite Husband* radio show about the husbands and wives switching roles,[14] but it adds in several classic slapstick centerpieces—like the women at the conveyer belt, which some say has its roots in Chaplin's *Modern Times*.[15] I, however, think there's a distinction. While both exploit a basic man-versus-machine tension, his film found bittersweet comedy in the inhumanity of man conforming to machine. *Lucy* heightens the hilarious humanity in our inherent being—or the notion that it may be impossible to conform.

But "Job Switching" is not just a testament to the show's physical comedy prowess—or the directing of William Asher (future *Bewitched* producer), in the first entry he helmed after replacing Marc Daniels.[16] It boasts a stellar, perfect use of the series' situation, for its plot hinges on the notion of a gender swap: the husbands will stay home and tend to the domestic duties typically reserved for women, while the wives will go out and earn the figurative bacon. From there, we get all the outrageous comic centerpieces and visual gags that make the episode such a hilarious tour de force—Fred bakes a cake that looks like a pancake, Ricky destroys his kitchen with an exploding chicken and overflowing pot of rice, Lucy gets into a messy slap fight with a chocolate dipper, and then the women have an iconic battle with a conveyer belt of chocolates.

Yet it's all attached to the story, which, here, stems from the central tension at the heart of the series' premise, via Lucy Ricardo's well-defined characterization, where there's something not fully satisfying to her about being only what she's expected to be, a homemaker. And in this case, given the setup, she's endeavoring to explicitly prove to Ricky, once and for all, that the confining role women face in the home is actually more of a struggle than what he experiences every day in the working world, which means that she is just as capable as he is of going out and earning a living. So, this "role reversal" angst is *I Love Lucy* at its thematic core—a quintessential display of the series. More than any other half-hour sample produced, *this* is what it's really all about.

Here, she's not going out and getting in show business—the clearest example (to her) of the most exciting life she could possibly have—but she *is* finally breaking out of the home and trying something new, asserting her belief in her own self-capacity. The conflict then comes from the fact that she's not used to working, and although these chocolate factory shenanigans—with the stern-faced Elvia Allman as the hilariously aggressive forewoman—are not necessarily caused specifically *by* her ineptitude, they do represent the basic notion that it would be a challenge for her to adapt outside the home, no matter where she tried. To that point, the status quo—the series' situation—is naturally restored, as expected, by the episode's end, when Lucy returns to the place where she's most comfortable, but her endemic discontent persists, and the show can continue to be what it promises to be, for both her and future story.

## Chapter Five. Like Lucy

**Ethel (Vivian Vance, left) and Lucy (Lucille Ball, right) with Elvia Allman as the forewoman in *I Love Lucy*, "Job Switching" (1952).**

Accordingly, I believe there is no better sample of *I Love Lucy*'s situation, which is upheld by its characters and how they exist in relation to one another, revealing their definitions through established details and specific objectives that motivate, inspire, and give depth to stories. It's the best of the best sitcom of the 1950s and thus the best sitcom episode of the 1950s.

## The Multi-Cam Movement

However, even as *I Love Lucy* was enjoying fabulous commercial and creative success, executive producer Desi Arnaz had bigger ideas. In the middle of *Lucy*'s first season, he made a deal for their company Desilu to shoot for CBS a pilot for the television adaptation of the hit radio sitcom *Our Miss Brooks*,[17] which had premiered in 1948 when it was initially set to star Shirley Booth before the role officially went to Eve Arden,[18] one of Ball's pals from their days together at RKO. Once greenlit to series, the TV version would become the second sitcom on air to utilize the multi-camera format as refined by Desilu and made famous on *I Love Lucy*, with the company's crew splitting time between both series. This was the ideal mode of presentation for *Our Miss Brooks*, as the multi-camera format allowed the show to retain the rhythm and sound it had in its hit radio incarnation, which continued throughout the concurrent TV run. And this naturally created a favorable association with *I Love Lucy*, which again was the most popular show on the air. So Desilu helped set up the television *Our Miss Brooks* for a good grade.

The TV version of *Our Miss Brooks* was essentially the same as on radio—following Arden's Connie Brooks, an unmarried high school English teacher who is head over heels in love with clueless biology instructor Mr. Boynton (Robert Rockwell on TV, the only actor not carried over from radio), and menaced by pompous, domineering principal Mr. Osgood Conklin (the bellowing Gale Gordon). Others in the main cast included her landlady Mrs. Davis (Jane Morgan), a daffy mother figure, and a young Richard Crenna, affecting a high-pitch nasal voice in the Henry Aldrich tradition, for the role of goofy student Walter Denton, Miss Brooks's young confidant and part-time romancer of Mr. Conklin's goody-two-shoes daughter Harriet (Gloria McMillan). In the peripheral ensemble, meanwhile, were Conklin's wife, Mrs. Davis's sister, an amorous male French teacher, a handful of ignorant students, and a rival for Miss Brooks in the form of Daisy Enright (the school's other English teacher, who also aimed to snag the bachelor Mr. Boynton for herself). Miss Enright was portrayed on TV (in just four scant appearances) by Mary Jane Croft.

With this setup, *Our Miss Brooks* was, as on radio, largely a workplace sitcom, for even the scenes at home with Miss Brooks and Mrs. Davis were largely dominated by figures associated with the school. The only real difference between the two versions of the series was, unsurprisingly, the freedom to indulge more physical comedy on TV as a result of the medium's visual opportunities. Arden was not as broad as Ball, though—her style was more verbal, or at least confined to the face, with a withering brow giving advance notice of a sarcastic quip.

As for *Our Miss Brooks*'s character work, the central figure has a basic objective: landing the beautiful but bashful Mr. Boynton. Like Lucy, this provides an engine for story to which she can be directly attached. But this core element of the situation proves not to be as fruitful as Lucy's, for the genre's necessary maintenance of a status quo forces these leads to be less emotionally realistic—especially in the case of Mr. Boynton, who has to remain somewhat cognizant of Miss Brooks's feelings, somewhat reciprocal in his affections, but always single and oblivious as to the extent of her crush. In other words, he can never learn information that any normal person would be expected to learn, keeping him therefore less mimetic, or believable. Take, for example, a very funny early episode called "Miss Brooks Play-Acts" (October 31, 1952) in which Mr. Boynton asks Miss Brooks to come over and pretend to be "Mrs. Boynton" as he interviews for a job. She thinks this is her chance to show him her potential as a wife, but what he really wants her to play is his mother. This cluelessness earns the comic story, but it can't last forever, and such episodes, while related to the leading lady's objective, can't help but remind us of the ways in which these regulars are *required* to be less believable in order to maintain the situation.

Accordingly, the show's capacity to make us emotionally invest in them is limited, and the characters—as a whole—fail to be nuanced or multifaceted, which constrains opportunities for story. This is an issue that accelerates during the run, as *Our Miss Brooks* also lacks *I Love Lucy*'s autobiographical flourishes and the attention to detail that can create an equally durable continuity of character. Their weaker believability is both exacerbated by, and the reason for, this limitation on the number of stories directly about Miss Brooks's core goal. Instead, most of the plots are farces built on misunderstandings—mild screwball comedies that sometimes use the school setting as the basis for their happenings, but sometimes don't even go that far. In simple terms, then, the show is narratively not as character driven or situation-based as *Lucy*, with the majority of *Brooks*'s plots tied only to background, or incidental, elements of the premise rather than the most important.

However, if the series' storytelling leaves something to be desired, *Our Miss Brooks* does boast some hilariously pitched characters—like Osgood Conklin and Walter Denton—and they all have unique relationships that reveal their delineated perspectives via dialogue specific to each of their depictions. And since *Brooks* remains a largely verbal enterprise, this means the majority of the TV series' comedy *is* coming from the regulars and their individual relational dynamics. That makes it, by the standards of this era, one of the most character-*centric* situation comedies on the air, regardless of story. It's an interesting contrast to another contemporaneous school-set teacher-led workplace sitcom, *Mister Peepers*, which started similarly broad and even more physical but slowly became more quiet and palpably human by the end of its 10-episode summer run, using its first full season (its second) in 1952–1953 to create a more sincere focus on its leads' relationships. *Brooks* is funnier than *Peepers* because its characters are more incongruous—with traits more exaggerated—and its misunderstanding-filled stories are bolder. But *Peepers* is more real, and it doesn't have to sacrifice too much humor to maintain that quality.

We'll talk more about *Peepers* later in this chapter. In the meantime, *Our Miss Brooks* is no less enjoyable than this other school-set classic, for it's a well-designed situation comedy as well, with pinpointable characters who have humorous personalities and relationships that *could* encourage story, a strong cast of talented performers, and the multi-camera format motivating it to be just as funny as (if not more than) it had been in its successful radio incarnation. This TV version's relatively high quality is as much a testament to its own premised design as to this assistance by Desilu, whose multi-camera configuration encouraged comedic triumph, even for shows that weren't quite as narratively or emotionally intelligent as *I Love Lucy*. In 1952–1953, *Our Miss Brooks* is at its best, for while many episodes were merely adaptations of some of the radio run's best scripts with added visual cues, its display of easy-to-understand leads, with precise traits and crystal-clear relationships, is worth celebrating—again, regardless of story.

▶ And there's greatness here. My favorite entry from the TV show's first season lands at **#15** on my top 50 list. It's "**Aunt Mattie Boynton**," which first aired on **January 2, 1953**. It was directed by **Al Lewis** and written by Lewis with **Joseph Quillan**.

Its story finds perennial rivals Miss Brooks and Miss Enright competing to show off their business administration skills.

"Aunt Mattie Boynton" is one of the most effective examples of *Our Miss Brooks* using its well-built ensemble dynamics within story, as it offers the television introduction of Mary Jane Croft's hilarious Miss Enright, who competes with Miss Brooks for a business administration position that Mr. Conklin is appointing—all in hopes of impressing Mr. Boynton, who insists that he wants to marry a woman just like his resourceful, household-running aunt. This setup, then, is not only predicated on Miss Brooks's pursuit of Mr. Boynton and his semi-clueless awareness, but it also factors in the competitive rivalry she has with Miss Enright, along with the way that she is both a nuisance to—and menaced by—the blustering Mr. Conklin.

What's more, the entry makes time for physical comedy, setting up a bit where Miss Brooks, at the advice of the dim-witted Walter Denton, thinks that she can impress her boss by buying cheaper fuel for his furnace, not knowing that he has just installed a new system that doesn't require the oil that she's had Walter load. Naturally, this yields a crude mess at the Conklin house—a climax that reinforces her strained relationship with the principal and is itself earned by Walter's basic stupidity. It evidences the series' penchant for misunderstandings, *all the while* keeping Miss Brooks's love for Mr. Boynton as the whole story's underlying raison d'être. As such, it's the series' most satisfying display of its main characters, and the relationships that inform its premised situation in narrative. Each year hereafter becomes less capable of cohesively demonstrating such straightforward situation comedy, as plots become more labored and detached.

At any rate, if *Brooks* is proof of how the Desilu style could be farmed out to sitcoms that were only somewhat similar, it would take a little while—a few decades, in fact—for the multi-camera format to truly become the industry's dominant standard. Of course, that didn't stop others from investigating its potential right away—including Phil Rapp, creator of another show that had its roots in radio but in the more liminal comedy-variety space: "The Bickersons." With a title that tells the basic premise—a bickering couple—this classic American reference began as a recurring sketch on several comedy-variety radio shows in the 1940s, mostly starring Don Ameche and Frances Langford and always written by creator Rapp.[19] "The Bickersons" officially made their jump to TV in the fall of 1950, as a regular attraction on DuMont's variety series *Star Time*, with Lew Parker now in the role of John Bickerson.[20] From there, *The Bickersons* had a brief run as a half-hour radio sitcom in the summer of 1951 and hung around TV throughout the next year, appearing on several different comedy-variety shows, now with Virginia Grey joining Parker.[21]

It has been erroneously reported elsewhere that, following the success of the half-hour radio sitcom iteration of *The Bickersons* in the summer of 1951, Rapp readied a TV version that he sold into first-run syndication for the 1951–1952 season.[22] In actuality, it wasn't until the summer of 1952 that Rapp attempted to film a pilot of *The Bickersons*, with Parker and Grey, at a local Hollywood theater using Filmcraft,[23] which was attempting to replicate the Desilu formula of shooting with multiple cameras in front of a live audience. Apparently, the results were unsatisfactory, for Rapp ended up a few months later at General Service Studios, the same place *Lucy* and *Our Miss Brooks* were being shot.[24] Now with Desilu's established facilities at Rapp's disposal, 13 half-hour episodes of "It's The Bickersons" were filmed into the early fall of 1952—four of which he began using as a pilot presentation for potential buyers.[25] But the series never got sold to a network, and I have found no evidence that it ever actually appeared in syndication either. Several entries circulate today, which is why there's confusion about whether it ever got formally run.

As on radio, the TV version of "The Bickersons," called "It's The Bickersons," is a joke-heavy affair that aims to derive the bulk of its comedy from the back-and-forth insults hurled by its titular pair. But these characters are kept, again, vague and generic, with not a lot of details giving them individual shape or much comedy supplied beyond the simple fact that they are prone to arguing. In this regard, the storytelling, like the comedy, is confined, and even though it must fill a half hour, the characters are not really pushing the plots based on how they are *uniquely* rendered. Also, while their bickering indeed is fueling the dialogue-heavy comedy, most of the laughs come from the heightened acidity of the lines themselves and not so much the individual characterizations saying them. Only in the sense that the Bickersons are *the* quintessential battling pair is there any value to this barb-filled but characterization-light affair.

By now, this genre demands more from its situation—its characters—especially in television, which, as we know, relies on more than just dialogue. That is one thing that Jackie Gleason quickly realized when he brought a similar sketch about battling married people to TV in the fall of 1951—"The Honeymooners," a recurring feature first on *Cavalcade of Stars* and later on *The Jackie Gleason Show*. We will talk about *The Honeymooners* and its history when it becomes an actual half-hour situation comedy in the 1955–1956 season, but it is worth noting here in relation to "It's The Bickersons" because of its comparatively better character work and, more simply, its sterling use of physical comedy, bringing the sketch-rooted sitcom out of radio's mores and into TV's. In the meantime, it is also worth noting again that sketch comedy does not require the same strong characters as a situation comedy, given the latter's need for weekly story, asking that a situation be connected to the generation of plot and therefore the leads themselves. In contrast, even when engaging domestic couple sketches, like "The Honeymooners" or "The Hickenloopers"—a more middle-class version of "The Honeymooners" that premiered on Sid Caesar's *Your Show of Shows* in 1950—their basically simplistic nature, suggesting one measly comedic idea for exploration over the course of a five- to 10-minute scene, is a step backward from situation comedy, due to the deemphasis on character and its relevance for story.

In the meantime, other sitcoms sought to replicate *Lucy*'s success not technologically but merely by looking at its premise, only without fully grasping *why* the

Arnazes' hit show was so special: its characters. Chief among these is *I Married Joan*, a vehicle for longtime radio comedienne Joan Davis, who had starred in a succession of sitcoms, or "modified sitcoms," throughout the 1940s.[26] After an unsold television pilot inspired by one of these radio shows, she eventually crashed into the new medium with a couple comedy obviously patterned after *I Love Lucy*, as Davis played Joan Stevens, a wacky housewife who causes grief for a husband who loves her anyway. It was loaded with outrageous slapstick, its modus vivendi, and the majority of episodes in its first season were directed by *I Love Lucy*'s own recently departed Marc Daniels. Associate producer Al Simon even brought over *Lucy*'s refined multi-camera format but with a significant difference—after the pilot, this show jettisoned its live studio audience.[27]

That technical distinction is notable—being forced to stage a show before an audience demands a theatrical quality that limits the storytelling by confining episodes to only a few sets and usually only a handful of people. This often instinctively pushes character to the fore. And indeed, the audienceless *I Married Joan* is a far less character-based show than *I Love Lucy*, regardless of its shared basic husband-and-wife premise and the variety of other big coincidences that suggest a deliberate patterning, like—beyond just Daniels and Simon—the many shared guest appearances from *Lucy* veterans, including Shirley Mitchell, Doris Singleton, and even the aforementioned Elvia Allman. Or the many similar comic centerpieces, such as in this first season alone, Joan's trouble in a ballet class,[28] the women's club show that goes awry,[29] and a very physical game of "charades"[30]—all ideas that had been deployed in the first season of *Lucy* but with much more character-based success, for while Joan Stevens could be a comic nuisance in the spirit of Lucy Ricardo, in the sense that she's always plotting and conniving like an adolescent for what she wants, there's a fundamental lack of definition by comparison because Joan is without the specific objective that explains *why* Lucy does the things she does. Joan's goals instead are stuck being episodic—she wants a new hat, wants to impress her friends, wants to lose weight: all things that Lucy has similarly wanted but with the backing of a sustained purpose: getting in show business or, more broadly, being more than what she's supposed to be.

This sustained purpose, which colors the entirety of her characterization, provides *Lucy* a bit of dramatic weight along with some continuity—not to mention, more of a situation for its storytelling. Because *I Married Joan* does not grant its leading character that foundational definition, it's far less satisfying as a situation comedy, for her generally conflict-making and difficult behavior feels more random and unnecessary than sympathetic and justified. One could perhaps say the pattern of her ridiculous actions suggests something of a consistency that in turn reflects the start of a characterization, but it's far less specific and therefore incapable of truly driving weekly story, as the Joan character is less directly attached to plots. In other words, yes, Joan is going to go after what she wants and not be afraid of doing so ridiculously, so you might say that's enough definition to provide a springboard for story, but it almost always feels like *any* sitcom wife could do the things she does and say the things she says—as opposed to Lucy Ricardo, who, even when pursuing relatable everyday goals, is doing so with a perspective that has been established to be more precise, and therefore special, enabling us to truly believe that *I Love Lucy* is about Lucy Ricardo and not just any wacky wife.

To that point, *I Married Joan* is a far less believable enterprise as a whole, for beyond just an objective to anchor its central character's depiction, the series is also without any of the attention to detail that helped make *Lucy*'s regulars feel more nuanced—the specifics that connect the dots (like Ricky's Cuban heritage, the Mertzes' past in vaudeville, Lucy's Jamestown childhood, etc.). This is partly because, aside from Joan Davis using her own first name, the show has no mimetic associations between the situation enjoyed by its performers and its characters, which as we've seen, can help make emotional investment more likely and also inspire confidence in their utilizations. For instance, look at *Burns and Allen*, whose premise is even more dependent on the real-life situation of its stars than *I Love Lucy*. It therefore gets away with being less specific and emotionally complex with its regulars' depictions, for its leads have *decades* of familiarity with an audience that recognizes their public personas doubling as the characters on the series, which then also has the implication of real-life "inspiration" to legitimize its otherwise silly storytelling.

Without help from real life—like, on a smaller scale, *Lucy*'s use of a truly married central pair or its repeated incorporation of details supplied by its performers—*I Married Joan* never has much inherent latitude with character. It's even more incumbent on the series' scripts to ensure that it's boasting leads who *can* be believed, both as a result of precision and consistency—that is, the all-important "aesthetic realism" (discussed last chapter), with hopefully some degree of emotional honesty undergirding it all: that is, some "literal realism" as well.

But the show is not interested in character—and Joan's husband Brad is indicative of this widespread problem, for while he's premised to be a judge whose career could possibly be threatened by Joan's antics, her antics are never a *specific* threat to his *specific* job. That is, *any* career could be ruined by a wife who is so randomly and unjustifiably prone to making a mess of things without cause. What's more, he's imbued with that tired, generic sense of stoic stability that probably seeks relatability but ends up being vague and benign, especially in comparison to a Ricky Ricardo, who actually has clear tics and quirks that make him unique. This lack of figurative color is especially shocking in *I Married Joan*'s case, for Brad Stevens is played by the hysterical Jim Backus, the longtime voice of cartoon icon Mr. Magoo and the future originator of Thurston Howell III on *Gilligan's Island*. (Incidentally, future *Gilligan's* creator Sherwood Schwartz wrote for *I Married Joan*.[31]) If this series were to actually give Backus the semblance of a character to play—with even just a few defined traits that could be exploited for comedy—he would play it ... and knock it out of the park. But there's little to grip onto with his characterization, so instead of his personality inspiring story, he ends up a neutral force. Backus does his best, but he's not given the chance that *I Love Lucy* provides Ricky Ricardo, via its maximization of Desi Arnaz. It's a big issue that speaks to an overall weakness with character.

As for story, writers like Arthur Stander and Frank Tarloff would eventually go on to reuse some of their funniest *I Married Joan* story ideas on later series, like *The Danny Thomas Show*[32, 33] and *The Dick Van Dyke Show*.[34] These ideas actually come across better on those future series, for they are better sitcoms with better defined characters and thus more of a capacity to let innately funny plots be threaded *through* an established situation, which supports them and therefore makes them feel more earned, especially as their leads provide distinction-making nuance.

Unfortunately, with such poor character work mitigating any concrete sense of the series' aesthetic realism, it should be no surprise that *I Married Joan* is not very literally realistic either, for if there's little thought as to how story can be motivated by, and believable for, character, then there's also not much concern (compared to other sitcoms) as to whether anything that happens is motivated or believable in the first place. In fact, scripts are fine being randomly ridiculous and not true to life, wavering inconsistently between everyday scenarios and off-the-wall hijinks, as long as Joan gets a chance to be funny, showing off her broad and often very physical comedy in the process. "Joan being funny" then actually seems to be the motivation for every story and gag—the only real continuity that exists on this series—more than anything actually in the situation, which is undermined as a result of its irrelevance.

This, of course, yields weak situation comedy, for in addition to not really using the situation—these characters, and specifically hers—in the cultivation of weekly story, *I Married Joan* also renders its situation—these characters, and specifically hers—less *useful* for weekly story, as their mimetic foundation is wobbly. Being so unmimetic, it would have been *impossible* for Joan Stevens to have 75 percent of TV owners tune in eagerly to see her go to the hospital in the culmination of a pregnancy arc. How could they invest in Joan if her own show doesn't?

In this regard, *I Married Joan* is to *I Love Lucy* what ground chuck is to filet mignon: it's a cheaper cut. It has the same basic husband-and-wife setup with a silly dame and a loves-her-anyway guy, a lot of the same wacky comic scenarios, and even many of the same funny faces. But its situation is significantly less developed and thus not deployable within weekly story, meaning the show isn't an ideal example of this art form. And, frankly, this is a shame, for Joan Davis truly *is* a brilliant slapstick comic—more naturally gifted and capable of making her work look even more effortless than Lucille Ball's. In fact, there's a bit here in this season's "Lateness" (April 8, 1953) where Joan gets a pair of mannequin legs stuck on her hands—it's one of the funniest routines I've ever seen. And there's at least one—if not two or three—deliciously played moments of slapstick comedy in almost every half hour from *I Married Joan*'s freshman collection, which is the most physical and therefore funniest of the series' three-year run. Episodes like "Acrobats" (December 31, 1952) and "Joan's Curiosity" (December 3, 1952)—the latter being the inspiration for a famous 1962 episode of *The Dick Van Dyke Show*[35]—will make you laugh out loud in appreciation of her genius. The problem is there's not much character anywhere and certainly not in thoughtful, consistent association with episodic plot. So we can't celebrate it as a great sitcom—and certainly not alongside the superior *Lucy*.

## Come on in, the Water's Fine

Meanwhile, beyond just *I Love Lucy* and Desilu, Lucille Ball's huge success in the television arena convinced other B-level stars to make the transition, as many had done with radio. One funny lady who followed suit post–*Lucy* was Ann Sothern, whom Ball had known, like Eve Arden, from her days at RKO in the 1930s. As *Lucy* was heating up in 1952, Sothern signed with producer Jack Chertok to star in a filmed single-camera sitcom called *Private Secretary*, which would air three out of every four weeks beginning in February 1953 (alternating with *Jack Benny*).

Unlike Ball and Joan Davis, who went in for the domestic format, Sothern (like Arden) opted for a workplace setting, its primary location being the high-rise office of Manhattan talent agent Peter Sands (Don Porter). Sothern would play an evolution of the Maisie character she enjoyed on screen and for several years in radio, Susie MacNamara, a former stage actress and WAC who was now Sands's personal assistant—a single woman with a big career in the big city. Stories sometimes would follow her private life (including romance) but usually revolved around her colleagues and job, for which she often had to pursue difficult clients. Others in the regular cast included Susie's best friend Vi (Ann Tyrrell), the receptionist, while recurring support usually came from their competitive switchboard operator frenemy Sylvia, portrayed by Joan Banks and introduced in the second season, along with under-handed rival agent Calhoun, played with verve by Jesse White.

This arrangement of characters allows for some basic sitcommery—with each lead offering elemental personality traits, like the demanding Mr. Sands or the slightly daffy Vi—and all the regular/recurring players boasting some clear relationship to Susie that could be reinforced in plot, as she's, for instance, either forced to scheme for or against her boss, conspiring with her best friend, being nice/nasty with her frenemy, or outright competing and trying to sabotage her rival. In this regard, the positions of the characters—their relationships—influence the storytelling and the comedy, meaning that there's *structurally* a mind for situation comedy here. However, beyond structure, the traits that these characters do have—particularly the three leads (Susie, Sands, Vi)—are relatively gentle compared to those on both *I Love Lucy* and *Our Miss Brooks*, with star Ann Sothern letting her character's personality coast more on her own charm than any specific attributes, let alone the kind of narrative objective seen on Ball's and Arden's sitcoms.

In fact, Susie's goal, which drives the majority of stories, is simply to fulfill the episodic terms asked of her by her boss—in other words, her job. And since her job is to court and flatter a variety of difficult clients, this means a majority of stories are dependent on guests—the people she's pursuing or making her work difficult—with essentially a different scenario every week, supported by the continuity of Susie's position as a private secretary for a popular Manhattan talent agent. This becomes a mediocre form of situation comedy, for stories and laughs start to come less from the regulars and the situation *they* suggest than from the weekly gimmicks allowed by the chosen premise or, in this case, the selected occupation. This tends to give the show a bit of a procedural, almost anthological feel, as Susie is on a different "mission" each week—sometimes even traveling. And instead of *Private Secretary* routinely calling on its leads and their relationships to propel and inspire plot—like the dynamic between Susie and Sands, which early entries, including the first season's flashback show from February 22, 1953, "Where There Is a Will," suggest to be the emotional core—it's sidelining them in favor of episodic narrative notions that connect, I suppose, to the premise but not to the way *the characters exist within* the premise.

As such, it's no surprise that with these regulars not being used for story, they're less helpful for comedy as well because they're never as actively defined, and we have fewer chances to learn about them. (Never mind that the series is also not inspired by Sothern's own reality, missing the metatheatrical mimesis implied by the casting of the Arnazes as the Ricardos.) This means the character work, overall, is limited, and while the series seemingly wants to mine humor from centerpieces with Susie, as Sothern is willing to dress up and scheme and improvise to get what she's episodically supposed to want, she's not a physical dynamo like Joan Davis, and she's a bit more protective of her movie star image than Ball. So while the few good episodes of *Private Secretary* tend to focus on the regulars' relationships and then afford some opportunity for Sothern to anchor a comic set piece, it's not usual that it happens, and rare for the show to be truly hysterical regardless. Thus, both in terms of situation and comedy, I'm afraid this is one of those efforts that fails to step into a routine of excellence. It's always middling.

But it's certainly notable. For one, it had a surprisingly heavy presence in early cable syndication, when Nick at Nite ran the series in the late 1980s under the title *Susie*, which it had been given in the 1950s, when reruns were sold while the show was still producing original segments. And it's also notable because, setting aside the more old-fashioned schoolteacher on *Our Miss Brooks* who was always pining for a man, *Private Secretary* is the first long-running sitcom to enter syndication with a premise about an unmarried working woman—who basically is okay staying an unmarried working woman—as its lead. This is a demographic that the genre would slowly embrace more and more in future decades with *That Girl* and *The Mary Tyler Moore Show*, although with far more comedic and character-based success. Additionally, *Private Secretary* employs a very classic "workplace" design—with an anchoring star who has a boss, a pal, and a couple of difficult nuisances with whom she has to deal on a regular basis—and like *Our Miss Brooks*, it's therefore an early model for this subgenre of sitcommery. So although not quite excellent, *Private Secretary* is a memorable series that offers a seminal example of several sitcom conventions that future classics will employ to more genre-affirming success.

Sothern wasn't alone. Other movie stars were similarly inspired to come to the small screen in filmed sitcoms, including Sothern's frequent costar Bob Cummings, who headlined a single-season single-cam endeavor for NBC called *My Hero*, which cast him as Ben Beanblossom, a ninny real estate agent working for a tyrannical boss. Beanblossom is something of a clumsy dweeb who somehow manages to always save the day, largely thanks to the secretary who loves him (Julie Bishop). The role was much closer to Mister Peepers than the Bob Collins for which Cummings would become better known on *The Bob Cummings Show*, where the element of an amorous secretary persisted, but Cummings would go from weirdo to womanizer, the latter better playing on his natural persona. However, it's nice to see the spark of a comic character here, even if it's dimmed by the real estate job that enables clients to dominate stories à la *Private Secretary*, never granting its leads the substance or experience necessary to develop traits conducive to motivating plots in a reliable form of situation comedy. What's more, there were behind-the-scenes conflicts that sparked creative turnover and resulted in Ben Beanblossom losing all the bumbling traits that actually made his character interesting[36]—the only wrinkle that allowed this show to be more watchable than the bland fare it otherwise resembled. So, *My Hero* is no gem, but fortunately, Cummings would be back a few years later with something better.

Also making their jump from the big screen to the small screen in 1952 were the famed comic duo of Bud Abbott and Lou Costello, who had their own radio show in the 1940s—a "modified sitcom," with some elements of variety. Like other slapstick screen comics such as Buster Keaton, they were really better suited for a visual medium such as television, where their physical humor could thrive as it had in the movies. And much like Keaton's 1951 self-titled sitcom, the single-camera laugh-track-laden *The Abbott and Costello Show*—produced by Hal Roach Studios and sold into first-run syndication beginning in 1952—was little more than an excuse to create a series of half-hour "short films" for TV, where the funny pair could re-create or offer mild variations on some of their most famous gags and routines, including the iconic "Who's On First?" sketch, which is performed in a later first-season entry called "The Actors Home" (1953). In fact, it is more like a series of shorts than a sitcom.

There's little by way of a situation—the leads don't exist beyond their already known personas of annoyed and annoyer, and unlike Burns and Allen, they're not well-entrenched in the low-concept trappings around them, which are thus never meaningfully relevant to weekly story either. Plots can basically go anywhere and do anything, with little maintained continuity, for nothing, not even the well-known comics' personalities, are really motivating the action consistently or believably. For that reason, this series—which yielded two years' worth of original episodes that could be sold to individual stations, counting initial runs during both the 1952–1953 and

1953–1954 seasons—is not a good example of the situation comedy genre, where situations matter. *Abbott and Costello* is just a venue for gags, and it's mostly worth noting as an early example of a series not broadcast by a major network but instead sold independently into first-run syndication—a growing phenomenon during the decade.

Meanwhile, another pair of movie stars taking the leap this season were Ozzie and Harriet Nelson, adapting their long-running radio sitcom into a filmed single-camera laugh-track-laden offering for the fledgling ABC network, which had the smallest reach in 1952 and was looking for amiable content that had a natural draw. Bringing over their reliable radio series starring this familiar family, with two boys—David and Ricky, who had been playing themselves since the 1948–1949 season[37]—was a no-brainer, and TV's *The Adventures of Ozzie and Harriet* would go on to a record-making 14 seasons and 435 episodes. (No live-action American sitcom has produced more episodes to date.) Running until 1966, the series changed a lot in accordance with other social and artistic trends, but it had also come a long way on radio as well. When it premiered in 1944, the Nelson couple offered a gaggy but mimetic sitcom where they played versions of themselves: two show biz vets now settling down into domesticity.[38] But a few years in, that show biz angle was all but dropped, and by the time their sons became permanent cast members, *Ozzie and Harriet* had turned into your basic, average, all-American suburban family sitcom—in the style that we associate with shows like *Leave It to Beaver*, *Father Knows Best*, and *The Donna Reed Show*.

Those family shows have a reputation for being boring because they are too benign, or rather, they're not incongruous enough, for their characters aren't defined with the kind of slightly caricatured traits that would make them funny. And since they generally don't have much comic definition, it's also difficult for the leads on these sitcoms to uniquely inspire story, which means that most of these are lesser examples of the art form, with episodic notions that aren't directly attached to their situations—their characters. Now, there *are* some exceptions. For instance, in a few chapters, we will talk about *Leave It to Beaver*, which took more care in how it presented the children at the center of its structure, giving them believable dialogue that naturally allowed them to be funny as well, emphasizing the relatable qualities common to kids their age, while they also lived inside comic stories that made sense based on said depiction. In this regard, that series found a way to be unique via its characters—a way to be a situation comedy. And *Ozzie and Harriet*, to its credit, actually claims at least one character who similarly has enough definition or, at least, occupies a position within the show's narrative construct that similarly allows him to be directly utilizable: Ozzie himself—another example of the fallible patriarch.

In contrast to Ward Cleaver of *Leave It to Beaver* and Jim Anderson of *Father Knows Best*, Ozzie is allowed to be made the fool in story—following the grand tradition of *Blondie*'s Dagwood, who was simply a goofball; Chester A. Riley, the working-class stooge who was put upon by the whole world; and even Stu Erwin, whose sitcom uses slapstick to illustrate how inept he is at running and maintaining the household. Ozzie Nelson (the character) of *Ozzie and Harriet* offers only some of the moralizing of Ward and Jim, and instead of being proven correct following some minor error committed by the lesson-learning children, it's often dad himself who childishly errs, as he dispenses advice and then is unable to practice it. This makes for a frequent narrative template, allowing for a link between Ozzie's actions and the storytelling. And it's interesting, for his character is lacking in a lot of the precise comic traits of a, say, Ricky Ricardo, which means Ozzie is therefore less comedically definable than he *should* be. But there are occasional details used—like his noted love of ice cream—to aid his believability and further the show's mimesis, which, of course, is also supported by the semiautobiographical nature of the premise—specifically the fact that he is *indeed* the patriarch of a nuclear family that includes these same people. This means that he feels far more human and therefore more connectable both as a figure in story and a purveyor of gentle laughs than so many of the aforementioned TV dads.

And yet, while the entire core Nelson foursome benefits from this real-life support, it's really only Ozzie whose narrative positioning makes him interesting. The kids are fairly generic, at least initially, as is Harriet, whose movie star status at the beginning of the radio run is entirely forgotten by the TV series—now she's the contented gatekeeper of domesticity, not prone to erring like Ozzie but seldom challenging him either. This, in a word, means that she—and the kids, too, in these early seasons—are pretty boring, mundane: a frequent critique of all the shows in this suburban family subgenre. And to that point, *Ozzie and Harriet* feels far more suburban than both *The Life of Riley*, whose working-class sensibility is all encompassing, and *Trouble with Father*, which is also set in suburbia but came about so early in the decade that it doesn't as definitively reflect the sense of homogeneity, and thus benignity, that came to collectively typify most of the other family sitcoms from the 1950s as they continued to increase in number, becoming more idealized and less truthful over time, especially without any real-life metatheatricality extending aesthetic realism as a potentially counterbalancing validity.

However, *Ozzie and Harriet*'s sense of suburban tranquility and idealized daily ordinariness has actually come to be seen as a point in its favor, with more contemporary critics calling it "a show about nothing" (in a reference to *Seinfeld*),[39] noting that the best episodes concern something very trivial and incidental that Ozzie then helps snowball. With this sense of mounting smallness becoming amusingly big, the series is often credited for its tight and imaginative plotting, where minor details weave together delicately and intelligently. And indeed, I think the notion of the trivial being emphasized—magnified—for the purposes of comedy is a fair description of how this series' best offerings distinguish themselves, for I would ultimately classify *Ozzie and Harriet* as being, in its entirety, an example of an "idea-driven" sitcom.

That's a term that exists in contrast to a "character-driven" sitcom, and while we'll really dive into the distinction between these two aesthetic descriptors in a few chapters, with regard to this series, you can start to get an understanding of what I mean by "idea driven," for essentially what *Ozzie and Harriet* suggests is that the more trivial, mundane, and benign an episode, the better, as that's how this show hopes to derive its comic incongruity, winking about its simple ordinariness and mining gentle laughs from the banality of its minutiae, which is exacerbated but sometimes only slightly. Accordingly, if the benign incongruity is coming from the small details of daily suburban life—the premised situation-based notions that form the start of a story—but not from strong regulars with benignly incongruous traits capable of propelling said story, then you can spot what the show is comedically and narrative prioritizing: its ideas, not its characters.

We will expand on this distinction soon. In the meantime, *Ozzie and Harriet* is a foundational example of idea-driven sitcommery, with writers like Jay Sommers, the mastermind of *Green Acres* (1965–1970), joining the staff in its second TV season and capitalizing on this concept of winking triviality by helping to extend the show's growing sense of surreal metatheatricality—the notion that this world is so benign that it actually might be absurd, with dreamlike gags (if not outright dream sequences) adding to the action as a self-aware comment that, yes, reveals a separation between the show's "reality" and this absurdity but only to draw parallels between the two—to mock or merely imply the artificiality of the premise's suburban sameness.

This makes *Ozzie and Harriet* unique among this subgenre, for while *Leave It to Beaver* will use its kids to upend adult benignity, and thus similarly manages to create comic distinction, other shows in this subcategory—specifically the dominating *Father Knows Best* and its distaff cohort, *The Donna Reed Show*—will depict this ethos sincerely, therefore losing laughs and credibility, defining this subgenre by its worst traits (a lack of humor, specifically), and not by how other samples genuinely *try* to uphold the sitcom's comedic and narrative requirements.

Ultimately, though, if *Ozzie and Harriet* is among the better examples of this very select category of shows, its everyday smallness, however gently mocked in practice, nevertheless becomes the series' guiding aesthetic by comparison, meaning that it ends up being a benign and less-funny-than-baseline example of a 1950s sitcom overall. And with its character work decidedly subpar, it's always mediocre. This mediocrity will also extend to when *Ozzie and Harriet* becomes a teen comedy with the goal of showcasing pop idol Ricky Nelson—a figure who will overtake Ozzie as the show's grandest presence but with less comic success because he will never display the incongruous traits that might allow him to be funny. And with no premise-connected way to be used in narrative—for example, as the fallible patriarch—it's even poorer situation comedy than what the show offers here, in 1952–1953, its first TV season (following a theatrical film that had been released in the spring, *Here Come the Nelsons*), where the series turns to some of its most successful radio scripts about parenting or Ozzie and Harriet's relationship, with only a minor acknowledgment of how the new visual medium of television can benefit the comic storytelling. There's more of a focus on Ozzie at this point, which is preferred, but the metatheatrical wink about the absurdness of its own benignity is only in embryonic (pre–Sommers) stages, meaning this isn't the best season of *The Adventures of Ozzie and Harriet*. We'll keep checking in on it going forward, though, with an eye on finding when it might possibly be at its most enjoyable.

As for where other fallible patriarchs stand here in 1952–1953, Stu Erwin's *Trouble with Father*, now in its third season, had come to look like a relic next to *Ozzie and Harriet* and other filmed single-camera sitcoms, which were now almost always using a laugh track to indicate their intentions with comedy, and seldom as cheaply produced. *Father*, in its second consecutive year of interspersing reruns with 26 original episodes was already losing steam, offering more stories featuring the kids but less of its initial calling card: the slapstick that centralized its eponymous father and helped suggest a faint characterization for him. By Season Three, with less physical comedy, there's less comedy overall, for none of the leads are well defined, and since the primary way this show used to exhibit both its situation and its comedy *was* the bumbling of its well-meaning but inept protagonist—evidenced most comedically *through* slapstick—*Trouble with Father* gets even lighter on both character and laughs, especially by the standards of this era, where there are more and better sitcoms on TV than when this series first premiered in 1950. So it's no longer worth mentioning, and indeed, it would sit the 1953–1954 season out, offering reruns before returning for a final batch of episodes—with elevated comedic intentions—in 1954–1955.

The 1952–1953 season also saw the return of one of radio's funniest fathers—the aforementioned Chester A. Riley from *The Life of Riley*, which had initially come to television during the 1949–1950 season with Jackie Gleason as its star, only because the role's originator, William Bendix, was contractually unable to appear in a filmed series.[40] Now that Bendix had become available, NBC-TV eagerly found a place for a new—more official—*Life of Riley*. It premiered in January 1953, by which time the quality of filmed (single-camera) productions had improved considerably, with a standard laugh track now encouraging scripts to at least guarantee more comedic moments and more fluid camera work to enhance the narrative pacing, reducing some of the awkward slowness of the Gleason iteration. Of course, all these technical improvements were relatively inconsequential compared to the simple fact that Bendix was back, and while Gleason was a very funny and kinetically watchable presence (now exhibiting his genius on his own self-titled variety series, where "The Honeymooners" sketches were rising in popularity), Bendix proves much more capable of adding a sense of gravitas to the role of Chester A. Riley, via an elevated pathos, and ultimately more authenticity, or at least the illusion of it, largely *because* of his history playing the role on radio for so long. This makes his Riley feel more sincere—more human—and therefore more capable of existing inside the weekly storytelling.

That is seminal, for what most distinguishes *The Life of Riley* from the other father-led family sitcoms is its working-class tenor, especially compared to the subgenre's idyllic suburban slant, evidenced on *Ozzie and Harriet* and soon typified by 1954's *Father Knows Best*. Oh, sure, Riley is still very much an elder cousin to Ozzie and, if not the morally untouchable Jim Anderson, then at least the blustery Stu Erwin because he is the most interesting character inside his own familial ensemble. But the primary source of his conflict largely arises in the form of "Riley versus the world," as Chester A. Riley, like on radio, is depicted as a working-class riveter, always struggling to do right by his family—either to improve their lot in life or, more simply, to provide some help in their daily predicaments. And, of course, he's constantly foiled—less so by others and less so by his own sometimes silly ideas but rather from a harsh reality wherein the little guy, and someone who so typifies it, is always going to finish last. This kind of attitude is evidenced by the character's catchphrase—"What a revoltin' development this is!"—and it's a persona that really depends on Riley having the kind of sincerity and, frankly, sadness, best embodied by the perfectly cast Bendix. So, as premised, this is a character who wants better from life.

Sound familiar? It's a setup where Riley has a bit of an objective, like Lucy's, that can be explored within story, for although it's more generic and he doesn't have the kind of granular consistency or the realism that the detail-oriented leads on *Lucy* have, there is a certain amount of history that the eponymous Riley brings with him after many years on radio, with Bendix's casting emphasizing this continuity. And he is certainly functional within narratives that make sense for his character, based on what the situation has established about his circumstances and his relatable, albeit less precise (compared to Lucy's or Miss Brooks's), goals. Unfortunately, if this makes him a character who can be reliably deployed within motivated plots, he gets very little assistance from the rest of the ensemble, who, even more than the Nelsons, are bland and personality-less—and without the emphasized anonymity of suburbia as a purposeful choice and semi-justification. No, this family of four—two kids and a wife, who is a little more outspoken than Harriet but not incongruously so—don't have consistent depictions. They're empty clichés.

Without their help with laughs and in story, Riley is left alone. And only sometimes is he inside ideas that flatter the working-class premise, indicating his characterization by suggesting some link between his persona and plot via his basic objective, with humor coming from how a script showcases Bendix's effortless portrayal. Usually, he's afforded an unideal form of sitcommery, featuring uninspired plots disassociated from anything specific to him or *The Life of Riley*'s situation and thus very few memorable episodes to show for it. Fortunately, in addition to Bendix's performance, the series is always written with a blue-collar edge—it's never as numbingly benign as *Ozzie and Harriet* and some other shows, for it aims to be jokey and fulfill its obligations to the genre, in accordance with its scrappier, more "of the people" sensibility. Thus, while *The Life of Riley* does not prove to be a great TV sitcom, it's far from the worst we're looking at in this book, and it's probably underrated as far as the family subgenre is concerned.

The 1952–1953 season was not all new shows, though. *Riley*, along with this season's other freshman filmed network comedies—*I Married Joan*, *Private Secretary*, *My Hero*, *The Adventures of Ozzie and Harriet*—joined some notable returnees, like *My Little Margie*, which started its second season with five initial episodes in the fall of 1952 before returning in January to run the rest of its output, offering more confidently elaborate farces but with less character-driven logic than before and even less elemental support from the series' central relationship.

Additionally, *The Amos 'n Andy Show* finished its second season on CBS, continuing to boast its now iconically broad characterizations inside stories swinging between ridiculous schemes and emotional declarations meant to humanize the leads, like the famous Christmas entry,[41] an annual tradition on radio that helped connect the sitcom with its serial origins, when most listeners had first discovered the show. Some of those listeners included members of the NAACP, which continued to speak out about the series' portrayal of African Americans, finally scaring away the sponsor in early 1953,[42] leaving the show's fate in limbo. That's for the next chapter, though. In the meantime, note that the season's funniest is the memorable "Kingfish Sells a Lot" (October 16, 1952), which offers hilarious sight gags inside another characterization-affirming Kingfish scheme, where he snookers the gullible Andy into buying a house—or rather, the facade of a house.

Also joining the roster of filmed sitcoms was *The George Burns and Gracie Allen Show*, which had completed two seasons of totally live alternate-week broadcasts that only survive as kinescopes. Following *Lucy*'s example, George Burns moved to film, and even adopted a similar multi-camera shooting process but without a studio audience present for the production. The films would then later be replayed for an audience whose laughter could be added to the soundtrack.[43] It was a big change for the famed comic duo. They had thrived for decades in front of an audience on radio, which had been an extension of their vaudeville origins. But with the company signing on to create 40 episodes a season, now on a weekly schedule, it was decided that staging scenes like a play (as always) but shooting them quickly like a low-budget movie would be easier, especially on Gracie Allen, who had most of the dialogue.

So the show moved to film, and while it would spend its next six years employing this style of production, there was a learning curve here in the first half of this season, as both the scripts and the stars adjusted. For George, this meant that his famous asides to the audience, performed while leaning on a stage proscenium during the live episodes, would transition into direct-to-camera addresses—a unique element that actually feels more disconcerting as the series sheds its initial theatricality for a more cinematic style that seeks to increase literal realism. This leaves George's asides as a more potent fourth wall-breaking device, at least visually, because he's still upholding our belief in the *characters*. And in so strengthening the characters—particularly Gracie, on whose well-known persona almost every single episode is predicated—he ends up strengthening the show as well. Eventually, his asides will gain the further wrinkle of the so-called magic TV set, but we'll save that subject for later.

As for Gracie, while her characterization is broad and somewhat vague compared to the high-water mark represented by Lucy Ricardo, with few of the details and emotional realism that *I Love Lucy* endeavored to marry to its vaudeville-inspired antics, her persona remains backed by so much pre–TV continuity—*history*, if you will—and again, with the couple's real-life relationship adding even more viability to the show's foundation of projected mimesis, she's a good character as far as the sitcoms of 1952 are concerned, and she's capably supported by funny people around her, including George of course, along with Harry Von Zell, Bea Benaderet, and Fred Clark, the last of whom would actually depart after this season, the first in the show's syndication package. To wit, switching to film gave the series permission to remake some of the best ideas initially performed live, such as two 1951 episodes where Sheldon Leonard played a gangster.[44, 45]

▶ Leonard appears twice here in Season Three, and both entries are fun. The best of these is the first—**"Silky Thompson; Gracie Writes 'My Life with George Burns,'"** which clocks in at **#45** on my list and first aired **December 11, 1952**. It was directed by **Ralph Levy** and written by **Sid Dorfman, Harvey Helm, Nate Monaster, Jesse Goldstein**, and **William Burns**. Its plot finds Gracie being visited by a gangster after she writes a false story in a magazine.

One of the most memorable examples of the "Gracie confounds a stranger" template, this installment is the first of two times that Sheldon Leonard plays a hood in Season Three—his third time overall. It's his funniest showcase on the series, as he has the most direct exposure to Gracie, whose perennial immunity to the threat of real danger (thereby suggesting the benignity of these threats to the audience) thoroughly unnerves Silky Thompson, who is visiting to restore his reputation, which has been diminished since she libelously claimed that her husband George Burns once beat him up. As in all of his appearances, Leonard's gangster ends up confused and irritated, with his initial plans to threaten and intimidate the Burnses giving way to his sheer desire to escape from this crazy broad who makes absolutely no sense. What I like best about this particular appearance, aside from the fact that Leonard and Allen get the most face time together—which means it's the best example of her annoying him—is that the story also stems from Gracie's actions, which means it's not a coincidence, like when, in the other Leonard episode (where he plays Johnny Velvet) she just so happens to witness a bank robbery. No, *she* starts the problem.

To that point, this segment offers a fine display of the series' storytelling, as its script weaves in a subplot about Harry Morton selling off a piece of swamp land (a bit set up in the prior entry[46])—utilizing some mild continuity to help earn a climax that compounds the mobster's terrible day with Gracie. So, while the bulk of the humor and the crux of the narrative hinges on her central characterization, there's support from the ensemble as well—not to mention the guest, who is iconic in his own right, helping to elevate this episode into a memorable sample of *Burns and Allen*, as it offers one of its best versions of a reliable template and, specifically, a familiar story. As the series settles into its filmed era, its presentation of good ideas only improves.

## Live, Love, Laugh—Emphasis on Live

Meanwhile, as filmed sitcoms came to be a dominant trend following the meteoric rise of *I Love Lucy*, television's live origins maintained their grip on the genre as well—with continued series coming now from both coasts. While the gentle *The Goldbergs* and the teen-centered *The Aldrich Family* were transmitted sans audience from New York, offerings like the laugh-seeking *My Friend Irma*, the slightly retooled *The Dennis Day Show*, and the now classic "modified" situation comedy—with variety elements still in evidence—*The Jack Benny Program*, all originated from Hollywood, where they were staged in front of audiences whose vociferous laughter mirrored the radio aesthetic. *Jack Benny*, in particular, is worth noting this year, for the veteran comic was still easing into the new medium, offering eight half-hour broadcasts throughout the season (alternating once a month with *Private Secretary* starting in February). But for the first time since its TV debut, more of Benny's showings relied on narrative scenarios inspired by his characterization—genuine sitcom scenes—as opposed to pure variety fare. So although still down his full radio ensemble, Benny's TV series is slowly becoming more relevant to our discussion.

Joining these notable live sitcoms this year were a very brief and no-longer-extant vehicle for young Eddie Albert (later of *Green Acres*) called *Leave It to Larry* and another adaptation of a radio sitcom, from Hollywood, and in front of an audience—*Meet Millie*, which, like *My Friend Irma*, centered on a young Manhattan secretary. Only instead of being about the romantic exploits of a dumb blonde, with the intermediary guidance of a wiser brunette roommate, *Meet Millie* focused its core relationship around a young woman and her intrusive mother, played by Florence Halop in "old lady" drag and with an appropriately exaggerated voice—on the opposite end of the age spectrum as Richard Crenna's Walter on *Our Miss Brooks* but no less broad and theatrical. Halop's performance of the show's central comedic characterization makes *Millie* a sillier and ultimately less realistic show than most of the other live sitcoms, but all of its core personalities are well delineated by the standards of this era, and the dynamic between mother and daughter seems capably felt in a majority of its chosen stories, so it *is* a moderately satisfying example of situation comedy—at least, based on the few surviving kinescopes that are available for viewing today.

*Life with Luigi*, another radio staple, made the move to television this season as well—also from Hollywood and also in front of an audience—but it didn't fare nearly as well. The premise's necessary ethnic humor, situated on a lovable Italian immigrant's efforts to adapt to life in Chicago, with humor coming from his foreignness to the American customs around him, didn't play sincerely in this visual medium without more authenticity backing up the performance. That is, while *Amos 'n Andy* smartly knew that the mimesis necessary for emotional investment in its TV iteration required actual Black actors to play the leads, *Life with Luigi* made the mistake of carrying over its star J. Carrol Naish (born in New York to Irish parents) in the role of Luigi, and as a result, his exaggerated characterization with a relative lack of nuance or dimension came to feel uncomfortable and alienating, for it was harder to suspend disbelief now that these stereotypes—unmoored from a more authentic portrayal—were staring viewers in the face.[47] So despite being scheduled in the cushy Monday at 9:30 p.m. slot after the remarkably popular *I Love Lucy*, the TV *Life with Luigi* was pulled from the schedule in December. Not even a retooling that bowed in April 1953 with an actual Italian actor, Vito Scotti, in the title role,[48] could salvage the series' bad first impression. Accordingly, *Life with Luigi* has gone down as a bad example of ethnic stereotyping in the early 1950s—as bad as *Amos 'n Andy*, which at least had an entire ensemble of wonderful African American actors whose work could be lauded as worthwhile.

Far less offensive—and more sincere—was 1953's adaptation of radio's *Ethel and Albert*, a couple comedy that had been created by Peg Lynch in the early 1940s, when it debuted as a sketch on a local Minnesota station.[49] By 1944, the sketch—which also starred Lynch, who was her series' head writer, à la Gertrude Berg—had expanded to a daily 15-minute network program, offering the everyday, trivial interactions of a husband and wife, whose naturalistic dialogue and effortless chemistry made their rapport believable, and these characters feel like humans. Most broadcasts were simply conversations, with minimal story, given the limitations of the time frame, and while they weren't serialized or serious in nature, they weren't really situation comedies as the other shows in the category, by 1944, would define the term either. At least not initially, for eventually *Ethel and Albert* indeed transitioned into a half-hour series in 1949,[50] with episodic stories and more of a comedic slant. But the heart of its appeal remained its simplistic rendering, with relatable scenarios anchored by a sort of "everyman" and "everywoman" couple.

This might sound a bit like the intentionally ordinary *Ozzie and Harriet*, but it's different, for while the latter emphasizes its benignity as a way of finding laughs via the insinuation that it's so benign as to be incongruous with what we'd find "normal," *Ethel and Albert*—which premiered as a half-hour TV sitcom in April 1953 from New York (after a brief stint as a sketch on Kate Smith's variety series)[51]—isn't nearly as self-conscious, with most comedy arising from its ever-so-slight highlighting of the things that are already funny in real life: the naturally occurring silliness. This is all a valid way to find humor—with minimal caricaturing, more reflecting. But in the case of *Ethel and Albert*, none of this is character based, for, again, unlike *Ozzie and Harriet*, where Ozzie's deployment in story helps suggest a basic comic characterization, this creator's efforts to keep her two leads relatable ends up denying them definition, affording them few comic traits that could be specifically identified and regularly reiterated by story. That's because Lynch's sights weren't actually set on making them funny or story providing; she was focused instead on the noble objective of having their dialogue and their light episodic plots remain rooted in real life, from which she always said to find inspiration.[52]

And to that point, yes, her leads are less cartoony than most in this genre—their dialogue is more naturalistic, and the performances by Lynch and Alan Bunce keep small, everyday ideas even more grounded in their palpable humanity. But while this is the foundation for all drama, and Lynch's writing is not without the everyday humor it seeks, this alone does not make for ideal sitcommery. Although one can certainly see how the series' projected realism could be a desirable counter to the artificiality of many entries in the sitcom genre, there's no obvious causational, correlational link between Ethel and Albert (the characters) to this series' stories or even its comedy, which again exists but only through dialogue and ideas that almost any married couple could convey. It's like a sketch, where ideas matter more than characters. Accordingly, Lynch is a very interesting presence in the sitcom genre at this time, and *Ethel and Albert* is often a warm, charming show—and, as one usually performed before a live audience, it *can* be funny, with the inherently comic Margaret Hamilton (best known as the iconic Wicked Witch from *The Wizard of Oz*) taking on a supporting role as Aunt Eva for much of its run. However, the episodes that are available just don't reveal the series to be a testament to what makes the situation comedy a true art form—the notion of having specific elements of a series' situation *directly* inspiring the comedy, as evidenced through weekly narratives that are also hinged on unique particulars.

Fortunately, there are other sitcoms that knew how to still create believable characters while also providing them the elemental reality-grounded traits that could then be spotlighted and caricatured *for* specific laughs and correlated story. While there's nothing left to study of *A Date with Judy* and the short-lived *My Son Jeep*, about an impish *Dennis the Menace*–like kid, there remains one terrific ambassador for all the live sitcoms produced in New York—one also staged in front of a live audience, but more successful at honoring the comedy that's implied. It's the previously discussed *Mister Peepers*, which had enjoyed such a smash success during its brief summer run that NBC-TV and sponsor Reynolds Metals were so eager to make room for it on the fall schedule that they pulled their filmed sitcom *Doc Corkle* (starring Eddie Mayehoff and Billie Burke) after only three weeks—just to reinstate *Peepers*, in which both had more confidence.[53]

Premiering in late October, *Mister Peepers* entered its second season with some smart tweaks, paring down its cast to Wally Cox's anchoring Robinson Peepers and the hilarious Marion Lorne's doddering Mrs. Gurney, along with two players who made guest appearances in a memorable entry from the end of the summer run: Patricia Benoit as Nancy, Peepers's good-natured love interest, and Tony Randall as Harvey Weskit, Peepers's best pal. This becomes the show's core four, and they're strong, helping to pivot scripts away from a wacky sensibility to a more relationship-driven focus, with funny characters but a palpable humanity as a result of believable performances inside roles that are, for the most part, allowed to be benignly incongruous. Benoit's Nancy remains the least comedically and narratively utilizable—she's just simply *nice*—but her romance with Peepers, who is awkward and shy around women and therefore naturally tense with someone like Nancy, provides an emotional hook for viewers, and their courtship offers its own narrative engine—culminating in their much-publicized engagement and wedding next season.

Interestingly, the show's sophomore year—its first full collection of episodes—provides a sort of preview of Peepers's upcoming arc with Nancy, for Randall's Wes spends the year dating, getting engaged, and then marrying Marge (Georgann Johnson), another mostly sweet and good-natured female love interest who nevertheless is depicted as a little more upper class and urban (she comes from the big city) than the rest of *Peepers*'s ensemble, thereby suggesting *some* traits that could be maximized for comedy. In actuality, they are only gently acknowledged, and this is something of a loss, just like Nancy's relative lack of color, for more comic contrast drawn between well-defined characters would create interpersonal conflicts that would allow for more story directly associated with their depictions and therefore the situation, beyond just the two formulaic romances. That is, something like the strong relationships seen on the school-set *Our Miss Brooks*, where every lead is so distinctly defined in a specific position that conflict between them can be naturally derived (or *could* be, if that show was more consistently written as well).

But the characterizations afforded to *Mister Peepers*'s leading ladies are not dire compared to everything else we've examined in this genre, for the two women's understated depictions add to the series' moderate, true-to-life air, and with other leads picking up the comic slack, the character work is far more commendable than not. Look, for instance, at Wes, who was introduced last season as a bit of a womanizing threat to Peepers. He slowly transitions at the top of this year into a more uptight, mannered "big brother"—qualities that make it easier for the pair to be unlikely confidants and friends and are also better suited to actor Tony Randall's own persona, which upholds his portrayal of the character. The same is true of both Marion Lorne and star Wally Cox—they, with Randall, inspire terrific characters with truth and comedy. And this makes the show far more realistic than *Our Miss Brooks*, which boasts bolder comic leads with clear and confrontation-making relationships but in a situation that forces them to be less emotionally truthful in maintenance of that series' status quo. It is not interested in evolving them through narrative developments, as the much more human *Mister Peepers* delights in doing.

Additionally, *Peepers* spends this season expanding its universe, introducing wonderfully unique side characters, like its hero's bookish sister (Jenny Egan), overprotective mom (Ruth McDevitt), and boisterous aunt (Reta Shaw), all of whom bring extra laughs and keep this gentle show—which still occasionally offers physical comedy but less as a narrative centerpiece than an affable display of Peepers's awkward characterization through story—from ever feeling too mundane, quiet, or benign. (McDevitt is especially great in an episode known as "The Summer College

## Chapter Five. Like Lucy

Course," which aired on June 28, 1953, and features the entire *Peepers* gang stopping over at his mother's house to spend the night.) And with all these characters having elemental definitions and easily understandable bonds that naturally enable believable story inside of a premise that is rapidly becoming relationship dominated, the series' storytelling feels totally unique to what it establishes—rich with personal interaction. It's not quite as character driven or boisterously uproarious as *I Love Lucy*, but it's filled with unique and mimetic leads and funny writing that honors the theatricality of the television medium's live New York–based roots, from which *Mister Peepers* hails as its finest ambassador—a respectable example of this genre and of the quieter qualities that typify the efforts on the opposite side and coast of *Lucy*.

So while this chapter has largely been about tracking *Lucy*'s influence, it's important to also celebrate fine episodic representations of a series that stands as its best rival—that's *Mister Peepers*, which also boasts fine characters but in a live production that comes from New York and accordingly displays radically different sensibilities regarding the tonal pursuit of humor. In fact, this is *Peepers*'s best season, for it's the best showcase for the series' strongest characters, with two particular episodes (both of which are on DVD) that I would put in my personal top 50.

▶ The first of these comes in at **#48**—the show's 16th episode, broadcast live on **November 30, 1952**. Often referred to as "**The Drive-In Movie**" by online sources, its plot concerns Mister Peepers's efforts to disrupt Nancy's date with a rival teacher at a local drive-in. **Hal Keith** directed, while the script is credited to **Jim Fritzell**, **David Swift**, and **Biff McGuire**.

It's a sweet show that builds the leading man's affection for his new love interest and with some visual gags that emphasize the meek-looking Wally Cox's natural physicality. In this regard, it's a vehicle for the series' core characterization, fueled by a remarkably unique performer who has his own natural idiosyncrasies, and it looks ahead to the relationship-led storytelling that will soon dominate *Peepers*, emphasizing the humanity that inspires emotional investment.

▶ The other entry I rank at **#31**—it's the series' 36th aired episode overall, broadcast live on **April 19, 1953**. Known online as "**Nervous Wes**," this half hour finds Peepers, Nancy, and Mrs. Gurney joining the soon-to-be-married Wes on a train ride to his wedding in Chicago. **Hal Keith** again directed, while this script was written by **Jim Fritzell** and **Everett Greenbaum**.

This installment addresses the season's central story arc of Wes's engagement—which, as with the above, proves how *Mister Peepers* could use narrative developments in its established relationships to make us emotionally invest in its leads and render them more palpably human, giving them a mimetic foundation that could form the basis of a character. The episode also offers great moments of comedy for the central players, including Tony Randall as the jittery Wes and Wally Cox as the jolly Mister Peepers, who is bounced around by the train itself in an example of how the show uses gentle slapstick in comic maximization of Cox's physicality, which again specifically adds to his persona. This is a common thread in all the best

114  Part II: Top Sitcoms and Episodes

Wes (Tony Randall, left) and Peepers (Wally Cox) in *Mister Peepers*, "Nervous Wes" (1953).

episodes of *Mister Peepers*, where the show capitalizes on what its leads bring to their roles, accentuating the comedic traits that help grant this otherwise gentle series the characterizations capable of making it a comedic contender, with genuine laughs that balance its more serious and sincere romantic beats.

From start to finish, this is a delightful sample of *Mister Peepers* that evidences all of what makes it special, including why it's a terrific encapsulation of the live, New York style of sitcommery, which, despite *Lucy*'s preeminence, was still a big part of the television landscape in 1952–1953. Of course, as you can already tell, that trend *was* shifting, and as we go forward, we'll continue to follow these changes—from live to filmed, New York to Hollywood—in large part *because* of Desilu and *I Love Lucy*, the most important situation comedy of the decade.

### JACKSON'S BEST SITCOMS FROM 1952–53

1. I LOVE LUCY (S2)
2. MISTER PEEPERS (S2)
3. OUR MISS BROOKS (S1)

### EPISODES FROM THE 1952–53 SEASON IN JACKSON'S TOP 50 FROM THE '50s

#1. I LOVE LUCY (S2): "Job Switching" (9/15/52)
#15. OUR MISS BROOKS (S1): "Aunt Mattie Boynton" (1/2/53)

#16. I LOVE LUCY (S2): "The Handcuffs" (10/6/52)
#31. MISTER PEEPERS (S2): "Nervous Wes" (4/19/53)
#34. I LOVE LUCY (S2): "The Operetta" (10/13/52)
#45. THE GEORGE BURNS AND GRACIE ALLEN SHOW (S3) "Silky Thompson; Gracie Writes 'My Life with George Burns'" (12/11/52)
#47. I LOVE LUCY (S2): "Lucy's Show Biz Swan Song" (12/22/52)
#48. MISTER PEEPERS (S2): "The Drive-In Movie" (11/30/52)

## *OTHER NOTABLE EPISODES FROM 1952–1953*

THE AMOS 'N ANDY SHOW (S2): "Kingfish Sells a Lot" (10/16/52)
I MARRIED JOAN (S1): "Joan's Curiosity" (12/3/52)
I MARRIED JOAN (S1): "Acrobats" (12/31/52)
I MARRIED JOAN (S1): "Lateness" (4/8/53)
THE ABBOTT AND COSTELLO SHOW (S1): "The Actors' Home" (1953)

CHAPTER SIX

# (Still) Like Lucy
## *The Best Television Sitcoms of 1953–1954*

The 1953–1954 season for sitcoms is largely an extension of the previous, with most new shows taking inspiration from prior successes and said successes looking to build on their own good fortunes. The headline of the year, though, has to be the continued saturation of film, both as a result of *I Love Lucy*'s maintained relevance and the continued production shift away from New York to Hollywood, which both accelerated and helped explain film's rise. Additionally, among the sitcoms that remained live, a divide continued to grow, with each coast really leaning into their divergent sensibilities—the live Hollywood sitcoms utilizing an in-studio audience and therefore prioritizing laughs like many of the radio comedies that inspired them, while New York's live offerings remained a paragon of theatrical intimacy, often eschewing an audience and offering a lighter form of humor, and sometimes ignoring the genre's cathartic demands in the process.

Many of the live sitcoms from Hollywood came out of CBS's Television City, which had opened in the fall of 1952 and was equipped for programs that wanted to be performed before a small audience—like a radio show. Among the series that had been shooting there were *My Friend Irma*, now in its third and final TV season, and *Meet Millie*, in its sophomore year—two adaptations of radio sitcoms with bold yet single-dimensional leads and a commitment to seeking laugh-out-loud comedy, evidenced via a present crowd that encouraged the writing and performances to play for visceral responses. Joining those two shows in the spring of 1954 was *That's My Boy*, an adaptation of the 1951 Jerry Lewis film, this time starring Eddie Mayehoff. No episodes are currently known to exist, but reviews at the time were mixed about its comedic prospects.[1,2]

Meanwhile, another new series that premiered in the 1953 season that was broadcast live from Hollywood, and in particular CBS's Television City, was also an adaptation of a radio program—*My Favorite Husband*, the show that once starred Lucille Ball and was partially adapted, particularly in terms of individual episodic ideas, for *I Love Lucy*. This formal TV iteration of the radio comedy that ceased production in 1951 but was still a known entity (especially given Lucille Ball's television success) starred Joan Caulfield and Barry Nelson as the leads—a silly wife and her solid husband who's got no choice but to go along for the ride. There can be laughs found in this evergreen setup, but they are seldom coming from the characters, for a look at this series only reiterates just how much *Lucy* improved on its template, as the wife here lacks the specific objective that later allowed Lucy Ricardo to be directly attached to story, motivating plots with a degree of character-based continuity that exemplifies the uniqueness of the situation comedy as an art form, where elements of a situation explicitly inspire the weekly happenings. What's more, the husband is generic and hard-to-define, with few comic traits that can be caricatured for laughs and nothing that's personally used from the actor's real life—like Desi Arnaz's Cuban heritage—to inspire a specific personality, someone who can respond to his silly wife while being both believable and funny, a character in his own right.

*My Favorite Husband* would switch to film in its third season—and recast its leads—but it's never on *I Love Lucy*'s level—just like many of the other filmed sitcoms that debuted immediately after *Lucy* and took some inspiration, including *I Married Joan*, a filmed sitcom without a live audience that was now in its second (and most watched)[3] season, toning down its slapstick in an effort to counteract criticisms about its ridiculousness, but with a still-broad and ill-defined lead inside the same clichéd female-focused couple construct where they, without unique definitions, can't uniquely inspire anything beyond the formulaic tripe that all domestic sitcoms with this format—the daffy wife and menaced-but-amused husband—inherently offer. Interestingly, there's also more effort this season to give the leading lady new scene partners—including Joan Davis's real-life daughter playing her sister, who has no personality, along with the structurally formulaic secondary neighbor couple, also bland. But this doesn't make it any easier for *I Married Joan* to showcase its leading lady's comic chops, and again, compared to *Lucy*, there's really no contest between the two shows' character work. The disparity is amazing.

The same goes for both the workplace-situated *Private Secretary* starring Lucille Ball's pal Ann Sothern and *My Little Margie* with Charles Farrell and Gale Storm—two filmed non-audience shows that continued being lesser forms of sitcommery, even as their leading ladies got to dress up in funny costumes and engage in hijinks—seemingly in the spirit of Ball's clowning. But with regulars who don't have a fraction of the definition and therefore can't or aren't given the chance to directly inspire story, it's not a fair comparison, and that stayed true in 1953–1954.

However, back to the year's new live offerings. There was one sitcom broadcast from Television City in Hollywood that actually resembled some of the qualities of the New York style, for it was considered far more natural and palpably human than those above, and it was set, like the dramatic *Mama*, as a period piece in the New York City of yesteryear, while also being based on a famous play that gave it some dramatic credibility—*Life with Father*. In fact, *Life with Father* genuinely looked like one of the domestic sitcoms that came from New York, boasting theatrical origins and a similar sense of heightened nostalgia but underplayed comedy, and yet, it indeed came from Hollywood and was shot in front of a very vocal audience to whom the writing and performances played, guaranteeing bigger laughs than one would ever find on *Mama*. A lot of these laughs initially came from the father—one of those fallible patriarchs that we have been discussing. But critical complaints about his early goofiness apparently forced the show to tame him,[4] muting his ridiculousness for a more gentle approach overall.

The second season in 1954–1955 began live as well, but 26 filmed episodes—shot by George Burns's company, McCadden—were mixed in for possible future syndication.[5] The show never fully caught on; it was still more obviously interested in venerating the comedic genre than the New York shows it better resembled. But it was quieter and less funny than other live Hollywood offerings, such as *The Duke*, a short-lived summer sitcom about a former prizefighter who tries to find culture and thus becomes co-owner of a nightclub. Broadcast for NBC-TV from the El Capitan Theatre, *The Duke* seems to have had a similar aesthetic to most of these brasher live audience Hollywood efforts.[6,7]

In contrast, New York's tended to emphasize gentleness, as actors who were honing their craft during the postwar era shared the theater's growing interest in underplayed realism, and they tended to champion properties where the laughs were secondary to the projected humanity. This was the case in shows like *Jamie*, starring 11-year-old stage actor Brandon deWilde as an orphaned kid who bonds with his grandfather. The series was renewed for a second season in 1954–1955 but canceled after two episodes.[8] What remains of *Jamie* is short on ha-has but big on warmth. In that same vein was a series probably more comedic but no less sentimental—*Bonino*, a half-season live sitcom starring Ezio Pinza as a widower concert singer who retires so he can raise his eight children. Although the premise made room for schmaltz (and weekly songs by Pinzo, the former star of the Broadway musical *South Pacific*), the cast also included Mary Wickes as the housekeeper and Conrad Janis as the eldest member of the Bonino family. So there were presumably some chuckles, even in spite of this premise, which incidentally was ahead of the curve—more nontraditional nuclear families would arrive later in the decade.

Another very gentle sitcom that came from New York—airing in the summer of 1954—was *The Marriage*, a couple comedy starring theatrical legends Hume Cronyn and Jessica Tandy in a semiautobiographical format where they also played a married couple with kids. It was adapted from a radio series and rooted in their own real-life circumstances, which made it thus very believable. But the show's comic interests were not as pronounced, as these creatures of the stage enjoyed more of the sensitivity we've come to associate with dramas, and their characterizations really weren't conducive to laughs. It was a less jokey *Ethel and Albert*, which continued to run this season but still without any recurring character traits to make the "everyday" scenarios seem tethered to something situation-specific beyond the generic setup. As to the notion of "everyday" life influencing comedy, one more interesting live sitcom that premiered out of New York in 1953–1954 that's worth mentioning is called *Take It from Me*, also known as *The Jean Carroll Show*, as it was a vehicle for standup comic Jean Carroll—one of the earliest women in that occupation (and one of the inspirations for the title character of 2017's *The Marvelous Mrs. Maisel*).[9] Unfortunately, no episodes of *Take It from Me* are known to exist today, but reviews indicate that her observational monologues were weaved through slice-of-life stories in a typical domestic structure—emphasizing the humor of the trivial.[10] It's not clear how the show depicted its characters, but it sounds fascinating, for decades later, a show like *Seinfeld* would engage a similar format for another stand-up comic looking to marry his established act to the sitcom form.

Meanwhile, a staple of these live New York offerings, *The Goldbergs*, remained one of America's foremost media brands, beginning on radio in the late 1920s and essentially running somewhere in some form since (with very few breaks), always guided by its affable star who helmed all the scripts, Gertrude Berg as Molly Goldberg. Let's check back in on the series. If you'll recall, *The Goldbergs* spent the bulk of its life as a daily radio serial but moved into the half-hour TV format in the spring of 1949. It ran on CBS through the 1950–1951 season, after which it was canceled due to Berg's support for her longtime costar Philip Loeb, who was being blacklisted.[11] The show returned in early 1952, now on NBC and with a new actor in the role of Molly's husband, for 15-minute episodes that aired throughout the 1952–1953 season, until the program expanded back into a half hour in the summer of 1953, by which time the part of Mr. Goldberg had been recast again. Then the series jumped once more, this time to the struggling DuMont network, where it ran for six more months of half-hour episodes, beginning in April 1954. Most of these DuMont episodes survive, and they reveal a show that had indeed changed since its TV debut in 1949.

Although it was still shot the same way—live from New York, no audience present—*The Goldbergs* grew less sentimental than it had been early on, embracing more comical ideas in line with the sitcom genre (like Molly learning to rumba,[12] going on a diet,[13] helping out in a kitchen[14]), thus emphasizing the slightly heightened attributes that make her a naturally humorous, albeit still human, character. Additionally, with the family's Jewish heritage providing the foundation for most stories, there seems to be a link between the series' situation and many of its plots. That is, only *The Goldbergs* could do some of these episodes or, at least, in this way. It makes for elemental sitcommery, and while the storytelling still seems like it would rather be a bit more serious than incongruously comedic, and not all the regulars are as wonderfully well realized as Gertrude Berg's Molly, I am not fully comfortable, as I am with the nostalgic *Mama*, rejecting it as a situation comedy. It's just a very mild one—a series that isn't trying to be *as* funny as the genre's best samples at this time. Indeed, the show would be canceled by DuMont after six months, returning for the final time in 1955 as a series of 39 filmed (single-camera) episodes made for first-run syndication, with a slight change of format and a switch in style (live to film) that suggests the defeat of the series' initial aesthetic—the end of an era. But more on that later.

As for the best of the New York sitcoms, there's still *Mister Peepers*, which stands out, like *Life with Father* on the opposite coast, because it doesn't adhere to the standards of its region's other offerings. That's mainly because it's broadcast before an audience that encourages the show to be laugh-out-loud funny, prioritizing humor in a more straightforward way, especially compared to programs like *The Goldbergs* and *The Marriage*, which perhaps don't consider laughter the singularly desired result of their pleasurable catharses. With this purpose and some strong characters in Mister Peepers (Wally Cox), Wes (Tony Randall), and Mrs. Gurney (Marion Lorne), each of whom have distinct traits that allow them to exist comedically in and out of story, *Mister Peepers* is able to match the live New York style's natural humanity *with* increased humor, thereby creating a more perfect balance. This is best evidenced here in the show's third season by its storytelling, as this is a big year narratively for the ensemble—the secondary couple (Wes and Marge) has a baby of their own (in an episode that aired on May 9, 1954—and based on its log line at UCLA, sounds absolutely hilarious), and more time is dedicated to exploring Peepers's funny family: his mousy sister, daffy mom, and boisterous aunt, all of whom recur.

However, the big story of the year is the central romance between Peepers and Nancy (Patricia Benoit), which culminates in a May 1954 engagement and wedding. This storyline, like Lucy's pregnancy the year before, earned the show a lot of positive publicity, and the big episode actually helped *Peepers* blow away its scheduled competition[15]—*The Jack Benny Program* (which was on every third week, alternating with *Private Secretary*). This was proof of just how much viewers cared about *Peepers*'s characters, and just like Lucy's baby—although to a far lesser extent—Mister Peepers's wedding was one of the earliest sitcom "events": a development the show had properly built toward, utilizing the genre's inherent continuity of presence to naturally maximize the audience's emotional investment, because the familiarity of the characters made them feel even more like real people, such that tuning into their wedding therefore became a more intimate obligation[16]—not just a hacky ratings stunt. Indeed, while *Peepers* would secure another season following this gimmick, it's a gimmick that nevertheless displays the series' charms accurately—as its characters are so believable that this arc feels more like an extension of their situation than a cheap ploy. And in the sense that the unique qualities of a situation comedy are always ripe for commodification, here's a great early example of it and with a show that really flatters our understanding of what both this genre and medium do best.

In terms of the wedding episode itself, the 95th original broadcast, often referred to online and at the UCLA archives (where it resides) as "The Wedding" (May 23, 1954)—it's got some great character laughs for both Peepers and Mrs. Gurney in the first half before a very weepy conclusion that is played straight, as Peepers walks down the aisle and is wed. It's not terribly ideal by our terms, as there's a long period where not a joke is even attempted, and that feels like a rejection of this art form's inherent promise, for here, it's not using its mimesis to earn a cathartic release of laughter, instead centering another emotion. Accordingly, it's important and memorable sample of this particular series but not an entry I can highlight as great.

## Are We Rolling?

At any rate, even though *Peepers* was never a ratings smash, it was well liked by critics,[17] and it seemed to inspire other series—including those on film. Among these was a new entry that popped up in 1953–1954 called *Meet Mr. McNutley*, a single-cam vehicle for movie star Ray Milland, who would also play a teacher, like Peepers, with a kooky, fumbling personality—in this case, a befuddled, absent-minded English instructor at a women's college. The pilot, by creators Joe Connelly and Bob Mosher (later of *Leave It to Beaver* and *The Munsters*, and previously of *The Amos 'n Andy Show*), was overly silly and slapstick heavy, and it got poor reviews, as did Milland for his heightened performance.[18] So, after a few weeks, that initially premised broad comedy was removed, leaving, well, absolutely no character for the lead whatsoever, just ensemble players like the understanding wife, the bachelor friend, and the mean dean. And they couldn't do much to cover for a lead with such a slight characterization, so plots instead became involved with generic domestic fare, most of it barely even related to his job. Season Two (1954–1955) then saw a revamp, with dropped scribes, a new title (*The Ray Milland Show*), a new last name for the leads (McNulty, not McNutley), new supporting characters with mild definition, and a move to a co-ed college where he now taught drama. This version of the show was even less comedic in tone, but stories remained equally situationless, more dependent than ever on guests and episodic stimuli. So, with scant character rewards, it was a far cry from *Mister Peepers*, which counted the use of its regulars *as* its very strength.

Of course, Peepers and McNutley weren't the only teachers on the air in 1953–1954, as *Our Miss Brooks*, starring Eve Arden, entered its second television season. There was no change to its format this year—the characterizations had been set very quickly after its radio debut in 1948, and the rigid maintenance of that status quo kept the situation easy to understand, albeit less believable, as the audience was forced to ignore traditional rules of human logic to accept Brooks's ongoing and unfruitful pursuit of the always seemingly clueless Mr. Boynton. Also, Richard Crenna's Walter is like Florence Halop's Mama on *Meet Millie*—a caricature with a funny voice who adds laughs and is well established but with the sensibility of vaudeville, where any potential for emotional investment from growing familiarity can be undermined because he's so broad and unmimetic. However, that's the same as it was last year, and these characters and their relationships are still as comedically defined as ever. And while the best radio stories are already starting to run out, forcing silly misunderstanding shows that have little to do with the situation of the characters, there *are* a handful of outings directly predicated on the leads and their dynamics.

▶ My favorite of these actually manages to make my top 50 at **#44**. It's "**Second Hand First Aid**," which first aired on **April 23, 1954**, and again finds Miss Brooks competing with her rival Miss Enright, as both are trying to avoid teaching an extracurricular first aid course that will monopolize their evenings and keep them away from the mutually desired Mr. Boynton. **Al Lewis** directed, and the script is credited to both **Al Lewis** and **Joseph Quillan**.

As with the previous season's "Aunt Mattie Boynton," this winning excursion, also based on a previously performed radio installment,[19] works because it's predicated on the established relationships of these well-defined characters, whose objectives are clear. Both Miss Brooks and Miss Enright are after Mr. Boynton, so having to manage a weekly first aid course for Mr. Conklin would limit their evening availabilities. This inspires an amusing slapstick centerpiece where Miss Brooks is determined to prove to Conklin that she is *not* the right woman for the first aid job—allowing her to drive the comic action and create a big, hilarious moment where all the involved characters shine in accordance with their personas. It's textbook sitcommery.

*Our Miss Brooks* was produced by CBS but shot by Desilu with its multi-camera live audience format. It was also a success, putting the company that refined this technological setup—combining the visual quality of film with the performative benefit of a live audience—in demand. In 1953, Desilu added several new shows to its roster, including a vehicle for dancer Ray Bolger (best known today as the Scarecrow in *The Wizard of Oz*), who signed with ABC for a sitcom that would allow him to showcase his talents. This resulted in *Where's Raymond?* (named after *Where's Charley?*), where he played a Broadway star with a habit of showing up late for performances because of his busy personal life, hanging out with his friends and family at home or at the nearby diner. The series was shot as a multi-cam but with a laugh track in place of an audience, for stories were little more than an amiable vamp until an expectedly intense dance routine by Bolger. As with *I Married Joan*, all character work took a back seat to the concern of showcasing what its star did best—in this case, fancy footwork. For the second season, the show was retooled, with an almost entirely new ensemble and a change in title to *The Ray Bolger Show*, and while he still got to perform every week, the switch to a multi-cam live audience format gave the series a chance to become *as* situation based as *I Love Lucy* and *Our Miss Brooks*. Of course, *The Ray Bolger Show*'s audience bumped up the comic energy, but it was always anchored by someone less interested in situation comedy than musical comedy, and thus, it's never a great sample of this genre—a lesser effort bearing Desilu's stamp of approval.

In contrast to *Where's Raymond?* was another new sitcom filmed by Desilu, beginning in the 1953–1954 season—and this one actually did take immediate advantage of its unique, live audience multi-camera format. Initially called *Make Room for Daddy*, this series was built for nightclub comic and singer Danny Thomas, with inspiration drawn from his real life, as the premise centered on an entertainer,

## Chapter Six. (Still) Like Lucy

**Mr. Conklin (Gale Gordon, left), Miss Enright (Mary Jane Croft, center), and Miss Brooks (Eve Arden) in *Our Miss Brooks*, "Second Hand First Aid" (1954).**

Danny Williams, who struggles to remain an active presence in the rearing of his children. In fact, the pilot was allegedly based on a real incident—his kids referring to him as "Uncle Daddy."[20] As with *Our Miss Brooks*, Desilu only shot the show, for it was produced and owned by Thomas, in association with Sheldon Leonard, who joined him early on in the first season. Together, this duo created a partnership that would go on to helm a handful of other important sitcoms, including spin-offs like *The Andy Griffith Show*, *The Joey Bishop Show*, and *The Bill Dana Show*, along with *The Dick Van Dyke Show*. (All but *Andy Griffith* also used Desilu's live audience multi-camera setup.) So, with many hits arising out of its success, *Make Room for Daddy*, like *I Love Lucy*, is a seminal work in the sitcom genre.

This series is also notable because it ran for a whopping 11 years, concluding in the spring of 1964 after a myriad of changes—such as the departure of Jean Hagen (best known today for her work in the film *Singin' in the Rain*) as Danny's first wife Margaret, who willingly left the show in the spring of 1956 and brought about a whole season where the leading man was a widower. This is also when the title changed to *The Danny Thomas Show*. In 1957, Danny got a new wife in the form of Marjorie Lord's Kathy, and the series moved from ABC to CBS, where it literally took *I Love Lucy*'s spot on the schedule. This is interesting, for I consider *The Danny Thomas Show* (referring to the series in its entirety) to be something of a connective tissue between the two most important sitcoms of their respective decades in terms of the genre's identity-affirming utilization of character—the 1950s' *I Love Lucy* and the 1960s' *The Dick Van Dyke Show*, the latter representing the next major evolution, from *Lucy*, in character-driven writing: simplifying the storytelling by making it even more true to life, removing a singular driving objective for its lead but maintaining a strong link between the regulars and motivated plots via the incorporation of *even more* credibility and continuity-supplying autobiographical details, along with an even stricter adherence to a mimetic foundation. Essentially, *Dick Van Dyke* became more literally realistic with its characters (compared to *I Love Lucy*), without sacrificing its laughs.

*The Danny Thomas Show*, even in its *Make Room for Daddy* era, has got elements of both *Lucy* and *Dick Van Dyke*, for although it offers less slapstick than either, it's another sitcom where the patriarch has a flashy job in show business around which some kind of tension hinges—either directly (as when Lucy challenges Ricky with her desire to join him in the industry) or more structurally, like here on *Daddy*, as the premised central conflict is that his job keeps him from being home with his wife and kids. In other words, Danny is caught between the two worlds. On *Dick Van Dyke*, that's not the guiding construct for interrelated conflict (it's a little too rigid for that series' more naturalistic scripting), but there's even more of a dual episodic structure there, as the lead, Rob, goes back and forth between his office and his house, with the best stories finding some way to associate the two spheres and unite all aspects of its situational design.

(This dual structure of the personal and the professional, and the intentional bridging of the two, will come to be a common template going forward, especially for the character-driven shows of the 1970s, many produced by Mary Tyler Moore's company MTM—including *The Mary Tyler Moore Show*, *The Bob Newhart Show*, *The Tony Randall Show*, and so forth. *Mary Tyler Moore* represents, like *Dick Van Dyke*, its decade's own advancement in character-driven writing—replacing slapstick with an emphasis on character-based interactions as comic centerpieces but with *even more* of a commitment to keeping their depictions emotionally truthful, essentially depending entirely on the leads. Not only do they drive story, but they *are* story. This is the arc of character-driven sitcoms from the 1950s to the 1970s.)

What these shows also share is the incorporation of autobiographical details that infuse their characters and plots with more believability. *Dick Van Dyke* is based on the life of creator Carl Reiner, not its star. But on both *Lucy* and *Danny Thomas*, there are elements of its performers' own real lives influencing the premise—only, for both, because they each have characters who work in the glamorous world of show business (to which most viewers could not directly relate), they consciously choose to make their leads a little bit less successful. They're not big-time movie stars, just regular middle-class families (or upper middle class). Yes, they're urban and not suburban (like the Petries on *Dick Van Dyke*), but their economic standing is meant to reflect as wide a reach as possible—keeping them from being rarified, no matter how much that would be the actual truth. And yet, in terms of initial design, *Make Room for Daddy* is more truthful than *Lucy*, mostly because more autobiographical details are applied.

That is, Lucille Ball is not playing an entertainer, like Desi Arnaz is, like Danny Thomas is, and that means, as a character, she's less rooted in her own mimesis. Thomas's Danny is more solidly analogous to Arnaz's Ricky because both are performers who have their ethnicities used to flesh out their depictions, inspiring both laughs and story—one, of course, is Cuban, and the other is Lebanese, with family members, especially Danny's recurring Uncle Tonoose (who debuts in Season Three and is played by Hans Conried), existing as an extension of this noted aspect of his characterization. And just as Lucy's hometown of Jamestown, New York, is oft-referenced, so is Danny's in Toledo, Ohio. In this regard, viewers can watch *Make Room for Daddy* and feel even more like they're watching Danny Thomas in scenarios that he directly understands. Of course, *Lucy* has the strength of its real-life couple carrying a lot of its realism—along with their incorporated pregnancy—so it probably evens out in actuality. But strictly on design, Thomas's show evolves this subcategory in the genre, like *Dick Van Dyke*, to something more premised as lifelike. That's a foundation that later shows will use to then ground even more outrageous comedy.

To that point, I wouldn't say that *The Danny Thomas Show* is quite as funny as either *I Love Lucy* or *The Dick Van Dyke Show*. Not only is this because it offers less viscerally physical gags but also because, in general, its characters are less incongruous. Not every regular here (particularly the wives) has clear comic traits that can be caricatured benignly for laughs. Additionally, *The Danny Thomas Show*—and particularly during its three seasons with Margaret and the two young kids as *Make Room for Daddy*—is far sweeter than these two counterpoints. This is due to the fact that more than those other two, *Make Room for Daddy* is a family sitcom and largely an extension of that growing trend. Both *Lucy* and *Dick Van Dyke* use kids in their ensembles and thus essentially have a family aspect that allows their writers to occasionally do stories on parenting, but they're more exclusively centered on the relationships between the adults. On *Daddy*, although the central relationship is husband and wife (just as it happens to be on those other two), its premise itself involves Danny's dynamic with his kids and his role to them as father. Accordingly, much of the conflict is centered on his parenting or lack thereof, and this puts him in line with the other fallible patriarchs that anchor most of the more obvious family sitcoms of the time (*Ozzie and Harriet*, *The Life of Riley*, *Trouble with Father*, etc.), where their imperfections as head of the household create comic conflict in story.

Fortunately, if *Daddy* is sweeter than those two classics surrounding it, rest assured that it is much funnier in the context of the family subgenre, for not only does Desilu's multi-camera format suppose an inherent desire to make the live audience laugh, but the characters are also designed to validate the premise, which is situated on the comic tension of Danny's role as husband and father. Danny is not only, as promised, inherently flawed (his temper is often cited as one of his big issues), but Margaret is also built to be confrontational in her own right, and the two kids—played initially by Rusty Hamer and Sherry Jackson (two of the best in the business)—are snappy and quick-witted, earning laughs while retaining some degree of humanity via their relative truthfulness. So with characters who can contribute comedically and validate the premise, which is built on conflict, the multi-cam *Make Room for Daddy* is not at all the benign series that most single-cam family shows sadly happen to be.

Now, with an 11-year run, *The Danny Thomas Show* goes through a lot of changes, and it's not always as worthwhile as it is interesting, for there's constant movement. We will be looking more at its trajectory in a few chapters, especially when it loses its matriarch and switches titles (1956), and then when it moves networks and finds a new leading lady—simultaneously inheriting *Lucy*'s old berth and adopting more elements associated with that series (1957). Eventually, in the early 1960s, the show even takes on traits unique to the structurally derivative *Dick Van Dyke*, which had come to eclipse the series creatively and represent a standard to which both *Danny Thomas* and the similarly designed *The Joey Bishop Show* would both aspire (and they all three shared key scribes during the overlap, like Garry Marshall).[21] So *The Danny Thomas Show* really comes to feel like the link between *I Love Lucy* and *The Dick Van Dyke Show*, existing between them as one of the only live audience multi-cams from the late 1950s, with a quality that isn't quite on either of their levels but is in the same figurative arena, especially compared to the rest of the genre (and subgenre) with which it is affiliated.

As for Season One, which is not in formal syndication (none of the Jean Hagen years are) but has some episodes available to find online, it's the collection that makes most use of the series' autobiographical premise, and the best episode I have seen is "Lost Dollar" (December 1, 1953), where Danny accuses Rusty of stealing a dollar. Danny's parenting, not to mention his hot temper, are subject to criticism in this story that evidences the premise by acknowledging just how unaccustomed its nightclub entertainer lead is to fulfilling his role as father. It also depicts him as the era's ever-popular fallible patriarch, when it's proven (as suspected) that Rusty did not take the dollar Danny accused and then punished him for stealing. Most family shows of this time have an imperfect dad, but none are as comedically defined and primed for relationship-based and premise-affirming conflict as Danny Williams of *Make Room for Daddy*, so this episode is both a testament to the era's trends as well as this series' own relative superiority. Also, you can see the series balance sweetness with comedy, delighting its live studio audience with laughs from fairly strong characterizations—not only Danny and Rusty but also recurring players like Louise Beavers as the family's housekeeper (she would later be replaced by another sitcom legend, Amanda Randolph) and Jesse White as Danny's agent, whose appearances faded out by the 1957 retooling. Indeed, tracking the show's evolution will be a focus of this book, especially as it becomes one of the finest sitcoms on the air.

As for Desilu, it also gave space this season to *The Jack Benny Program*, then in its fourth year on television and now being shown every three weeks (alternating with *Private Secretary*) for a total of 13 episodes, eight of which leaned into the situation comedy format, offering a narrative scenario inspired by Jack Benny's established situation and either his relationships with other recurring presences or his generally well-defined characterization in a somewhat motivated story scene. Of the remaining five broadcasts, two took their centerpieces from dream sequences—a blend of situation and sketch comedy, perhaps—while three were outright variety shows, utilizing comedy skits in which the star was not totally playing Jack Benny or motivating plots inside of his typical world. However, the ratio of sitcom to sketch is fairly high this year, and even as the TV series remains a less ideal example of its concurrent radio iteration (which boasted a more concrete regular ensemble that made situation comedy easier and more likely), we can see the rise of this genre in the medium of television *through* the Benny program. There's nothing great here, at least not in the sitcom episodes (the sketches have some hilarious moments), but there may be soon.

In the meantime, it's more pertinent to note another trend reflected through the series, for, as mentioned, Desilu gave space at its facilities to Benny this year, as the comic decided to film a few of his shows.[22] (His old cohort Dennis Day, incidentally, had his own sitcom—*The Dennis Day Show*, which switched from all live to entirely filmed in this, its final season.[23]) Now, contrary to popular belief, *Jack Benny* did not take full advantage of Desilu's capabilities. These were filmed without a studio audience, even though the live broadcasts still had one. There's no good reason why Benny resisted the *Lucy* setup—it would have given him an ideal aesthetic.

The next year, Benny put some more episodes on film—this time using his pal George Burns's company, McCadden, which—as previously noted—started branching out in 1954 beyond its flagship, *The George Burns and Gracie Allen Show*, now in its fourth season here in 1953-1954. This was *Burns and Allen*'s second on film, still using a multi-camera setup to shoot but similarly without a live audience or the help of Desilu and its refinements. However, this did not matter, for just as the series adjusted to its new filmed format at the end of the prior season—dropping some of its theatricality and embracing more narratively involved ideas, all of which were delightfully predicated or complicated by the comic Gracie Allen persona—this particular year is filled with gems, offering the official, syndicated versions of some early live plots that are seldom seen (if not entirely lost forever), such as Gracie's visit to a psychiatrist,[24] or her scheme to buy items wholesale.[25] Additionally, the season is also blessed by a new husband for Bea Benaderet's Blanche—well, not a new husband; it's still Harry Morton but a very different Harry Morton, now played (for the duration of the run) by the fourth actor to take on the role: Larry Keating (perhaps best known today to TV fans for his work as Addison on *Mister Ed*).

He replaced the outgoing Fred Clark, who had been an improvement over the first two men to depict Harry because he helped the role develop a trait that could be emphasized for comedy—his voracious appetite. This was a running gag from which character-based jokes could arise. Fortunately, Keating accelerates the part's capacity for comic utilization even further, with a totally different characterization based on his own innate sensibility. His Harry is similarly frugal but now with a tenor of haughty sophistication and ego-based aggrandizement—a specific, exaggeratable perspective that make his reactions to Gracie more *uniquely* unnerved and even colors his dynamic with George to whom he looks down his nose. In a year or two, Larry Keating's instilled personality for Harry Morton will not only be creating character-rooted laughs; it'll also be helping shape story in a way that no prior iteration of Harry Morton could *specifically* do, rendering him a better realized tool in the show's situation comedy arsenal and a walking embodiment of the series' continued ascension into being fuller sitcommery, using its characterizations—not just Gracie's—in the cultivation of plots. So Keating's arrival here marks a "leveling up" for the series' situation, just as it's also employing the definitive, filmed takes on some of its best ideas.

▶ That said, Gracie remains the main attraction, and there are a handful of memorable *Burns and Allen* outings in its fourth season. My pick for the best makes it to **#21** on my top 50 list: **"An Elephant Sits on Gracie's Fender"** in which nobody believes Gracie's outlandish story about how her car got dented. It was first broadcast on **April 5, 1954**, directed by **Frederick De Cordova**, and its script is credited to **Sid Dorfman**, **Harvey Helm**, **Keith Fowler**, and **William Burns**.

Most episodes of *Burns and Allen* deploy Gracie's centralized persona in either one of two ways—either her warped, literal perspective drives a kooky scheme that creates hijinks, or her warped, literal perspective is contrasted against a confused outsider whose responses create the hijinks. This episode is fairly unique, for it doesn't use either of those basic templates, instead utilizing the other *regulars'* impressions of Gracie's established character to create the conflict. Specifically, George, who usually is all-knowing (especially in later seasons with his so-called "magic TV") but is behind the viewer this time, as we already have more information and are aware that Gracie is telling the truth about, as the title says, an elephant sitting on her fender.

The comic complications come, in this episode, not directly from Gracie but from the reactions to her based on the continuity that both the regulars and we associate with her character, thanks to the series' longtime consistency with her depiction. In this framework, the episode reverses the show's usual narrative emphases, even though the Grace Allen persona is still kept centralized, giving a chance for other leads on the show, particularly George, to respond directly to her persona, and causing conflict because, for once, he happens to be wrong. This is great situation comedy because it's totally inspired by what we know of Gracie, and even though the elephant story may be ridiculous, it's exactly the kind of tale that Gracie *might* tell, or to go further back, include in a Burns and Allen vaudeville exchange. So we buy its usage on this show—just as we buy George's disbelief in its veracity, for he knows

Gracie Allen (left) and George Burns in *The George Burns and Gracie Allen Show*, "An Elephant Sits on Gracie's Fender" (1954).

Gracie, just as we do. And again, that is a tribute to the show's sitcommery—it's the kind of story that could only happen with characters defined as such.

As for other filmed sitcoms this year, there was another new nuclear family series with a fallible patriarch, joining ABC's *The Adventures of Ozzie and Harriet* and NBC's *The Life of Riley*—both of which enjoyed second seasons in 1953–1954 with few qualitative tweaks from their first. *Riley* is probably a little less broad and also less premise-connected this year, but its character work in story remains just as nondescript outside of its lead and his ingrained working-class tension, while *Ozzie and Harriet* is still using a lot of old radio scripts for two parents and two young kids, with the show's wink about its own benignity never more pronounced than its actual benignity. This new show, also on ABC, is *Pride of the Family*, a filmed single-camera sitcom (with heavy laugh track) that is best known today for starring screen siren Fay Wray (*King Kong*) as the matriarch and a young Natalie Wood as her daughter. Otherwise, *Pride of the Family* sort of steps into the space previously occupied by *Trouble with Father*, which was airing an entire season of reruns ahead of one more slate of new episodes in 1954–1955. Like *Trouble with Father*, *Pride of the Family* has another clumsy and inept dad in Paul Hartman and a family that's even more suburban and average than the showbiz-adjacent Nelsons or the working-class

Rileys, whose economic status colors their situation entirely (and should be fodder for story).

It's not as heavy on physical comedy as *Trouble with Father* used to be, but there are some really broad, silly stories and an occasional boldness with humor that differentiates *Pride of the Family* from the quieter *Ozzie and Harriet*. Thematically, it's not as interesting as the others—there's no economic angst or a tongue-in-cheek agreeance about its own triviality—but it tries to avoid the overt moralizing of, for example, *Father Knows Best* and (some years of) *Leave It to Beaver*. I wish I could see more of the series' output to form a more concrete opinion about how it reliably stands as an example of the sitcom. It seems fairly typical for the family subgenre, and its mere existence indicates the growing prominence of suburbia as another rising sitcom trend.

## *You Have a Face for Syndication*

Speaking of trends, this continued increase in filmed programs brought about an elevated awareness that television shows might have life beyond the networks. And a new market opportunity started becoming more common: selling shows to individual TV stations sans the intermediary backing of a major broadcast network. We call programs that are explicitly produced to air directly on stations to which they have been sold, and not to a network who delivers programs to their affiliates, shows that debuted in "first-run syndication." In the last chapter, we touched briefly on *The Abbott and Costello Show*, which was sold to specific stations across the country that began airing the program at the end of 1952, with its two 26-episode orders premiering during the 1952–1953 and 1953–1954 seasons. This became a more viable option for TV producers and production companies following the end of the Federal Communications Commission "freeze" in 1952, when licenses for new television stations were now available again and thus a rush of new broadcasters came on the airwaves, some without a formal affiliation to one of the four major networks: NBC, CBS, ABC, and DuMont.[26]

In addition to *Abbott and Costello* in its second and final first-run season, 1953–1954 saw several more sitcoms premiere like such in syndication, including a TV version of *Duffy's Tavern*, the long-running workplace/hangout "modified" sitcom from radio set in a city bar. This single-camera TV iteration kept some of the radio version's regular characters—including Ed Gardner as bartender Archie—but the new medium demanded a little more fidelity to the situation comedy format than the original property was ready to supply, for without regular musical numbers and a revolving door of special guests, all this version of *Duffy's Tavern* had were its leads, and while they've each got basic personas, they were not well-accustomed to motivating story, and they're thus not good at it. Accordingly, the TV *Duffy's Tavern* wasn't the radio show that audiences once loved, and after 39 episodes (which debuted in first-run syndication beginning in 1954, up through the 1954–1955 TV season), this failed radio-to-TV adaptation closed up shop. But, of course, because it was on film, it could also remain in syndication thereafter as well.

Also available to stations in first-run syndication during 1953–1954 was a comedy called *Life with Elizabeth*, a vehicle for a local Los Angeles television personality by the name of Betty White. Yes, *that* Betty White. Her career in TV began during the 1948–1949 season,[27] and she soon became a fixture on the local L.A. station KLAC-TV as a daytime talk show host alongside star Al Jarvis. Many more opportunities came her way during the early 1950s, including several evening variety shows that she either hosted or cohosted. In 1951, she began appearing on one of these variety programs with writer George Tibbles (whose best known credit is *My Three Sons*) in a series of sketches casually called "Alvin and Elizabeth," about a silly and impish newlywed with her often amused but adoring husband.[28] This eventually expanded into its own half-hour series, *Life with Elizabeth*, on KLAC in May 1952, with Del Moore by now opposite White in the role of Alvin.[29] To sustain the half hour, this new series consisted of three individual sketches, or vignettes, all featuring the two leads in everyday, realistic scenarios, with maybe one guest star and a couple of sets. Although only locally seen, this live series—staged at a theater before a live audience[30]—was well received in Hollywood, as was its affable leading lady, who even won a regional Emmy in 1953.[31] That same year, White and Tibbles, with producer Don Fedderson, decided to create a version of *Elizabeth* for a national audience—selling the program to various stations across the country and effectively putting the show in first-run syndication.

Sixty-five episodes of *Life with Elizabeth* debuted during the 1953–1954 and 1954–1955 seasons, offering Americans outside of L.A. their first regular exposure to a woman who would spend the next sixty-five years on television. In fact, by 1954, White was already being dubbed with a moniker she'd keep for the rest of her remarkable career, "America's Sweetheart"[32]—so earned not just because of *Elizabeth* but also her first network program, *The Betty White Show*, a daytime talk/variety series that debuted nationally on NBC in January of that year.

As for the quality of *Life with Elizabeth* as it pertains to our study of the sitcom form, first let it be said that there is some debate about whether the show should even be *called* a situation comedy, for this new filmed version—shot single-camera without an audience—retained the format of the live local version, with each episode boasting three vignettes, each usually one scene (maybe two at most) and with a different idea. In this regard, the series never offers a fully plotted episodic story—the kind encouraged by the half-hour format—and it might even seem like it would better be called a sketch show. And yet, each sketch uses Alvin and Elizabeth and their basic "situation" as newlyweds, so like earlier 15-minute series with the sitcom label—ones that seem sketch-like in terms of narrative—the continuity of character is at least maintained through each episode and each individual vignette as well. Plus, it's definitely not a serial—the radio form from which 15-minute comedies sprung—for there's no continuity of plot, and it's tonally lighthearted. As such, it has a consistency of character but not plot and is temperamentally more a comedy than anything else. Under those terms, I am fine with discussing it *as a version of* a situation comedy.

However, it is structurally always going to be subpar, for the characters and their situation can never be explored in story because there *is* no story—each episode is but three self-contained sketches with barely any conflict, let alone regulars acting and reacting in accordance with their established personas. And because they don't have a half hour's worth of story encouraging them to take on some revealing definition, Alvin and Elizabeth are incredibly bland as characters, directly inspiring their own laughs as seldom as they inspire their scenic notions, which are also very bland, seemingly concerned with everyday trivia but without the natural dialogue of Peg Lynch's *Ethel and Albert*, for *Life with Elizabeth* revels in its own idealistic falseness—perhaps as an extension of its newlywed premise—and instead of striving for a caricatured mimesis, it merely wants to be warm and cute, not even mimetic. In this regard, the show is neither great comedically nor situationally clever, for it's not very funny, and none of its established elements have much definition, as there's no specific, regular link made between the characters and its ideas. Beyond the basic hook that she is livelier than her more rigid husband—"Elizabeth, aren't you ashamed?" the announcer would ask once a week, after she's made some "joke" or done something silly—there's nothing here. And even that comic attitude, you'll note, is totally dependent on White bringing her own natural charm and charisma to the role. Outside of White, *Life with Elizabeth* would not be worth watching at all. Her true sitcom triumphs came later.

Last, another sitcom that wound up in first-run syndication during the 1953–1954 season was *The Amos 'n Andy Show*, which got pulled from the CBS schedule after the NAACP successfully applied enough social pressure to make its sponsor flee.[33] Thirteen additional episodes were produced in the spring and early summer of 1953 in hopes that a new backer would save the program and it would return to the schedule, but that proved to be in vain. So, beginning later that summer, as reruns of the 52 network *Amos 'n Andy* episodes were sold to individual stations, there were 13 new segments included in that package, and they started making their debuts. There's really no change in style between these next 13 and those before, although one funny installment, called the "Vacation Show" (premiered 1953), counted a memorably outrageous Kingfish scheme—as he takes the gullible Andy "camping" in Central Park. Instantly popular in syndication, talk of a resurrection was immediate—this time under the title "The Adventures of Kingfish." A new network order never came, but 13 more episodes were produced and folded into the *Amos 'n Andy* syndication package, starting in 1955.

So although *Amos 'n Andy* finally left the network's schedule, it was still very much a part of the TV landscape in 1953–1954, which continued to be dominated by the country's most popular program, *I Love Lucy*, then in its third season and perhaps at the peak of its cultural phenomenon, as the year—1953—started with the coordinated birth of Desi Jr. and Little Ricky and also saw a blitz of publicity for the television couple's new joint motion picture, *The Long, Long Trailer* (released in 1954). The show's—and couple's—popularity was so great during this season that they were able to survive a moment that's been cheekily dubbed the "Red Scare," when Lucille Ball's previous registration with the Communist Party publicly came back to haunt her as it was revealed that she had been questioned by the House Un-American Activities Committee.[34] Although the pair feared the possibility that her career might never recover, even the simplest of explanations—she registered for her kooky grandfather, not knowing what she was doing[35]—was enough to quell any doubt, for America loved *Lucy* no matter what, and this incident—magnified by biographers and filmmakers since—had no effect on their Nielsens.[36]

Nielsens aside, how was the show holding up? Well, in Season Three, there are approximately just as many episodes as there were in the year before dealing with Lucy Ricardo's specific objective of getting in show business—only here, there is no pregnancy or "'spectin'" arc to justify the shift in focus. Rather, ideas directly related to that one individually premised goal of Lucy's are no longer as fresh or abundant as they were in seasons past. Instead, this is the year that must really extrapolate from this core desire other episodic motivations that still make sense for her character, relying more on the larger implied themes—like her yearning to be more than a "typical" housewife and mother, longing for a life that's not ordinary but glamorous and exciting, the best of everything. And this extrapolation is possible, mind you, *because* she first had that objective and its associated subtext as a foundation, for in seeing her pursue this specific show biz want in story, larger desires could then be inferred. Additionally, with a growing continuity as a result of both consistency and mounting details, the Lucy Ricardo character—heck, all the regulars on *I Love Lucy*—feel more believable than ever. So it's more possible to read more human motivations into her pursuits in narrative—to a degree that we cannot do, for instance, with Joan Stevens on *I Married Joan*, who feels less realistic and doesn't have the reliability of Lucy's initial "want" as a touchstone for everything else she goes after in plot.

Now, without Lucy's objective being explored as uniquely or frequently and no other narrative arcs to steal focus, *I Love Lucy*'s third collection has often been perceived as the show's most boring year, with somewhat routine domestic/couple ideas that other shows could employ—you know, like stories about jealousy over perceived infidelity,[37] or the business partnership that goes awry,[38] or a misunderstanding over a surprise party.[39] But I see it differently. I see this as the year where the show *proves* the value of its characters, for when they don't directly inspire the generation of plots, they significantly shape the beats that influence the storytelling.

For instance, the infidelity story is motivated by the mechanics of Ricky's chosen career—a publicity stunt—and there's indeed affiliation then to the unique premised aspects of the series' situation, and its characters specifically. And the business partnership that goes awry—in this case, a diner that the two couples go into together—is not just a temporary get-rich-quick scheme, like it might be on other sitcoms. No, on *Lucy*, it's motivated by Ricky's dissatisfaction with show business—another part of the premise and his character—and putting the women, particularly Lucy, in the workplace also addresses her broader desire to find meaning for herself beyond the home and the roles she's expected to fulfill. And as to the surprise party, the reason there's a conflict is because Ricky's specific career has made nights at home with Lucy a luxury, and in his pursuit of a normal life (again, a premised aspect of his characterization), he longs for a quiet anniversary with just his wife, who sees the intimacy of their secret one-on-one rendezvous as an exciting and glamorous prospect. It's totally character validating—not to mention emotionally buyable, supported by the mimetic foundation of their relationship, and the audience's awareness of how the Ricardos are, in *some* part, a reflection of the Arnazes.

Accordingly, this is the season I would point to when convincing others of the superiority of *I Love Lucy*'s character work—and the use of its situation overall. In enlivening otherwise more predictable, unoriginal stories via the leads' established definitions and the particulars of their premised existence, they confirm their own value and in turn corroborate the situation comedy as a unique art form, one where these primary elements—the characters—are the main attraction, uniquely satiating both the genre's need for episodic conflicts and its inherent comedic requirement. Thus, while other seasons are more popular and have more classic episodes—and as we'll see soon, Season Four finds a way for Lucy's specific objective to be more often invoked, or at least *tangentially* invoked, in story on a more reliable and believable basis—this is a collection of half-hour ideas that no sitcom from this era could do better.

I have four entries that I want to mention. The first is a straightforward example of Lucy pursuing her goal of getting into show business. It's "Home Movies" (March 1, 1954), with a story about Lucy and the Mertzes producing their own TV pilot for a potential sponsor who is interested in Ricky. The centerpiece is a terribly edited (by Lucy) combination of Ricky's pilot, her pilot (a Western), and boring home movies of Little Ricky that have accidentally been spliced in as well. It's a hoot—all related to Lucy's objective and the hasty zeal with which she pursues it, even at Ricky's expense. Other episodes like "Lucy Is Envious" (March 29, 1954) don't use a specific show biz angle but still show Lucy as being dissatisfied with her existence via her efforts to project, or perform, a heightened degree of class or sophistication. In this story, that manifests itself as a donation to a snobby friend's charity and thus a quick need for cash she doesn't have, leading to a stunt where she and Ethel dress up as aliens on top of the Empire State building to promote a forthcoming film. It's a big, broad beat—but Lucy's wants propel her decision-making.

▶ This yearning for more also manifests itself in a classic entry that I personally rank as **#26** on my list—"**The Million Dollar Idea**" in which Lucy and Ethel attempt to go into business together selling salad dressing. It debuted on **January 11, 1954**, and was again directed by **Asher**, with a script by the busy trio of **Oppenheimer**, **Pugh**, and **Carroll**.

There are several episodes, even in this season, where Lucy and Ethel explore going into business for themselves—a running theme that speaks directly to Lucy's dissatisfaction with a "typical" existence, which, for her, means being stuck in her middle-class home as a wife and mother *only*. In this entry, she's not pursuing a career in show business but with salad dressing, something more domestic—something on which she and Ethel should theoretically be experts. However, their lack of business understanding gets them into trouble when they underestimate the demand for their product and fail to set the proper prices. It's a simple dilemma that helps re-earn the status quo in a believable way, taking advantage of the characters' ambitions and limitations simultaneously. Narratively, it's good sitcommery. But it's hilarious as well—with two great centerpieces. The first is a parody of daytime ads directed toward women, when Lucy and Ethel do a commercial for their product on a local TV station. It's a chance for Ball as Lucy to play an *especially* daffy housewife who can't help guzzling the delicious dressing. (This makes a winking contrast to the actual Lucy Ricardo character, who is much savvier.)

The second great bit is their second commercial, when the pair has gotten so many orders that they go back on TV in an attempt to *unsell* the product, this time with Lucy playing a less put-together woman, who looks like she was literally plucked from the street. She tastes the product, physically and vocally registers immediate disgust, and urges buyers to "Cancel! Cancel!" Naturally, the ad is viewed as comedic, and the stunt backfires. But it was a good idea—a typical Lucy scheme, evidence of her conniving intelligence, and the central goal that motivates her very choices, getting her into these kind of comic predicaments in the first place.

▶ However, my pick for the season's best, at **#13**, is "**Lucy Tells the Truth**." It debuted on **November 9, 1953**. **Asher** directed, and **Oppenheimer**, **Pugh**, and **Carroll** wrote the script about Ricky and the Mertzes betting Lucy that she can't go a full day without telling a lie.

Challenging a character to avoid lying is an idea that will be funny in most circumstances, for, as human beings, we know that frequent dishonesty is not moral behavior, even though it's impossible to get through life without bending the truth. In fact, it is socially more acceptable to tell white lies every now and again than to be uncompromisingly candid. So the log line for "Lucy Tells the Truth" is one that many sitcoms could—and have shown they could—employ, like a lot of the stories here in *Lucy*'s third season. Heck, the idea was based on a 1951 *My Favorite Husband* radio script—"Liz Stretches the Truth"—which of course has its roots in *Nothing But the Truth*, the Frederic S. Isham novel that has since been adapted into every medium.[40] It's not new.

But what makes *I Love Lucy* a great sitcom is *how* it uses its situation's elements—its characters—to support the idea and render it therefore unique enough to the show. For instance, Lucy Ricardo's penchant for lying is not a convenient trait that arises to justify this story; no, we've seen her repeatedly fib over the course of the last two years, especially in pursuit of her ultimate objective—being in show business. Giving Lucy Ricardo a goal to pursue in story has created a pattern of behavior—tactics—that have become established aspects of her characterization. And so, this conflict—Lucy being forced not to lie—is already situated on a known aspect of her persona, made funnier and more believable from the continuity.

What's more, the show uses some of its recurring fixtures—like Lucy's frenemy Carolyn Appleby, played with straightforward nice-nastiness by Doris Singleton—to ensure that it is a challenge for her to successfully avoid untruths. And then the climax, which was rewritten during production week, really puts Lucy in a situation-supported dilemma, as she goes to an audition and is made to either tell the truth and be rejected or lie and have a chance at the job. In other words, Lucy can pursue her macro objective of getting in show business or the micro objective of winning this episode's bet. Naturally, she chooses the former, and the physical climax involves Lucy becoming a victim of her own lying, as she's bluffed into standing in as the quivering and unwitting accomplice to a professional knife thrower. So that's the centerpiece—a performance by the hungering performer and a consequence of her own well-established flaws, the subject of this entire narrative. Interestingly, the original script involved Lucy and an IRS agent—Desi Arnaz rejected it because it was just after the "Red Scare."[41] Thank goodness! The filmed version is affiliated with the series' show business trappings, allowing it to be more *fully* an example of how *I Love Lucy* maneuvers its situation—its leads—to enliven even ordinary episodic stories.

## *Hi, Concept*

Now, before we move to the next chapter, there are two more sitcoms I want to highlight. Both are departures from the previously discussed shows, which tend to be simple and largely true to life, with mostly relatable scenarios: couples, families, workplaces. These last two are a little more specific and less mimetic for audiences. The first is *Colonel Humphrey Flack*, a live sitcom broadcast on the struggling DuMont network from New York, where, in accordance with that style, it was not staged before a live audience and was thus less concerned with broad laugh-out-loud humor. Its unique premise concerns a modern-day Robin Hood (played by Alan Mowbray) who dupes cons so that he can pay back folks in need. The regular cast consists of just the title character and his assistant—otherwise there are few recurring players, making it procedural, almost an anthology show: every week a different story with different characters and circumstances motivating what the regulars do. Yes, there's a situation—a premise and a lead with his sidekick—but the leads themselves are not influencing the ideas, and they are barely shaping the beats or earning laughs (which are few). Therefore, it is not great sitcommery. (Incidentally, these live episodes would later be filmed for syndication in the 1958–1959 season as *Colonel Humphrey J. Flack*. If you remember the show, it's likely from those remakes.)

The other, similarly less relatable and true-to-life entry is *Topper*, a filmed single-camera comedy inspired by the popular movie (franchise) that was also adapted as a radio sitcom briefly in 1945. It didn't work in that audio-only medium because its premise is about ghosts only being visible to one guy and nobody else—so, much of the humor is dependent on sight gags. This TV adaptation, which ran for two years on CBS, is this medium's first supernatural comedy—a trend that would become more popular in the escapist 1960s with shows like *My Favorite Martian*, *Bewitched*, and *I Dream of Jeannie*. *Topper* is their forerunner, and it actually has a few things going for it. For instance, the series boasts a strong ensemble foursome (Anne Jeffreys, Robert Sterling, Leo G. Carroll, and Lee Patrick) with the same basic roles as in the film. But the hook here is that the mortal couple has moved into the ghosts' old home, and only the mortal man, Cosmo Topper, can see them. Also, there's some fun with the addition of the ghosts' also-deceased dog, who likes to drink, and Kathleen Freeman, who's on hand in Season One as the mortal couple's maid—struggling to comprehend Cosmo's odd behavior. She's a riot.

As for the ghosts themselves, while the mortal twosome (the Toppers) each have elementally distinct personas, the deceased duo (the Kirbys) is sort of singular in definition, evidenced by their collective usage in plot. This is not dissimilar from their depictions in the original 1937 film, but on a sitcom, where differences between personalities make characters clear for the audience and theoretically open up more story possibilities, this is less satisfying.

While that may be a flaw inherent to adapting the film to this new format, the TV series is also down two things that the movie *did have*. For starters, these ghosts do not have a specific objective. In the film, they stuck around haunting Cosmo because they needed to do a good deed to get into heaven. In the TV series, they merely say they want to make Cosmo more fun. But that is hardly ever explored *specifically*, and it's kind of a generic excuse that allows them to just rile him up, with little unique motivation. So all of their actions feel less justified than in the film, and their ties to story are less personal. That speaks to the second point: the ghosts had a preexisting relationship with Topper in the film. In the series, they share no history, and that means there's lower emotional stakes and a very limited capacity for character-driven conflict between them as a result of their bond's lightness and triviality. Again, they don't care enough.

All this show is then, in terms of story, is mortals living their lives and a ghost couple messing around with them, while only Cosmo knows it—forcing him to cover and explain, as the other mortals continue to remain oblivious. There are very few details or specifics about them as individuals used to help support the situation narratively and give it some character-based individuality beyond those conceptual givens. *Topper*'s sitcommery is therefore limited.

A smart question to ask here: is the premise itself the problem? Not necessarily, for this kind of show can work. You see, *Topper*—like *Colonel Humphrey Flack*, actually—is what we would call a premise-driven, or "high concept," show. A high-concept show is one that we can typically summarize in a sentence because it's got an obvious, unique premise. This is in contrast to low-concept shows, which are harder to define because they are more about individual characters and how they interact in relationships—essentially, the regulars *are* the premise. Although *I Love Lucy* and *Our Miss Brooks*, to use two examples, have precise conceptual particulars—like the former's show biz conflict and the latter's high school setting—both are considered low concept because their stories aren't about that exactly; they're about the people within those constructs, whose relational dynamics don't just uphold the situation, but are it. These low-concept sitcoms also tend to be more literally realistic, with smaller everyday surroundings that imitate life in a more natural, expected way.

You can see how this differs from *Topper*, which is about ghosts haunting the owner of their new home—and this ridiculous, heightened premise is what defines both story and comedy, more so than the individual objectives, perspectives, and flaws of the characters, in relation to each other. Many more of these high-concept shows would come about in the 1960s, not only via the supernatural efforts mentioned previously, but also in premise-led offerings like *The Beverly Hillbillies* and *Green Acres*, which find conflict in a growing urban versus rural divide. Note, however, that many of those 1960s classics, including *Bewitched*—the best of the supernatural lot—may be high concept, but they're still supported by great characters and relationships, whose goals and dynamics *support* the high-concept premise, giving it personalization. That is, *Bewitched*'s characters enable and enliven the high concept, based on their individual definitions and specific relational tensions. Again, this is where *Topper* naturally falls short—not because of its high concept, but because its character work is not good enough to support that high-concept premise in the way this genre prefers.

In a few chapters, we'll dive into the similar notion of character-driven sitcoms versus idea-driven sitcoms. High-concept efforts like *Topper* are all idea driven because they're led by a strong premise—or, at heart, an idea. However, we will find that not *all* low-concept shows are character driven in return because not all low-concept shows have good-enough character work to genuinely let their characters drive story. Therefore, it's important to remember that whether low concept or high concept, idea led or character led, the best sitcoms, as always, depend on their regulars to anchor a situation and inspire plots that yield humor because, again, characters are what provide the imitation of life (even supernaturally). That's the basis for *all* Drama, especially comedy.

With regard to *Topper*, its leads have some definition, but it's just not set up for them to uniquely aid the premise, which is otherwise driving story in a limited and unsatisfying capacity because it doesn't have more precise details about them from which it can create episodic ideas. So not only is it a mediocre sitcom; it is a mediocre example of a high-concept, idea-driven sitcom. And not even a very young and pre–Broadway Stephen Sondheim, credited with cowriting 11 of Season One's 39 produced offerings, is able to elevate the proceedings, which get worse in Season Two, as the show becomes even less rooted in its own situation—traveling around on Topper's job and removing the home setting as a consistent element of its identity.

Yet if *Colonel Humphrey Flack* and *Topper* represent some of the earliest high-concept sitcoms on TV, the 1953–1954 season is still mostly concerned with the same types of low-concept domestic shows discussed earlier in the chapter. This year, in particular, continued the same, previously accelerating trends—as more series moved to film, and television production came to join the movies, hopping more and more from the East Coast to the West Coast. As for the sitcom as a genre, it continued to be on an upswing because of *Lucy*'s fast success, and next season would mark the peak of its stature in the 1950s—with more sitcoms airing original episodes on network or in first-run syndication than any other year during this entire decade. The new medium was not so new anymore, and it had found a tested programming template. Of course, as we have seen, the sitcom is an art form, and not all efforts are artistically great.

### JACKSON'S BEST SITCOMS FROM 1953–54
1. I LOVE LUCY (S3)
2. THE GEORGE BURNS AND GRACIE ALLEN SHOW (S4)
3. MAKE ROOM FOR DADDY (S1)

### EPISODES FROM THE 1953–54 SEASON IN JACKSON'S TOP 50 FROM THE '50s
#13. I LOVE LUCY (S3): "Lucy Tells the Truth" (11/9/53)
#21. THE GEORGE BURNS AND GRACIE ALLEN SHOW (S4): "An Elephant Sits on Gracie's Fender" (4/5/54)
#26. I LOVE LUCY (S3): "The Million Dollar Idea" (1/11/54)
#44. OUR MISS BROOKS (S2): "Second Hand First Aid" (4/23/54)

### OTHER NOTABLE EPISODES FROM 1953–54
MAKE ROOM FOR DADDY (S1): "Lost Dollar" (12/1/53)
I LOVE LUCY (S3): "Home Movies" (3/1/54)
I LOVE LUCY (S3): "Lucy Is Envious" (3/29/54)
I LOVE LUCY (S3): "The Diner" (4/26/54)
MISTER PEEPERS (S3): "The Wedding" (5/23/54)

# Chapter Seven

# The Sitcom Boom

## *The Best Television Sitcoms of 1954–1955*

There were barely 10 original sitcoms airing new episodes on national television when the decade began in 1950–1951. Now, by the 1954–1955 season, I count more than 40—the most of any year here in the 1950s, unmatched again until the mid–1960s. As we move into the final half of this decade, we will track the decline in this genre's popularity and highlight some of the reasons why it took so long for the sitcom to reach such quantitative heights once again. But first, we must discuss the original sitcom boom—a movement that had essentially been developing since the quick success of *I Love Lucy* in the 1951–1952 season, when Desilu's first TV endeavor finished the year as the country's third-most-watched show, ascending into the coveted #1 slot during 1952–1953, 1953–1954, and again here, in 1954–1955.[1] From the moment the sitcom genre had its first hit unique to this new medium, many looked to *Lucy* as an inspiration for possible success, accelerating already burgeoning trends, like the shift of programming from live to film and the accompanying transition from New York to Hollywood as the industry's hub. The sitcom certainly reflected these changes, with *I Love Lucy* as the most sterling and therefore guiding example, demonstrating this to be an incredibly lucrative form.

Of course, our study has proven that the sitcom is an art form hinged on a set of standards—specifically, that the established elements of some situation should inspire both the episodic narratives and the pursued comedy. Accordingly, quantity does not equal quality—that is, the more sitcoms there are, the clearer it becomes how difficult it is to find ones that actually validate the form's unique terms and the artistry that makes it beautiful. What we find with most sitcoms—and most of the ones that existed in 1954–1955, during the genre's first peak—is that they fail to be great or even good because they are unable to create a regular, reliable link between their weekly storytelling apparatus and the elements that make up their sustaining situations (propped up most especially by character). The shows that can manage to put in practice a definitive association are the ones worth watching, and they are made more brilliant by their seeming scarcity—even within a TV season like this, where the schedules were overflowing with young samples.

*I Love Lucy* remained the genre's high-water mark for a reason. In its third season, the series had started to run out of stories directly related to Lucy Ricardo's central objective of pursuing a career in show business. Instead, scripts had to branch out to plots that otherwise revealed her wider objective of escaping the confining bounds of typical housewifery. This kept the show in top shape, but today, Season Three is less favored by fans. For Season Four, *I Love Lucy*'s scribes—still Jess Oppenheimer; Madelyn Pugh; and Bob Carroll, Jr.—found a way to reinvigorate the series by strengthening the connection between character and story *through* the original show biz tension, offering a narrative arc about Ricky Ricardo testing for a part in a Hollywood movie, landing it, and then taking the family (plus their friends, the Mertzes) cross-country to California, where he would work at the studio over a period of several months. This proved to be an incredibly popular storyline—like the baby shows of Season Two, it's a narrative arc with an endgame goal that provides focus for episodic plots, giving scripts a temporary addition to the series' situation and another way to engage with an established element for story. It also provides slight serialization; episodes themselves are complete, but a larger narrative idea persists.

Yet this arc is even better than the baby, for it involves Ricky's career, and given Lucy's guiding objective of making it in show business as well, this storyline forces direct conflict related to these foundational aspects of both their characterizations. Therefore, this isn't just a new wrinkle to the situation—it's a wrinkle that speaks to the series' central premise, as evidenced by the characters who define it. For that reason, this is indeed one of the best seasons of *I Love Lucy*, and in fact, of the seven episodes from the 1954–1955 season that make my top 50 list, all of them belong to this series—nothing else is *as* excellent here, even during this sitcom boom.

Installments like "Ricky's Movie Offer" (November 8, 1954) and "Ricky's Screen Test" (November 15, 1954) are great examples of how this opportunity for Ricky naturally ignites Lucy's ambitions, creating episodic problems directly motivated by her goal and this seminal aspect of her characterization. Then, following a handful of stories that continue this narrative thought—with preparations to travel cross-country leading to a three-week stint on the road—the foursome finally arrives in Hollywood for a classic offering where Lucy makes a fool of herself by gawking at celebrities in the famous Brown Derby, before trying to avoid further embarrassment for Ricky when William Holden, the star she slighted (with a pie in the face) at said eatery, shows up in their hotel room. It's one of the series' best-remembered episodes and the highlight of this year.

▶ Unsurprisingly, "**L.A. at Last!**" comes in high on my list—at **#9**—for its story about Lucy embarrassing herself at the Brown Derby represents a new way for the show to invoke its premise via her characterization. It was, of course, written by **Jess Oppenheimer, Madelyn Pugh,** and **Bob Carroll, Jr.**; directed by **William Asher**; and first aired on **February 7, 1955**.

Now, its story may seem to have nothing to do with Lucy's original objective; hunting stars may seem like an episodic desire for a run-of-the-mill nuisance that's more in the spirit of Joan Stevens of *I Married Joan* than Lucy Ricardo of *I Love Lucy*. But there *is* a definite association between this motivation and Lucy's ultimate desire to be in show business, for even this chance to rub elbows with the rich and famous in the iconic Brown Derby restaurant offers Lucy the kind of excitement and glamour she seeks in her everyday life, reminding us of her obsession with this elite industry, while making her feel important by proxy—a desire at the heart of her being. Again, the crux of most *I Love Lucy* outings is the tension of Lucy Ricardo wanting to be more than just the "typical" housewife and mother. So when Lucy goes crazy star hunting (and harassing) in Hollywood, the show is not only indulging weekly stunt casting gimmicks as it enters the latter half of its life (and let's be clear, this kind of movie star stunt casting *is* a gimmick, even if the series' show biz situation supports it), but it's also better attaching itself again to Lucy as a story-driving character via the invocation of her show biz–specific aims. "L.A. at Last!" is a particular gem because it is the funniest and simplest representation of this new type of story, which is enabled by the show's move to L.A. as part of this believable, rejuvenating narrative arc.

▶ Lucy's feverish crusade to meet the stars becomes a running part of her characterization throughout the show's stay in Hollywood, growing into another core facet of her comic identity. It's not only evidenced in the classic "L.A. at Last!" but also in "**The Star Upstairs**" in which Lucy goes to great lengths to sneak upstairs for a peek at hotel guest Cornel Wilde, who plays himself. It first aired on **April 18, 1955**, and shows up on my list at **#27**. **Oppenheimer**, **Pugh**, and **Carroll** are again responsible for the script, while **Asher**, as resident director, staged the action.

"The Star Upstairs" is best remembered for the hilarious sight gag that begins when Lucy, who has ignored Ricky's wishes and sneaked up to Cornel Wilde's penthouse by masquerading as Bobby the bellboy, ends up trapped outside on his balcony. As she tries to lower herself down to the Ricardos', where Ethel waits to assist her, Ricky enters his room and Ethel is forced to distract him from the sight of Lucy, swinging aimlessly in the background on a rope made out of clothes. It's absolutely riotous, made hysterical by Vivian Vance's frenzied performance when Lucy falls. This is one of the funniest moments of the entire series—a centerpiece earned by Lucy's objective of meeting Cornel Wilde, all because she so craves to be even close to this glamorous industry.

▶ There are many other character-driven stories that result from this arc as well. Lucy also takes this time in Hollywood to naturally further her own dreams, as seen in episodes like "**Lucy Gets Into Pictures**," which first aired on **February 21, 1955**, and comes in at **#11**. Like everything from this season, it was written by **Oppenheimer**, **Pugh**, and **Carroll** and directed by **Asher**.

This is another popular entry that features a big physical comedy centerpiece, as Lucy is cast in a film where she's tasked with playing a showgirl who gets murdered. But descending down a set of stairs while wearing a giant headdress proves difficult—a physical reminder that the intensity of her desire to make it in show biz is not matched by actual talent or ability. It is a necessary story for the Hollywood arc, giving Lucy a chance at what she's always wanted—not even Ricky is standing in her way this time—only for her to screw it up with her lack of experience. It's pure Lucy Ricardo, and Ball does some of her best physical comedy ever here.

▶ Lucy actually has more success as a performer when she dances with Van Johnson in "The Dancing Star" (May 2, 1955), an affable entry where she's less motivated by show biz dreams than the mere delight of one-upping her frenemy and housewife rival Carolyn Appleby (Doris Singleton), who also appears in the well-remembered "**Harpo Marx**," where Lucy brags about her Hollywood lifestyle and then must make good by producing a star. These two segments are rooted in another key aspect of Lucy's characterization—her efforts to *seem like* she's more than what she is, which imply an image consciousness that recurs in her depiction. And the latter, which aired on **May 9, 1955**, makes my list at **#42**—a tour de force for Ball as she does the famous "mirror routine" with the eponymous Harpo Marx, one of the funniest clowns of the century.

Yet another type of story in this era revolves around Lucy's attempts to further Ricky's career—that is, her efforts to use her own assets and drive to move *him* up in the world, thereby elevating her station as well. This is evidenced in entries like "Don Juan Is Shelved" (March 21, 1955) and the especially hilarious "Ricky Needs an Agent" (May 16, 1955), where Lucy's plan masquerading as Ricky's agent accidentally get him released from his studio contract. It's also a great showing for Ricky as well, who shines in a centerpiece where his hot temper explodes.

All of these episodes reveal the Hollywood arc to be a strong collection for character and comedy, granting the series a boost of energy from a reconnection with the premise's original show biz trappings, which better activate the Lucy characterization, specifically, for conflicts explicitly related to her central objective, which is naturally at the fore when she's rubbing elbows with movie stars. For that reason, this is a candidate for the best season of *I Love Lucy*. And it's hard to quarrel with the episodic results. Heck, even before the cast gets to Hollywood, the show is firing on all cylinders. Offerings like the aforementioned "Ricky's Screen Test" and "Lucy Learns to Drive" (January 3, 1955) help set up the trip with stories that mine their laughs from known aspects of the Lucy character, earning big comedic centerpieces because of this support.

▶ And then as the foursome goes cross-country, there are lots of ha-has in entries like the gag-heavy "First Stop" (January 17, 1955) and the Ethel-centered "**Ethel's Home Town**" in which the characters stop in Albuquerque and discover that Ethel has told her family that the reason she's going to Hollywood is to make a movie of her own. This outing, which first aired on **January 31, 1955**, is a standout excursion (there's no other like it) and it makes my list at **#41**.

"Ethel's Hometown" is unique because it centralizes Vivian Vance's Ethel, the former vaudevillian whose Albuquerque upbringings, themselves inspired by Vance's own past, have been referenced throughout the run of the show. This entry is thus supported by the continuity surrounding her character and what we know of it. Its conflict is also show biz-related, for her lie about her MGM fortunes plays into the ongoing arc and naturally irks the others—her vaudeville partner, the star who's really going to Hollywood, and the housewife who wants nothing more than to be in show business herself. So when the script wisely creates a concert climax starring the now big-headed Ethel, it's a chance for the bitter trio to upstage her in a comedic set piece that features them all well, while validating their histories *and* the very specific thematic tension that doesn't only exist because of Lucy and Ricky but is also aided and abetted by the Mertzes.

▶ Ethel also shares the spotlight in "**Ethel's Birthday**," which has a simple story about a fight that erupts between the two best pals when Ethel unknowingly insults Lucy's taste. First aired on **November 29, 1954**, this installment is **#24** on my top 50 list.

"Ethel's Birthday" has nothing to do with the year's Hollywood arc and it may sound more generic—like something any show could do with two best friends. But just as with many of the best offerings from the previous season, *I Love Lucy* tailors a fairly ordinary idea to its characters. That makes it genius when the specifics of this situation inspire the laughs and the story. It starts with Fred asking Lucy to pick out Ethel's birthday present for him because Ethel's never satisfied when he, the well-known cheapskate, is left to his own devices. Lucy decides that Fred should get Ethel a pair of "hostess" pants—a garish garment that doesn't resemble anything else in Ethel's wardrobe. When Ethel finds the hidden gift and opens it in front of Lucy, she naturally begins to insult "Fred's" taste, not realizing who really picked them out. This sparks a fight where the ladies insult each other—an argument that only works because we believe that Lucy and Ethel have different ideas of what's fashionable, based on who we know them to be.

That is, flashy Lucy differs from the more practical Ethel, who would have preferred a toaster, and that's at the heart of their disagreement—rooted in an elemental contrast that's been evident for the entire run of the series. There's also the added layer of what the gift says about their views of each other—would Lucy actually wear such an odd outfit, or is that merely her perception of what *Ethel* would think is fashionable? And what *does* Ethel really think about wacky Lucy's taste? This becomes a character conflict, you see, and a revealing one at that. Of course, the best pals reunite by the half hour's end—when they are stuck sitting next to each other at a Broadway show: a show bizzy device that locks this entry even more firmly into *I Love Lucy*'s ethos. So although "Ethel's Birthday" starts out seeming like an ordinary sitcom episode, it's really a deft display of *Lucy*'s precise situation via its precise characters.

▶ And that's not even all. I have one more episode from this gem-filled season that makes my top 50 list and needs to be highlighted. It's another selection not related to the Hollywood arc—"**Mr. and Mrs. TV Show**," which aired on non-CBS affiliates that were carrying the series on **November 1, 1954**, but was first shown on most CBS stations, with a flashback open, on **April 11, 1955**.² Its plot is about Lucy and Ricky being cast in a husband-and-wife morning TV show. With such a ripe foundation for comic conflict, this entry makes my esteemed list at **#10**.

"Mr. and Mrs. TV Show" is quintessential *Lucy*, as the title character's ambitions propel her to create an opportunity for both her and Ricky to star together on a morning TV show, where they would essentially play versions of themselves. Ricky is loath to the idea of appearing on television with Lucy and insults her. But when the sponsor is adamant that she be included (along with the Mertzes), he is forced to pretend that he wants her with him after all. The show seems to be going well in rehearsal—it's a chance for the *Lucy* scribes to spoof this very niche genre of programming: the artificial chat/news morning show—until Lucy learns of Ricky's deception. Ever the schemer, she aims to get back at her husband by embarrassing him and the sponsor during the dress rehearsal. However, what she thinks is the dress rehearsal is actually the broadcast. This mistake is perhaps a convenient way for Lucy to bungle her chance at success, but it's set up well by Ricky—with a motivation that makes sense—and her failure is indeed earned by a known aspect of her characterization: her childlike habit of vengeful scheming, which we've seen her do frequently in pursuit of her goals. Here, it backfires, and in a show biz story where Lucy could have gotten everything she ever wanted—fame in show business alongside her husband.

It's a hilarious entry, and it's not even part of the Hollywood arc, which, though a great way for the series to open up new opportunities with regard to its title character and her unique objective, implies a little bit of atrophy within the storytelling. Uncoincidentally, the next two seasons of *I Love Lucy* will go on the road more often and traffic in even *more* guest star cameos. They inevitably reframe our understanding of this Hollywood venture as the first in a trend—the first example of the series literally changing its locale to create fresh story, which is otherwise getting harder to conceive. Of course, compared to the European tour, the Florida trip, and the country move, this Hollywood stay is *Lucy*'s most successful—the most believable, the most rooted in the series' identity. But it still represents the fact that this show is no longer comfortable staying at home in its characters' usual situation for a long time. It essentially marks the end of *I Love Lucy*'s original form—there aren't many gems like "Mr. and Mrs. TV Show" ahead.

Nevertheless, the fact that this series remains as excellent as it does throughout the duration of its run *despite* these gimmicky maneuverings is a true testament to the leading players and how they can help support story by making even unmotivated changes to the situation showcase their specific, well-defined personalities. And as for Season Four itself, even if I think its choices do not augur well for the series' *future* health, I must reiterate that it is a total triumph as far as this year is concerned, allowing *Lucy* to, once again, be the toast of the season: the finest sitcom on TV. And there are more than a dozen classic half hours of comedy in this collection alone as proof.

## The Film Industry—of Television

With *I Love Lucy* still on top, the Arnazes continued to expand the Desilu empire, contributing to the year's sitcom boom with several more of their own, including shows that they merely helped film (for other companies), like *Our Miss Brooks*, now in its third TV season for CBS, *Make Room for Daddy*, now in its second season for Danny Thomas's company (with Sheldon Leonard), and the newly retitled *The Ray Bolger Show*, which was produced by Ray Bolger but entered its second and final season with more help from Desilu, adopting the multi-camera live audience format.[3] This live audience boosted the energy and was a natural fit for a star who had a theatrical background, but even with this change in style and a tweak in the ensemble cast to accompany this slight retooling, the series remained merely a vehicle for its song-and-dance man to sing and dance, with situation comedy—characters rendered comedically in episodic story—taking a figurative back seat. As for *Our Miss Brooks*, the TV adaptation had run out of good radio scripts by this point in its run and was already growing narratively stale, struggling to concoct stories that could emphasize the central relationships. Too often now, it engages silly plots for which the depictions of the leads are largely irrelevant. In fact, the following season will find *Brooks* undergoing a major retooling of its own—an attempt at rejuvenating a concept that had lost its freshness in the seven years since its radio premiere.

*Make Room for Daddy*, a sophomore offering from ABC, was in much better shape than the two above, continuing to enjoy all its original premised constructs but with gradually less sentimentality, as the kids were already getting more to do—bursting the bubble of "cuteness" that so often allows sitcoms heavy on children to avoid being funny. No, *Daddy* always wants to have laughs—perhaps not as much as *I Love Lucy*, but as these parenting sitcoms with fallible patriarchs go, this one remains one of the best, with children who add to the series' comedic charms. Thomas's show also continues to enjoy its established show business gloss as well—one of the qualities often associated with Desilu sitcoms (like *Lucy*) and very evident in another of the company's own produced offerings, *Those Whiting Girls*, a 13-episode multi-cam live audience effort that took *Lucy*'s spot on CBS's schedule during the summer of 1955.[4] It was built for the Whiting sisters—successful chanteuse Margaret and her little sister Barbara, who wanted so much to be like Margaret. There's not much to the situation of the series beyond this basic arrangement, which allows Barbara to be a menace to her older sister and their mother (played by Mabel Albertson, later of *Bewitched*), with room for other celebrity guests and, of course, a weekly song by Margaret herself. Little changed when the show was brought back for another 13-week run in the summer of 1957, now with Jerry Paris (later of *The Dick Van Dyke Show*) as Margaret's accompanist.

As for the quality of *Those Whiting Girls*, the series was created by Bob Carroll, Jr. and Madelyn Pugh of *I Love Lucy*, and like *Lucy*, the premise used autobiographical details of its star's life (although keeping her less successful, more economically relatable) and enjoyed the multi-camera format's comic push. What's more, it also gave one of its characters a similar objective—Barbara wants to be in show business just as much as Lucy does, given that her family member is in it. Accordingly, you might expect *Those Whiting Girls* to be a decent sitcom, for it enjoys so much of what made Lucy structurally poised for excellence. But unfortunately, Barbara's motivation is not as well attached to story as Lucy Ricardo's—that means, too many episodic plots are merely keeping her a Joan Stevens–esque nuisance as opposed to a woman with a *want*—and the cast as a whole is not nearly as helpful. Barbara Whiting is not nearly as strong an actress as Lucille Ball, and Margaret is way too bland and undefined to be like Desi Arnaz's Ricky, leaving the character work, en masse, relatively vague and underdeveloped compared to *I Love Lucy*.

Speaking of show business, Desilu also managed to inject an industry backdrop into another new series they produced—*Willy*, a multi-cam that premiered in September 1954 as a vehicle for June Havoc (sister of Gypsy Rose Lee), playing a former vaudeville star who's since changed her life and become a small-town lawyer in rural New Hampshire. The ensemble cast included her father, a judge (Lloyd Corrigan), her widowed sister (Mary Treen), and her veterinarian boyfriend (Whitfield Connor). Initially in a terrible 10:30 p.m. slot, the series failed to catch on and was rescheduled and retooled mid-season, with the eponymous Willy moving to the big city to represent a vaudeville troupe—an added show biz element that, perhaps given Havoc's own background, might have made more sense for her from the beginning. This new cast boasted Harold Peary and Sterling Holloway,[5] but it was too little too late, and the series was canceled after this one season. Today, despite being filmed, very little of the show circulates among collectors, so it's difficult to get a full picture of *Willy*'s strengths and weaknesses. But based on what I've seen and researched, I'd say the design of the ensemble didn't give Willy enough support from her situation in episodic story, forcing the show to rely too much on her lawyerly job and the "case of the week" (or the guest star of the week, when she moves to New York).

However, if *Willy* proved to be a flop, Desilu had much greater success with another new sitcom that premiered in the fall of 1954. This one was free of show biz motifs, and it actually didn't need them, for it was simply at the right place at the right time—right behind *Lucy* on CBS's Monday night schedule, to be exact. The show in question was *December Bride*, a mediocre radio sitcom created by Parke Levy (*Duffy's Tavern* and *My Friend Irma*) that managed to eke out a five-year-run on TV because it spent its first four seasons right next to the country's most popular comedy, reaping the benefits of this proximity. It starred the nevertheless affable Spring Byington as Lily Ruskin, who moves in with her daughter and her daughter's new husband—only there's a catch: this mother-in-law actually *gets along* with her son-in-law! Now, one might be tempted to think this is a refreshing choice—avoiding the common clichés—but this premised congeniality ultimately proves foolish, for it mitigates situation-based relational conflict, especially because both of the "kids"—married couple Ruth and Matt—have no personality whatsoever and therefore no way to inspire story on their own. Unfortunately, their living arrangement—the very premise of *December Bride*—proves to be a narrative dead end as well since none of their relationships are allowed to have any inherent dramatic tension that could also spark conflict. As it stands, all the show has for episodic fodder is Lily's basic personality trait—she's a touch daffy—and the fact that she's searching for another husband. That objective is used most often here in Season One, but it fades over time, and it's seldom of major importance, while again, there are no interpersonal clashes that give weight to story inside of the series' own premise.

The best parts of *December Bride* are the other two main players in its ensemble, one of whom is Harry Morgan (later of *M\*A\*S\*H*) as wisecracking neighbor Pete Porter—a Fred Mertz–like figure who makes mother-in-law jokes about his own wife Gladys, an unseen shrew who would remain off-screen until their 1960 spin-off series, *Pete and Gladys* (which proved to be another *I Married Joan*—with a manic wife who causes weekly problems for her dispirited husband, just because she's a general nuisance). Pete is reliable for peripheral ha-has, and considering that this is a multi-camera live audience Desilu sitcom, the show does endeavor to be laugh-out-loud funny. Fortunately, it also has another ringer in its ensemble with Verna Felton as Hilda Crocker—added a few weeks into the TV run as a sidekick for Lily. Felton was a popular character actress of the day—best known in the sitcom world for playing Dennis Day's overbearing mother on his and Jack Benny's shows, with a booming, menacing voice that the Disney Studios also frequently employed, and a matronly figure that, on *December Bride*, contrasted well against Hilda's spry and youthful verve, especially with regard to her own romantic pursuits. She is a material elevator—someone who improves what's on the page by the sheer force of her performance and is even game to offer some slapstick, all to boost the series' humor quotient.

So the funniest episodes of *December Bride* tend to make smart use of either Hilda or Pete—the series' only two comedically defined characters—but it's otherwise a sitcom with not enough "sit." It's light on conflict and too many of its leads are fatally bland, which means story is often unoriginal and not tailored to them specifically. Despite a handful of agreeable elements—Byington's presence and the work of both Morgan and Felton—it is always far below its lead-in, *I Love Lucy*, in terms of merit. And there's nothing episodically great here in its first season; well, there's nothing episodically great in any season. But we'll keep track of it anyway.

Meanwhile, the Desilu influence continued to extend beyond just Desilu. As we have noted, there were other shows that tried to cash in on *Lucy*'s success, such as *Private Secretary*, a workplace comedy anchored by Ann Sothern, a glamorous movie star and contemporary of Lucille Ball. Now in its third season during 1954–1955, the show was still chugging along, neither as hilarious nor character-rooted as its simple design should have encouraged. Even worse were *My Little Margie*, another single-camera filmed sitcom that took the basic idea of a female aggravator and her constant scheming, and *I Married Joan*, which employed the beleaguered husband and screwball wife setup—both of them failing to link their stories to the well-motivated choices of well-defined characters, opting instead for silly, broad comedy that does not always play well, for unlike *Lucy*, it's not grounded enough by the continuity of a regular situation with strong regulars. It's just ridiculousness for ridiculousness' sake. That remains true in *Margie*'s fourth season and *Joan*'s third— both of their final hurrahs. (*Private Secretary* has two years left.)

Additionally, other previously discussed single-cams that ended this season include the high-concept supernatural sitcom *Topper*, which had an interesting premise not backed by a strong enough use of its leads in story, and the retooled second year of the renamed *The Ray Milland Show*, which was just as starved of character as it was as *Meet Mr. McNutley*. Joining them on the exit ramp was *Trouble with Father*, now in its fourth and final season following an entire year of reruns. After a season away, the show was returning to a landscape that had essentially outpaced it. At one time, it was television's only example of the domestic family sitcom with a bumbling, fallible patriarch, but stories can no longer satisfy that notion as well as they had in earlier years, especially now with increased competition. This season got more of a budget, however, and also found the series adding in a laugh track—adopting what had since become the industry standard for filmed single-camera shows— while plots follow the engagement and marriage of Stu's (recast) eldest daughter and the elevated Sheila James as tomboy Jackie.

But the central premise—the comic notion of a father not being an effective head of house—was no longer as novel for story, particularly since the medium had cultivated a regular place for better, more interesting bumbling dads, like radio's more formative example, Chester A. Riley of *The Life of Riley*, now in its third season with original star William Bendix, whose pathos continues to infuse the role with the working-class angst that makes him relatively unique in this subgenre. Sadly, stories are not as adept at hitting those class-based themes as in earlier years. It's only because of the central character's long continuity on radio that *Riley* still manages to feel more fully realized than the otherwise bland example of a rote family sitcom it actually evidences.

However, the best of the father-led family subgenre during this time is *The Adventures of Ozzie and Harriet*, which, it must be remembered, is still benign in comparison to this era's other great sitcoms, for there's not as much ridiculousness or incongruity with either the characterizations or the storytelling—meaning it's not as well poised for big, boffo comedy, let alone big boffo comedy linked to these regulars and their situation. And yet, because the series is always benign, the best episodes are not the ones that endeavor *not* to be—those inherently fail. No, the best episodes are the ones that lean into this benignity, offering episodic ideas *so* trivial, *so* low stakes, and *so* dramatically irrelevant that the show is almost winking about its low-concept simplicity, mocking its stylistic inertia and thereby deriving humor from a subtle commentary about the way in which it's benign—pointing out that it's *so benign it might as well be ridiculous.* This allows the series to actually be funny,

**Harriet Nelson (left) and real-life husband Ozzie play versions of themselves in *The Adventures of Ozzie and Harriet*, "The Furnace" (1954).**

and when it uses its one well-defined characterization, the fallible patriarch Ozzie, a conservative yet neurotic head of house who is full of advice that he has trouble following himself, *Ozzie and Harriet* truly is able to deliver unique situation comedy, supported by the continuity of his gentle, yet pinpointable, characterization.

This season, the series' third, is even better about offering enjoyable sitcommery than its predecessors, producing a handful of episodes that smartly utilize Ozzie within trivial stories that emphasize the show's unique comic identity. The best entries are "The Furnace" (October 22, 1954), where Ozzie and Harriet disagree over the temperature of the house—a small, relatable argument that becomes ridiculous because of Ozzie's motivated scheming; "Odd Bolt" (December 10, 1954), where Ozzie's obsession with something so trivial creates an ironically small adventure that makes for series-validating comedy; "Individuality" (January 28, 1955), which expressly rails against the suburban sameness that most of these 1950s family shows collectively embody; "The Sports Car" (March 11, 1955), where laughs are derived from the juxtaposition of Ozzie's (and his show's) conservative persona against the ostentatiousness of a flashy sports car; and "Thorny's Piano" (May 6, 1955), in which the series plays with Ozzie's need to be right by haunting him with a nightmare—a frequent device that *Ozzie and Harriet* likes to deploy, for it offers another way for the series to comment on its own action and reveal a comedic commentary.

None of these are as expertly crafted as the highlighted *Lucy* segments from earlier in the chapter, but they succinctly explain how *Ozzie and Harriet* manages to be a cut above the rest of the other father-focused single-cams in this domestic format, both because of how these stories contextualize their inherent benignity and also by how they find a way to deliver—through Ozzie—some form of situation or character-specific credibility to otherwise small notions. Naturally, *Ozzie and Harriet* may not seem hilarious when compared to *I Love Lucy*—or several of the classics we will discuss in the next half of the book, like *The Honeymooners* and *The Phil Silvers Show*—but there are other patriarch-centered suburban family shows from this era that prove the Nelsons' comic dominance by contrast. I am referring specifically now to *Father Knows Best*: the nadir of uncomedic benignity within this specific subgenre, giving the entire 1950s decade—which is best remembered *for* these types of bland family shows—a bad, anti-sitcom reputation.

## *Pleasantville and the Cummings Rebuttal*

*Father Knows Best*, a filmed single-camera sitcom starring Robert Young and Jane Wyatt as a suburban couple with three kids, survived an early cancellation by jumping networks, ultimately enjoying a six-year run as one of the most Emmy-nominated television programs of the decade.[6] It's since helped define a lot of what we still think about today when imagining 1950s comedies, which, in media references like *Pleasantville* (1998), have become synonymous with picture-perfect suburban domesticity, reflecting a lifestyle that many Americans in the postwar era were practicing, as urban flight increased and the baby boom tied a plurality of citizens (nearly 45%)[7] into a similar nuclear family structure. The shows that embraced this design—however idealized—have thus come to symbolize this era of the sitcom as well, for most studies of this genre look outward-in, deriving value from social commentary as much as, or more than, artistic merit. Of course, when using *Father Knows Best* as a primary text, I understand why: artistic merit is hard to find.

It's a "sitcom" that actively rejects opportunities to be funny because its characters are intentionally benign, for they are not allowed to have traits that would make them too ridiculous. It's a "sitcom" that does not have stories motivated by its leads, for they do not have traits that would *allow* them to directly inspire plots, which instead are unoriginal and banal, but without the winking impulse of *Ozzie and Harriet*. And it's a "sitcom" that, frankly, could not ever represent this genre well as a case study, for it's anchored by a stern patriarch who is less a comic figure than a moral compass for a passel of kids who must learn repeatable lessons in the course of their growing up. Okay, *Leave It to Beaver*'s Ward Cleaver will follow in Jim Anderson's footsteps, but otherwise, we've seen that a goofy, imperfect father—Stu Erwin, Chester A. Riley, Ozzie Nelson—is the more common trope. The head of the house tends to be the head of the comedy, particularly if he's also the star. That's sort of expected.

Robert Young endeavored to buck this trend,[8] intentionally moving away from the early radio iteration of his series, which was performed in front of a live audience and thus courted bigger laughs via a more caustic, sarcastic father character who made the *Father Knows Best* title ironic,[9] someone less perfect or all-knowing than the dad on this consequently more serious TV update, where he starts in Season One with a few rare but noticeable traces of a rough edge before it's smoothed out for the rest of the run so that he's completely straightforward and unerring—no more irony. And with no one in the cast well-defined either—comedically or otherwise—all stories quickly become confined to domestic clichés, rotating between the kids. Now, I could try to *squint* and generously say that Elinor Donahue's Betty maybe cares too much about her image and that is her defining trait, that Billy Gray's Bud is perhaps clumsy and awkward and that most colors his usage, and that Lauren Chapin's Kathy is possibly precocious from time to time. But frankly, they seldom (if ever) act in ways that are not common to every other kid or teen in fiction, so even if we're reading between the lines to find a continuity of characterization for them, it's all so relatively generic and not tied to individualized details that it doesn't matter. The character work is scant and not well-evidenced within narrative anyway.

Also, it goes without saying, but Jim's wife Margaret has *absolutely* no definition—zero personality, barely any history, no unique way of existing in plot. Contrary to her depiction and the similarly confining model of happy suburbanism as spoofed in *Pleasantville* and all post-1950s representations of this era in entertainment, she is not the way most 1950s sitcom women were rendered; she gives them all—Lucy and Miss Brooks and Gracie—a bland, inaccurate name, for she is simply the blandest of an entire cast that is similarly pitched.

This handicap is caused by the fact that Robert Young demanded these characters not be contorted in ways actually conducive for laugh-out-loud comedy.[10] A laugh track was added per the industry's current standard for filmed half hours, but many episodes are not even slightly comedic, with a humorlessness guaranteed by the blandness of the leads and the too-earnest storytelling, which occasionally branches out into outright drama, thereby confirming an even more macro problem: there's seldom a link between the weekly plots and these regulars' situation, because they're not well-defined enough for that to even be possible. For instance, scripts about a son trying to leave home,[11] a teen elopement misunderstanding,[12] a kid raising a bird[13] could exist on *any* family show, funny or not, and there's little personalization. In fact, *The Donna Reed Show* would eventually crib a handful of scripts from this series, but with a focus around the matriarch, making it a sort of distaff *Father Knows Best*—yet both equally dull.

Otherwise, this lack of comic color does render *Father Knows Best* an outlier in the mid 1950s. Unlike *The Life of Riley* with its working-class angst, or *Ozzie and Harriet*, which had Ozzie, its wink, and eventually the pop sensation of Ricky Nelson, or *Leave It to Beaver*, which boasted two really funny kids at the center, *Father Knows Best* does not care if comedy is a low priority every week, and it's therefore light on both comic characters and funny, motivated stories. So there is nothing here that I can recommend. All I want to do is castigate it for being allowed—in media—to symbolize this era's sitcoms so unfavorably. And again, inaccurately, for very few shows are as willfully allergic to the habits necessary for laughs, preferring instead something more tranquil and pleasant, with all quirks or extremes rooted out.

To that point, even if the false perfection of the unfunny *Father Knows Best* is somewhat countered by those fallible patriarch sitcoms constituting the more dominant trend in this subgenre, they nevertheless still honor the nuclear family as a popular ideal. Sure, they tease the world gently and highlight silly things in it, but they draw a contrast between ridiculous characters and their otherwise happy status quos. And they all exemplify a certain homogeny. Was there anything else?

That is the tantalizing question at the heart of a new sitcom that premiered during this same season. It was produced under a leg of George Burns's company McCadden, which in 1954–1955 was still filming *Burns and Allen*, then in its fifth season and in good-but-not-great shape. The company's flagship series was running out of new ideas and trying to fill the void by introducing Blanche's mooching brother as a recurring foil, not really offering fresh situation comedy for its funny regulars, namely Gracie, who needed better stimuli. Fortunately, the following season would take inspiration from *I Love Lucy*, bringing the show cross-country and introducing a major change in format (debuting Ronnie Burns) that would boost its fortunes. We will discuss that more later. In the meantime, while *Burns and Allen* temporarily was going through the motions, McCadden was otherwise booming by following Desilu's lead and expanding its production empire, taking over the filming duties of previously live Hollywood sitcoms *Life with Father* and *That's My Boy*, both of which completed their second and final seasons in 1954–1955. Like *Burns and Allen*, they were both shot with multiple cameras but like a single cam, and not in front of a live studio audience.

However, the crown jewel of McCadden, aside from *Burns and Allen*, was this new show to which I alluded above—premiering in January 1955 as a counter to the idealized family depicted on dreck like *Father Knows Best*. It's *The Bob Cummings Show*, more commonly known in syndication as *Love That Bob*, a showcase for movie star Bob Cummings, who a few years earlier had headlined a single-season flop called *My Hero* (see Chapter Five). This new series suited him much better, affording him the chance to play a role more matched to his natural persona. Cummings was now Bob Collins, a swinging bachelor photographer and air force reserve officer whose life has recently changed since he agreed to take in his widowed sister Margaret (Rosemary DeCamp) and her teenage son Chuck (Dwayne Hickman), for whom he now serves as a proxy father and inspiration, as Chuck idolizes Uncle Bob and his sexy, glamorous world.

The conflict, then? Bob has essentially been *forced* into a domestic structure and the role of patriarch—choices that are at odds with his existence as a perennial playboy. Now everyone, it seems, is determined to upend his lifestyle—like Margaret, who hopes to find him a nice woman and settle him down, or his now-married friends, like Harvey (King Donovan), who wants to saddle him with the same responsibilities they've taken on, or the many elderly women in the neighborhood, who adore Bob and want to pair him off with one of their many daughters/nieces. And then, of course, there's Schultzy, played by Ann B. Davis (later of *The Brady Bunch*), who loves Bob and feverishly pursues him, all while he himself hunts gorgeous models and tries desperately to get the rest of the world off his figurative back—especially Schultzy and Margaret, both of whom he hopes to pawn off on anyone except his horny pal Paul Fonda (Lyle Talbot), who's a "wolf" like Bob.

To that point, watching *Bob Cummings* in the context of today's social understanding often raises issues of sexism and misogyny, as women on the show are essentially categorized in three ways—they are maternal and must be protected (Margaret), they are homely and make for best pals (Schultzy), or they are desirable and only for casual fun (the models, including Joi Lansing's recurring Shirley). However, with so much of the show predicated on sex, the men get similarly categorized as to perceived standards of virility—the puppy who has a lot to learn (Chuck), the wolf who can teach him (Bob), and the neutered dog who got leashed (Harvey). What's more, Bob Collins seldom gets the girl when he lies, and if it seems like scripts are going out of their way to make women the butt of the joke more often—particularly Schultzy or Nancy Kulp (later of *The Beverly Hillbillies*) as the recurring Pamela Livingstone—it is Bob's shallow way of viewing the opposite sex that often gets him in trouble. Rest assured, he is punished for his sins. In fact, the series' foundational tension stems from his refusal to change—his unwillingness to bend to the dominant way of life in the postwar era: the nuclear family, with the contrast between *Bob Cummings* and all those other domestic shows, such as *Father Knows Best*, a subliminal but intended frame of reference, for in being a sitcom with funny, well-defined leads, this is a much more enjoyable, lively series to watch—a fact that has the perhaps unintended effect of celebrating Bob Collins's resistance, or at least allowing his lifestyle to come across as fun and exciting, mining comic drama from the clash of expectations—what is "normal" and what is "Bob."

In this regard, *Bob Cummings* is a fascinating sitcom because it really uses its era's ideals—reflected in many other series of the 1950s, like those aforementioned—to predicate the benign incongruity of its premise, allowing Bob to constantly fight the "normal." And although perhaps seldom achieving his episodic goals, he *is* able to routinely prove that this incongruity is *okay* by maintaining his affable status quo—where, yes, he is forced to act as a proxy-patriarch for his sister and her teenage son, but he is also allowed to have a full dating life or, rather, sex life, pursuing the kind of women and at least *part* of the lifestyle he prefers. Thus, the inherent clash of perspectives within the concept is maintained, and the series smartly roots natural conflict in a notion that is always comedic, thanks to his inherent but benign incongruity. Thematically, then, this is one of the smartest sitcoms of the 1950s—atypically positioning itself against the time's main ambassadors and ridiculing them via the obvious contrast in entertainment value, even as there's also laugh-yielding ridiculousness in this show *from* its characters as well (especially Bob himself).

Accordingly, *Bob Cummings* is a testament to great character writing, for it is not an idea-led satire merely critiquing the domestic ideal suggested in *Father Knows Best*. Rather, it is having fun caricaturing someone who resists said lifestyle, and by simply making him such a rich, interesting character in his own right, both he and his show—which represents said resistance—come across as more dynamic, more fun. If those actual nuclear family sitcoms, like *Father Knows Best*, allowed themselves to have stronger leads, with traits that actually *allowed* them to be funny and address naturally benign incongruities of their suburban life (some of which *Ozzie and Harriet* is occasionally able to find), perhaps the stereotypical depiction of domesticity that is fought by Bob Collins, and remembered by viewers today who think derisively of all 1950s sitcoms, would not be so ripe for challenging in a comedic context. That is, *because* it lacks funny characters, *Father Knows Best*—and everything it represents to viewers who remember or ponder this era of sitcommery—isn't compelling.

But *The Bob Cummings Show* is. This is because, of course, the series does have funny characters and, in fact, gives them all something to seek in story, which means that there's a terrific attachment between the elements of *Bob Cummings*'s situation and the episodic narratives—the weekly practice of identity. Although the depths of their characterizations may vary—for instance, we get a lot less of Margaret's psychology in the text than, say, Schultzy's—their different positions within the premise are unique enough to ensure that they can all help inspire different types of plots. In fact, every character ends up defined, and every story is related to at least some aspect of the series situation. The best of these are focused on the nuclear family in which Bob finds himself trapped, but *any* use of these ensemble relationships can make for a terrific genre-affirming example of sitcommery. And one of the things that this series does especially well is its commitment to continuity, not only as far as episodic narratives are concerned but also in its ability to reference past events and previous characters, sometimes in multi-episode story arcs. This helps build the show's sense of aesthetic realism and allows us to invest in these regulars and the reliability of their depictions. They do not have quite the same level of detail as *Lucy*'s leads and there is less of a grounding autobiographical component, but the show is not quite as comedically associated with the vaudeville-rooted slapstick of the early 1950s either, so there's often less broadness to ground.

Now, that is not to say *Bob Cummings* is not comedically broad or big. On the contrary; as a property from McCadden that was created by Paul Henning, who had written for the first two (and some change) seasons of *Burns and Allen*, those sensibilities are very much felt. Henning is the scribe who would go on to helm the rural trilogy of *The Beverly Hillbillies*, *Petticoat Junction*, and *Green Acres* in the 1960s, and a lot of the qualities embodied by those shows—including an aforementioned regard for narrative continuity—are already on display here: primarily, a strong situation with bold characters and an emphasis on comedy. The main difference is that those shows (specifically *The Beverly Hillbillies* and *Green Acres*) are high concept and thus a little more premise dominated than *Bob Cummings*, which thematically has its juxtaposing lifestyles as a similar underlying situation but is otherwise more consumed in the week-to-week happenings by low-concept plots that explore specific relational dynamics between members of the regular or recurring ensemble. Of course, as in all great sitcoms, Henning's characters are his strong suit, and that is the biggest carryover from his work here and in those later classics.

As for *The Bob Cummings Show*'s five-season run, the series improves as continuity accrues in future seasons but before star Cummings takes too much of the behind-the-scenes reins and foists too much of his own ideas into scripts—like the cartoony Grandpa Collins, a character also played by Cummings but in old-age drag. Grandpa Collins, who is essentially an extra horny Bob, only appears once here in Season One (1954–1955), but he'll soon be overused—a threat to the rest of the series' aesthetic realism and a broad gag that the show does not need, for it does not serve the other relationships within the series' central premise as well.

Fortunately, if Grandpa Collins is a negative, pretty much everyone else is a positive, like Chuck. He is Bob's nephew, played by Dwayne Hickman—the era's ultimate teen, the guy who would go on to anchor the whimsical *The Many Loves of Dobie Gillis*, a series we'll be discussing in a few chapters. His increased inclusion is great for *Bob Cummings*'s premise, especially when Bob is forced into the role of unintended parent, imparting wisdom and copyable behavior that, well, we would never ever get from the upright and uptight Jim Anderson.

The best parenting episode from this freshman collection is "Bob Gives Up Girls" (February 13, 1955), which plays right to the series' premise, as Bob attempts to stop dating women in an effort to spend more time with his nephew. This, of course, proves to be a challenge, and it isn't long before Bob is scheming to dump the boy so he can run off with a date—a goal that, unbeknownst to Bob, Chuck is trying to do as well. The narrative is a perfect display of a central conflict—Bob must sacrifice the way he wants to live in order to be a stand-in daddy—and it's one of the first entries here in Season One to play to the specific relationship between uncle and nephew, a vital (and growing) part of the premise. Other entries from this first season that I especially enjoy include "Bachelor Apartment" (March 20, 1955), where Bob literally gives up his duties to the household by moving out, and "Schultzy's Dream World" (May 15, 1955), where a series of fantasy sequences explore Schultzy's romantic obsession with her boss—an affection that will ramp up in later years.

However, the primary standout of this shortened season is an offering called "The Air Corps vs. Marriage" (April 17, 1955). In this episode, Bob's married friend Harvey and their pal Sid (Lee Miller) attempt to get Bob to finally take a wife by drafting a bogus letter that says, because he's unmarried, Bob must report to active duty. Bob catches wind of their scheme and decides to have some fun with the duo by recruiting saucy stripper Boom Boom Laverne (Evelyn Russell) to pretend she's

Bob (Bob Cummings, left) and his married friends, played by King Donovan (center) and Lee Miller, in *The Bob Cummings Show*, "The Air Corps vs. Marriage" (1955).

his bride-to-be, launching an audacious performance that ends with them refusing to let him walk down the aisle. It's a great example of how this first season so effortlessly uses the series' established situation in story, as Bob actively fights the urge to settle down, like everyone in his life wants him to do. In this case, the driving force for the first half of the entry is his married buddies, but that role rotates throughout the series, often involving Margaret and/or Schultzy.

Meanwhile, the incorporation of Boom Boom Laverne is incredibly bold—the kind of raunchy, bawdy comedy that not even *Lucy* would be inclined to offer, let alone the antiseptic *Father Knows Best*, which has about as many laughs in its entire first season as Boom Boom earns in five minutes. So this is a very funny entry that uses the show's primary conflict, centralizing Bob in a plot where he motivates the climax. Although the series will improve in later years, it's already in good shape, and we will continue to track its trajectory going forward.

## *Remember, Quantity Is Not a Synonym of Quality*

While *Burns and Allen* and *Bob Cummings* proved to be McCadden's best efforts, George Burns's company also helped shoot this season's four filmed episodes of Jack Benny's half-hour TV program,[14] now in its fifth year and airing every other week (rotating with *Private Secretary*), for 16 total episodes—with most coming live from Hollywood. Of the entire 16-episode output, approximately 12 skew more to the sitcom form than the series' variety roots, offering scenes where the stars on the show, particularly Jack, are acting and reacting in character to a specific set of circumstances. This represents an ongoing shift for the TV program – even though it must be noted that most of these sitcom scenes are classic centerpieces that had been used many times before on his radio series (now in its final year), including Jack's trip to the grocery store,[15] his adventures at the train station,[16] his journey to the fair with the Beverly Hills Beavers,[17] etc. And much of this is sitcommery focused entirely on his character because, unlike on radio, he lacks the full ensemble that also helped inspire story via their individual personas and unique relational dynamics. Accordingly, the situation that can be explored is limited—there's Jack and maybe one or two others who can join him in any given scenario. For that reason, there is nothing here that is really great or competitive with this season's finest, but as always, we will keep our good eye on it—and see if anything pops up in the back half of the decade.

Truthfully, *Jack Benny* will always be something of a "modified" sitcom—existing in the liminal space between variety comedy and true situation comedy. But it isn't alone this year, for with the genre growing in prominence as a result of several big successes, fledgling variety series like *The Imogene Coca Show*—a single-season vehicle for Sid Caesar's hilarious former partner—and even the declining *The Red Buttons Show* temporarily adopted sitcom elements throughout the year in an effort to boost their ratings (just like Alan Young had tried last season). And like *The Ray Bolger Show*, another filmed sitcom anchored by a famous song-and-dance man, the single-season *Here Comes Donald* for Donald O'Connor was little more than an excuse for its star to croon and hoof, with a flimsy situation built around these otherwise more important musical centerpieces. So even in shows that were not necessarily predisposed to be sitcoms, the network brass was eagerly injecting elements of the genre into their proceedings, hoping this would help. Naturally, half a sitcom is not as satisfying as a full sitcom, especially when a situation only exists as a peripheral afterthought, subordinated to other interests.

Sometimes it's hard to find the correct priorities even in *actual, full* sitcoms, including several new series that also indulged the growing popularity of show business settings—a trend not specific to *Lucy*, given the longtime success of shows like *Burns and Allen* and *Jack Benny*, but a testament to the potency of autobiographical elements: writers writing what they know. This is how 1954–1955 ostensibly saw a handful of new filmed Hollywood-set sitcoms, like *So This Is Hollywood*, a single-cam laugh track series that premiered in January 1955 and claimed to focus on a stunt woman, her up-and-coming actress friend, and their two beaux. Unfortunately, none of these characters is well defined with story-pushing personalities beyond some obvious career pursuits, and the series proves to be little more than a chance to spoof the industry and its clichés, dominated by guests and comic notions that were already tired, even by the mid–1950s.

Even worse, meanwhile, is *Hey, Mulligan!*, another filmed single-camera sitcom (with laugh track)—this one starring thirtysomething movie star Mickey Rooney as a page for a fictional TV network. It's a highly specific workplace setup that, like *So This Is Hollywood*, we expect to offer winking spoofs of the industry. But it turns out that this series' situation actually is relevant in fewer than a third of its produced stories, which are otherwise all over the place, putting Mickey in a hodgepodge of scenarios that have little to do with this premise or the other leads ("Mickey builds a robot,"[18] "Mickey becomes a detective,"[19] "Mickey enters the boxing ring"[20]). It's bad. And while Rooney has decent chemistry with pal Joey Forman and guest Pat Carroll, who appears a few times as his occasional date, there's really only one episode that skewers TV and uses the Mickey character to do it—it's called "The Average Man" (February 26, 1955), when the bosses decide that Mickey is the personification of the typical viewer and therefore has valuable expertise for when they make all their new programming decisions. It's a cute idea and works within the premise, unlike so many of the others, which set this bar so dreadfully low.

From these efforts, we can see a growing interest in workplace constructs, or at least, sitcoms that utilize specific jobs and careers as a launching pad for story, as opposed to domestic familiarity. Obviously, this is not a new development; *Our Miss Brooks, Private Secretary,* and even shows that merely split their time between work and the home reveal a precedent. But in this 1954-1955 Sitcom Boom, there's a wider variety now of professions being used to predicate sitcom concepts. Take, for instance, another single-camera filmed entry, *Dear Phoebe,* which ran for one year and starred Peter Lawford as an advice columnist working under a female name. For maximum irony, his love interest was a female writer (Marcia Henderson) covering sports with a male nom de plume—a setup that also includes crusty Charles Lane as their boss, and thus seems like a great foundation for relationship-based stories about conflicting characters who could be well-defined via their juxtaposition, especially since their jobs are positioned as competitive. Unfortunately, scripts lean too much into the profession itself, as there is a revolving door of news stories, personalities, events to cover, taking focus away from the relational dynamics inside of this otherwise fixed situation. It would be like if *I Love Lucy* was more about the different themed shows Ricky was putting on at the club every week rather than the Ricardos' marriage. This is a common problem in many workplace sitcoms, where the job and its duties are prioritized above the regulars, and both story and laughs are derived from episodic one-offs instead of the established elements. And in the case of *Dear Phoebe*, it's a shame because the elements were there.

Speaking of single-season workplace-focused sitcoms, this year also offered *The Halls of Ivy*, a single-camera adaptation (that only intermittently used a laugh track)[21] of a radio favorite created by *Fibber McGee and Molly*'s Don Quinn. It was about a college principal and his wife, a former musical theater star, as they run both a household and a university. Both the TV show and the earlier radio incarnation featured Ronald Colman and his real-life wife Benita Hume, who had showcased their sitcom chops for years by playing versions of themselves on *The Jack Benny Program*, and they were joined here on television by Mary Wickes and Ray Collins as a maid and faculty member, respectively. Not many episodes of this TV version circulate for study today, but from what there is to see, it seems to be a mildly comedic (not *un*comedic) series that nevertheless appreciates a gentler and occasionally dramatic timbre. Stories tend to be more about the running of the school than the relationships between the characters—which means it might not be as good an example of a sitcom as some others—but it's a wildly different take on the school-set comedy of which we have seen a handful, and it remains an indication that the television medium was still looking to the then-dying radio for material that it could potentially consume.

Incidentally, we can also spot radio's influence on television in the growing first-run syndication market, which in 1954–1955 was not only debuting the final original segments of Betty White's filmed vignette-filled sitcom *Life with Elizabeth* but also the end of the single-season 39-episode adaptation of radio's original workplace/hangout comedy *Duffy's Tavern* and the last ever produced installments of TV's *The Amos 'n Andy Show*. The latter was reignited in hopes of a new network run under the title of "The Adventures of Kingfish,"[22] but the NAACP's pressure was still high, and when the new series fell through, these extra 13 segments were merely folded into the *Amos 'n Andy* syndication package, bringing the total count to 78. The new episodes boast Jay Sommers (of *Ozzie and Harriet*; later of *Green Acres*) as a writer, and many include bigger, broader ideas. However, while they intentionally center on the Kingfish, the change between these segments and those earlier is slight. There's merely better sitcom competition now—nearly five years after the TV show's premiere, there are smarter shows with characters who are better able to drive story and do not seem *as* rooted in potentially unflattering stock types.

After these final episodes debuted in early 1955, the series remained in syndication until 1966.[23] That means, for over a decade, *Amos 'n Andy* and *Beulah*, which had ended during the 1952–1953 season, were the only filmed and thus syndicated sitcoms starring Black actors until *Julia*'s premiere in 1968. And even then, the last episodes were debuting here, in 1954–1955, before the Montgomery bus boycott and many of the important events in the civil rights movement that changed history, a history not reflected on the sitcom during this time. Sadly, this decade that initially started as more inclusive—with shows about Black families, Jewish families, Italian families, etc.—was turning more homogenous, not only in its subject matter, but in its characters as well. And this is never good for situation comedy, which thrives on funny people who are unique and exist in contrast. (For example, Lucy and Ricky Ricardo!)

At any rate, the first-run syndication market that absorbed more *Amos 'n Andy* also got a few more single-camera filmed properties around this time, including *His*

*Honor, Homer Bell*, which was about a widowed judge raising his niece—a very gentle affair—and *The Mayor of the Town*, a TV adaptation of a sleepy radio program whose genre affiliation is dubious. Both lasted only one season. Additionally, 1954 also saw the single-season syndicated resurrection of *Meet Corliss Archer*. This was not the first television adaptation of radio's long-running teen comedy, as there had been a live version broadcast on CBS-TV in both 1951 and 1952. But this was the first time the series was on film and with a largely new cast—only Robert Ellis carried over in his role as Dexter Franklin, the lead's steady boyfriend. The new *Corliss Archer*—the sole version available to screen now—is a bouncy, youthful affair with animated interstitials, a jokey narrator, and occasional asides directly to the camera (not unlike a future Mr. Dobie Gillis would enjoy).

Unfortunately, this appealing style cannot quite make up for the fact that its depictions of the regulars are vague—vaguer than on radio—for despite a strong contentious dynamic between the stern Mr. Archer and the geeky Dexter, which can occasionally provide fodder for stories that work because they're rooted in a well-established aspect of their situation (like a segment called "Quaranteen" where they're directly paired)—most of the plots feel like they could happen on any teen sitcom, regardless of character definitions or the circumstances of their family arrangement. Also, Ann Baker is weak as the titular Corliss, who is too often irrelevant to laughs and story. So although this is touted as a teen sitcom—and indeed was one of the first on TV, following *The Aldrich Family*—it doesn't quite explore or focus on the teens in story like others in this subgenre will, including the aforementioned *Dobie Gillis*, which we'll discuss soon. Until then, note that the teen subgenre—so popular on 1940s radio—never became the same phenomenon on 1950s TV, with the four-season live run of *The Aldrich Family* (1949–1953) being the closest to a replicated success. In this era, most sitcom depictions of teens were relegated to the family shows—*Father Knows Best* and *Ozzie and Harriet*—where they were poorly defined support for the adults. Although, in the case of the latter, a takeover was soon to occur.

But I digress. In the meantime, there are two other filmed single-camera (with laugh track) sitcoms to highlight, both of which aired on NBC. The first is *It's a Great Life*, a nontraditional family series that puts a wrinkle in the era's typical suburban-set formula via a unique premise about a widowed matriarch (Frances Bavier, later of *The Andy Griffith Show*) who lives with her young adult daughter and her lazy, loafing brother (James Dunn) before deciding to take in some boarders to make ends meet. They wind up with a pair of off-duty servicemen (Michael O'Shea and William Bishop) who need a place to stay as they get back on their feet. So all five of these people live together in one small house—a notion ripe with interesting conflict. And coming from Ray Singer and Dick Chevillat, two scribes who penned radio's *The Phil Harris–Alice Faye Show*, a ribald sendup of the typical father-led family fare, this series seems to be in the right hands, for these folks know how to manipulate and find laughs within the natural tension of the domestic format, especially from characters who otherwise don't seem suited for it. That is, the two main characters, like Bob Collins, are wild men who have seen the world (or at least, Korea—a war that lasted from 1950 to 1953) and now they, unlike the marriage-averse Bob, are indeed trying to settle down.

There is a lot of possible story in that setup, related to the interplay of different types of people. Unfortunately, none of these characters are well-defined enough for the show to seize these opportunities, and despite some strong performers—like Bavier, Dunn, and O'Shea—they simply cannot overcome the fact that the two soldiers are fairly generic. One is a little wilder, the other a little more sensible, but they otherwise tend to operate in story as a duo—or a trio, if the lazy uncle gets involved—and this makes it difficult to delineate and distinguish individual personas. They are essentially a collectively unemployed nuisance, bouncing around to odd jobs that, of course, make the storytelling less tethered to a situation. And even once they get seemingly steady employment as vacuum cleaner salesmen, episodic plots remain routine and not well associated with who they are, let alone the realities of this premise—that they are living a strained domestic life with a bunch of strangers. Sadly, the sitcommery never improves during the series' two-season run; in fact, it actually gets worse, as the daughter leaves about two-thirds of the way through this first year, further limiting story opportunities about the combination of people within this house and the struggles of acclimating men of the world to the rules of 1950s suburbia. Season Two then goes for bolder episodic notions, increasing the weekly yuks, but with still no affiliation to anything unique in the series' situation and its characters' main conflict. So it remains a big disappointment, especially given the premise's inherent potential.

The last filmed single-camera sitcom (with added laugh track) that I want to mention is *Norby*, which was created by *Mister Peepers*'s David Swift and premiered in January 1955 as a fairly unimaginative fallible patriarch sitcom with a heavy helping of workplace angst at a local bank—both halves of which are boring because they are not enlivened by special characters. The thing most notable about *Norby*—then and now—is that it was the first sitcom to film every single episode in color,[24] a technological advancement that the networks were experimenting with more frequently during the 1954–1955 season. But color was a gimmick that only few could enjoy,[25] and it seems little thought was put into the construction of this series' situation and how it would exist as a memorable, unique sitcom—you know, like *Mister Peepers*, which was now in its fourth and final season as one of the last live comedies coming from New York, still counting charming characters whose palpable humanities did not preclude big laughs but in fact fueled them, thanks to benign incongruities supported by personal sincerity.

Unfortunately, the year's storytelling left something to be desired. After the previous season married the central leads (Peepers and Nancy), stories here are less sure what to do with them, opting to have the pair travel more—perhaps, a *Lucy*-esque move—but without as much character-motivated or, at least, character-explorative opportunities provided by this gimmickry. (The nadir of gimmickry is an entire episode where Wally Cox plays himself, in his own "life story"[26]—something that has nothing to do with *Mister Peepers* and does not belong in it.)

Accordingly, the final season of *Mister Peepers* seems not as good at using its situation for story—not only its school setting but also the established relationships between its main characters—and as such, their strong definitions are no longer as well featured on a weekly basis. The show would eventually flunk out at the end of this season, offering a huge blow to the live sitcom operation in New York, which, at this point, was otherwise upheld by the wry *Ethel and Albert*, the Peg Lynch series that considered itself deliberately amusing but with less well-defined leads. In fact, the only new series worth mentioning this year that came live from the East Coast was *Honestly, Celeste!*, a 13-week vehicle for Celeste Holm, casting her as a midwestern journalism teacher now in Manhattan pursuing a career as an actual journalist. Despite having *M\*A\*S\*H*'s Larry Gelbart as a creator and later input from a young Norman Lear as a replacement scribe,[27] the show never caught on. According to Holm herself, her character was not very well drawn.[28] So with *Peepers* going, New York lost its best ambassador. After this, live sitcoms from New York would be rare.

Hollywood, meanwhile, still had a handful of live sitcoms of its own, including the reliable *Meet Millie* and *My Favorite Husband*, the latter of which would recast its leading lady and switch to film (for Desilu, ironically enough) in the following season. Both were produced at CBS's Television City in front of a live audience, along with the single-season newbie *Professional Father*, which premiered in January 1955. It was another fallible patriarch sitcom but with an even more specific premise about a child psychologist who was great at his job but far less competent when dealing with his own kids, who were otherwise much better handled by their mother, played by a pre–*Leave It to Beaver* Barbara Billingsley—a much sassier and smarter take on her eventual June Cleaver. Very little of this live series survives, but what *is* viewable indicates a good setup with some solid comic ideas. I cannot tell if there really is much definition supporting the stories and the laughs—particularly in terms of the kids, who seem fairly ordinary—but it doesn't seem as benign as most in this subcategory. If McCadden had filmed the whole series, as it did the pilot, more of the show would probably exist today and we'd have a fuller impression of it.[29]

Lastly, there's one other live sitcom from Hollywood that I want to mention—the last new sitcom from this chapter—it's *The Soldiers*, which, after its pilot, was broadcast live in front of an audience during the summer of 1955.[30] It stars Hal March (you may remember him as the very first Harry Morton on TV's *Burns and Allen*) and Tom D'Andrea (who was temporarily leaving his spot as William Bendix's sidekick on *The Life of Riley*) as a pair of malcontent, complaining soldiers in a workplace buddy comedy notably produced by Bud Yorkin (Norman Lear's future partner) and frequently staged by Jackie Coogan (later Uncle Fester on *The Addams Family*).[31] The series developed out of a sketch that the pair had frequently performed on *The Colgate Comedy Hour*, just as *The Honeymooners* would spring next season from another variety program, *The Jackie Gleason Show* (and *The Cavalcade of Stars* before it). It's also a military sitcom—one of the common workplace settings of the 1950s and 1960s—hitting the airwaves before the perhaps quintessential entry in this subgenre, *The Phil Silvers Show*. In this regard, *The Soldiers* shares elements of two important sitcoms that we are about to discuss in the following chapter—*The Honeymooners* and *The Phil Silvers Show*—both of which, interestingly enough, came from New York and were shot on film, despite similarly having live TV (and comedy variety) roots.

As for the quality of *The Soldiers* itself—which lasted only 13 weeks, largely due to the chronic bickering between its stars[32]—the show is like most sitcoms that expand from sketches (including *The Bickersons* and *Ethel and Albert*, which were previously discussed): its characters have an intrinsic thinness that makes it hard for them to be dimensional enough to motivate believable story week after week. Instead, more value is placed on comic notions—"Is there a funny idea to support this extended 24-minute sketch?" We will really dive more into what that means in the next chapter, as we finally examine the direct differences between character-driven and idea-driven sitcoms, using *The Honeymooners* and *The Phil Silvers Show* as the decade's two most seminal and influential representatives of the latter form.

*The Honeymooners* and *Phil Silvers*, with *I Love Lucy*, represent the decade's three finest sitcoms, and their brief coexistence during the 1955–1956 season will make it the peak year for 1950s American situation comedy, for even though we'll note a contraction in *quantity* from the sitcom boom of 1954–1955, most of the shows next year are in better shape, more handily making a regular connection between their weekly storytelling and the established elements of their situations. This has been the most common problem with "bad" sitcoms up to now, and with so many of them to examine here, this chapter has contained more examples than any other. Again, though, quantity has never equaled quality—this is also why the sitcom's reputation has long been mired in unfortunate and inaccurate samples, like *Father Knows Best*, which also symbolizes what we think about this period in America and its entertainment (whether actually true or not). Ultimately, good sitcommery is like good art: it's special. And fortunately, some of the best of the best is still ahead. Stay tuned.

## *JACKSON'S BEST SITCOMS FROM 1954-55*

1. I LOVE LUCY (S4)
2. THE BOB CUMMINGS SHOW (S1)
3. THE GEORGE BURNS AND GRACIE ALLEN SHOW (S5)

## *EPISODES FROM THE 1954-55 SEASON IN JACKSON'S TOP 50 FROM THE '50s*

#9. I LOVE LUCY (S4): "L.A. at Last!" (2/7/55)
#10. I LOVE LUCY (S4): "Mr. and Mrs. TV Show" (11/1/54 and 4/11/55)
#11. I LOVE LUCY (S4): "Lucy Gets Into Pictures" (2/21/55)
#24. I LOVE LUCY (S4): "Ethel's Birthday" (11/29/54)

#27.  I LOVE LUCY (S4): "The Star Upstairs" (4/18/55)
#41.  I LOVE LUCY (S4): "Ethel's Home Town" (1/31/55)
#42.  I LOVE LUCY (S4): "Harpo Marx" (5/9/55)

**OTHER NOTABLE EPISODES FROM 1954-55**
THE ADVENTURES OF OZZIE AND HARRIET (S3): "The Furnace" (10/22/54)
I LOVE LUCY (S4): "Ricky's Screen Test" (11/15/54)
MEET CORLISS ARCHER (S1): "Quaranteened" (1954)
I LOVE LUCY (S4): "Lucy Learns to Drive" (1/3/55)
I LOVE LUCY (S4): "First Stop" (1/17/55)
THE BOB CUMMINGS SHOW (S1): "Bob Gives Up Girls" (2/13/55)
THE BOB CUMMINGS SHOW (S1): "The Air Corps vs. Marriage" (4/17/55)
I LOVE LUCY (S4): "Ricky Needs an Agent" (5/16/55)

## Chapter Eight

# The Golden Age
*The Best Television Sitcoms of 1955–1956*

Despite a reduction in the total number of sitcoms from the peak of 1954–1955, 1955–1956 is the best year of the decade for this genre. For one, it is the only year where this era's three best sitcoms are all running: *I Love Lucy*, *The Honeymooners*, and *The Phil Silvers Show*. Additionally, it is the center of the 1950s and singularly contains all the trends we've highlighted so far—including the death of live TV in favor of film, the transition from New York to Hollywood, the rise of the syndication market, and the ascension of the multi-camera format as common among the best and funniest comedies. It also looks forward to the trends we will examine in the latter half of this decade, including the increase of bland domestic family shows and the dwindling popularity of sitcoms as a result. The 1955–1956 season also offers the best opportunity to present the central thesis in my theory of sitcom analysis—the aforementioned notion of character-driven sitcoms versus idea-driven sitcoms. We touched on this briefly several chapters ago in relation to *Topper*, which as a high-concept supernatural comedy fits easily into the idea-driven category.

As a reminder, a high-concept show is one whose premise can be stated in a sentence, largely because it is important, specific, and sometimes unusual or not naturally mimetic. This is in contrast to low-concept shows, which tend to be based more simply on relationships inside more inherently relatable, familiar, and common scenarios—like a generic workplace or a traditional nuclear family. Because of their notable premises, high-concept sitcoms must use their weekly stories to honor the major conceptual aspects of their situation, and this ensuing focus on particular trappings above the actual characters is precisely what makes them, first and foremost, idea driven.

Specifically, idea-driven sitcoms are sitcoms whose episodic successes are most predicated on the strength of their episodic ideas (as situation fulfillment), rather than the strength of how they display their characters (as situation fulfillment), which is the focus of character-driven sitcoms. Of course, because the sitcom is a form that intrinsically depends on sustaining characters, all idea-driven efforts must also rely on their characters—to uphold stories that allow for the kind of ideas necessary to satisfy a situation. But it's a matter of prioritization. Are characters being used to procure good ideas, or are ideas merely the conduit for displaying the characters? In other narrative forms, you may have heard the term "character driven" contrasted against "story driven" or "plot driven" or even "premise driven," where the narrative itself is more important than the exploration of a character. But I use the term "idea driven" because it is broader—it applies not only to heavy narrative setups (like those high-concept shows) but also to a focus on certain themes, styles, structures, perspectives, or even types of story: any kind of ideological, identity-revealing marker that viewers can expect every week *in addition to* the regulars, whose individual definitions are not the singular, primary concern of a situation's weekly projection.

I draw a marker between character-driven sitcoms and idea-driven sitcoms because I believe they are the two dominant approaches to the genre, existing in aesthetic opposition to each other since the 1950s, which helped create a divide that would persist in every decade thereafter. For instance, this clash certainly extends into the 1960s, where that era's high-concept comedies—like *The Beverly Hillbillies* (about poor mountain folk moving to the mecca of wealth and glamour) and *Bewitched* (about a human man marrying a lady witch)—are contrasted against low-concept domestic comedies like *The Dick Van Dyke Show* and *He & She*, where stories are more about everyday, relatable characters in their mostly common familial and/or workplace relationships.

This divide is also very pronounced in the 1970s via the revolutionary comedies of Norman Lear, whose efforts are at their best when dealing with topical issues and reflecting a specific ideological perspective. They are most contrasted by the very character-oriented work plus home comedies from Mary Tyler Moore's company MTM, where the exploration of characters juxtaposed against each other in specific but familiar relationships holds prominence and inspires episodic story. That's similar to the divide as evidenced in the 1990s, where shows like *Seinfeld* thrive on funny trivial ideas ("Where does a comedian get his material?") told in a very specific and highly stylized plotting, while sitcoms like *Friends* merely explore their leads as if in a romantic comedy and therefore with a focus on relationships as a plot engine. You can see the contrast in these examples—it's the prioritization of ideas versus the prioritization of characters.

And yet, if character-driven sitcoms and idea-driven sitcoms are markedly different and every show is more like one style than the other, it is not necessarily true that their principles are mutually exclusive. Most shows have elements of both, like the 1980s' *The Golden Girls*, which follows strongly defined leads in motivated stories that can also be idealogically focused in accordance with its premise. Also, while it seems like I may personally prefer character-driven sitcoms because of this book's character-centered definition of the sitcom, let me be clear: characters only get exploration within some kind of narrative framework or a set of ideas, and ideas can only capably get explored when propelled by the right set of characters.

They are of mutual import, then; the reason every sitcom wants strong characters is so that they can inspire smart ideas that fulfill the genre's comedic and narrative requirements, and no idea-driven sitcom can accomplish its goals without using its characters in exhibition of its situation, just as all dramatic works, even comedies, definitionally require figures who uphold a story by personifying the foundational imitation of life. If there's a qualitative difference between the two, it's that the sitcoms we can point to as being character driven naturally have their priorities aligned with the elements of a situation that most set up the genre for success, while idea-driven sitcoms must go through the extra step of ensuring that in the process of projecting whatever their conceptual goals may be, their characters are also being meaningfully engaged—and this most vital aspect of any situation, of utmost importance in any dramatic work but especially comedy (and *especially* the sitcom), is never being ignored.

In other words, the best idea-driven sitcoms are ultimately like the best sitcoms, period: they use their characters to support their ideas. For instance, *Bewitched* puts its leads in direct conflict, while exploring its high-concept "witch married to mortal" premise, and this naturally showcases their contrasting definitions (unlike the similarly fantastical, high-concept *Topper*, which didn't distinctly define its leads well for story). Similarly, Norman Lear's best sitcoms (like *All in the Family*) marry sociopolitical clashes to strong contentious relationships, supporting topical debates with personal and relatable emotional stakes. And *Seinfeld* deliberately depicts its regulars as minutiae focused so that they help earn the funny, trivial episodic ideas that satisfy the "where does a comedian get his material?" premise as earned by observational Jerry Seinfeld.

To that point, I need to make an important distinction. While all high-concept shows are inherently idea driven because they have unique premises to acknowledge above their characters, not all low-concept sitcoms can be called character driven. *All in the Family* and *Seinfeld* are good examples of why not—one is a simple family show, the other a "hangout" comedy featuring a group of friends. Those setups are low concept and *could* be character driven, but they choose not to be. Fortunately, they're still great though, both due to the strength of their ideas *and* their use of characters to support those ideas, thereby honoring the macro definition applicable to all situation comedy, with genre-affirming laughs further cementing their excellence relative to others. However, they are exceptional—most low-concept sitcoms (idea-driven or otherwise) *don't* use characters well. We've already seen a lot of examples.

In fact, let's back up. If these two separate sitcom aesthetics are trackable going forward, the first question is, where do they begin? Well, frankly, like the sitcom itself, it's hard to find a pinpointable start, but we can trace this schism back to our very definition of the genre and how it came into being on radio. For the purposes of our analytical study, this divide is most clearly delineated in the 1950s by 1955-1956—the center of the sitcom's first decade on TV—and by its best. And if you're still confused about the difference between character-driven and idea-driven sitcoms, these next examples should be clarifying. For instance, *I Love Lucy*, with its lead's strong objective driving story and its use of autobiographical elements plus attention to detail, all of which ensures her emotional credibility and surrounds its star personality with well-defined support, can easily be called the 1950s' best ambassador for the character-driven sitcom. Indeed, it is the first *great* character-driven sitcom on TV with, as we explored in Chapter Four, all its laughs and stories being channeled *by* and *for* its regulars. In this chapter, we will contrast the character-driven *Lucy* with the era's two best representatives for the alternative idea-driven ethos: *The Honeymooners*, which helps reveal the origins of this rival aesthetic, and *The Phil Silvers Show*, which best displays how this rival aesthetic would influence future generations.

For starters, the ideological discrepancy between character-driven sitcoms and idea-driven sitcoms begins with the way the sitcom genre developed on radio. As we explored in Chapter One, the sitcom came about in the convergence of tenets from three other genres: the anthology drama (which had episodic, or self-contained, stories), the serial drama (which had sustaining characters), and comedy-variety shows (which were presentational and clearly laugh seeking). In those early days, some of the best comedy shows on radio we labeled as "modified" sitcoms because they maintained more of an affiliation than the genre later would to those foundational variety elements. Some of these early "modified sitcoms" include the formative *Fibber McGee and Molly*, which we called the first long-running radio example of situation comedy despite its lingering attachment to its stars' original vaudeville sensibility, and the incredibly funny *The Jack Benny Program*, which had top-tier character work but was still engaged with songs and skits as a presentational variety show. (This would remain true throughout his TV run, as we've seen.) Now, I wouldn't call *Jack Benny* idea driven, given its excellent use of well-defined leads in narrative scenes that suggest situation comedy, but idea-driven sitcoms similarly differ from their character-driven counterparts by leaning more into the variety aspects of the genre's origins—and specifically, the comedic sketch, which, ironically, is a dramatic form far more narratively slight than the sitcom.

A sketch is typically a self-contained comic scenario that only lasts for a limited amount of time—usually between 5 and 20 minutes. It arose from vaudeville, found itself in Broadway revues, and then came to radio in the comedy-variety shows of the 1930s. Many sketches were parodic in nature but not always—they could just be a simple domestic idea: a shortened and noncontinuing version of what we would identify as traditional sitcom fodder, with a husband and wife and some minor conflict. Sketches didn't necessarily have to be one scene either—just one self-contained idea—and as radio folks moved over to TV, the popular comedy-variety shows continued to use sketches as a staple of their weekly offerings. In fact, during the early part of the 1950s, the most popular comedy shows on television were indeed variety programs, hosted by the likes of Milton Berle and Sid Caesar.[1] Here, as on radio, the programmatic, ongoing nature of these shows allowed for something that would not have been possible on the stage: *recurring* sketches—a feature that maybe wouldn't happen every week but would appear as a frequent and reoccurring attraction in *most* weeks, like "The Hickenloopers," a husband-and-wife sketch on Sid Caesar's *Your Show of Shows*. Some of the recurring sketches that we have previously discussed in this book include "The Bickersons" and "Ethel and Albert"—both of which began on radio variety shows, expanded into their own half-hour sitcoms, and first made the jump to TV back on variety shows (on *Star Time* and *The Kate Smith Hour*, respectively), before they were again fleshed out into their own half-hour television packages.

As with the similarly sketch-born *The Soldiers*, which we examined last chapter, these sketch-to-sitcom adaptations have all been disappointing, for they all have fairly thin, undefined characters, and each episode is therefore more dependent on some kind of disconnected comic idea—now stretched to the length of a half-hour sitcom, instead of a five-to-twenty-minute scene (or set of scenes) that does not require as much actual story or support from the characters. Whether tacky and clichéd, relying on generic insult comedy, like *The Bickersons*, or deliberately muted and erroneously striving for realism via a generic (and therefore not personalized) relatability, like *Ethel and Albert*, these sitcoms could not help but reveal their sketch-like origins, where characterizations inherently did not matter as much, for the singular idea predicating each scene's existence remained prominent, barely altered by this genre's differing needs. Even with a recurring presence allowing for continuity, these examples' obvious sketch-rooted sensibilities make them akin to idea-driven sitcoms, for something(s) is/are being prioritized other than the leads, who are but a means to an end—satisfying whatever the comic purpose of the sketch is: an over-the-top bickering couple, a wannabe realistic couple, or in the case of "The Hickenloopers," a way to showcase stars Sid Caesar and Imogene Coca as a pair somewhere tonally between the warring *The Bickersons* and the down-to-earth *Ethel and Albert* (just like Caesar and Nanette Fabray in the suburban-set "The Commuters" sketch from his followup show, *Caesar's Hour*). All of these sketches, incidentally, made their TV debuts out of New York—broadcast live, like most of the comedy-variety shows of the 1950s.

## *The Honeymooners*

"The Hickenloopers" and "The Bickersons" both came to TV in 1950.[2, 3] The following year on DuMont's *Cavalcade of Stars*—a live variety show hosted by Jackie Gleason from New York—a new recurring husband-and-wife sketch debuted. It was "The Honeymooners," and it cast the rotund, bug-eyed Gleason in the role of Ralph Kramden, a beleaguered bus driver living in a tiny Brooklyn apartment with his wife Alice, initially played by the sourpuss Pert Kelton. The title of the sketch was ironic—these were not newlyweds, and they certainly weren't lovey-dovey like honeymooners, for their life was drab and miserable, not blissful, and they constantly sparred.

What made them different from "The Bickersons" and all the rest, however, was their class—the others were in the middle, neither rich nor poor (even though "The Hickenloopers" also lived in a small apartment, it was in Manhattan, not Bensonhurst). The economic plight of the Kramdens—visually made clear by the sparse setting for their "love nest"—fueled the title's sarcasm, mocking the false sitcom ideal marital bliss and abundance. It was that very idea on which the sketch was founded: mocking the ideal of marriage, especially for those in the blue-collar sector. Expanding on this notion were Ed and Trixie Norton—the Kramdens' best friends and neighbors, played by the rubber-faced Art Carney and, initially, Elaine Stritch, the gruff Broadway star who was quickly replaced by the more feminine Joyce Randolph. Norton was a sewer worker—another dirty blue-collar job that, like Ralph the bus driver, could hammer home the idea of a meager, harsh existence.

Now if this all sounds miserable and unpleasant, Gleason—whom you may remember as the original Riley on the first filmed version of *The Life of Riley*—helps by bringing a lot of pathos to the role, in addition to his kinetic physical comedy, which Carney also offers in a less tragic, more goofy way. So there are a lot of laughs (visual too—the best kind for TV) and far more nuance than "The Honeymooners" sketch-born concept would have us believe. Indeed, the reason, ultimately, that the half-hour version of *The Honeymooners* is a great idea-driven sitcom and the best of these sketch-to-sitcom examples is not just that, like all great idea-driven sitcoms, it has very funny ideas. No, it's also a great showcase for its star, whose characterization does the heavy-lifting for stories that, like all sketch-to-sitcom outings, are otherwise relatively slight and not well supported, especially by character.

To that point, although Carney matches Gleason in comic stylings and therefore is another material elevator, the two wives are painfully undefined. Alice always has a basic attitude—brusque when played by Kelton, stoic when played by Audrey Meadows, who took over the role when the sketch moved over to *The Jackie Gleason Show* in 1952. But there's really not much to her: no recurring objectives, no clearly reiterated history, no pronounced comic traits, and no sense that she exists beyond her thin, predictable dialogue. Additionally, Trixie is one of the most undefined characters you'll ever find on a great sitcom. Okay, occasional references—on the variety show—are made to her once being in vaudeville, but that never informs the way she speaks or the things she does, and she never gets any kind of exploration in story. Ever. And needless to say, all four of these leads are denied the kind of attention to detail that would help make them feel more believable and more actively utilizable in weekly plots à la the leads on *I Love Lucy*.

That said, the economic straits of the Kramdens and Nortons *do* sort of give them a collective recurring objective in story: the desire to pull themselves out of this drab lifestyle by getting rich quick: the "American dream." It's the kind of goal shared by leads on *The Life of Riley* and *Amos 'n Andy*, two other blue-collar sitcoms of the era, and it's a helpful "want," just as it is on those shows, but the fact that it exists there should clue you in on its relative genericness—it's far less specific than the goal given to Lucy Ricardo, which is directly tied to her relationship with Ricky and actually quite personal. This discrepancy—the generic versus the personal—is one manifestation of the difference between a sketch and a sitcom, and more broadly, the difference between character-driven and idea-driven sitcoms, the latter of which "The Honeymooners" did not become for several years. That is, after a year on *Cavalcade of Stars*, Jackie Gleason got his own variety show, Pert Kelton was replaced by Audrey Meadows, and "The Honeymooners" continued as a recurring feature for the next three seasons on CBS's *The Jackie Gleason Show*. Most of the *Jackie Gleason* "Honeymooners" sketches survive today via kinescopes taken as they were being broadcast live, still from New York, growing from under 10 minutes in 1952 to nearly 40 by the end of 1953.

You'll note that 40 minutes is longer than an actual sitcom episode, often requiring more story beats than a half-hour show. But instead of turning to the characters to help support these more developed narratives, most of the sketch's ideas are very basic comic scenarios—funny no matter what, with emphasis remaining on the notions themselves, just like a sketch. That said, while there's a lot of reliance here on externally conceived comic ideas, the scripting is above average, and the performances—especially by Gleason and Carney—are riotous, adding needed humanity (via laughs and pathos). Also, the basic idea of "The Honeymooners," with their premised economic struggles, does influence the weekly happenings, making it something we can enjoy as a situation that's being satisfied. Particularly by the end of the 1953–1954 season and during the 1954–1955 season of *The Jackie Gleason Show*, the 31-to-42-minute "Honeymooners" sketches are a delight—they're worth checking out, if you're a fan, and similar to the sitcom version that would premiere the following season, in 1955–1956.

That's right. Due to the success of these sketches, Gleason agreed to a half-hour series of *The Honeymooners*. His contract was for two seasons with an option for a third, but only one year of 39 episodes ended up produced.[4] These are commonly called the "Classic 39," and they're the only actual sitcom episodes of "The Honeymooners" ever. To replicate the style of the sketches, which were performed live in front of an audience (like most comedy-variety shows), the new sitcom would be filmed in New York at the Adelphi Theater in front of a live audience with multiple cameras[5]—using a variation of Desilu's multi-camera format specifically patented by DuMont (the fourth-place network that was about to die), whereby an image could simultaneously be recorded on film and broadcast live to a source.[6] This kept the proceedings spontaneous and very theatrical—as if it *was* an extended sketch broken out from a comedy-variety show. And for as much as I have criticized the sketch form compared to the sitcom form, maintaining this variety-rooted look was wise, for that was part of "The Honeymooners" style—its aesthetic situation, the maintenance of which would thus be key to its success, even implicitly.

These episodes are called the Classic 39 for a reason. They're the peak of "The Honeymooners" format, which incidentally, Gleason would revive on his variety show during the 1956–1957 season and again throughout the 1960s. However, never before or after these 39 are the ideas as comedically clever, and never again are its performances as pitch perfect, building out these relatively thin characterizations so that we don't constantly notice their slight definitions. Although Harry Crane and Joe Bigelow had created the sketch on *Cavalcade of Stars* in 1951, scripts for "The Honeymooners" as they reached the Classic 39 were by now written by three pairs— with one of the scribes being Leonard Stern, who would go on to work on *The Phil Silvers Show* and then in the next decade would also create several of his own sitcoms while serving as head writer for *Get Smart*, another beloved idea-driven gem.

These six scribes kept up a high level of quality—most of their funny ideas find some way to tap into the continuity of Ralph Kramden's character, like his membership in the Raccoon Lodge; his noted jealousy and possessiveness with Alice; his hot temper and how that negatively affects his relationships; and more broadly, all the characters' dire economic fortunes, leading to his and Norton's shared desire for a windfall. As for the best of the Classic 39, entries where Ralph teams with Ed for inevitable shenanigans while in pursuit of a get-rich-quick, or economic, objective are the most satisfying, for they most attach the series' central characterizations to story. Again, it's a generic goal, but one at least rooted in the situation established for these leads. And while Alice is not a great story partner because of her lack of definition, Ed *is*, thanks largely to the material-elevating work of Art Carney, who helps make "Kramden and Norton" a duo in the Lucy and Ethel variety, or Laurel and Hardy, or Abbott and Costello—with the classic image of "the fat guy" and "the skinny guy" evoking memories of great comedic teams. Accordingly, while this is the kind of show where every fan has a favorite episode, many of the best—the ones that most reveal the series' identity—pair the two men for a comedic narrative idea where they pursue a clear economic goal.

▶ Among these is the entry that I rank at **#6** on my top 50 list. It's "**The $99,000 Answer**," which was first broadcast on **January 28, 1956**. The story parodies the mid-1950s' quiz show fascination as Ralph tries to land a windfall by competing on a *Name That Tune* type of show. It was directed by **Frank Satenstein** and written by **Leonard Stern** and **Sydney Zelinka**.

This is a famous excursion—to a certain generation, it's as iconic as some of *Lucy*'s best hijinks, particularly for its big comedic climax, where Ralph goes on a live TV show to compete for the grand prize of $99,000 but is unable to guess a single tune: the very one that Ed Norton has nonchalantly been playing repeatedly throughout the episode—"Old Folks at Home." It's a great gag that allows for the expected maintenance of the characters' economic status quo, tragically dashing Ralph Kramden's dreams but with big laughs that also involve the goofy Norton and their relationship, plus the series' financial situation. Also, it's a great example of what idea-driven sitcoms tend to enjoy because it's a notion that would be funny regardless of series, as the benign incongruity resides in the person's inability to detect a very common, ubiquitous tune after studying far more niche, difficult options. That would be true with any character, before it is then made especially funny with Kramden and Norton, two perennial losers whose failure is, again, baked into their series' situation.

▶ This funny duo is even better partnered in an entry that I place even higher—at **#4**! It's **"Better Living Through TV"** in which Ralph and Ed hope to get rich by advertising a kitchen tool on live television. **Frank Satenstein** again directed this episode, which first aired on **November 12, 1955**, and with a script credited to **Marvin Marx** and **Walter Stone**.

"Better Living Through TV" is another memorable installment where, in accordance with the basic economic objective that provides the most continuity for how these characters can motivate story, Ralph and Ed decide to go into business together on the "Handy Dandy Kitchen Helper"—a multipurpose gadget that they are sure is going to make them rich. Under this delusion and against their wives' better judgment, the pair shells out money to advertise this gadget on TV. Of course, as expected, their TV spot is a disaster, both because the product does not work properly and also because of Ralph's performance jitters—a running trait for his character that goes back to "The Honeymooners" sketches (in segments like "Ralph's Sweet Tooth" from 1954).

What's most impressive about this particular entry is that the men drive the funny idea with a pursuit that is rooted in their class struggle and therefore part of the sketch's original premise—which initially related to the husband-and-wife relationship but now is more broadly applied to Ralph's entire unglamorous existence. Their failure here is also more directly attached to their own personal flaws than in "The $99,000 Answer," where Ralph is a loser because of irony and bad luck. Here, he's an idiot with terrible judgment and uncontrollable nerves. What's more, this one's got a more physical centerpiece too, taking advantage of both Gleason's and Carney's strengths as broad comics, especially when together. As a result, this is, I think, the best display of *The Honeymooners*' identity in story during the Classic 39—the only period where it formally adheres to the sitcom format, with real character concerns and corresponding plots.

Of course, there are many other well-remembered favorites as well. Some worth noting here include "A Matter of Record" (January 7, 1956), which contains Ralph's iconic "BLABBERMOUTH!" outburst to his mother-in-law; "Young at Heart" (February 11, 1956), which reengages the original sketch's romantic focus in a story that also makes room for physical comedy; "Head of the House" (March 31, 1956), where Ralph and Alice feud over control and both he and Norton get to do a drunk routine; and "Dial 'J' for Janitor" (September 15, 1956), which puts Ralph in a very visibly blue-collar position as he becomes the building's maintenance man and gets stuck while trying to fix the pipes. These are but a few great offerings and they're all hilarious—I could list a dozen more, and I am sure there are *Honeymooners* fanatics reading this whose favorites I have failed to mention. This is a testament to the show's reliable comedy, which helps give almost every episode something great to recommend for it (much like *I Love Lucy*).

*Chapter Eight. The Golden Age* 175

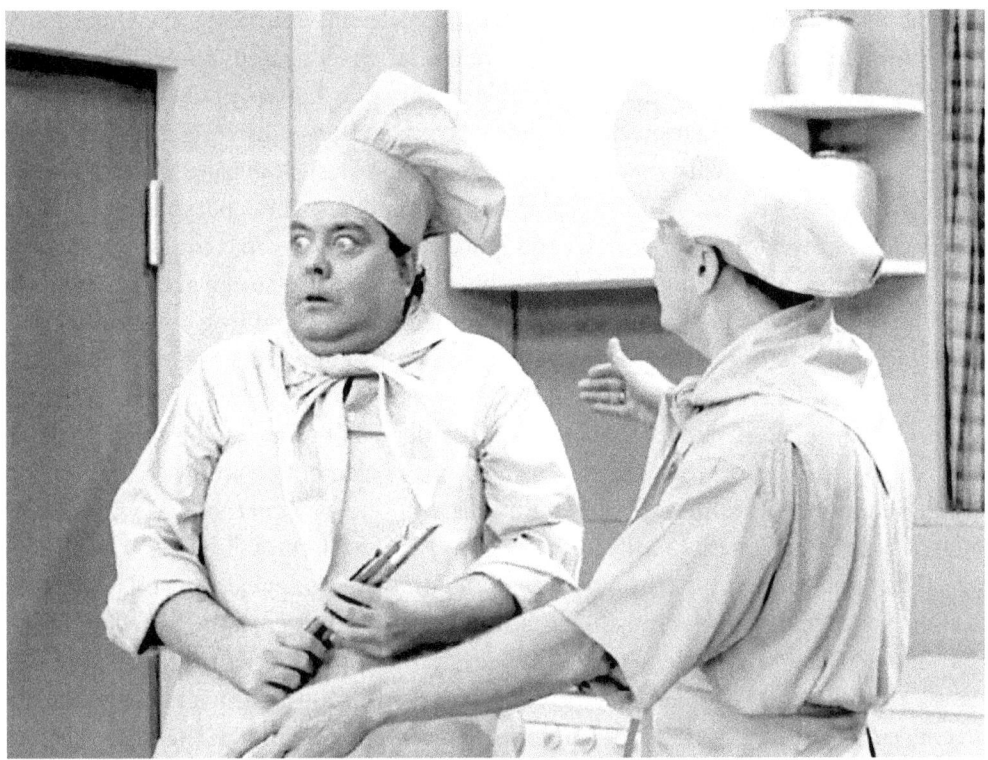

**Ralph Kramden (Jackie Gleason, left) and Ed Norton (Art Carney) in** *The Honeymooners,* **"Better Living Through TV" (1955).**

▶ But the last of the Classic 39 to make my top 50 list is "**The Golfer**." I rank it at **#19**, and it first aired on **October 15, 1955**, with a script by **A.J. Russell** and **Herbert Finn**. The story has Ralph pretending that he can play golf in order to impress his boss. **Satenstein** directed.

"The Golfer" contains a memorable physical centerpiece where Ralph, clad in his own idea of golf attire, attempts to practice his swing in the Kramdens' tiny apartment, with Norton—of all people—giving him tips. It's another comic tour de force for Gleason, the Great One, who mines every single laugh he can find in this simple scenario. But what's most impressive about this entry—and why it's a great sample—is because it's very smartly set up within the series' situation and, specifically, the leads' low economic fortunes. That is, as part of Ralph's repeated efforts to improve his lot in life, he is goaded by Norton into pretending that he's proficient at golf—a sport he's never played—all in hopes of impressing his boss and gaining the inside track to a needed promotion. Accordingly, everything that happens is rooted in what we know of these characters and their world. And while this is much better than the series' usual storytelling, it nevertheless does evidence the elevated character work—primarily within the generation of plot—that indeed makes the sitcom version of *The Honeymooners* superior to its sketch origins.

Of course, even though it's an improvement, the limitations that dog this sitcom because of those sketch origins are also evident. Primarily, the thinness of these regulars in relation to those on more character-conscious shows, like *I Love Lucy*, is glaring and hard to avoid when the two are now both part of the same genre and directly comparable (especially as multi-cams that visually resemble each other and comedically exist with the same physical sensibilities). That is, we know so much more about the Ricardos and Mertzes—their histories, their personalities, their desires—than we do the Kramdens and Nortons, and the former foursome accordingly feels more well rounded and believable, not only because of a greater attention to detail but also because of the autobiographical elements adding emotional credibility. That's missing on *The Honeymooners*, and its characters are less functional as a result. As for episodic story on *The Honeymooners*, while my favorite offerings grant Ralph a generic but at least situation-connected objective so he can help drive the action—and most other plots use *some* kind of element we know as inspiration (the Racoon lodge, Ralph's job, his temper, etc.)—the way character is viewed episodically is very different on this idea-led show than, well, the character-driven *Lucy*.

Here is a direct comparison between *Lucy* and *The Honeymooners* on terms that feel fair: both had episodes in which their main comic duos got handcuffed together. As we discussed in Chapter Four, "The Handcuffs" (October 6, 1952) segment of *I Love Lucy* is entirely rooted in character. From Fred's vaudeville past, to the tension between Lucy and Ricky because he works and she does not, to the theatrical climax where Lucy gets in the act, there is always some direct connection to what we know about these leads and how they exist in relation to each other. Meanwhile, on *The Honeymooners*' "Unconventional Behavior" (May 12, 1956)—a great entry for this show in the same way "The Handcuffs" is a great *Lucy*—Ralph's objective is actually resolved at the midpoint, when he and Norton are not able to sneak off to their convention without their wives knowing, as was their original goal. Act Two, then, is relatively plotless but still in need of a crescendo to help validate the situation's comedic reputation. So the script—also by Marvin Marx and Walter Stone—calls on this tried-and-true handcuff bit. After all, this spot needs a centerpiece that shows off Gleason (and Carney, serving as his comic partner).

In this case, the presence of the handcuffs and how they get on the two men is "explained" by Norton being extra prankish and silly, which is not unbelievable based on his childlike characterization, but it's a motivation that's conveniently simple and less situation-backed than what we saw on *Lucy*, where her actions psychologically predicate themselves on a major, specific part of her characterization and how she regularly exists in narrative. She's being explored, not the idea. Instead, the way these handcuffs pop up in *The Honeymooners* reveals that attaching plot points (and comedy) to character stakes is far less a concern, for *this* series is driven only by its want for the funny moment itself—the good idea—and not so much from the elements in the situation who might earn it. Motivation is exposition, not exploration. This is a perfect and uncomplicated example of the difference between character-driven and idea-driven sitcoms—where contrasting priorities are exhibited by what's being focused on: the funny character who earns the funny idea or the funny idea itself.

Now, with all that noted, if the show is not *as* specific to its characters as *Lucy* and those that exist as its descendants in the character-driven school, note that *The Honeymooners* uses its leads—or at least Ralph Kramden—better than so many other idea-driven sitcoms. Heck, better than so many sitcoms. For there is still something we know about him attached to every story—like above, his affiliation with the lodge and the corresponding shenanigans of which Alice disapproves. That's a huge part of why this series is great—like all sitcoms, it's using what we know about its regulars to help deliver boffo laughs, even as it's more focused on the ideas it's employing rather than the character connections. Also, it's not character driven, but Ralph and Norton are comedic, and Alice can be as well. Scripts don't prioritize them above their funny propositions, yet the leads are still featured in such a way that they *are* instrumental to these propositions' appeal. And this fundamental satisfaction of the genre's requirements, along with every script's uproarious humor, makes *The Honeymooners* a great sitcom—one of the best of the decade, even with only 39 episodes: a single gem-filled collection.

## *Nat Hiken, Sgt. Bilko, and the Idea-Driven Promise*

But while *The Honeymooners* is a fine exhibit to examine in a discussion of idea-driven sitcoms because of its sketch origins and the qualities it therefore reflects, the next series we must study is a little more fully formed—it's *all* sitcom, and always was. And because of that, it's perhaps an even better example for spotting these idea-driven attributes in practice. In fact, it is one of the genre's most influential offerings in total: *The Phil Silvers Show*, subtitled *You'll Never Get Rich* during its original run but perhaps better known colloquially as "Sgt. Bilko." That moniker pays tribute to the center of this series—another iconic character, this time a classic army con man played by former vaudevillian Phil Silvers.

*The Phil Silvers Show* was a multi-camera comedy filmed in front of a live audience but from New York (like *The Honeymooners*), not Hollywood, and it is similarly low concept, essentially premising itself as an ensemble workplace comedy set on a Kansas army base and focusing around the aforementioned Sgt. Bilko, who leads the base's motor pool and has a predilection toward scamming his pals and superiors for sport—a trait that provides the narrative through line and most common spark of story for the series' 143 episodes.

Yet if that seems like a well-defined Lucy Ricardo–esque motivation, what makes this series more affiliated with the idea-driven camp is the way it consistently projects qualities more similar to *The Honeymooners*: less attention to detail regarding character (especially for anybody outside of Ernie Bilko, as everyone else is basically one-joke support), little emotional continuity and believability for the leads (their relationships are underexplored and not specific—perhaps the strongest is between Bilko and his boss, Colonel Hall, who clashes with Bilko because of his positioning in the workplace, but it's not at all as nuanced and original as the tension between Lucy and Ricky), and storytelling that is less focused on exploring the regulars and what they're doing, instead emphasizing the funny ideas being offered every single week. Indeed, the real brilliance of *Phil Silvers* comes through in the strength of its unique comic ideas and the fast plotting that keeps them rolling—a style, or rhythm, that is *as much* a part of this series' identity as its characters.

These concerns—both the individual comic notions and the overarching style that is itself an ideological necessity for the unique projection of the series' identity, or situation—make this show idea driven, and it's the kind of idea driven that future sitcom lovers can find echoed, for instance, in *Seinfeld*, a 1990s classic that was similarly focused on finding amusing (trivial) ideas and then arranging them in a heightened way, where the tension could mount and plotlines could intersect—a construct that's spiritually close to *Phil Silvers*'s deliberately fast-paced cadence, in which beats build on each other, with a chosen storytelling template emerging as one key part of the show's defining charm. Unsurprisingly, *Seinfeld*'s head writer Larry David has called *Phil Silvers* his favorite sitcom[7] and specifically referenced this series' influence on his work.[8] (This is as opposed to *The Honeymooners* or *Lucy*, the two other 1950s sitcoms that future sitcom auteurs frequently cite as formative.)

Now, a look at *Seinfeld* is more suited for a book on 1990s sitcoms but bringing it up in this context is meant to consider the legacy of *The Phil Silvers Show* and indicate why it remains a cornerstone of American sitcommery—especially now in the twenty-first century—for *Seinfeld*'s own sphere of influence, rippling throughout the genre, has by proxy kept *Phil Silvers*'s reverberating today as well. For instance, we can see the legacy of Bilko in recent classics like *Curb Your Enthusiasm* and *Arrested Development*—sitcoms that are overly concerned with their amusing ideas, and the faster, narratively specific storytelling patterns that reinforce them.

Here is an example of what I mean regarding *Phil Silvers*'s style and story—using the character-driven *I Love Lucy* and its own narrative aesthetic as a contrast. For this comparison, let's look at *Lucy*'s and *Phil Silvers*'s second filmed episodes—when both series had stated their identities but were still discovering how to best showcase them in story. This will give us an indication of the differences between how Lucy Ricardo and Ernie Bilko, two schemers, have their respective schemes laid in plot. On *I Love Lucy*, when Lucy wants to get back at Ricky and Fred for going to an escort service in "The Girls Want to Go to a Nightclub" (October 15, 1951), she and Ethel arrange to show up, in disguise, as the guys' hideous dates. On *The Phil Silvers Show*, when Bilko wants to get back at a trio of soldiers for taking money from a new recruit in "Empty Store" (September 27, 1955), he buys an empty storefront, allows gossip to accrue about why he bought that storefront, watches as the trio sucks up to him to get in on the deal, and then rents a third of it out to each of the three before revealing that it is otherwise worthless. For *Phil Silvers*, this constitutes a relatively simple story, but compared to a typical *Lucy*, it's plot heavy, hitting more beats and leaving less room for peripheral comic character moments outside the plot because said plot, and the presentation of it, is the attraction, just like on *Seinfeld*, where narrative dovetailing became a sign of comic dexterity and a vital display of its own situation—another element of identity that viewers were conditioned to expect every week.

As for the stories themselves, let us compare both series' best episodes—arguably, each show's most famous individual offerings. In *I Love Lucy*'s "Job Switching" (September 15, 1952), as we've examined in Chapter Five, Lucy tries to prove that she's just as capable as Ricky of earning a living. That is a rich character goal because it's tied to her overall objective of proving her value outside the home, as Ricky does, which thus creates the central conflict between the two. Therefore, the comic centerpiece in "Job Switching," of Lucy being inept at the chocolate factory, is supported by the series' situation—her own eagerness to be working in the first place *and* her shortcomings as a homemaker who has never really been out in the real world, in a factory, on an assembly line, enduring a true daily grind. Contrast "Job Switching" to *The Phil Silvers Show*'s "The Court Martial" (March 6, 1956), where Bilko has to defend a chimp that has accidentally been inducted into the army, and you see a huge difference. This is a very funny setup for an episode, yes, and it showcases the Bilko characterization in spots by forcing him to "sell" something that is ridiculous, like the carnival barker he is. However, the idea itself is not motivated by *his* actions within plot, and it has nothing to do with any of his overarching wants or needs specifically. That is, the story is not born out of the Bilko character.

Okay, to be fair, most *Phil Silvers* episodes *do* have him pushing the action along somehow with his money-making schemes. But like *The Honeymooners*, this is a relatively impersonal goal compared to Lucy Ricardo's more specific objective, which is also conceived for her *in relation* to her husband and his characterization. In contrast, Bilko's persona sort of exists independently of any other element within his show's regular construction, which means it's less supported, both by his sitcom's structure and by the weekly narrative happenings, where he is always crucial—and in fact centralized—but not with the same totality or specificity, whereby he might be, as Lucy is, the principal means through which her show orients its situation. *Phil Silvers* orients itself through its stories, its ideas, and he follows suit as their leading contributor.

The scripts for these two sterling and ideally exemplary samples reveal that key distinction: "The Court Martial" is not concerned with displaying Bilko's comedic definition as a character. It's committed to the wild, silly things that happen as a result of its unfolding narrative—a processing error that is beyond his individual control and doesn't exist on this show *because* of him. This is the exact opposite of Lucy Ricardo in "Job Switching." Lucy may herself lack control over the raucous conveyer belt, but she is only in this factory predicament, where she is expected to fail, *because* of her clearly defined character, which is thus well-displayed throughout.

Again, this reveals the difference between focusing on characters as the propulsive comic force versus specific ideas as their own propulsive comic force, even when they have some basic support from a star's persona to enable existence within the sitcom genre.

Please note: this is not a critique of the idea-driven sitcom, or its finest ambassador. The *Phil Silvers Show* is brilliant—again, one of the best of this decade—*because* of the strength of its ideas and the excellence exhibited by its unique, creative, situation-establishing storytelling, centered by Bilko, who crucially upholds it. It's great sitcommery. And all of this is thanks to its creator, Nat Hiken, a terrific writer whose primary credits on comedy-variety shows gave him a natural familiarly with the sketch comedy aesthetic to which many of these early idea-driven sitcoms are affiliated. Specifically, Hiken had written for Fred Allen on radio and both Milton Berle and Martha Raye on TV, and he even had some sitcom experience before—creating a funny but short-lived radio sitcom called *The Magnificent Montague*, another idea-led comedy with one singular star characterization acting as a conduit for a season's worth of funny episodic notions. However, with his background consumed mostly by variety, Hiken's experience with sketch comedy is of course felt on both *The Magnificent Montague* and *The Phil Silvers Show,* via his prioritization of funny ideas. This sensibility paired particularly well with Silvers' history in vaudeville— one of the forms that gave rise to comedy-variety shows in the first place.

Hiken was *Phil Silvers*'s head writer and guiding creative force—with his name on every single script—for the entirety of the series' 34-episode first season. He then tried to reduce his workload in the second year (1956–1957), ultimately staying fully hands-on but splitting his script assignments with other scribes, including Leonard Stern from *The Honeymooners*. Other *Honeymooners* scribes and even the great Neil Simon came to write for the show in its last two years, after Hiken had departed. But the series' quality can really be mapped alongside Hiken's involvement. It is at its best when he's most engaged and declines as his control diminishes. I attribute this correlation to Hiken's sheer imagination with these episodic ideas and the fact that the storytelling's unique rhythm comes directly from his own personal ethos. In fact, he is one of the few genuine auteurs in the sitcom genre of the 1950s—a clear forebearer to Larry David, who again was directly inspired by this and Hiken's later *Car 54, Where Are You?* This affiliation is also made clear via the distinctness, or obviousness, of their own styles, which became so overwhelming that they essentially are embedded within their shows' DNA.

To that point, another link between David and Hiken and another way we can track *Phil Silvers*'s influence is via its metatheatricality—its acknowledgment of the bounds of its own fiction, or performance. That is, there's a show biz angle to this series that isn't necessarily warranted by its situation—an ensemble workplace comedy at a Kansas army base. The show biz focus can only be justified by a generous extrapolation to Silvers's own persona and the notion of media/entertainment as an easy industry in which one could scheme and "get rich" quick. But again, that's a generous reading, for these shows don't exist to explore Bilko (this is not a character-driven sitcom, after all); they exist to explore their funny ideas. And this show biz awareness is just a convenient recurring interest, as illustrated by the frequent stories about some kind of entertainment and specifically the self-referential medium of television.

The final episode—"Weekend Colonel" (June 19, 1959)—is the best example; it's the culmination of this running metatheatricality, with a story that finds cameras being installed on the base and characters watching each other as if on a TV show. It's overly clever, and throughout the run, there are many entries where these characters indeed get a chance to perform—an unusual running source of story for soldiers who otherwise work in the motor pool. Now, I think some of this show biz fascination is a New York trait, as *Honeymooners* has some of it as well, although not to this extent, and without the *Lucy*-esque justification of having a lead, like Ricky, directly involved in the industry. Also, it's interesting to note the marriage of idea-driven sensibilities with a fourth wall-defying wink—that in itself is a joke, an idea, extending beyond character.

This metatheatricality streak—now very much part of many television sitcoms, from *Seinfeld* to *The Office*, with the latter literally constructing itself as a faux documentary—will actually become more prominent as the run progresses, and it's not as clear yet in its first season, which, due to the freshness of Nat Hiken's ideas and the novelty of his ingenious storytelling, is otherwise the series' best, with the most consistent quality and the highest number of gems. Like *I Love Lucy* and *The Honeymooners*, everyone has their favorites. Four installments from Season One make my top 50 list, but really, there are a dozen or so worth highlighting.

▶ I'll start with the aforementioned "**Empty Store**," which was first broadcast on **September 27, 1955**. It's the series' second aired episode, written by creator **Nat Hiken** and directed by **Al De Caprio**. With its plot about Bilko waging psychological warfare by merely renting out an empty store front, it's a terrific display of the show's storytelling and how Bilko's characterization feeds an idea-driven ethos where fast-paced plots create comedy and inform the situation. I rank it at **#25** on my top 50 list—you can read more about it earlier in this chapter.

Other great episodes include "Dinner at Sowici's" (February 14, 1956), where Bilko tries to dissuade his casual girlfriend from wanting something more serious by subjecting her to a night with the battling Sowicis, and "The Eating Contest" (November 15, 1955), which guests Fred Gwynne from *The Munsters* and Hiken's own *Car 54, Where Are You?* and employs a frequently used narrative template—as Bilko attempts to exploit someone's natural talent.

▶ Another gem that *does* make my top 50 at **#38** is "**The Twitch**," first broadcast on **December 13, 1955**. It was written by **Nat Hiken**, **Terry Ryan**, and **Barry Blitzer** and directed by **Al De Caprio**. In this one, Bilko gambles on the results of a classical music lecture.

This entry guests the hilarious Charlotte Rae (future star of *The Facts of Life*) as a lecturer who is brought in to speak to the motor pool about Beethoven—an activity that they're forced to attend as punishment for their rampant gambling, of which Bilko is naturally at the center. But Rae's character is eccentric and has a nervous twitch when she speaks, and Bilko, ever the opportunist, manages to find a way to make money on the lecture, taking bets on how many times she'll exhibit her tic during the speech. It's an absolutely riotous idea, and it's motivated by the driving aspect of Bilko's characterization. Additionally, it's supreme evidence of Nat Hiken's creative genius, for this is not a narrative notion that we would find on any other series here in the 1950s. That sheer imagination—which yields terrific comic ideas for story—is a huge part of *The Phil Silvers Show*'s appeal as a comedy, and it's thus an important part of its situation.

▶ Yet another identity-revealing entry is "**Bivouac**," which comes it at **#35**. Also directed by **Al De Caprio** and written by the trio of **Nat Hiken**, **Terry Ryan**, and **Barry Blitzer**, "Bivouac" first aired on **November 29, 1955**, and it's about Bilko's efforts to fake sick during a mandatory drill.

As with many of this series' best episodes, "Bivouac" follows a Bilko scheme, but this one directly concerns his position in the army, which is a part of the series' situation via its chosen setting. Accordingly, this story takes advantage of what's been established, both for the character and his general surroundings. However, it's special because it depends on the dynamic between Sergeant Bilko and Colonel Hall, who is essentially Bilko's boss, played by the easily flustered Paul Ford. Their interactions, as natural antagonists who are often positioned against each other in weekly plots despite a nevertheless mutual respect, suggest the strongest relationship on the series. And although not a lot of stories make exploring their complicated rapport a focus, the ones that do gain points for not only better emphasizing character but also for making use of a key aspect of the series' design—where this positional bond is important. "Bivouac" is the first entry—and one of the best—to deploy Bilko and Hall in relation to each other, and it's thus an effective display of the series' situation, especially with a good idea driving it.

▶ Of course, my favorite *Phil Silvers* is the classic installment that best reveals the show's identity—the one recently cited in comparison to *I Love Lucy*. It's "**The Court Martial**," which I rate highly as **#3** on my list—a true sitcom classic and *the best* episodic example of an idea-driven sitcom in the 1950s. It first aired on **March 6, 1956**, and was directed by **Al De Caprio**, with a script by creator **Nat Hiken** and **Coleman Jacoby** and **Arnie Rosen**.

"The Court Martial," which we just discussed, has an easy reason for being the best: on this idea-driven sitcom, it has the best idea. It's the funniest, most ridiculous, most memorable. Its success is predicated, like almost everything in an idea-driven sitcom, on a hilarious sketch-like log line—something that would play in any venue. This one comes courtesy of Hiken's brilliant imagination, and it's of course aided by its script's clever plotting and its above-average utilization of the Bilko persona as a defense attorney for the primate, "Private Harry Speakup," whose army induction

*Chapter Eight. The Golden Age* 183

**Private Harry Speakup (Zippy the Chimp, left) and Phil Silvers as Sgt. Bilko in *The Phil Silvers Show*, "The Court Martial" (1956).**

is a huge systemic accident after Colonel Hall streamlines the process. In this regard, even though it's a funny idea that would work well in any venue—a chimp in the army?!—enough particulars from *The Phil Silvers Show* are engaged to make it feel emblematic of the series itself, simultaneously featuring many members of the army ensemble—including Paul Ford, Allan Melvin, and Harvey Lembeck. They fill out *The Phil Silvers Show*'s regular cast, along with the doughy Maurice Gosfield as Doberman, plus Billy Sands, Herbie Faye and—starting in Season Two—the hysterical Joe E. Ross (also of *Car 54, Where Are You?*) as Ritzik. (These folks will get more chances to shine in the years ahead.)

Ultimately, this episode—like all the other highlights I've chosen to cite as fine examples of *The Phil Silvers Show*'s sitcommery here in its peak first season—deploys Bilko smartly in support of Hiken's brilliant story notions and trademark storytelling, such that our definition of "sitcom" feels validated. In other words, we know what to expect of *Phil Silvers*, and every week its laughs and its episodic plots—like here in "The Court Martial"—meet those expectations by using the regular attributes inherent and unique to its own success. It might not be stemming from a character or characters primarily, but this laugh-yielding use of concepts or ideas that give the series definition, *with support* from its characters, is why *The Phil Silvers*

*Show* is among the best-written shows of the decade. It's a sitcom so hilariously poised that many forthcoming series would honor it stylistically, almost as an equal to *I Love Lucy* in that regard, for if not as technologically influential, it could at least claim to be so textually due to its professed priorities and how it incorporates conceptual markers of identity (ideas) as commensurately important tenets of its situation, *with* an iconic character supporting those notions. No other idea-driven sitcom in the 1950s does this as well or is as worthy of being modeled.

Together, the iconic *Honeymooners* and influential *Phil Silvers* represent the best of what this decade has to offer in idea-driven sitcoms, or sitcoms that derive success beyond just the application of their characters but from the application of elements *beyond* their characters, who are instead used even more in a supportive capacity. As the first great idea-driven sitcoms of the genre in this new medium, they reveal the origins of how this style came to be (and why it differs from the character-driven alternative). And their excellence allowed them to exist as templates for many series that followed, inspiring future generations. Paired with *I Love Lucy*, which contrastingly embodies a sensibility more entirely hinged on the depiction of its leads and how their narrative presentation defines a situation, these three are the finest sitcoms of the 1950s, and it's no wonder why they remain both relevant in TV history and popular with viewers today.

## *Now, What Else Is Going on?*

The 1955–1956 season is not just great because of those three sitcoms. This season also proved to be a banner year for some of our old favorites as well, including *The George Burns and Gracie Allen Show*, which had completed three full years on film and found itself in a bit of a rut, for although casting Larry Keating as the new Harry Morton in 1953 added a strong characterization to the ensemble, giving more comedic support in story to Gracie Allen's sustaining persona, the series had exhausted its best ideas for showcasing her by the 1954–1955 season (even remaking some of its live gems), and the introduction of Blanche's sleazy brother as a recurring narrative device wasn't much of a salve—he did not have enough relevance to George and Gracie or their dynamic. Itching to bring the series back to its roots, the writers added a vaudeville "after piece" for the duo at the end of every episode starting in May 1955. And going into 1955–1956, two even bigger changes were made. The first involved the setting—just as the Ricardos and Mertzes had gone east to west, the Burnses and Mortons would go west to east, spending their entire sixth season at a Manhattan hotel, transferring the show and all its stories.

This is a burst of creativity, as the series' self-referential show biz aesthetic thrives in New York, where there's more of a connection to the stage and, in this case, the couple's real-life vaudeville origins. Also, Gracie has new people to confound—including the hotel staff and other assorted blue-blooded New Englanders, like Doris Packer, who recurs as society matron Mrs. Sohmers. Accordingly, while California suburbia was George and Gracie's real-life stomping grounds, they get a jolt of energy by being back in New York, with new opportunities that make the season fresh *but also* still helpful for the Gracie character and this series' comic sensibilities.

Another reason for the show's reignited spark is the addition of a teenage son for the couple—Ronnie Burns, played by the duo's real-life kid, Ronnie Burns. The continuity here is wonky—Ronnie showing up out of nowhere without being previously referenced harms the series' illusion of reality and wouldn't be acceptable, for instance, on a show like *I Love Lucy*. But because he really *is* their son, it actually feels like *Burns and Allen* is becoming more honest, not less, adding more autobiographical details that enhance the characters' emotional credibility. Also, like New York itself, Ronnie invites fresh stories. Of course, we still care most about Gracie—she's the centralizing comic force and still the only reliably hilarious presence (outside of Keating's take on Harry Morton). Fortunately, Ronnie brings with him new guests and recurring figures whom Gracie can vex, and thus new ideas in which her comic persona can be featured in accordance with the series' situation—where she is a lovable nuisance. By that same token, stories about Ronnie's acting ambitions—like all Ronnie stories—work best when they relate to his parents and their established relationship, sometimes even giving Gracie a motivation (helping her son's career). When such scripts earnestly try to turn him into a teenage sensation (à la one of the Nelson boys) by showing off his subpar acting skills, it's neither funny enough nor connected enough to the primary aspects of the situation about which we are most invested: his folks.

Ultimately, though, Ronnie does more good than harm because he's a satellite of them, and with both the new kid and new locale making *Burns and Allen* feel like a rejuvenated but still reliable *Burns and Allen*, it's a great season. Some of its best offerings include "Harry Morton's Cocktail Party" (October 31, 1955), where a farcical scenario develops while George Burns is promoting his own new book—a blending of fact and fiction that further asserts the situation's solidity—"The Stolen Plants" (March 12, 1956), where Gracie's naivete confuses new types of bureaucracy; "The Switchboard Operator" (September 24, 1956), a memorable outing with a set piece where Gracie and Blanche run amok on the switchboards; and three sublime entries with Doris Packer as the hilarious Mrs. Sohmers: "The Ladies' Club" (February 27, 1956), "Questions and Answers" (September 10, 1956), and "Mrs. Sohmers Needs a Psychologist" (September 17, 1956). These segments showcase how Season Six's tweaks to the series' situation breathe new life into the proceedings by benefiting the established characters, setting *The George Burns and Gracie Allen Show* up for a strong last few seasons, where a few more changes will be made.

▶ In fact, the season is so good that I can't avoid putting an episode from it on my list. It's **"Mrs. Sohmers Needs a Psychologist,"** which was held to air at the end of the summer on **September 17, 1956**. Written by **Norman Paul, Harvey Helm,**

**Keith Fowler**, and **William Burns** and directed by **Frederick De Cordova**, it finds the unnerved Mrs. Sohmers (Doris Packer) visiting a therapist because she's been so thoroughly mixed up by Gracie. I ranked it at **#37**.

Now, the interesting thing about this idea—the crux of which is a misunderstanding where Gracie shows up to Blanche's appointment with a psychologist, leading the doctor to think that Blanche is kooky and in need of psychiatric care—is that it was done back in the show's live days in 1951.[9] And it was great. Then it was done again in 1954,[10] now filmed, and it was arguably just as great. But this iteration tops them all, for it still keeps the basic comic complication, and yet it's more comedically dexterous, better involving the rest of the ensemble. For instance, this one predicates its story on a new element of the series' situation, introduced here in its unique sixth season: the hysterical Mrs. Sohmers, who has been driven mad by Gracie at every turn, especially now that she's reluctantly let Gracie into their literary club. Also, this script includes the expected beat where Harry Morton thinks his wife is ill, but it instead straightens out that mix-up quickly—for an even *bigger* centerpiece where the doctor mistakes Harry Von Zell for George Burns, and the doctor himself comes to think that he too, just like Mrs. Sohmers, has been rendered insane because of his involvement with the bizarre Gracie. It's a fuller exploration of the idea, with more jokes and more of the show's moving parts—the best version of a reliable logline, which is already strong for incorporating Gracie's persona and how she naturally confuses others. And it's character-driven, for it can *only* exist to showcase a characterization like the centralized Gracie's.

Meanwhile, George and Gracie's friend Jack Benny also had a good season, as his comedy-variety series with roots as a "modified" sitcom is probably at its strongest here. It's the first year where Benny was not concurrently offering his long-running (and superior) radio series, and exclusively dedicated to TV. Still alternating every other week and mixing live broadcasts with filmed shows, the number of pre-shot half hours increased from four to six,[11] while the rate of sitcom or sitcom-dominated scripts held strong at about three-quarters. This is the best that this TV iteration of *Jack Benny* will ever be *as* a sitcom, for its ideas ahead are not as fresh and original as those in this sixth season—where there's a mix of classics (i.e., Jack getting mugged—"your money or your life?"[12]) and fun stories rooted in the Jack Benny persona, like his bad violin playing, or his exasperation when dealing with Frank Nelson, a longtime menace who pops up in a variety of roles. In tracking this series' trajectory, I was hoping to highlight a specific segment—in tribute to how formative the radio series was via its depiction of character—but this year is just too competitive; nothing here is top tier. I can still praise it, though, as a fitting peak season for a show whose use of character, even in a modified form that hews closer to comedy variety, remains a model for the *entire* genre. And there just may be a highlighted entry in the chapters ahead.

Another show that remained in good shape was *Make Room for Daddy*, now in its third and final season under its original title, as wife Margaret, played by Jean

Hagen, would depart the series after finishing these last 30 episodes, making Danny a widower, and evolving the original premise. Here, it's still in its initial conception—a work-versus-home sitcom where Danny is caught between his personal and professional duties—and there are no signs of it losing steam. In fact, with kids Rusty and Linda getting older, they're able to participate more in the action, and as they age, the show becomes a little less sentimental, more comedic, with home-set stories that use them more as characters than devices. Additionally, there continues to be above-average continuity and attention to detail supported by autobiographical truth, like Danny's Lebanese heritage, which gets creatively personified this year via the introduction of Hans Conried in "Terry and the Sorority" (February 27, 1956) as boisterous Uncle Tonoose, the mustached patriarch of the family who has strict opinions about what everybody ought to be doing, especially his favorite nephew. Tonoose will become a more prominent recurring presence in later seasons—broader than the regulars, but because he reflects Thomas's actual ethnicity and allows for the kind of humor that the star comic himself frequently utilized in his act as a proud first-generation American, Tonoose's presence is situation corroborating—another familiar character-rooted element for the show to hold on to as it undergoes some big changes with the departure of its leading lady. But just wait—it'll all prove to be a blessing, as the best is yet to come with Danny.

Speaking of autobiographical detail, *Ozzie and Harriet* has another one of its best years in 1955–1956, following a great third season in 1954–1955, for it continues to focus on Ozzie's own foibles, recognizing that in this terribly benign series, the more intentionally benign an idea—playing up small trivia to the point of near absurdity—the more likely it is to actually be funny, especially when supported by Ozzie, the only well-defined comic figure. Next year will see the show start to split its time with the teens, vacillating between scripts about the boys and scripts about the adults (including Don DeFore's Thorny, who fades out in 1956 but is already less visible this year than he was before, slowly replaced by other figures, like Parley Baer's Darby). But those scripts about the boys will not be great because of the boys' lack of comic qualities and thus fewer opportunities to inspire appropriate story. Without characterizations, the show has nothing to attach situation comedy, instead offering generic fare merely designed to create time for Ricky Nelson to sell his records and David Nelson to plug his movie career. It's not good.

But Ozzie's trivial nature can often be amusing, and because it's the primary focus of Season Three, and here again in Season Four, these years are the most comedically favorable—the best collections of situation comedy from this mediocre low-concept but otherwise idea-driven series focused on domestic minutiae. Standouts from this batch include "Man Across the Street" (November 11, 1955), which introduces Darby; "The Eclipse" (December 16, 1955), which boasts an appropriately trivial narrative idea; "A Day in Bed" (March 23, 1956), an Ozzie-focused remake of an earlier radio script with a simple structure; "A Beautiful Day" (April 13, 1956), another radio remake centered on Ozzie and his moods; and "The Honest

Face" (April 20, 1956), yet another Ozzie-centric entry built around aggrandized trivialities.

As for other domestic shows from the period, the blue-collar *The Life of Riley* is actually in a bit of a transitional phase—it's without its secondary couple, the Gillises, as Tom D'Andrea had left to star in the short-lived *The Soldiers*, which premiered and ended in the summer of 1955. There are new neighbors, but they are blander and have less of an emotional history with Riley, who more often now is paired with the wispy-voiced Waldo, portrayed by the inherently amusing and unique Sterling Holloway. Meanwhile, daughter Babs gets engaged, then married, then discovers she's pregnant this year—but instead of being emotionally exciting, it's all by the numbers and not fleshed out by specifics, for this has never been a great character-focused or detail-providing show, especially for the kids and the wife, and they are therefore unable to exist within weekly plots that feel directly associated with them and the low-concept situation they individually and collectively inhabit. As such, this is another below-average year of a below-average domestic sitcom, with not as much comedy and fewer stories that suggest the premise of a fallible patriarch in economic distress, trying to elevate his family's station—like Ralph Kramden, whose show is much funnier.

Of course, *The Life of Riley* is still not the worst of this era—it's still not as bad as *Father Knows Best*, where father is essentially *infallible*—erring very rarely and even then, only slightly and only very benignly. Naturally, this is because he still knows much more about everything than his children. This doesn't prime him well for comedy. However, there are a few notable episodes here relative to the rest of the series, like one segment where the family is actively amusing in their disdain for Margaret's relatives—"Family Reunion" (March 14, 1956)—and one intentionally comedic entry called "Father Is a Dope" (November 2, 1955), where Robert Young actually allows his character, Jim Anderson, to be the butt of the joke but in a metatheatrical plot that acknowledges Young's own desire to *usually* contrast his characterization against the bumbling dads typical of TV sitcoms (like Riley and Ozzie), therefore upholding his own self-righteous and ultimately anti-sitcom perspective. But that is a rare exception of humor (via an external idea, metatheatricality), for *Father Knows Best* remains what it always wants to be—a lighthearted gentle drama, seldom willing to contort or tweak anything for true laugh-out-loud comedy.

Meanwhile, the tranquil domesticity of suburbia got an additional and unlikely booster from another series—a former titan, returning after a year away, now in a new format with a new premise. Following the cancellation of the long-running half-hour version of *The Goldbergs* in 1954, Gertrude Berg wrangled that cast to film 39 more episodes for syndication. These segments, which debuted in 1955, deliberately broke with the continuity of the series' 25-year run by having the family move out of the Bronx and into the Connecticut suburbs. Critics have since come to view this move as something of a negation of situation—specifically, the end of their Jewishness, enabled by their displacement from their traditionally Jewish enclave and the other Jewish characters who existed within it.[13] But with a fish-out-of-water premise—or *gefilte fish*–out-of-water premise—their ethnicity could have remained reinforced. In fact, the opposite could have been true, as the series' new setting actually sets them up for a real clash of cultures, accentuating the family's heritage by contrasting it against the homogeny of a white and implicitly non–Jewish suburbia. Unfortunately, the storytelling (in scripts still written by Berg herself) lets this idea down, for while elements of Molly's ethnic-based persona remain—especially via her extended family—plots seldom deal with conflicts related to her integration, as a Jewish woman or even just a former urbanite. (Only the series' second entry, "Social Butterfly," depicts Molly's struggle to fit in.)

Also, an arc about son David getting married seems like it could have been an excuse to play up the family's culture through an ongoing storyline where the Goldbergs would be forced to interact with a different clan, but those opportunities are not seized on either. Instead, the syndicated version of *The Goldbergs* traffics in by-now-generic sitcom plots that could exist on any suburban series—some have more of a comedic bent, but most are sentimental, emphasizing the long-running series' pathos. In general, these 39 episodes *do* try to be funnier than their live counterparts, but they're just never hilarious. And with so much of what made the series special gone—namely, the element that most defined the leads, rendering them unique within the television landscape—plus the dramatic opportunities suggested by this new premise left unexplored, it's disappointing in a way the earlier live series, while gentle, was not. Thus, this is a sad coda to one of the longest running media franchises of the era. Gertrude Berg would play Molly Goldberg twice more in variety show appearances during 1957,[14] and she would return to the sitcom format for *Mrs. G. Goes to College*, a single-season comedy in 1961–1962. But by and large, the only thing that remained visible in the following decades were these filmed episodes. And they're not a fair representation of what *The Goldbergs* had really been as an early TV staple.

However, the end of *The Goldbergs* corresponds with several connected trends we have been following, including the slow death of live television and the slow death of television in New York, which only got a brief reprieve as a TV hub this season thanks to filmed sitcoms like *The Honeymooners*, *The Phil Silvers Show*, and the short-lived *Joe and Mabel*. Otherwise, the end of New York's *Mister Peepers* and Los Angeles's *My Friend Irma* left very few live sitcoms on air. All New York had was *Ethel and Albert*, now in its own final season and no better off than it was before, and all Los Angeles had was *Meet Millie*, also in its final season and given a last-minute reprieve ostensibly because of a Screen Actors Guild strike that delayed production on the aforementioned *Joe and Mabel*.[15] The previously live show *My Favorite Husband* actually made the jump to film this year—shot by Desilu (the company co-headed by the woman who starred in the original radio series) but not in their usual before-an-audience style[16] and with Vanessa Brown now as Liz. Of course, the same problems remained—the characters are undefined, so the storytelling is generic and unoriginal. Those shortcomings are not removed simply by changing the production technique.

Another sitcom shot by Desilu this year was the second season of *December Bride*, which again aired behind *I Love Lucy* and got high ratings by default, even though the conception of its premise and its lack of strong characters—aside from material-elevating performances from sidekicks Harry Morgan and Verna Felton—forever kept it from being a great sitcom. Oh, there is one memorable episode worth pointing out here—"Sunken Den" (February 20, 1956)—but that is only because it guest stars Desi Arnaz and therefore affiliates itself with a much stronger show. Interestingly, Arnaz also played himself this season on an episode of the struggling *Our Miss Brooks*, which, now in its fourth and final year on TV, opted for a change in format, dropping all of its regulars except for Miss Brooks, her nemesis Mr. Conklin, and her landlady Mrs. Davis (plus Mrs. Davis's recurring sister Angela), and transferring the titular lead to a California middle school with a new ensemble consisting of folks such as Bob Sweeney, Nana Bryant, and William Ching.

The strength of the low-concept and character-driven *Our Miss Brooks* was always its well-defined relationships, so with most of those gone, the series was inevitably left to flounder, attempting to replicate past successes by creating new interpersonal dynamics but without the bank of emotional history and support that helped her previous situation be more credible with story and more reliable with laughs. These growing pains led to even more changes, as Bryant and Ching got replaced mid-season by Isabel Randolph and Gene Barry, with Nancy Kulp recurring a few times as Sweeney's girlfriend. This is actually a very funny cast that could have thrived under different circumstances. But *Brooks*'s further instability only made it harder for the show to settle into a satisfying status quo with its new characters and their relationships, so good ol' Mr. Boynton was brought back for the final few episodes—right before the release of the 1956 film *Our Miss Brooks*, which had been shot in late summer of 1955[17] and utilized the old format (and characters). Of course, this was way too late, and the series was not renewed—again, marking a sad end for a radio and TV staple, an important ambassador for the genre and the Desilu multi-camera style.

Meanwhile, Desilu also shot (but didn't produce) a new multi-camera live audience sitcom from the *Make Room for Daddy* camp—namely, writer Arthur Stander and director Sheldon Leonard. And indeed, *It's Always Jan* was similar—a show biz–related star vehicle for performer Janis Paige, playing a single mother (a war widow) who works in a nightclub as a songbird and then goes up to her kid and two roommates, essentially hopping back and forth, like Danny Williams, between her work and her home—with the conflict between those obligations yielding the most premise-related story. Others in the cast include amusing folks like future *Danny Thomas* regular Sid Melton as Jan's agent, Arte Johnson as the neighborhood deli owner, and Merry Anders as one of the roommates. All are strong, as is Janis Paige, who exhibits a natural flare for comedy and, like Thomas, gets a chance to sing every week. And yet, despite a fine cast and funny writing in the *Make Room for Daddy* vein, the storytelling for *It's Always Jan* does not end up being *as* driven by its characters, especially Jan's, as it's more narratively consumed by guests and comic circumstance. You could say, then, it's a low-concept sitcom that *should* be character driven but nevertheless ends up more enamored of its episodic ideas, making it idea driven. Whatever the case, it was a promising show that never quite rose to the occasion of *Make Room for Daddy*. Incidentally, the same could be said about *It's a Great Life*, in its second and final season during 1955–1956. We discussed it last chapter—it boasted a promise-filled premise not capably explored in story. That doesn't change this year, rendering it another show that lets itself down.

In terms of other new sitcoms that are worth noting, this season also offered the filmed, syndicated version of radio's long-running *The Great Gildersleeve*, which debuted in 1941 as a spin-off of the influential *Fibber McGee and Molly*. This video update starred Willard Waterman (who'd been playing the role on radio since 1950)[18] instead of the original Harold Peary, and with a lesser cast overall, it couldn't but feel like another disappointing attempt to recapture old magic without some of the elements that made it possible in the first place. Much like the filmed and syndicated television iteration of *Duffy's Tavern*, it isn't competitive within this new landscape. Not even the strong Gildersleeve character can compensate for tired, unimaginative storytelling and plots that simply don't feature him or the premise well.

Additionally, the summer of 1956 saw two more filmed audienceless sitcoms hit the airwaves—one was the previously cited *Joe and Mabel*, another adaptation of a radio series from 1941,[19] this one about a taxicab driver and his manicurist girlfriend. The show was supposed to premiere in the fall of 1955 but got delayed by a Screen Actors Guild strike,[20] thereby allowing *Meet Millie* a last-minute reprieve and bumping *Joe and Mabel* to the summer, where it was far less likely to succeed. In terms of its quality, the series is a working-class sitcom anchored by a streetwise couple who aren't yet married, despite her best efforts to pester him (Larry Blyden) into a proposal. Star Nita Talbot is fun as the eponymous Mabel, instilling in her role a droll wiseacre quality that contrasts well against the fundamental daffiness necessary for the plots, but to that point, the stories are generic and uninspired, not often engaging the premised relational dynamics, and without the simplicity and elevating performances of *The Honeymooners* cast, for instance. So *Joe and Mabel* is another forgettable, middling entry—I wish its leads were able to contribute more actively to story.

The other new summer sitcom was *The Charlie Farrell Show*, a vehicle from Hal Roach Studios for the eponymous *My Little Margie* alum, casting him as the manager of a Palm Springs Hotel and racquet club (mirroring the actor's real life) with a decent supporting cast—including Charles Winninger, Richard Deacon (later of *The Dick Van Dyke Show*), and Kathryn Card (of *I Love Lucy*). Unfortunately, the hotel setting provides a premised excuse to focus on guests more than the regulars and their relationships, so the series' use of its situation—its characters—leaves a lot to be desired. Again, it is a shame, as there was potential in its setup and with its strong casting.

Speaking of potential, perhaps the most interesting new sitcom of the year was NBC's *The People's Choice*, a funny, one-of-a-kind single-camera comedy created by *The Life of Riley*'s Irving Brecher but mostly written this year by Alan Lipscott and Bob Fisher and coproduced by George Burns's McCadden. Starring former child actor Jackie Cooper, *The People's Choice*'s high-concept premise centers on Cooper's Sock, a bird-loving ornithologist from a small California city who lives in a trailer with the aunt who raised him and is thrust, in the series premiere, into small-time local politics by Mandy, the mayor's daughter who loves him. There are a lot of interesting possibilities for story in that log line, with a decently unique lead at the center. Here's the problem: none of the other regulars are inherently amusing (except perhaps the mayor himself—played with bluster by Paul Maxey). So the series is forced to scramble—creating the role of a weird French artist who disappears mid-season, before stumbling into the best remembered part of this off-beat, atypical format: the narrated thoughts of Cleo, Sock's basset hound, voiced for most of the run by *I Love Lucy*'s and *Ozzie and Harriet*'s Mary Jane Croft. Cleo is a gimmick meant to add easy laughs, for while a communicated perspective makes her something more of a character than most sitcom animals, Cleo doesn't exist in story like a lead—she does not drive action or make choices. She's a device—providing the jokes on which to end scenes.

In story, the situation is not well realized either; instead of exploring the fun of Sock's ineptitude at local politics, most plots are episodic and related to some guest and/or episodic circumstance not caused by Sock or his pals. The romance, fortunately, is better handled—even though Mandy's rather bland, there's a sweetness to their rapport, and the plotting of this first season progresses their relationship believably so that we look forward to upcoming developments. Accordingly, *The People's Choice* is special—it's a high-concept sitcom that doesn't do well by its high-concept premise but instead has more success with the individual relationships supporting it—the reverse of the usual. And it is only Mandy's lack of comedic definition that ultimately precludes character-based greatness within their dynamic. Otherwise, it's cute—it has promise, including some narrative continuity within the episodic apparatus that also makes the series seem smarter than its storytelling otherwise proves it to be. That is, episodes move the situation forward but their plots are not well connected to the individual characters and how they're defined. And as the show will continue to evolve its situation in the two seasons ahead, it never improves—the leads never get more helpful. Only the series' second episode, "How Sock Met Mandy" (October 13, 1955), evidences much character-based comedy in narrative.

Fortunately, if the sitcom genre always has its middling and subpar efforts—like *Private Secretary*, still trucking along in a successful but mediocre fourth season—1955–1956 asserts its overall strength through a few other shows that are in good, maybe even great, condition. One of these is the network-hopping *The Bob Cummings Show*, now in its first full year—second season overall—and in even better shape than it was before, evolving its understanding of its situation courtesy of a terrific roster of supporting players, including all our favorites from last year and now Kathleen Freeman in the recurring role of Schultzy's friend Bertha Krause. Meanwhile, the series' premise remains well invoked, so much so that head writer Paul Henning is already having fun playing on or against our expectations—specifically in an arc where Bob is actually given a *real* love interest, someone for whom he has genuine feelings that might indeed end his perennial bachelorhood and stifle his attempts at avoiding this era's typical domestic responsibilities. She is Kay Michaels (Lola Albright)—sister of his bachelor buddy Paul Fonda (Lyle Talbot), and her handful of episodes serve to deepen Bob's character by showing that he has a capacity for love. Although their romance never settles him down—the "status quo" is therefore not disturbed—he does feel like a more dimensional and lifelike figure for having shown the potential to change.

Another example of the series' brains this season can be found in its introduction of Ruthie (Mary Lawrence), Bob's married pal Harvey's domineering wife. She starts recurring in the latter half of Season Two, and all her episodes tend to be winners, for she is the walking personification of the restricting married life Bob seeks to eschew by remaining single and playing the field. We'll see much more of her next season in, no coincidence, what is ultimately the series' strongest showing. But her introduction, just as with the Kay Michaels arc, reveals a brilliant understanding of the series' premise and how to play up to it in story. This intelligence pairs well with some growing comic imagination, yielding more fantasy sequences that comedically comment on the action. So, even more than last season, CBS's *Bob Cummings* is one of the funniest shows on the air, and some of its best episodes this year include "Bob Falls in Love" (October 20, 1955), where Bob is gaga over Kay Michaels, "The Sheik" (December 29, 1955) in which Nancy Kulp shines as Pamela and Schultzy has a fantasy about Bob, and "The Sergeant Wore Skirts" (May 10, 1956), which looks forward to next year's funnier and even more narratively pointed Ruthie stories.

Speaking of best, I think it is fitting to end this chapter by checking back in on the year's most popular sitcom, *I Love Lucy*, still the era's paragon of character-driven writing, which has been contrasted so far against the best of this season's idea-driven lot: *The Honeymooners* and *The Phil Silvers Show*. This is the only year where the three coexist, alone elevating 1955–1956 above its peers. And indeed, *Lucy* remains in solid form—it's just, unlike those freshmen, not at its *best* here, struggling more than ever before to find stories that take direct advantage of Lucy's central objective or finding episodic plots that at least can be extrapolatable based on all the established traits associated with her depiction. While last season's Hollywood arc breathed new life into the premise by reengaging scripts with show biz trappings that could uplift episodic narratives, this year, Season Five, is less rejuvenating. It opens with four shows still set in Hollywood—including a two-parter where Lucy and the Mertzes steal John Wayne's footprints from Grauman's Chinese Theater: the ultimate manifestation of her star obsession—a running characteristic directly related to her aggrandized aspirations. (Both "Lucy Visits Grauman's" and "Lucy and John Wayne"—from October 3 and October 10, 1955, respectively—are classic half hours.)

But once the company returns home to New York City and their brownstone apartment, the writers—which now include Bob Schiller and Bob Weiskopf, joining veterans Madelyn Pugh and Bob Carroll, Jr., as head scribe Jess Oppenheimer was planning to step away from his duties at the conclusion of this season—prove themselves to be less inspired. So they quickly shoehorn the characters into another vacation arc, which makes sense since the Hollywood trip was so successful. This time, it's a European tour, with Ricky working, Fred serving as his cheap tour manager, and the wives tagging along after some prodding. Hopping from England to France to Italy naturally creates new stimuli for story based on the locations alone, but that's just it: these ideas aren't *as* steeped in the show's specifics as they were at its height. And while Lucy still drives the plotting of individual episodes, and the big comic centerpieces *are* motivated by her consistent characterization, a lot of the impetus for scripts are coming externally and not so much from the leads and their relationships. This feels less character driven and in fact gimmickier—as if the show *needs* this trip to continue generating worthwhile offerings.

Now, if that sounds weak, it's not. It's still *I Love Lucy*, and that strong foundation of character always exists, so there remains many classic episodes with memorable bits that are hilarious and earned by her characterization. Aside from the aforementioned two-parter, some of the best include "Lucy Gets a Paris Gown" (March 19, 1956), where Lucy's desire to be more than the typical housewife finds her pestering Ricky for a fancy Parisian gown, which Ricky and Fred decide to give to their wives—well, sort of—leading to an amusing centerpiece that emphasizes the way in which the two women, especially Lucy, is concerned with how she's viewed in society, and "Return Home from Europe" (May 14, 1956), which is more enamored of a comic idea than a great character objective but nevertheless *is* supported by continuity: the lengths to which we know Lucy will go to get what she wants—in this case, a souvenir.

▶ And there are still two episodes from this season that make my top 50 list. One of them, at **#20**, is "**The Great Train Robbery**," which was first broadcast on **October 31, 1955**. Its story has Lucy trying to catch a jewel thief who is apparently riding with them on the train back from Los Angeles to New York. **James V. Kern** directed, while the script was written by this year's staff: **Bob Schiller**; **Bob Weiskopf**; **Madelyn Pugh**; **Bob Carroll, Jr.**; and **Jess Oppenheimer**.

Narratively, this is an unusual selection, for it's not only got a one-off episodic setting that makes the whole thing feel gimmicky and more disconnected from the regular situation, but it also claims a story where the drama is derived from some kind of external force and not specifically the relationships between the leads. However, its comic centerpieces—including the gag of Lucy repeatedly pulling the emergency brake and irritating the ever-irritated Frank Nelson—are just too good to ignore. And more important, Lucy behaves entirely in-character, specifically when she's tasked with helping catch an apparent jewel thief—a mission that calls on her to *perform*, which is what she wants to do anyway. More broadly, she feels important when she has an outside purpose, and it satisfies the character's ego—what she wants and who she wants to be. Accordingly, it's a showcase for the Lucy persona, and her brand of comedy is at the fore.

▶ However, the best offering from this season is one of *Lucy*'s all-time classics—coming in at **#5** on my list. It's "**Lucy's Italian Movie**," where Lucy visits an Italian winery after being cast in an Italian film. First broadcast on **April 16, 1956**, it was also directed by **James V. Kern** and written by the same crew—**Oppenheimer, Pugh, Carroll, Schiller,** and **Weiskopf.**

"Lucy's Italian Movie" is probably better known as the "grape-stomping episode," but while the memory of that iconic centerpiece—where Lucy gets into a physical brawl with an Italian woman while stomping grapes in a vat—is hysterical, some may forget how she gets there: a famous Italian director spots her being dramatic on a train and decides she would be perfect in his movie, casting her in a film that she learns is to be called "Bitter Grapes." This opportunity is what she's always wanted—directly attached to her core desire of being in show business—and her actions thus make sense, for in her overzealousness for a career that is now within reach, she goes off to a local winery for some research so she will be well versed in the film's subject matter. This, of course, sets up the bit. But the plot itself remains rooted in Lucy's objective, and the act of getting to the winery is motivated, based on the consistency of her depiction.

So this is the kind of character-driven setup that, even as it's not *as* common on the series as it was in years past, continues to distinguish it as a jewel of the decade, right up there with *The Honeymooners* and *The Phil Silvers Show*—the two idea-driven classics whose sensibilities would come to represent a counter-aesthetic to *Lucy*'s. They're always more focused around the funny idea than the characters and relationships that allow them to exist. It is the opposite of the way that "Lucy's Italian Movie" works—*only* with a character like Lucy Ricardo.

Of course, both *The Honeymooners* and *The Phil Silvers Show* have memorable characters who help support their funny ideas as well, giving weight to other elements within their situations. Comparing these two styles of writing, then, is satisfying in 1955-1956, for this is a season with compelling ambassadors—and the two divergent but never mutually exclusive paths that the sitcom will follow in the decades ahead are nevertheless delineated. Many shows indeed took cues from these outstanding efforts: a trio of classics that brilliantly exemplify why the sitcom is a challenging but rewarding art form, capable of evoking just as much laughter today as in the 1950s.

But this is the top. From here on out, the sitcom genre will essentially be in decline for the rest of the decade, because after peaking in prominence during the 1954-1955 season and excelling via a handful of its finest representations here during 1955-1956, the loss of this era's best shows and the senseless popularity of terrible examples of sit-commery like *Father Knows Best*, which established this era's reputation for laugh-lite benignity, would leave the form both artistically restrained and, due to imitations of lesser products, commercially undesirable compared to alternative types of programming. In fact, as we will explore over the next few chapters, the television sitcom would go through its first metaphorical "drought"—a period of unpopularity, directly correlated to the relatively lower quality of the situation comedies that did exist on the air. It would take until the early 1960s for a full recovery to occur.

## JACKSON'S BEST SITCOMS FROM 1955-56

1. THE PHIL SILVERS SHOW (S1)
2. THE HONEYMOONERS (S1)
3. I LOVE LUCY (S5)

## EPISODES FROM THE 1955-56 SEASON IN JACKSON'S TOP 50 FROM THE '50s

#3. THE PHIL SILVERS SHOW (S1): "The Court Martial" (3/6/56)
#4. THE HONEYMOONERS (S1): "Better Living Through TV" (11/12/55)
#5. I LOVE LUCY (S5): "Lucy's Italian Movie" (4/16/56)
#6. THE HONEYMOONERS (S1): "The $99,000 Answer" (1/28/56)
#19. THE HONEYMOONERS (S1): "The Golfer" (10/15/55)
#20. I LOVE LUCY (S5): "The Great Train Robbery" (10/31/55)
#25. THE PHIL SILVERS SHOW (S1): "Empty Store" (9/27/55)
#35. THE PHIL SILVERS SHOW (S1): "Bivouac" (11/29/55)
#37. THE GEORGE BURNS AND GRACIE ALLEN SHOW (S6): "Mrs. Sohmers Needs a Psychologist" (9/17/56)
#38. THE PHIL SILVERS SHOW (S1): "The Twitch" (12/13/55)

## OTHER NOTABLE EPISODES FROM 1955-56

I LOVE LUCY (S5): "Lucy Visits Grauman's" (10/3/55)
I LOVE LUCY (S5): "Lucy and John Wayne" (10/10/55)
THE PEOPLE'S CHOICE (S1): "How Sock Met Mandy" (10/13/55)
THE BOB CUMMINGS SHOW (S2): "Bob Falls in Love" (10/20/55)
THE GEORGE BURNS AND GRACIE ALLEN SHOW (S6): "Harry Morton's Cocktail Party" (10/31/55)
FATHER KNOWS BEST (S2): "Father Is a Dope" (11/2/55)
THE PHIL SILVERS SHOW (S1): "The Eating Contest" (11/15/55)
THE HONEYMOONERS (S1): "A Matter of Record" (1/7/56)
THE BOB CUMMINGS SHOW (S2): "The Sheik" (12/29/55)
THE HONEYMOONERS (S1): "Young at Heart" (2/11/56)
DECEMBER BRIDE (S2): "Sunken Den" (2/20/56)
MAKE ROOM FOR DADDY (S3): "Terry and the Sorority" (2/28/56)
I LOVE LUCY (S5): "Lucy Gets a Paris Gown" (3/19/56)
THE HONEYMOONERS (S1): "Head of the House" (3/31/56)
THE HONEYMOONERS (S1): "Unconventional Behavior" (5/12/56)
I LOVE LUCY (S5): "Return Home from Europe" (5/14/56)
THE HONEYMOONERS (S1): "Dial 'J' for Janitor" (9/15/56)

CHAPTER NINE

# The End of the Beginning
*The Best Television Sitcoms of 1956–1957*

By the time the sitcom entered the 1956–1957 season—the seventh of the 1950s and the tenth for this genre on television (counting *Mary Kay and Johnny* as its first example in 1947)—the form had really matured. No longer a niche entertainment for only the 10 percent of the population who could afford it (as in 1950), television now reached over 70 percent of American households.[1] As the country embraced TV as a daily routine, the television sitcom became a familiar distraction—and many reminders of its unsure early years were starting to fade away. Indeed, this year would see the end of the half-hour weekly version of *I Love Lucy* and leave only two comedies on the air that predated it—one being the "modified sitcom" hosted by Jack Benny and the other *The George Burns and Gracie Allen Show*, which like so many examples from this era, was deliberately reinventing itself, transitioning into something creatively new.

Now in its seventh season and returning to the couple's redesigned Beverly Hills home, *Burns and Allen* continued its previous attempts to build up new regular Ronnie Burns, playing a version of himself, as a teen sensation. But as always, unless George and in particular Gracie, the comedic anchor, are well involved, the show isn't using the core aspect of its situation. In fact, this year ends up being a middling one, with weaker ideas and not enough of the star. However, Ronnie remains beneficial in the same way he did last year—his inclusion strengthens the series' relationship with its own autobiographical details and its corresponding aesthetic realism. This sense of increased literal truth is especially welcome now that the show is ramping up its willingness to play up its own metatheatricality. That is, it's willing to be less subtle in acknowledging its "fourth wall"—its own bounds as a sitcom, which, yes, is also taking more cues from its stars' real life but still contorting them to enable narrative fodder for the TV show on which they are appearing. Heck, the TV show they're on almost becomes *part* of the series' formal situation here in Season Seven with the introduction of something that viewers have termed George's "magic TV"—a literal television set that George, in the show, uses to watch the show itself, allowing him to view the action, comment on it, and sometimes intervene.

Of course, "modified" sitcoms have always been intrinsically metatheatrical, and George has always stepped out of a scene to address the audience—in the live years, he did so while leaning on the proscenium of a stage, very theatrically. During the earlier filmed years, he spoke right to the camera—a direct address, like a monologue. And he always had intel about episodic plots, made jokes about the show as entertainment, and even deliberately interjected himself to complicate the action. Now, though, while he still speaks right to camera, the apparatus that gives him all this information is his TV—which means *Burns and Allen* is now contextualized as a television show, graduating from its theatrical, vaudeville roots and the simple implications of film into this unique medium where the sitcom, as a form, has become established enough to inform a series' actual situation, for its status as a TV comedy can now be considered a vital part of its identity—something viewers can expect to find regularly reiterated through George's own screen, as a program he, the character, watches. With this move, *Burns and Allen* completes its trajectory of embracing the sitcom genre and, specifically, the sitcom genre on television, and this "magic TV," a cool device introduced in "The Missing Stamp" (November 12, 1956), is a symbol of this evolution in the medium at large, for now television is firmly ensconced in the lives of its viewers and its subjects. But we'll talk more about this special "magic TV" next chapter, so stay tuned.

## New York Fights Back

As *Burns and Allen* reflects the maturation of the sitcom, 1956-1957 did boast one blast from the past—the only official full-scale sitcom this season totally broadcast live to air, and from New York. As we have tracked, live TV was a vestige of the medium's initial technical limitations and necessary New York–centricity. But as film became the preferred means of production via enhanced quality and network connectivity, the industry moved out to Hollywood, where the greatest talent for filmed products resided. By 1956–1957, almost every network sitcom was shot in California, and this was the only true live effort—coming from New York City and produced by *Your Show of Shows* and *Caesar's Hour*'s Max Liebman. It's *Stanley*, starring comic Buddy Hackett as the eponymous Stanley, a mama's boy who works at the newsstand of a Manhattan hotel. Writers for the program included many of Caesar's scribes, among them Lucille Kallen, the Simon brothers—Neil and Danny—and a young Woody Allen. Meanwhile, the cast boasted a dewy Carol Burnett as Stanley's understanding girlfriend Celia, debuting in the fourth episode, and Paul Lynde, who initially recurred as the voice of the unseen hotel owner.

Despite a great cast and crew, *Stanley* is never great—Hackett and Burnett bring a lot of charming big energy to their performances, but their characters are fairly nebulous in comparison to those on, say, *Mister Peepers*, the best study-able live New York sitcom, which counted great leads in Peepers, Wes, and Mrs. Gurney (among others). But *Stanley*'s scripts and stars do ham it up more in pursuit of laughs, and their efforts to enhance the comedy are therefore noble for this genre. That objective also pairs well with the show's own liveness, as the forced confinement of story to only what's theatrically possible encourages more reliance on characters in simple conversation. This would be a recipe for success if, again, the leads were better defined and not so dependent on the actors themselves to make interesting material out of pretty banal texts.

▶ That said, it's just fun to see these stars play together in scripts by great writers who are all pursuing a comedic goal, so it's a show that has us rooting for it. And hey, there *are* a few memorable entries, the best of which is Burnett's debut, "**Celia Goes to a TV Show**," also known as "Stanley Gets Jealous" from **October 22, 1956**, where the show parodies the new Elvis Presley fascination by having Celia erupt into hysterics when she's in the live audience of a TV program with a similar singing idol—a wild demonstration of fandom by Burnett that's uproarious and, of course, causes Stanley to turn into the proverbial green-eyed monster. Written by **Russell Beggs**, **Lucille Kallen**, and **Woody Allen** and directed by **David Brown**, this entry is **#30** on my list.

It earns this distinction because, as a show that struggles to be character driven, this entry at least starts with a funny idea, and the performers really sell it, implying characterizations as a result of their big choices. Narratively, it misses a good climax, and in that regard, it's little more than an extended sketch—as many idea-driven sitcoms are, even low-concept ones that *should* be more character driven (like *Stanley*). But it's clever, TV literate—acknowledging the medium in the same way that *Burns and Allen* was now doing—and very watchable, for, again, the laugh objective is pronounced, thanks to two stars who emphasize the unique theatricality that only comes from live TV. Unfortunately, the series was not a hit, and Liebman's endeavor to reassert liveness (and New York–ness) as a viable option going forward was a failure[2]—rendering this the last *major* live sitcom from New York, and the 1950s' penultimate example in that category.

The only other sitcoms that were still occasionally broadcasting live in 1956–1957 came from Hollywood and were in the "modified-sitcom" category—that is, a little closer to their comedy-variety show roots, with songs and sketches. One, of course, is *The Jack Benny Program*, now in its seventh season and with a commensurate ratio of sitcom outings to variety outings compared to last year and still a mixture of live and filmed half hours—four of which were actually shot on location in Europe.[3] These gimmicky on-location episodes are especially bad because while they intend to be sitcoms, they mine a lot of yuks and story from their unique settings, not from the characters and their relationships. In general, this season is also not as fresh as others—most of the good ideas have been done before and better. Meanwhile, the other occasionally live "modified sitcom" was very much in the *Jack Benny* camp—*The Marge and Gower Champion Show*, a new comedy built around the eponymous pair of married dancers, incorporating so many musical set pieces that it's as much a musical as a sitcom, elements of which are but a means to this tuneful end.

Celia (Carol Burnett, left) and Buddy Hackett in *Stanley*, "Celia Goes to a TV Show" (1956).

Like *Benny*, the show came from Hollywood and alternated between live and filmed segments.[4] Never again would the West Coast offer a fully live weekly sitcom, even one on "modified" terms. That died the previous season with the end of CBS's *Meet Millie*, leaving the Champions' show to be a hybrid postscript.

As for New York, Jackie Gleason, who had previously filmed *The Honeymooners* there, opted to return to his self-titled variety show for 1956–1957, folding "The Honeymooners" back into weekly sketches, some of which were now hour-long musicals about a trip to Europe—a terrible idea-driven example of, like Jack Benny's vacation, using a new locale and accompanying gimmicks to spark story, rather than any character- or premise-based source of regular identity. This left *The Phil Silvers Show* as the most prominent filmed comedy from New York. Now in its second season, this classic idea-driven sitcom was still in terrific shape, offering hilarious ideas unique to the show and its situation, capably aided by the star characterization of Sgt. Bilko. Additionally, the season's output still boasts a prime display of creator Nat Hiken's fast-paced, whip-smart storytelling—not to mention, per the era, its increasing metatheatrics, which shows up in episodes where the series comments on its identity as a sitcom, like in "Sergeant Bilko Presents Ed Sullivan" (December 18, 1956), or merely when fixated on show business and performance as a narrative concern, like in "Sergeant Bilko Presents Bing Crosby" (January 22, 1957), despite having a regular situation that's otherwise not show biz related.

Speaking of Hiken, he remained in control of the series during Season Two but sought to eventually reduce his involvement, hoping to groom a protégé to replace him. Initially, Hiken's choice was *The Honeymooners*' Leonard Stern, who left mid-year to lead Steve Allen's comedy-variety show after realizing it was impossible to write *The Phil Silvers Show* as well as Hiken himself could.[5] Other scribes, like Billy Friedberg—who had earlier contributed to *Stanley*—would come to realize this as well, as he officially took the wheel from Hiken in the following season.[6] Of course, the show's annual quality tracks with the level of Hiken's involvement—its best ideas and most situation-validating sensibilities are most consistently offered in Season One and still evident here in Season Two. But they've already become a little less ingenious and a little less reliable in accordance with his own loosening grip. And then the final seasons—while still good for the genre—are not nearly as brilliant or one of a kind as their predecessors. Season Two, then, is the show's second best.

And it has a lot of hilarious episodes—most of them in the first two-thirds of the year, prior to when the show stopped shooting live before an audience, dropping that sketch-related, theatrical, and very New York part of its identity for the sake of a smoother, easier production.[7] This trade-off would alter the series' rhythm and strip away some of its authenticity as far as its aesthetic is concerned—right ahead of Hiken's departure. But that's more a problem for the years ahead. In Season Two, there are many classics. Some of my favorites include the best of the metatheatrical entries: "It's for the Birds" (September 25, 1956), which spoofs the TV season's quiz show craze in a way that again acknowledges the medium, and "Bilko's Television Idea" (February 12, 1957), which literally winks at the idea of its own existence as a sitcom, in a way that only "modified sitcoms" (or even variety-rooted ones like *Burns and Allen*) tend to do.

The year also has several hilarious entries built around the comic presence of Doberman (Maurice Gosfield), someone who isn't terribly well defined but his looks and moves are so innately funny that we're willing to fill in the blanks in classics like "The Face on the Recruiting Poster" (October 16, 1956) and "The Big Scandal" (May 14, 1957).

▶ The best of this year's Doberman-focused offerings makes my top 50 list at **#46**. It's "**Doberman's Sister**," which first aired on **November 20, 1956**, and is about Bilko's efforts to con one of his men into dating Doberman's sister. **Nat Hiken** wrote the script with **Billy Friedberg**, **Tony Webster**, and **Leonard Stern**. **Al De Caprio** directed.

Although this popular entry is largely remembered for its hysterical climax, where Maurice Gosfield dons drag to play his character's sister, it makes my list because it's actually a terrific showing for Bilko, the perennial schemer, who invents a bogus legend called "Musselman's Law"—which says, "the uglier the brother, the more beautiful the sister"—all in an effort to convince a member of the platoon to ask out Doberman's visiting sibling. It's another clever Bilko maneuver—and the idea itself, unsurprisingly for this idea-driven sitcom, is hilarious, especially given

**Sgt. Bilko (Phil Silvers, left) and Maurice Gosfield as Doberman's sister in *The Phil Silvers Show*, "Doberman's Sister" (1956).**

the final reveal. So, for using the lead character well in support of this funny notion, it's an easy classic.

▶ This season also has great Bilko schemes centered on Joe E. Ross's Ritzik. The best of these is **#33** on my list, **"A Mess Sergeant Can't Win."** It was written by the same crew as above—**Hiken, Friedberg, Webster**, and **Stern**—with **De Caprio** directing. First airing on **November 13, 1956**, its story has Bilko trying to trick Ritzik into winning *back* his gambling losses!

Now, this is obviously a primo idea for *The Phil Silvers Show* because it plays against our expectations—instead of its lead trying to bilk one of his men out of money, he actively tries to help him win it back. And this proves to be a much more impossible task. That's not only very funny, but it also only works with a character who is defined like Bilko, for the comic notion is predicated on our understanding of how he usually operates. Also, viewers tend to appreciate this story because it presents Bilko a little more multidimensionally, as his episodic goal is altruistic, for the benefit of someone else. That someone else is Ritzik, who is introduced here as a replacement for the first year's Sowici. Also married, Rizik, played by the unpredictable Joe E. Ross, is one of the only tangible improvements between the otherwise superior first year and this mostly great sophomore collection, for he's a lot more comedically nimble than his predecessor, and his rapport with Beatrice Pons as wife

Emma is so electric that Hiken would reuse the two—as another pair of bickering spouses—in his next sitcom, *Car 54, Where Are You?* This is the first indication of just what comedic gold they'll manage to be later, and it's a standout.

▶ However, my pick for the best *Phil Silvers* episode of the season is the frenetic "**Love That Guardhouse**," which was first broadcast on **January 15, 1957**, and lands on my list at **#17**. **Al De Caprio** directed, and the script, by **Nat Hiken**, **Billy Friedberg**, **Arnie Rosen**, and **Coleman Jacoby**, is about Colonel Hall's efforts to prevent Bilko from getting Ritzik's Las Vegas winnings.

"Love That Guardhouse" makes the best use this season of Bilko's character, courtesy of a stellar idea—a story firmly rooted in the series' premised situation, about a chronic gambler stationed at an army base. It's well supported by the established relationships between the regulars—specifically, their collective and individual histories with Bilko—and the script allows Bilko to plot and scheme. Here, he's trying to circumvent the precautions Emma has beseeched Colonel Hall to put in place (namely, locking Ritzik in a guardhouse), so that he can be alone with the weak-willed Ritzik and cheat him out of some Las Vegas winnings. This makes for the best showcase of the series' central characterization, evidenced through his actions, and the reactions to him by everyone else, which are able to motivate a unique and fast-paced story in demonstration of Nat Hiken's one-of-a-kind idea-driven style. So, this segment is a sublime display of *The Phil Silvers Show* at large, and best of all, its character work is artful as well.

## *Glorifying the White Picket Fence*

*The Phil Silvers Show* is especially brilliant when compared to some of the other long-running sitcoms of the year—primarily the domestic entries, including the bland *Father Knows Best*, in a particularly uninspired third season, and even *The Life of Riley*, whose fifth season is better than its direct predecessor because the neighboring Gillises are back and NBC threw more of a budget at the show, shooting several entries in color,[8] and allowing scripts to be more creative (like in a Hawaiian trip arc). But it's still not really taking advantage of the things that make it unique in story—its blue-collar bent and how that can inspire Riley's objectives. It's still generic. Fortunately, that's less true right now of *The Adventures of Ozzie and Harriet*, also in its fifth season and undergoing something of a transitional era, as Ozzie's best friend Thorny (Don DeFore) is phased out, forcing the leading man to branch out more with Darby (Parley Baer) and the newly introduced secondary couple, the Randolphs (Lyle Talbot and Mary Jane Croft).

More to the point, though, this is the start of *Ozzie and Harriet*'s teen domination, as Ricky Nelson's first single was released in spring 1957,[9] and the show promoted it by having his character croon it in the pivotal "Ricky the Drummer" (April 10, 1957). From here on out, the series will split its time being a show about the adults and a show about the two young adult sons, both of whom see their outside career endeavors pushed, primarily Ricky as a new pop star, whose newfound celebrity rejuvenated the show and kept it running until 1966. This was good for the bottom line but not so good creatively, for the boys, like Harriet, remain incredibly bland, and just because Ricky's now singing every other week and stories are starting to be set on the college campus doesn't mean anyone has magically developed personalities. If only that were true! No, they are still vague, and Ozzie remains the only funny regular, with some support from his mildly amusing adult friends—specifically Clara, portrayed by the funny Mary Jane Croft, a very busy performer this season. Accordingly, with this shift in the show's understanding of itself starting to occur here in Season Five, this year offers less situation-validating sitcommery, even though there still are segments that stand above the fray—all of them adult led, including "The Fishing Lure" (June 12, 1957), which is so appropriately trivial and detail-oriented that it's funny, presenting the notion that a trinket on a fancy hat could be a good "bait" when fishing.

Another sitcom in a transitional season was the newly titled *The Danny Thomas Show*, which changed its name from *Make Room for Daddy* because it lost Mommy, as Jean Hagen decided not to renew her contract and her character was written out—leaving Danny Williams now a widower, forced to raise his two children all alone. This is a fascinating wrinkle added to the show's situation, which had heretofore been based on the autobiographical conflict of Danny trying to balance his responsibilities as both performer and parent. Now he's the only parent, and thus the conflict is pushed even more to the fore. In fact, it's almost the culmination of this series' premise as it originally existed, for Danny has no choice now but to *make* a choice—his priority is decidedly at home. Of course, that was always the case, but with the kids continuing to grow up and therefore becoming more viable scene partners, there's also more story and comedy opportunities in the home and more incentive to remain there almost exclusively. So even as the hilarious Mary Wickes recurs this year as Danny's press agent and a de facto mother figure for the kids, the bonds between the Williamses are already more developed and utilizable for episodic plot than anything else, especially with the widower angle allowing for related conflicts, some that are sentimental, which is okay when it's directly attached to the situation, and some that naturally deal with a structural reality: most sitcoms about families offer the traditional "nuclear" arrangement, with a mom, a dad, and their kids. And even though this show is urban and show bizzy, it still wants to be a family sitcom too, so finding another mother is on its immediate to-do list.

This means that Danny actively dates this season—in fact, Barbara Billingsley, a few months prior to June Cleaver, even plays one of his love interests—before the final four episodes of the year introduce the woman who'll eventually become his wife and the show's leading lady in its following season: Marjorie Lord as Kathy, a widowed nurse (with a young daughter) who clashes with Danny when she comes to care for a measles-ridden Rusty. Her debut episode, "Danny Meets Kathy" (April

4, 1957), is the best of this season due to the excitement of their chemistry—which is contentious and therefore suggests both comedic and narrative opportunities, especially because this iteration of Kathy is someone who can go toe to toe with Danny, with her Irish heritage matching the established Lebanese part of his persona, a nice autobiographical touch.

Speaking of autobiographical, Thomas broke his leg at the start of the season, so scripts had to write it in as well—another little detail that makes this show seem realer than its counterparts and, like *Lucy*, focused on little things that help its characters feel well defined. With such attention to detail, they're now more conducive to whatever story arises, as generic ideas can draw on specifics to look more precisely tailored to them. Indeed, as these characters become more interesting (amid the kids' continued growing up), this year's forced widower tweak in the show's situation actually plays directly into its original premise, and with a tone that's balancing both humor and heart in an earned way, this is the best year of this series yet. However, further heights will be reached next season when the show jumps from ABC to CBS and literally replaces *I Love Lucy* on the schedule, assuming that titan's position as the Tiffany Network's most important comedy.

Meanwhile, other shows shot by Desilu during 1956–1957 besides *The Danny Thomas Show* and the aforementioned *I Love Lucy* include *December Bride*, now in its third season and still no better—indulging a copycat cross-country trip like *Lucy* did a few years back but with nothing great to show for it—and the second season of *Those Whiting Girls*, which originally aired in the summer of 1955 and was back for the summer of 1957, now with Jerry Paris added to the cast but still no improvement from the basic shortcomings that existed before. Also during this season, Desilu helped shoot a new live audience multi-cam starring Gale Gordon and Bob Sweeney called *The Brothers*—a buddy comedy for those two *Our Miss Brooks* alums that cast them as a pair of opposites, living together in San Francisco. With delineated personalities that allowed for a clear relational dynamic and a nice comic rapport between two strong performers, *The Brothers* had potential. I have seen only two episodes, but they indicate a proficiency with comedy (including slapstick) via help from character, which is better than most short-lived efforts of this decade.

Like, for instance, *Date with the Angels*, which premiered in May 1957 as a vehicle for Betty White, "America's Sweetheart," whose syndicated comedy *Life with Elizabeth* had wrapped production in 1955.[10] *Angels* would be her first network sitcom and her first multi-cam filmed before an audience. She was cast in an Elizabeth-like role, as Vickie Angel, another cutesy newlywed. Yet there was a hook to this otherwise unoriginal low-concept premise, and it was inspired by Elmer Rice's play *Dream Girl*: its heroine would have an active imagination that could allow for fantasy sequences. This would permit the show to flex its comic and creative muscles, not just offering typical domestic scenarios but tweaking them based on her fears, insecurities, goals, and desires. Unfortunately, after the pilot—shot by Desilu in 1956[11]—this *Dream Girl* angle was dropped, leaving the series to become the banal husband-and-wife affair it originally did not want to be (think the Lucy-less *My Favorite Husband*), and even with recurring support from funny folks like Burt Mustin, Maudie Prickett, and Richard Deacon, who enliven sketch-like ideas in segments such as "Shall We Dance?" (June 21, 1957), *Date with the Angels*—produced by Don Fedderson—never cultivated a way to be funny with its leading couple, either in this 12-episode summer run or its 21-episode second season in 1957–1958. The series simply failed to meet the central requirement of all sitcoms: defining its characters. Not even Betty White could overcome that hurdle. In fact, after such a tough experience, she took her time returning to the grind of regular television sitcommery.

With more and more productions like these adding to the Desilu roster, playing the Ricardos every week and maintaining their series' top quality was starting to become difficult for Lucille Ball and Desi Arnaz. That's ultimately why they ended the weekly *I Love Lucy* and instead committed to a series of five hour-long specials in 1957–1958. More on that decision in the next chapter. In the meantime, the show's sixth season here in 1956–1957 found the characters back from Europe and with the same problem faced in Season Five: a shortage of ideas related to the show's original New York–set situation. And with original head writer Jess Oppenheimer gone, this creative conundrum was now left up to the four remaining staffers, two of whom had only joined the year before. Season Six, then, was essentially an exercise in finding ways to reignite the show's creative spark. Its first solution, going into the year, was to finally cast Little Ricky as a speaking role, thereby giving scripts an opportunity to offer stories featuring his character.

Keith Thibodeaux was chosen for the part, but while his prodigious drum playing made him a buyable choice as Ricky Ricardo's (and Desi Arnaz's) son, he was no Rusty Hamer by way of acting and comedy. That is, it's ultimately helpful to see Little Ricky every now and then to affirm his existence within the situation, which therefore aids the show's aesthetic realism, but the less we hear of him, the better, for like most children in sitcoms, he's not a true character, just a narrative device. Nevertheless, Little Ricky is more additive than subtractive, for *I Love Lucy* knows better than to rely too heavily on him. That's only an *aspect* of the situation for these adult characters—their personalities, objectives, and relationships with each other still remain more seminal to its weekly identity. Now they just have another speaking role in the mix, a new tool to help inspire related story.

The next way that this season tries to recharge its creative engine is with another trip. Just like the Hollywood and European stints opened up new narrative avenues, that's the purpose of this year's Florida vacation, which actually consists of three amusing entries—none of them are all-timers, but they nevertheless find ways to get attached to some well-known aspect of the Lucy characterization. And because they are self-limited to only three weeks instead of half a season, it doesn't feel quite as labored as, say, the European tour. What's more, the Florida trip is followed by an entry that's set in Cuba, as the Ricardos and Mertzes take Little Ricky down to meet Ricky's family. That episode itself—"The Ricardos Visit Cuba" (December 3,

1956)—lacks a great comic centerpiece à la other *Lucy* classics, but it's a terrific idea for the series, as Ricky's ethnicity is a huge part of his characterization and one of the things imparted from Desi Arnaz's real life that lends credibility to the show and his character, affording him a linkable detail-oriented history and perspective that fills out his depiction. By taking us to meet Ricky's Cuban family—something unique to his character and therefore unique to this series—the show's situation is well invoked. It's smart and *Lucy* specific, even if comedically average by the series' own standards.

Last, the third and most major way that *Lucy* tries to recharge itself in Season Six occurs at its midpoint—its last 13 episodes—when the show decides to have its lead characters leave the city and move to the country, more specifically to Connecticut, and a version of suburbia that's perhaps more rural than the neighborhoods on *Ozzie and Harriet*, *Father Knows Best*, and *Trouble with Father*. But it feels like suburbia nonetheless—with a manicured house instead of a modest apartment. This move is fascinating, for it's almost as if *Lucy* cannot help but indulge the 1950s' rising reputation for celebrating the white picket fence, thereby reinforcing the dominance of this iconic subgenre, particularly in our collective consciousness. Of course, more Americans were indeed moving to suburbia at the time,[12] and this shift is as much a TV trend as it is a social one—that is what's being reflected. And yet, regardless of the impulse, this move in these final 13 weeks *does* creatively open up the show's possibilities for episodic story, and for the most part, the selected ideas *are* more original than those on other suburban shows, which have lesser characters.

Oh, sure, "building the barbecue" is reminiscent of an entry from the first season of one of the earliest suburban TV sitcoms, *Trouble with Father*,[13] and most ideas *have* existed in a similar form elsewhere—that's true for most half-hour stories, by the way—but these regulars still have unique, well-defined personalities, and they're strong enough to make the application of these perhaps familiar ideas feel customized to the situation, even via small details. So *Lucy*'s opportunities are indeed expanded—even by way of supporting characters, such as in the introduction of new recurring pals, the Ramseys, played by Frank Nelson and Mary Jane Croft (yes, her again!), both of whom add energy to the ensemble and allow for some conflict between the Ricardos and Mertzes. So there's a sense of freshness here at the end of Six that validates the move for basically accomplishing its goal—there are many new, funny ideas enabled by this change in setting, and most of them are enjoyable, for they still allow the characters to shine.

This is perhaps unexpected because the move to the country symbolically indicates the death of *I Love Lucy*'s original premise and specifically the unique objective afforded to Lucy Ricardo that allowed her to drive story. No longer is she in New York (or Hollywood) and actively close to entertainment venues that could afford her regular opportunities to assert herself as more than a homebody in the same way Ricky does every working night of his life. Now she's moved to Connecticut, and both she and the show are literally separated from these narrative concerns in episodic plot.

Crucially, there are very few entries during Season Six that directly address Lucy Ricardo's original objective, particularly in these final Connecticut shows, and it's almost like the character herself has given up: *she* has settled down and decided to be a typical wife and mother, no longer striving for more. Oh, sure, every story can still be extrapolated out in some way to stem from traits we know about Lucy Ricardo *based* on the previous pursuit of show business ambitions, and there are occasional reminders of it—like in the classic "Lucy Does the Tango" (March 11, 1957), which hinges on the idea that she and Ricky are performing together for the PTA. But it's not as present and guiding as it used to be. This almost seems like a defeat—for the character. Lucy Ricardo has been domesticated, subjugated, and she not only does not seem to mind, but with the end of the half-hour show, it's effectively positioned as her happy ending.

Neither the writers nor the viewers would have been thinking about the end of the show in this way—after all, Lucy is still a wacky schemer, and Ricky is still in show business. Stories are now just about their life in the country, raising the children and the chickens. It's still funny. But in terms of the storytelling, since *I Love Lucy* formally moves away from its lead's primary and heretofore situation-defining goal, then it's a good thing it ends where it does, here in Season Six, which reveals the show to be tiring. Fortunately, because of its strong foundation and concerted tweaks, it's still capable of producing excellent entries in spite of its decline. Some of the funniest include "Lucy and Superman" (January 14, 1957), a New York offering with a cameo by George Reeves, a physical centerpiece for Lucille Ball, and a plot that's motivated by her character's relatable desire to come through for Little Ricky and one-up recurring frenemy Carolyn Appleby; and "Lucy Raises Tulips" (April 29, 1957), a wonderfully suburban excursion that emphasizes Lucy's competitiveness (this time with Betty Ramsey) while also allowing Ricky a rare opportunity to be the screw-up. Also, the latter has a terrific bit of slapstick comedy as Lucy runs amok on a lawn mower—a quintessential display of how her character's bumbling physicality still exists, even though she's chosen domestication.

▶ However, the year's most famous entry—and the only that makes my top 50 list, coming in at **#12**—is the aforementioned **"Lucy Does the Tango,"** which was first broadcast on **March 11, 1957**. Written by **Bob Schiller**; **Bob Weiskopf**; **Madelyn Martin**; and **Bob Carroll, Jr.**—with direction by **William Asher**—its story finds Lucy and Ethel trying to keep their husbands from fighting now that they're working together as heretofore unsuccessful chicken breeders.

This selection is emblematic of the show's country move and the series' standing here in Season Six as a whole, with a plot that uses particulars of this new environment—like the chickens—along with the newly cast Little Ricky, who plays a larger role in the second act, when he hides the birds around the neighborhood in an effort to keep them from being sold. But this entry is interesting because it's most remembered for what happens in its funnier and more character-driven first act, where the script establishes the idea that Lucy and Ricky are doing a tango for an upcoming PTA show—which makes sense because he's still a performer, and this is a lingering reminder of her old objective, making it rooted in character—before carefully laying the groundwork for a scenario where Lucy and Ethel are attempting to hide store-bought eggs under their own chickens so that they can keep the peace between their husbands, who are growing increasingly frustrated and blaming each other. That sets up a scene where Lucy and Ethel try to sneak the eggs out to the barn, just as a busy Ricky wants to do a quick rehearsal of their tango.

As you can guess, this yields the most famous physical centerpiece of *Lucy*'s season, where Lucy is forced to do the tango while hiding dozens of eggs in her blouse. It's a hilarious two minutes, as the audience eagerly anticipates the climax where Lucy embraces Ricky and all her eggs break. But beyond just being a delicately crafted bit of unique physical comedy, look at how it's all set up by the characters—specifically, Lucy and Ethel, who are scheming together in the name of friendship, all in an effort to save their core foursome: a key aspect of the series' situation, even here amid all the changes from this strong-but-not-strongest final season.

## *There's Something High Concept About You*

The end of *I Love Lucy*, however, marks the end of the first great television sitcom—and it's perhaps the end of an era in its own right, as many shows from this period took lessons from *Lucy*, even though most of them failed to apply these lessons in the right way. One such series was *Private Secretary*, now in its final season and still a ratings success.[14] But it was forced into retirement because of a dispute between star Ann Sothern and producer Jack Chertok, who sold the series without her input.[15] Interestingly, I think this may be one of the best years of *Private Secretary*'s run, only because there seems to be more thought given to the relationships between ensemble members instead of the individual episodic story gimmicks. Sothern's next series, the self-titled *The Ann Sothern Show*, will actually continue this forward shift into a more relationship-focused place, never becoming as truly character driven as *Lucy* but at least improving on the standards of *Private Secretary*. There'll be more about this in a few chapters. Stay tuned.

In the meantime, as this season said goodbye to *Private Secretary*, another female-led ensemble workplace comedy that undermined its regulars and their relationships in favor of flashy episodic guests and one-off anthology-esque narratives was gearing up—*The Gale Storm Show*, subtitled *Oh, Susanna!* It was Gale Storm's follow-up to *My Little Margie* and another single-camera comedy from Hal Roach Studios. This time, instead of centering on the relationship between an impish daughter and her spry father, Storm's new series went full idea driven and premise focused, casting her as a cruise director traveling around the world in a theoretical workplace, depicting her as a Margie lite or a more mature Margie—still an impulsive schemer but not quite as often and with not quite as much wild-eyed exuberance.

*The Gale Storm Show* actually gives its star a better supporting cast, though, with Roy Roberts as her boss and the particularly amusing ZaSu Pitts as her sidekick—a more equal partner than Storm ever had on *Margie*. Unfortunately, this new show was just not interested in setting itself up for motivated situation comedy either, as it overindulges its high-concept cruise ship setting, spotlighting instead mere guest-star-of-the-week or flashy location-of-the-week fodder, with little comedy or story coming from the regulars and their specific relational constructs—that is, the low-concept character-driven elements. Additionally, since, like *Margie*, the show's writing is not interested in much detail-oriented continuity (of the *I Love Lucy* or *Danny Thomas* variety), there's no sense of aesthetic realism binding its situation together—every week, there's a new concern, like a new guest or a new song to sing. The best episodes spare themselves of one-off gimmicks and do more with the leads, but those are few and far between, rendering *Gale Storm*'s four-season run essentially mediocre and only slightly less ridiculous than *My Little Margie*.

Similar to *The Gale Storm Show*, or *Oh, Susanna!*, is *Hey, Jeannie!*, a single-camera vehicle on NBC for British musical comedy star Jeannie Carson, casting her in the role of a naive Scottish émigré just getting accustomed to New York. The show lasted only one year, but it would be semi-revived, in a completely different format, for a syndicated run that finally premiered during the 1959–1960 season. Like *Gale Storm*, it's idea led, with a cutesy leading lady falling into weekly predicaments that have nothing to do with her characterization or her relationships, such as those with the cabbie and his wife who take her in—Allen Jenkins and Jane Dulo, both affable and funny performers deserving of better material. What's more, the show doesn't take advantage of its premised opportunities to posit her as a "fish out of water" in any real sense. While the notion of her being a Scottish transfer is noted in dialogue, it's barely apparent in story. Every week is a new concern with little continuity coming from the leads—someone new to befriend, somewhere new to visit, a new job to tackle in a new location. And Carson sings on the show even more than Storm on hers, so working in those musical numbers often takes priority over situation comedy.

Meanwhile, proving again that television is always about copying past successes, another new sitcom that premiered in 1956–1957 is *Blondie*, the first TV version of the classic radio comedy, based on the film that was in turn based on the comic strip. Those origins are felt in this single-season series, which premiered in January, as the show—produced by Hal Roach Studios—essentially depicts its lead, the original goofy patriarch, Dagwood (Arthur Lake), as a larger-than-life cartoon, even more heightened and ridiculous than most sitcom characters of this era. This makes him hard to believe. On the other hand, at least he has comic definition, which is more than can be said for his wife Blondie, who, very much like on the radio series, has absolutely no personality whatsoever. This contrast, despite existing in every iteration of this property, is especially jarring in *this* medium's more evolved understanding of what's needed for situation comedy, for while scripts truly endeavor to be funny, the storytelling is really hacky, with generic routines and clichéd plots that the leads don't meaningfully inspire based on who they are and how they interact. In 1957, we expect better of a sitcom. And while Florenz Ames, Harold Peary, and Elvia Allman are decent support, this show is just not fun to watch given the poor calibration of its characterizations and its lame storytelling, both of which feel ignorant to the genre's best.

Smarter, although still no better with character, is *The People's Choice*, now in its second season and with an evolved situation that places the series at its most memorable, for early in the year the leading couple, Sock and Mandy, secretly elope and don't tell anyone. The next two-thirds of the season follow their attempts to keep this secret from her father, the mayor, particularly once his new wife, Sock's aunt, finds out. And with this secret being kept under wraps, scheduling a honeymoon proves to be tough as well—made no easier by the fact that the couple also takes in a boarder, Sock's old army buddy, a mooch played by *Bob Cummings*'s Dick Wesson—another wrinkle added to the show's ever-evolving situation. How does this all fare? Well, the narrative hook of keeping their marriage a secret is fun in theory but none of the leads gain any definition—and in fact, Sock regresses, for the initial premise of a dweebish bird studier now being thrust into the role of small-town politician is pushed further from view. Now he's just a married man pretending he isn't. Thus, the series remains mediocre, for the interesting relational dynamics complicated by this arc don't do a good job of coloring story due to the series' innate blandness with regard to character—the most important part of its situation, which remains underbaked and now more obscured. And funny voice-overs from Cleo the dog—provided by Mary Jane Croft; another role for this busy lady!—are not enough to compensate. Actually they're an overused gimmick.

As for other higher concept sitcoms, 1956–1957 offered a few more, including a single-season entry called *The Adventures of Hiram Holliday*. Based on the book of the same name, this single-camera sitcom starring *Mister Peepers*'s Wally Cox is a radical departure from his earlier gem. While that classic was live and relationship based, this one is filmed and idea driven. The premise has a newspaper proofreader being awarded a trip around the world, alongside a reporter meant to cover all his stops. Everywhere he goes, he—Hiram Holliday—solves crimes and fixes things—for he has many skills and, evidently, comedically so, given his otherwise meek stature and persona. In this regard, it's a bit like *Get Smart* with a Peepers at the center, which is itself a comic idea, and Cox indeed does have a persona he's bringing into the character. But every story takes up a new narrative concern with no sustaining relevance for the leads, and although attached to the basic traveling premise, none of it is driven *by* character or revealing for him. This might as well be an adventure series—an episodic drama/crime show or even an anthology-esque procedural, with a different case each week. It's not unfunny—Cox is innately humorous; it's just an inherently deficient situation comedy, especially compared to *Peepers*. Oh, and it comes from Phil Rapp of *Topper*, which goes to say it doesn't have any of the genius of *Get Smart* (which was helmed primarily by Leonard Stern, of *The Honeymooners* and *The Phil Silvers Show*).

Fortunately, a far more successful high-concept sitcom premiered at midseason. It's *Mr. Adams and Eve*, a single-camera effort from Four Star Productions for real-life couple Howard Duff and Ida Lupino, who play versions of themselves— or, rather, not literally themselves like Burns and Allen but movie stars, and the show's situation is very much about their careers and how this affects their personal lives. That's why it's high concept—the career is specific and assumes focus in story, so this isn't an ordinary domestic "husband-and-wife" show. And yet, *Mr. Adams and Eve* is fairly relationship conscious in its first season, which is less gimmicky than the second of 1957-1958, as it initially aims to follow how this pair navigates such a strange industry.

As for the characters, Ida Lupino's Eve is a typical movie star diva—and lots of fun because of the rich comedic possibilities suggested by this bold, easily amusing persona. Duff plays a little bit of a colorless straight man opposite her, but there's a decent recurring cast who builds out their world, and stories genuinely use the situation of their professions intruding on their personal lives, if not to craft multidimensional leads who then directly drive story, then at least to satisfy the premise, ensuring that even routine plots feel *of* the series. So, for this era, it's an idea-led, high-concept show that's got its head in the right place, using some autobiographical details to aid our emotional investment and increase the illusion of reality, and with scripting that genuinely seeks to be comedic, giving play to characters within a unique relationship, as premised. It's no classic, but as high-concept short-lived 1950s sitcoms go, it's among the best—at least here in this truncated first season, which is sadly not as widely available as it should be.

## *The Last Rebel*

Also not as widely available (as of this writing) as it should be is one of 1956-1957's continued success stories—the third season of *The Bob Cummings Show*, which is the series' best, featuring a bevy of episodes related to the established premise of Bob's fight against settling down and all the ways in which the recurring characters and this ensemble's established relationships complicate his ideal bachelorhood. Paul Henning's scripts are as funny as ever, and as Bob Cummings himself assumed more of the directorial duties, there's more of a briskness to the filmed product that enhances the comedy on the page. In terms of story, Season Three offers plenty of Harvey's domineering wife Ruthie (Mary Lawrence)—and these installments where she clashes with Bob, or he attempts to subvert her, are terrific because she is the series' most menacing personification of marriage and domesticity: the very things Bob is trying to avoid. With her as an avatar for this premised conflict, the show's situation feels especially well invoked.

Meanwhile, Dwayne Hickman's Chuck goes to college this year and is more prominent in story—with an attempted backdoor pilot about his school days airing in February 1957[16] and serving as a proto–*Dobie Gillis*, one of the few gems of the late 1950s that we'll discuss soon. His elevated presence helps keep Bob's domestic obligations centralized. As for notable episodes, some worth citing here include: "Bob Meets the Mortons" (March 21, 1957), where the characters from *Burns and Allen* (also produced by McCadden) cross over, and "Bob Escapes Schultzy's Trap" (April 4, 1957), where Ann B. Davis's Schultzy has fun trying to snare Bob with help from the comedic Hans Conried (now recurring as Uncle Tonoose on *The Danny Thomas Show*). And then there's Ruthie, Bob's chief antagonist, on whom he actually turns the tables in the memorable "Bob Uncovers Ruthie's Past" (December 27, 1956).

▶ However, the best of the Ruthie shows rounds us out at **#50** on my list. It's "**Bob Tangles with Ruthie**" from **February 14, 1957**. It was written by **Paul Henning** with **Dick Wesson, Shirl Gordon**, and **Phil Shuken. Bob Cummings** himself directed. The story finds Bob battling Ruthie in a proxy war when she forbids his nephew Chuck from seeing her niece.

It's a fun show because of what Ruthie represents to Bob—the typical domineering wife, who determines exactly what her husband can and can't do, thus quashing the very freedom that Bob, the bachelor and air force reserve officer, seeks to preserve in his life. This is despite encroaching obligations from his sister and her son, who, incidentally, looks at Bob as something of a father figure, even though, as here, he might not always be teaching him the right lessons. Thus, this is a story that, more than any other *Bob Cummings* segment, showcases the conflict at the heart of the series' situation, for Bob's efforts to avoid domesticity have him fighting battles for others, including his best pal and his nephew. There's also a comedically clever "Caesar and Cleopatra" fantasy sequence with Harvey, Ruthie's husband, as a whipped Mark Antony.

▶ Also, there's one other episode from this season that makes my list, the risqué "**Double Date**," where a promise to double date with Chuck on his 18th birthday conflicts with Bob's own plans. Appearing on my list at **#28**, it was written by **Paul Henning** with **Phil Shuken** and **Shirl Gordon,** directed by **Norman Tokar,** and first broadcast on **November 15, 1956.**

In this episode, Bob's swinging bachelor lifestyle is put in direct conflict with his duties as an uncle and surrogate father figure to Chuck, who has finally turned 18—a legal adult—and alerts Bob that he was promised a double date for this occasion. The problem is, Bob already has a date lined up that evening with a notorious stripper named Boom Boom Laverne, whose exaggerated Mae West sexuality makes plain the dilemma facing Bob—sex or responsibility—and asserts *The Bob Cummings Show* as still one of the boldest and funniest sitcoms on the air, rejecting the era's reputation for bland domestic conformity via episodes like this, which reveal the pleasures directly opposed to the über-benignity of *Father Knows Best* or even *Ozzie and Harriet*. Additionally, with so much of the series' situation at play in a character conflict, this is great sitcommery, and in coming from a season where even the once defiant *Lucy* seemed to finally be acquiescing to the decade's reputation for suburban propaganda, an episode like "Double Date" feels more like a comedic, rebellious victory than ever.

The sitcom genre would need more of this going forward to maintain its relevance. Unfortunately, such comic chutzpah—such boldness—would prove harder and harder to find.

## *JACKSON'S BEST SITCOMS FROM 1956-57*
1. I LOVE LUCY (S6)
2. THE PHIL SILVERS SHOW (S2)
3. THE BOB CUMMINGS SHOW (S3)

## *EPISODES FROM THE 1956-57 SEASON IN JACKSON'S TOP 50 FROM THE '50s*
- #12. I LOVE LUCY (S6): "Lucy Does the Tango" (3/11/57)
- #17. THE PHIL SILVERS SHOW (S2): "Love That Guardhouse" (1/15/57)
- #28. THE BOB CUMMINGS SHOW (S3): "Double Date" (11/15/56)
- #30. STANLEY (S1): "Celia Goes to a TV Show" (10/22/56)
- #33. THE PHIL SILVERS SHOW (S2): "A Mess Sergeant Can't Win" (11/13/56)
- #46. THE PHIL SILVERS SHOW (S2): "Doberman's Sister" (11/20/56)
- #50. THE BOB CUMMINGS SHOW (S3): "Bob Tangles with Ruthie" (2/14/57)

## *OTHER NOTABLE EPISODES FROM 1956-57*
THE GEORGE BURNS AND GRACIE ALLEN SHOW (S7): "The Missing Stamp" (11/12/56)
THE BOB CUMMINGS SHOW (S3): "Bob Uncovers Ruthie's Past" (12/27/56)
I LOVE LUCY (S6): "Lucy and Superman" (1/14/57)
THE PHIL SILVERS SHOW (S2): "Bilko's Television Idea" (2/12/57)
THE DANNY THOMAS SHOW (S4): "Danny Meets Kathy" (4/4/57)
I LOVE LUCY (S6): "Lucy Raises Tulips" (4/29/57)

CHAPTER TEN

# Where's Lucy?
*The Best Television Sitcoms of 1957–1958*

The 1957–1958 season is the first since 1950–1951 without *I Love Lucy*, and this loss of the genre's best and most popular sitcom left a bit of a vacuum—one that other new shows and some old favorites sought to fill. But where was the sitcom going in the post–*Lucy* era? Unfortunately, if this season's new efforts were any indication, it would be doubling down on bland domestic fare—with characters who are deliberately generic and therefore neither funny nor conducive to inspired story—and with slightly high-concept premises, or idea-driven "wrinkles," meant to compensate. Ultimately, as we'll see, this will harm the sitcom's reputation, further accelerating its overall loss in popularity following the 1954–1955 "sitcom boom" and the following year's creative peak. That is, in the last half of the 1950s, American tastes veered away from the sitcom, embracing other forms instead, like westerns and crime dramas (and for a while, quiz programs), all because, frankly, the comedies being offered weren't as great as they needed to be. In fact, it would take until the early 1960s for the genre to get out of this "bear market" and return to its *Lucy*-inspired bullishness. And in addition to suggesting why the genre was less popular at the end of the 1950s, the output from this particular season also foretells some of the trends that we can expect in the remainder of this decade.

Of course, when labeling this era "post–*Lucy*," that specifically means the half-hour sitcom called *I Love Lucy*, for actually, the Ricardos and Mertzes still continued to exist on television—not only in syndicated reruns but also in *The Lucille Ball–Desi Arnaz Show*, a series of hour-long specials that ultimately yielded a total of five offerings during the 1957–1958 season. These shows continued the "situation" of *I Love Lucy*'s final season, with the two couples living out in the Connecticut countryside, but now with special guest stars in every episode. Lucille Ball and Desi Arnaz made the choice to scale back in this way—even though *I Love Lucy* went out as the most-watched show on TV and the network wanted more[1]—so they could focus on building their empire. In addition to producing other shows and offering their production services to many more, Desilu was now expanding its studio space, via their late-1957 acquisition of the old RKO lot (where the couple, incidentally, had first met in 1940).[2] It was simply no longer feasible for Ball—and specifically, Arnaz—to keep up the weekly responsibilities of *I Love Lucy*, especially as the pair's volatile relationship slowly began to unravel behind the scenes.

So *The Lucille Ball–Desi Arnaz Show*, known today under its syndicated title of *The Lucy-Desi Comedy Hour*, kept the married performers still working together in their classic format but on a far less frequent basis and with major guest star support. From design, these shows are inherently less worthwhile—not only are guests a collective gimmick that distracts from the main characters and their relationships, but also an hour-long episode is close to a feature film, and the pacing of the sitcom genre, with its episodic stories, far prefers half-hour run times (over longer or shorter). And yet, they still have the well-defined Ricardos and Mertzes, and even though scripts—by the same writers—are no longer making good use of Lucy's central objective, it's still reverberating through her characterization, especially in the second of these specials, "The Celebrity Next Door" (December 3, 1957), which boasts hilarious stage diva Tallulah Bankhead, who temporarily becomes the Ricardos' neighbor.

This is the best segment of the *Comedy Hours* because it's the most like *I Love Lucy*, and it's essentially two half hours paired together. The first is about Lucy putting on airs for a famous stage actress, recruiting the Mertzes to play her butler and maid so that she can pretend to be more socially elevated—a manifestation of her own desires to be more than "typical," rubbing elbows with the entertainment glitterati—and the second half finds Lucy and Tallulah feuding during a PTA show in which the entire cast appears, an idea that inherently involves show biz and thus makes sense for *Lucy*. It's a consistently funny, situation-affirming hour.

Of the other four, the only one that really plays with the characters and their relationships is the premiere, which got a special 75-minute slot, "Lucy Takes a Cruise to Havana" (November 6, 1957)—a flashback entry that reveals how Lucy met Ricky. Although we heard different versions of this story throughout the years, the continuity is fairly good by the standards of this era, and the choice to use a flashback to reveal a seminal moment in these leads' lives is enhanced and enabled by both their emotional credibility and our investment in their shared history (made possible by the autobiographical details informing the premise). Yes, it's overlong, and the guests are more distracting than additive—including Cesar Romero, Rudy Vallee, Hedda Hopper, and Ann Sothern, the last of whom doesn't play herself but plays her *Private Secretary* character Susie McNamara in a post-series crossover. But it explores Lucy and Ricky's backstory and therefore feels valuable to them as characters. It's solid sitcommery, and it got good ratings,[3] like most of these specials. In fact, they were so well received that Ball and Arnaz agreed to offer more of them in the following season—but only under the umbrella of a Desilu-produced anthology series *The Desilu Playhouse*, or *The Westinghouse Desilu Playhouse*. Five *Lucille Ball–Desi Arnaz Show* episodes for Westinghouse would be offered in 1958–1959 and three more came to be in 1959–1960, as the anthology program was canceled and the Arnazes' marriage finally fell apart.

Together, all 13 hour-long episodes would be rerun starting in the summer of 1962 as *The Lucy-Desi Comedy Hour*.[4] There are some decent segments in this collection ahead, but the further the cast and crew got from *I Love Lucy*, the harder it was to stay affiliated with that classic's great character work and the understanding of how these leads could best be exhibited in story. At any rate, I don't consider it fair to measure *The Lucille Ball–Desi Arnaz Show* (or whatever you want to call it) against other half-hour sitcom episodes because they were irregularly scheduled like specials and twice the length. And just as I did not count daily programs or 15-minute comedies as fair game for this study of the genre's best, I'm recusing these hour-long *Lucy*s—they're worth discussing but fundamentally don't represent the sitcom format fairly or ideally.

## *Families—Nontraditional and Otherwise*

Meanwhile, without *Lucy* on the weekly schedule, CBS eagerly sought a replacement. The solution? Snagging ABC's best comedy—*The Danny Thomas Show*, now in its second year under that title and fifth season overall—to specifically fill the Monday berth vacated by *Lucy*. The pick of *Danny Thomas* makes sense—it's another laugh-seeking multi-cam filmed by Desilu with an urban show biz veneer and a sense of aesthetic realism aided by autobiographical elements that lend credibility to the characters and indicate an attention to detail revealed through the storytelling. In short, it's probably the series most like *Lucy* on the air in 1957–1958, and indeed, this move from the lowest-rated network to the highest-rated network—and its best slot—vaulted *Danny Thomas* to the top of the Nielsen charts. It would come in at #2 for the 1957–1958 season, as the country's most-watched sitcom—an honor it would hold for the rest of the decade.[5]

That commercial success kept the show running into 1964, and it would never leave the top 15.[6] However, this wasn't just due to a good time slot. The show was also funny—in fact, it's at its best here in the last three TV seasons of the decade but particularly 1957–1958, where Marjorie Lord is officially added to the regular cast as Danny's new wife Kathy, whom he met at the end of the previous year. Now she's a regular, bringing along a young Angela Cartwright as her daughter Linda. They join Danny and his two kids—played by Rusty Hamer and Sherry Jackson—to create perhaps the first *blended* nuclear family on an American TV sitcom, with a married couple who live together as parents to their children, all from prior unions.

This is fascinating, especially because this season (and the next, to a lesser extent) explicitly acknowledges their "blended family" arrangement as part of the situation, deriving episodic conflict from this motivated and relatable source of comedic and dramatic tension. For instance, many stories here involve the kids getting used to having a new mom (or a new dad) or Danny and Kathy adjusting to a life together. The lovebirds also mingle their larger families as well, including his

Uncle Tonoose (Hans Conried), and her equally proud father, played by William Demarest, who recurs this year, adding to this emphasized familial integration. In this regard, the season utilizes a recent development—Danny's second marriage—to present stories that directly involve these characters and their new, specific relationships inside this situation, making this is the best and most genre-validating form of situation comedy ever offered on *The Danny Thomas Show*.

And it's a welcome change, for if you remember, the original premise of Danny being caught between his work and his home already climaxed when he was forced, as a widower, to become both father and mother—the ultimate drama related to that idea. Now that he's with Kathy, an accommodating newlywed who doesn't put up as much of a fight as Margaret did over Danny's career (perhaps that's also why her personality is not as sharp or spunky as she was first introduced to be at the end of the fourth season), that initial conflict simply doesn't play. So this "blended family" wrinkle thus provides a new framework that simplifies the show's work-versus-home situation around the home more exclusively, with the continued inclusion of guests, musical numbers, and other show biz reminders from Danny Thomas' smartly autobiographical premise maintaining the series' ethos, but in a more peripheral capacity.

In terms of merit, *The Danny Thomas Show* has always been above average—even when it was *Make Room for Daddy*—but compared to *I Love Lucy*, its embracement of tropes associated with other 1950s family sitcoms has sometimes rendered it overearnest or treacly. Such serious and sometimes maudlin sentiment was really on display last year—the widower season—although most of that *was* earned by the change in the characters' situation. Even still, one of the reasons Season Five is such an improvement is because it sees the show turning back toward comedy and away from self-indulgent schmaltz. Oh, yes, that still exists and will always be a part of its DNA—more so than on *I Love Lucy* or *The Dick Van Dyke Show* (a 1960s sitcom produced by these same folks that counts a similar premise yet boasts even better, funnier scripting)—but it's less felt.

Fortunately, in assuming *Lucy*'s old spot, *Danny Thomas* on CBS becomes an even more consciously laugh-out-loud series, more readily offering bigger centerpieces and bolder comic narratives. This shifting sensibility asserts its obviousnesses in the following two seasons, which, incidentally, fade out the "blended family" arrangement to the point that by 1960–1961, the show is acting as if Danny and Kathy were always married. This is certainly less wise—the show ignoring its own history—for established details help inspire more character-specific stories. And that's another reason why *this* funny year is so good—it's got more of a situation to grip.

Some of the best episodes this season that explore these new elements within the series' situation are "Terry vs. Kathy" (October 14, 1957), which literally roots its conflict in the evolving household dynamic, and "Parents Are Pigeons" (November 4, 1957), where the youngsters—Rusty and Linda—play their respective stepparents off each other for personal gain.

*Chapter Ten. Where's Lucy?* 219

From left: William Demarest as Mr. Daly and Hans Conried as Uncle Tonoose make life difficult for newlyweds Danny and Kathy Williams (Danny Thomas and Marjorie Lord) in *The Danny Thomas Show*, "Uncle Tonoose Meets Mr. Daly" (1958).

▶ However, the season's finest episode is also my pick for one of the series' finest. It comes in at **#32** on my top 50 list and first aired on **March 3, 1958**. Titled "**Uncle Tonoose Meets Mr. Daly**," its story has Danny and Kathy caught in the middle of a feud between two visiting relatives: his uncle and her father. **Sheldon Leonard** directed the script by **Arthur Stander**.

"Uncle Tonoose Meets Mr. Daly" is the best episodic exploration of this season's uniquely offered "blended family" premise, for this is where the senior patriarchs of both clans meet and feud, creating a very funny half hour that takes direct advantage of the expected struggles of merging two separate groups, especially through the prism of two distinct ethnicities, which is always part of *Danny Thomas*'s situation, as his Lebanese heritage is a true autobiographical detail that has, since the series' start, lent emotional credibility to his characterization and contributed character-specific laughs. These laughs are exacerbated when Danny's family—his very history—is personified by the larger-than-life Hans Conried as his recurring Uncle Tonoose, and with William Demarest as Kathy's proud Irish father playing an extension of her, evidencing this show's use of cultural identity (like with Ricky on *I Love Lucy*), both leads themselves feel represented. Accordingly, the simple presence of these ambassadors for Danny's and Kathy's backgrounds adds to our understanding of them, turning a perhaps generic *Abie's Irish Rose*–esque in-law battle[7] into a series-corroborating display of character-driven conflict. It's smart and comical—unique to this season, which is the best showing of *Danny Thomas*—one of the finest sitcoms in the post–*Lucy* 1950s.

At the same time, a new sitcom that debuted this season also took on the idea of a nontraditional family, but this one wasn't blended and instead utilized a more familiar notion: the single relative who takes in a parentless teen. I'm referring to *Bachelor Father*, which alternated weekly with the eighth season of *The Jack Benny Program*. It starred John Forsythe as the eponymous bachelor, who takes in his niece (Noreen Corcoran) and is forced to adjust his lifestyle now that he's thrust into this role of proxy father. In this regard, it's similar to *The Bob Cummings Show*, where another bachelor was forced to become a de facto daddy for his nephew—with domestic duties that put a crimp in his swinging, carefree lifestyle. But this comparison does *Bachelor Father* no favors, for it's not nearly as comedic or designed for situation-affirming conflict as *Bob Cummings*. That is, although Forsythe's Bentley, like Bob, pursues women, it's clear here that the kid comes first, not his lifestyle. Therefore, the tension between these two aspects of his life is muted and not exhibited well through character conflict. And while stories do a decent job of using this premise for story—that is, the bachelor trying to both date and parent—it's all toothless: never really dramatic and certainly not hilarious. It's, frankly, benign.

This is in large part because the characterizations are more generic and not as bold as those on *Bob Cummings*. Most of the laughs come from the Asian "houseboy," Peter, played by Sammee Tong, whose role builds over the course of Season One, eventually becoming, in later years, much more of a comedic and narrative presence. At the time, the very inclusion of his character was considered socially progressive.[8] Now it plays a little more stereotypical and one-dimensional, and unlike *Amos 'n Andy*, whose leads have emotional depth and actually push both laughs and story, Peter feels even more slight—a peripheral joke with no agency. Nevertheless, this isn't a terribly written show as far as its situation's exploration is concerned; it's just not funny enough, shying away from any bold comic conflicts, ultimately championing domesticity in a way *Bob Cummings* doesn't but other bland domestic shows like, most especially, *Father Knows Best*, do.

Speaking of *Father Knows Best*, its fourth season portrays the show as still dire with respect to enjoyable situation comedy, for even though it tiptoes closer to more comedic ideas, it still is written as if it prefers to be a drama, refusing to maximize traits that could be seen as comedically ridiculous for its leads. More enjoyable but only marginally (because it at least *wants* to be funny) is *The Life of Riley*, now in its sixth and final season. Nothing has really changed here either except there's less of married daughter Babs and a niece is brought in to allow the show to continue having two kids under its roof. It thus remains formulaic, and the elements that made the premise unique—specifically its title character's dogged pursuit of a better life, given his blue-collar and working-class entrenchment—is less often addressed. This

## Chapter Ten. Where's Lucy?

marks an unfortunate but predictable end for a series that always should have been better than it was, never fully rising to the occasion.

Meanwhile, our other benign suburban offering, *The Adventures of Ozzie and Harriet*, was thriving in contrast, for now that it had a bona fide pop star in its ensemble, it knew to showcase him in at least half of its episodic output, ensuring not only that Ricky Nelson would sing every other week but that many of the stories would be about the boys and their collegiate antics. As with before, these aren't great because the kids are so undefined that they're bland. The Nelson boys have no discernible personality traits, and while Ricky used to be *sort of* mouthy and precocious, now that he's a teen heartthrob, he might as well be a crooning cardboard cutout.

Far more enjoyable, as usual, are the adult episodes, featuring Ozzie and Harriet, the Darbys, and the Randolphs. Their stories are not as trivial and therefore so benign they're funny as they were in previous years, but there are a few outliers that really get the idea. Indeed, two of the show's best-known episodes come from this season—both involving Ozzie's well-established love of ice cream, a trivial detail that suggests some rare personalization. They both also employ dream sequences—a frequent device that these benign domestic sitcoms use to imply a form of creativity that's typically absent. But *Ozzie and Harriet* tends to do them better, both because of its fixation on minutae and because of Ozzie's own wide-eyed persona, which is more naturally conducive to comedy.

▶ "Ozzie's Triple Banana Surprise" (November 20, 1957) delights in its dream mechanics and is worthwhile for its silly subject, but even more iconic is "**Tutti-Frutti Ice Cream**," which I've made room for on my list at **#49**. First aired on **December 11, 1957**, this entry—written by **Jay Sommers**, **Don Nelson**, and **Ozzie Nelson** from a story by **Perry Grant** and **Dick Bensfield**—was directed by Ozzie himself and concerns his all-night quest to find some tutti-frutti ice cream.

Unlike the even more dream-heavy "Ozzie's Triple Banana Surprise," the more character-driven "Tutti-Frutti Ice Cream" merely features a dream sequence as a singular set piece for the family, including Ricky, where he sings and helps set up Ozzie's pursuit of this ice-cream flavor—a specific and therefore trivial objective that is comedic because it's so ordinary, so benign, so unimportant. Accordingly, it's actually a perfect example of *Ozzie and Harriet* at its best: not hilarious but so simple and ordinary that it's *not* simple and ordinary. It's weird and thus amusing. And with Ozzie driving the action, the proceedings are brisk and light and somewhat colored by his character—even in this show's otherwise colorless, idealized world. Oh, and with the musical dream notably included, both the series' penchant for this "creative" device *and* its growing musical identity are both present and accounted for as well. It's one of the show's most beloved episodes, and with so much of its overall situation on display, that reputation is deserved.

At the same time, there were two more family comedies added to the genre's roster this season—with slight differences in concept meant to differentiate them from the more straightforward examples we just discussed. One of them, like *Bachelor Father*, employs a nontraditional nuclear family format. It's *The Real McCoys*, a single-camera comedy coproduced by Danny Thomas's company and led by movie star Walter Brennan with *Our Miss Brooks* alum Richard Crenna. It follows a family of West Virginia ranchers who move to California after inheriting a sizeable portion of land. Brennan plays the irascible Grandpa Amos, the focal point of the series, while Crenna is his adult grandson Luke, who is married to Kate (Kathleen Nolan) and raising his two younger siblings (Lydia Reed and Michael Winkelman). Others in the main cast include the ranch's Mexican hired hand (Tony Martinez) and the MacMichaels, an elderly brother and sister who live next door—Grandpa's frenemy George (Andy Clyde) and frequent paramour Flora (Madge Blake), respectively. What's most interesting about *The Real McCoys* is twofold—the first thing is the unique family setup, resembling but tweaking the traditional nuclear clan.

The second interesting thing about the series is that it's decidedly rural. While comedies about country folk have been prevalent in other mediums—think the *Ma and Pa Kettle* film series—the sitcom genre on TV has heretofore been fairly urban, with a lot of shows set in or around the places they originated: New York or Los Angeles. And if they weren't urban, then they were suburban. *The Real McCoys*, on ABC, is the genre's first notable comedy about people who live outside the city—far outside, where they both visually and verbally reflect the kind of folks who would be found in those environs: on the farm, on the ranch, or simply in the small towns that make up Middle America.

Now, perhaps it makes sense that most early television programs were reflected as either urban or suburban, for TV's reach was contained. But as its access continued to grow—by 1957, it is estimated that nearly 80 percent of American households had at least one set[9]—these middle-American viewers became a bigger audience. Accordingly, the 1960s would find the networks seemingly catering more to the middle of the country with down-home shows about regulars who were definitely not city slickers. The most famous of these sitcoms would come from *The Bob Cummings Show*'s creator Paul Henning, whose interconnected rural trilogy—*The Beverly Hillbillies*, *Petticoat Junction*, and *Green Acres*—proved to be highly popular, along with 1960's *The Andy Griffith Show*, another entry from Danny Thomas's production company.

In this regard, *The Real McCoys* is a precursor to the next decade's popular hits. However, it's still quite different, especially from the high-concept premise-driven *Beverly Hillbillies* and *Green Acres*, which are both about "fish out of water" (country folk moving to the city and vice versa). Those shows are upheld by well-defined characters who are uproariously funny, but satisfying the central premise is their scripts' paramount concern. That is, because they're high concept, they're also fundamentally idea driven. This is not true of *McCoys*, which merely takes its leads from one rural spot to another and instead functions—like at least half of *Andy Griffith*—as one of the era's traditional family sitcoms, nontraditional setup notwithstanding.

In other words, it's a low-concept sitcom about relationships among family members, and it's tonally not as funny as the best of the Henning trilogy or even *Andy Griffith*, which also boasts a workplace setting with Don Knotts as Barney Fife—whose scenes give that series its biggest laughs. No, *The Real McCoys* is often warm or, to use a less generous term, mild—like the worst of the family comedies. And I'm afraid there's a lot of similarities between this and the worst family sitcoms of this era, especially early in its run, where the humor is so gentle that this might as well be a drama—*Father Knows Best* but on a ranch and with a nontraditional nuclear family.

This is partly because none of the McCoys—with the exception of Brennan's Grandpa Amos—are well defined, so there's a genericness to the proceedings that, well, is shocking, given that the rural setting and unique family arrangement should be better at inspiring story and encouraging conflict between characters, since they're relatively fresh wrinkles. But no, all there really is to find here is Brennan being a lovable curmudgeon with a bunch of interchangeable scene partners—and the best entries merely are those where he is firmly spotlighted.

In fact, most enjoyable are the ones where Amos is paired with the neighbors—his pal/rival George or his girlfriend Flora, for their dynamics are specific and more conducive to chuckles than those with his comedically nondescript family members. And to that point, there are installments that stand out in the series itself, but nothing deserves to sit with the best sitcom samples of this season. I suppose that speaks to *McCoy*'s elemental mediocrity, for despite things that make it special and more watchable than other sitcoms from the late 1950s, it's just another bland family effort at its core, not doing what it should on behalf of its characters. For as much as I'd like to celebrate Brennan and the conceptual hooks within the premise that do indeed suggest a true and distinct situation, there just aren't great results to show for it.

Much better on this metric is the other new family sitcom that premiered in the fall of 1957—this time on CBS. It's *Leave It to Beaver*, an iconic nuclear family sitcom that's often been associated with the likes of *Ozzie and Harriet* and *Father Knows Best*, as Ward and June Cleaver (Hugh Beaumont and Barbara Billingsley) have become cultural points of reference when discussing the falsely tranquil and idealized brand of suburban domesticity often depicted on television in the 1950s. I wish I could more firmly dispute this condescending reputation, but it's not totally undeserved. However, they are not this show's focus, for what makes *Beaver* unique—the wrinkle in its otherwise familiar existence—is that it's centered on its kids: Theodore "Beaver" Cleaver (Jerry Mathers) and his older brother Wally (Tony Dow). Stories follow the boys and, in these first few seasons, scripts are fairly skilled at believably replicating the alternately naive and precocious nature of baby boom children, whose world at this young age mostly revolved around their friends and peers, while adults—parents, neighbors, teachers—were merely friendly, or ancillary, talking heads. To wit, the best part of the series, are the boys' friends and peers—Beaver's clumsy friend Larry Mondello (Rusty Stevens) and Wally's rascal pal Eddie Haskell

(Ken Osmond), the latter of whom is the funniest because of his precise depiction: a weasel who thinks he's fooling the adults but isn't; they know he's a "creep."

These young characters—especially the anchoring Beaver—feel optimistically mimetic in these early years written by Joe Connelly and Bob Mosher (former *Amos 'n Andy* scribes). For instance, while their entire world is wide eyed and idealized, the things they say make sense for their ages and are congruous with what we expect from them, given how they're positioned in the low-concept nuclear family premise. There's not necessarily a lot of continuity in the characterizations, as small recurring details or sustaining character motivations aren't ever pronounced—perhaps through no fault of their own, for children on sitcoms *typically are* more like narrative devices: conflict-makers to which adults react, without a clearly communicated understandable decision-making process, since, well, realistically their decision-making processes are still developing. With that in mind, *Beaver* is surprisingly adept at ensuring its young characters are more like actual characters than most sitcom kids and that they exist in story they *help* drive—maybe not based on unique, sustaining specifics but on general and relatable terms associated with boys their age: crushing on a teacher, going to a girl's party, seeing a scary movie, etc. Most plots are narratively appropriate for them and, more granularly, propelled and upheld by dialogue and behavior that's amusing in its relative naturalness, feeling like it *could* be true to life and thus character corroborating, if not individualized and character revealing.

In this regard, *Beaver* is funnier than most of these other family sitcoms— certainly funnier than other suburban efforts like *Father Knows Best* and much more satisfying than this year's other new family shows, which seek differentiation through their premises/settings—aka ideas—not through a focus on specific characters, who, in this case, happen to be the kids. To that point, if the kids are this show's strong suit, the blandness of the adults—and the relative benignity of the overall world, which fares well against *Father Knows Best* but not, for instance, *The Danny Thomas Show*—is a hinderance, indicating shortcomings that still exist with character. Sadly, never are the adults on *Beaver* afforded much of anything, although it's interesting to note that here in Season One, while Ward is typically an example of the infallible patriarch who knows so much more than his kids and often has to gently teach them lessons, there *are* a handful of outings this year where he has an emotional arc—meaning, through watching the antics of his children, *he* learns something about humanity or parenting. This story template isn't abundant, but it's noticeable—especially because this is the only season where it exists. After this, *Beaver* becomes a more straightforward series of "lessons," before ramping up its comedic chops in its middle era and then, eventually, in the 1960s, struggling to write these characters as they grow.

As such, Season One (the only year on CBS) is one of *Beaver*'s best, especially by way of the kids, who are at their youngest and most precious—allowing for stories that really take advantage of these scribes' innate ability to write believably for children. Some of the funniest—most of them from the beginning of the season—include the character-establishing series premiere that introduces the regulars and the recurring themes beautifully, "Beaver Gets 'Spelled'" (October 4, 1957), along with the first produced "Captain Jack" (October 11, 1957), which boasts a memorable log line about a pet alligator that the boys put in their toilet tank, and "The Haircut" (October 25, 1957), where Beaver disastrously gives himself a haircut. All of these entries offer relatable stories that make sense for boys of Beaver and Wally's maturity. And they're funny, both because of their ideas and for how the boys are depicted—sincerely, with the kind of curious personalities only the young can have. Of course, when simply seeking excellent sitcommery, *Beaver* will never compare to the best of what we're highlighting—it's just not funny or character-specific enough. But of all the single-camera suburban family comedies of the mid-1950s, only *Leave It to Beaver* and *Ozzie and Harriet* find ways to genuinely be comedic within their domestic benignity. And *Beaver* does it through the depiction of a few regulars—the kids.

Speaking of domestic benignity or, rather, the lack thereof, *The Bob Cummings Show* continued to be bold in its fourth season, now back on NBC. There's less of Dwayne Hickman's Chuck and more of Ann B. Davis's Schultzy (Davis won her first Emmy this season[10]), as stories more frequently become about the main women in Bob's life (Schultzy and Margaret), scheming against Bob to keep him from satisfying his carnal whims. This injects a little more formula into the storytelling but with just as much relevance for the main character and the relationships existing within the strong ensemble—an ensemble that continues to expand, like with former vaudeville star Rose Marie, who joins the recurring cast near season's end as Martha, another one of Schultzy's friends and accomplices. We'll see more of her in Season Five. In the meantime, this is the show's second-best year overall, especially with Cummings himself as director, ensuring a sense of tonal continuity with every episode, in addition to Paul Henning's inherent affinity for some slight narrative serialization, or at least multi-week arcs. If last year was the series' peak, that's because the premise felt better invoked with Chuck around more often to remind us of the central dilemma, pitting Bob between, essentially, freedom and family. Now that Chuck is aging and the episodic emphasis is shifting, the situation isn't *quite* as full or strong.

As for this year's best, Ann B. Davis shows off her comedic chops in "Bob Gets Schultzy Into Pictures" (October 1, 1957); Bob is back up against that old avatar for stifling domesticity, Ruthie, in the memorable "Bob and Harvey Go Hunting" (January 7, 1958); Don Knotts guest stars as a prospective beau for Schultzy in "Bob and Schultzy at Sea" (April 29, 1958); and there's a very basic thesis-fulfilling story in "Bob's Forgotten Fiancée" (June 17, 1958), which is all about Bob trying to avoid another one of the ensemble's attempts to trap him into domestic tranquility.

## *They Still Don't Get It, Do They?*

Yet while *Bob Cummings* was narratively coasting but still churning out solid episodes, many of the other sustaining series back for this season weren't in top form—if they ever were. While the second season of *The Gale Storm Show* (or *Oh, Susanna!*) is set more on the boat and uses more of the main cast, its stories are still focused on episodic ornaments—not its leads or their relationships. Additionally, the unique *Mr. Adams and Eve* with Ida Lupino and Howard Duff as a movie star couple has by now devolved into a series of one-off gimmicks, with fewer stories about how their situation affects their life together. And the second season of Betty White's *Date with the Angels* remains just as bland and character-starved as before.

The same can be said for both the fourth season of *December Bride* (now airing after *Danny Thomas* on Monday nights) and the third and final season of *The People's Choice*, which again evolves it situation—but not for the better, as the original premise all but evaporates when Sock and Mandy, whose marriage is no longer a secret, move from the town where he was in public office into a neighborhood where he, though a recent lawyer, becomes a salesman for the housing community. The mayor and his wife (Sock's aunt) still appear but less so, and oh yeah, the main relationship hops from newlywed bliss to expectant parenthood: predictable beats on a by-the-numbers course—nothing to do with the specifics of these characters, who are more generic than ever now that there's nothing tethering them to the initial idea, which was more high concept. In fact, the show has slowly become more low concept but without the strong characters who could justify this transition and make it worthwhile within episodic story. All of these shows are subpar, depicting the situation comedy genre as a lame collection of middling, seldom-funny efforts.

Meanwhile, in new sitcom news, *Our Miss Brooks*'s Eve Arden came back to the genre in a multi-camera live audience effort filmed by Desilu called *The Eve Arden Show*, casting her as a widowed mother of twin girls caught between her personal and professional duties when she embarks on a career as a self-help author and teacher. Arden's sardonic persona remains intact, but in this new setup, she's without Connie Brooks's clear objective, and while stories do indeed predicate themselves on the old "career versus family" dilemma at the heart of other sitcoms (like *Danny Thomas*), the character work just isn't good enough here to yield big laughs or memorable story. More poised for success, meanwhile, was mid-season's *Love That Jill*, which reunited former *Topper* costars (and real-life couple) Anne Jeffreys and Robert Sterling as rival modeling agents who have an attraction. Seemingly built on their relationship, the show's episodic story ultimately disappoints because the characterizations, again, aren't ever allowed to directly inspire the proceedings uniquely. And not even their premised rivalry is well channeled.

At the same time, high-concept idea-driven shows also remained in the pipeline—one of which was *Sally*, a single-camera sitcom starring *My Favorite Husband*'s Joan Caulfield as an unmarried department store clerk who accompanies her boss's daffy wife—played by *Mister Peepers*'s Marion Lorne—on a trip around the world. Unfortunately, stories on *Sally* aren't about these characters or their relationship but about the episodic locations and the shiny new attractions that appear every week inside these outlandish plots, with porous aesthetic realism and no sustaining emotional continuity. When this proved unpopular, the last seven weeks found the two women back in New York, and the show transformed into an ensemble workplace comedy in a department store, with Gale Gordon, Arte Johnson, and Johnny Desmond now in the cast. But that was too little too late: *Sally* had squandered its chance to prove its worth to audiences. Similarly, *Dick and the Duchess* was also a high-concept and idea-driven effort—a single-camera sitcom produced in England about an American insurance investigator (Patrick O'Neal) who marries a duchess (Hazel Court). Once again, instead of character-driven comedy about their clash of cultures—the "situation" that exists between them as people—stories were in the dramatic, episodic vein, as he would have to investigate something and she would help à la Nick and Nora Charles. So this was also not a good example of sitcommery—comedically or narratively.

Fortunately, there was one other new sitcom this season and it's far more fascinating. It was produced jointly by 20th Century–Fox and NTA (National Telefilm Associates), which was a new attempt at a fourth network following the demise of DuMont. NTA started offering programs in 1956, and by that time, 20th Century–Fox was its majority owner[11]—providing syndicated films and filmed shows to independent stations across the country and landing over 115 affiliates at the network's peak,[12] with many agreeing to schedule NTA's offered shows in coordinated slots. This was NTA's first sitcom, released in the fall of 1957—*How to Marry a Millionaire*. Based on Fox's own 1953 movie, this filmed single-camera comedy was about three women in Manhattan who pool their resources to rent a penthouse and court millionaires. Originally, the up-and-coming Lori Nelson was set to be the series' star, but she quickly got outshone in early episodes by young Barbara Eden (later of *I Dream of Jeannie*) as Loco, a character crafted from both the Betty Grable and Marilyn Monroe roles in the film—a ditzy fashion model with terrible nearsightedness. Rounding out the trio was Merry Anders's Mike, ostensibly based on the Lauren Bacall part—supposedly a wisecracking Wall Street secretary. Unfortunately, Mike never receives the kind of attention that would make this definition obvious, and I include that description to be generous, as an indication of how this premise *could* have worked. Even worse, however, is Lori Nelson's Greta—a quiz show hostess who, I *guess* we could say is a little more regal, classy—a personality that, again, had it *actually* existed might have led to more creative situation comedy.

Others in the cast include the recurring elevator man (James Cross) and the girls' mean landlord, played for most of the run by Joseph Kearns (later of *Dennis the Menace*). As in everything he does, Kearns's high energy is conducive to comedy, even when it doesn't really exist on the page. And true to her future reputation, Eden's screen presence is undeniable. Together, they make the show fun to watch. But otherwise, with two of the three leading ladies not well defined at all, the TV version of *How to Marry a Millionaire* ends up being another bland and mediocre affair, even when stories actually let them pursue their objective. It's just not as supported by character as the best sitcoms of this era, and its ideas are not as unique or funny. The only logical reason to seek it out is to study a nascent Barbara Eden develop her craft—which is even more on display in Season Two. To that point, we can revisit the series and the fate of NTA—a syndication service trying to be a network—next chapter.

## Lucy's Elders: Benny, Burns, and Allen

Now that we've gotten all the duds and mediocrities from 1957 to 1958 out of the way, we can look at three of the season's finer offerings—one of which is a longtime "modified" sitcom: *The Jack Benny Program*, now in its eighth season on TV. Still airing every other week and offering 16 episodes total—six of which were shot on film at Revue, while the other 10 continued to be broadcast live[13]—this year's scripts hew more to sitcom scenarios than comedy-variety set pieces, at a ratio of about three to one. This is commensurate with the last few seasons—with no improvement one way or the other. In fact, the show is still a shell of its former iteration on radio, where a more well-rounded ensemble allowed scripts to deliver more character-based situation comedy with established regulars in relation to one another. And the ideas utilized here, well, they've been getting less and less fresh since the TV show's 1955–1956 peak (which is the first season where Benny was exclusively on television, following his exit from radio). However, because the series is such a stellar example of character-based comedy, even amid its "modified" variety-rooted design, its charms are hard to ignore. I couldn't make a top 50 list and leave out something so seminal as *The Jack Benny Program*, for it's got *the* Jack Benny.

▶ Accordingly, I am selecting, at **#18** on my list, an entry called "**Christmas Shopping Show**," which was first broadcast live on **December 15, 1957**. Written by **George Balzer**, **Hal Goldman**, **Al Gordon**, and **Sam Perrin** and directed by **Ralph Levy**, this show finds Jack at a department store shopping for Christmas gifts to give to his friends.

Fans of Jack Benny's radio program know that "Christmas Shopping" became a nearly annual tradition during the 1940s, with a pretty set narrative formula in which Jack would go to a department store and be both menaced by, and a menace to, several of the workers there—all of whom would be played by frequent *Jack Benny* guest stars, such as Frank Nelson and Mel Blanc. This recurring story template became a holiday staple because it was such a great showcase, not only for the peripheral ensemble but also for Jack's centralizing characterization—and in particular, his cheapness, one of the most crucial aspects of his comic persona. This episode—the first time this extended routine was performed for television—largely plays with the best bits from previous versions, especially as Jack increasingly agitates the nervous Mel Blanc. And, in fact, this script would be reused, with few changes, for 1960's "Jack Goes Christmas Shopping"—which was filmed and is thus currently in syndication, unlike this 1957 predecessor. But it's also very funny, and if you've seen the 1960 filmed installment, you understand why this earlier version (available at UCLA and the Paley Center) deserves to be on a list of the 1950s' best sitcom samples—it's such a tribute to one of the most formative, iconic characters in this genre. Of course, Jack Benny's character isn't always afforded legitimate (narratively supported) situation comedy, but when he is, his precise definition makes him a walking tribute to this form's unique rewards—*he* is an established comedic situation. And this classic story setup—where he bounces off recurring foes—is his best exhibit in TV's first full decade. So I had to single it out, just to single him out.

Also worthy of some praise this year is *The Phil Silvers Show*, now in its third season and still shooting with multiple cameras but without a studio audience. It's also without creator Nat Hiken, who finally turned over the reins of his idea-driven gem. As previously discussed, Hiken was directly responsible for the strength of this hilarious sitcom's winning episodic notions in its earlier seasons, along with the fast-paced and intelligent storytelling for which its scripts were known. Without him, the show indeed becomes less sharp—the ideas are not as clever, the plotting is slower, more pedestrian. And yet, the energy of the leading Bilko characterization and the writers' maintained understanding of the series' idea-based identity are enough to keep the cast and crew delivering weekly rewards, including the popular "Doberman, The Crooner" (January 14, 1958), where Bilko schemes to exploit his friend's talent, just as he does in "Hillbilly Whiz" (October 1, 1957), a memorable entry that guest stars a young Dick Van Dyke as a baseball prodigy.

Additionally, there are some classic Bilko schemes in "Bilko and the Flying Saucers" (December 31, 1957), "Bilko's Pigeons" (February 4, 1958), and my favorite, "Bilko, The Genius" (March 14, 1958), which not only features the Bilko characterization well but also uses aspects of the series' premise—namely, its military workplace setting—to further ensure that its story is firmly entrenched in the specifics of *The Phil Silvers Show*, making for a well-rounded display of this sitcom's situation that proves its excellence by offering something only it could do. Nothing makes my top 50 list this particular season, but "Bilko, The Genius" is a highlight.

Of course, *Phil Silvers* also continues to offer show biz–related metatheatrical outings as well. And speaking of metatheatricality, *The George Burns and Gracie Allen Show*—one of the pioneers of this aesthetic—presented its final season here in 1957–1958, as Gracie Allen decided that she was ready for retirement.[14] Allen's pending farewell hangs over the season—at least in its latter half—as this year goes for broke, showcasing Gracie Allen at the peak of her powers within some of the show's best comic ideas, many of which are tried and true. The season is especially bold with its comedy—and this starts right from the beginning, with a TV-literate arc about Harry Von Zell trying to pitch George on a western show, now that he knows sitcoms are losing their popularity in favor of this growing genre. Such self-reference has always existed in some form or other on this series—after all, everyone in the main cast but the Mortons are playing versions of themselves—but it's on high alert this year, now that George's "magic TV" is more frequently used, contextualizing all the weekly happenings within the literal bounds of a television screen and thereby suggesting a wink to the audience—a self-awareness that's meant to communicate intelligence and create an intellectual rapport with the viewer. It's a potent device, and even today, metatheatricality tends to invoke sophistication, for a lot of sitcom characters aren't self-aware, so for a sitcom to insist that it itself *is*, it's giving itself extra permission to caricature its mimesis via the acknowledgment that it's only a peformed reflection.

Now, sometimes this can be a gimmick, providing a crutch for mediocre character work. But metatheatricality has always been part of *Burns and Allen*'s premise, and the George character has always exhibited some kind of all-knowing influence on weekly plot. Thus, his "magic TV" *adds* to his utilization and makes him a more fully present sitcom figure. For that reason, the TV—more than just a sexy gag—is an extension of the show's situation, its identity. And it's a lot of fun, especially in this last season, which, again, is better than its predecessor at showcasing Gracie, who is back in the spotlight for more entries than she was last year—once more serving as the primary narrative engine and taking some of the burden off the affable but vanilla Ronnie, who nevertheless continues to exist as a generic but helpful story lubricant.

▶ One of my favorite Gracie-focused entries of all time is "**A Hole in the Carpet**," which aired on **December 16, 1957**. Written by **Norman Paul**, **Harvey Helm**, **Keith Fowler**, and **William Burns** and directed by **Rod Amateau**, this story concerns a confused department store that thinks Gracie has suffered injuries after tripping on their carpet. It's **#14** on my list.

As with a handful of offerings here in Season Eight, "A Hole in the Carpet" uses the same story as a well-liked episode from earlier in the filmed era—namely, a winning Season Three excursion known as "Gracie at Department Store" (August 17, 1953), which similarly follows a misunderstanding that develops when Gracie trips at a store and assumes she's financially liable for their carpet, even though the store is most concerned with paying her off so she doesn't sue, a concern that heightens when the claims adjuster visits and believes that her damages are worse than they imagined—she's obviously suffered brain trauma. It's a hilarious idea that speaks to Gracie's own personality and how she vexes strangers—a classic template that hinges on her characterization. But this application of the winning narrative setup is even better than the previous, both because this year's sensibilities are bolder when it comes to comedy (with George making mischief using his metatheatrical "magic TV") and also because the story is now even more associated with the show's particulars—specifically, Ronnie, who is now an employee of the store as well. So, this is the strongest, most "sitcom" version of a great character idea for one of the decade's great characters.

There are also classic farces this year as well, in outings like "An English Tea" (October 21, 1957) and "Ronnie Finds a Friend an Apartment" (January 13, 1958). However, the year's best—and the best of the entire series—is an iconic two-parter that definitely makes my list.

▶ It's **"Hypnotizing Gracie"** and **"Gracie Is Brilliant,"** which I rank at **#8** and **#7**, respectively. They aired on **February 24** and **March 3, 1958**, respectively, and were helmed by the same crew as the above—written by **Norman Paul, Harvey Helm, Keith Fowler,** and **William Burns,** and directed by **Rod Amateau**. They follow what happens when Gracie suddenly becomes intelligent.

In this remarkably imaginative but character-specific storyline, Gracie Allen is intentionally turned upside down after she's hypnotized by a specialist and suddenly becomes a genius. This is a gorgeous comic notion because it plays with our expectations of her 25-year characterization as a Dumb Dora—a subversion of the norm that can only exist *if* there's first a strong understanding of who she usually is. That is, when her intelligence becomes the comic incongruity here, it only works because it's based on the fact that she's, typically, dumb. Knowing this, Part I lays the foundation for her switch using hypnosis—a silly, broad way to earn the idea, but one that's actually applied with shrewdness, for it explicitly reminds us of Gracie's regular depiction, via the fear that maybe her personality is *too* strong to subdue. And this is great—it's a testament to her durable, clear definition that stories are able to state who she is and then play against it, reinforcing her regular depiction through the precise out-of-character contrast.

In the second half of this two-parter, the consequences of Gracie's newfound intelligence have wider implications, for now she and George can no longer be a comedy act. This metatheatrical danger—speaking to the off-camera reality that soon this duo *won't* be performing together anymore—is a fascinating display of an important part of the series' own identity, and the ways in which scripts continue to have fun blending autobiographical truth with intentional comic fiction, specifically by way of character. Speaking of character, Part II is where the leads really shine—for when Blanche is accidentally hypnotized into being like Gracie, it's yet further confirmation of what a strong comic persona the sitcom version of Gracie Allen has, as the scene's comedy is again predicated on the basic incongruity of her characterization, thereby emphasized when it's seen in the body of her typically sensible friend, played by the rock-solid Bea Benaderet, who doubles the incongruity because of her own status quo being temporarily disrupted. So this episode, in so venerating the Gracie characterization by highlighting it in relation to other elements of the situation (both George and Blanche), is a perfect sample of *Burns and Allen*, whose success has always depended on the utilization of its star, including the "meta" connection to her real-life circumstances. With such thematic perfection, this would have been a fitting series finale.

It's *not* the series finale, mind you, but simply by existing in this final year, it helps *Burns and Allen* go out on a high note—a note that would sadly be soured the following season, when everyone in this company, minus Gracie, returned for the disappointing *The George Burns Show*. More on that later. In the meantime, *Burns and Allen* was one of the 1950s' last great examples—the only sitcom older than *I Love Lucy* to outlive it. (Along with *Jack Benny,* but that's a "modified sitcom" that's

Gracie Allen (left) and guest John Stephenson as the quiz show host in *The George Burns and Gracie Allen Show*, "Gracie Is Brilliant" (1958).

only half-countable given its heavy variety elements.) Its trajectory has embodied the ascent and acclimation of the sitcom form within this now-matured medium of television. And with both *Burns and Allen* and *Lucy* no longer championing the genre on TV with regular success, sitcom excellence would be sparse for the decade's remainder. Sure, *The Danny Thomas Show* and *The Phil Silvers Show* continued past 1957–1958, but with fare like *Father Knows Best* and *The Real McCoys* offering "sits" that were not delivering a lot of "com" and sadly representing too many of the genre's other efforts via unideal tenets, it's clear the sitcom was headed in the wrong direction. 1957–1958 is the last season in this decade where the strong shows are somewhat able to combat the stink of the bad ones. Without obvious delights, the art form's merit becomes harder to argue.

### JACKSON'S BEST SITCOMS FROM 1957–58
1. THE GEORGE BURNS AND GRACIE ALLEN SHOW (S8)
2. THE DANNY THOMAS SHOW (S5)
3. THE PHIL SILVERS SHOW (S3)

### EPISODES FROM THE 1957–58 SEASON IN JACKSON'S TOP 50 FROM THE '50s
#7. THE GEORGE BURNS AND GRACIE ALLEN SHOW (S8): "Gracie Is Brilliant" (3/3/58)

### Chapter Ten. Where's Lucy?

#8. THE GEORGE BURNS AND GRACIE ALLEN SHOW (S8): "Hypnotizing Gracie" (2/24/58)

#14. THE GEORGE BURNS AND GRACIE ALLEN SHOW (S8): "A Hole in the Carpet" (12/16/57)

#18. THE JACK BENNY PROGRAM (S8): "Christmas Shopping Show" (12/15/57)

#32. THE DANNY THOMAS SHOW (S5): "Uncle Tonoose Meets Mr. Daly" (3/3/58)

#49. THE ADVENTURES OF OZZIE AND HARRIET (S6): "Tutti-Frutti Ice Cream" (12/11/57)

## OTHER NOTABLE EPISODES FROM 1957-58

THE PHIL SILVERS SHOW (S3): "Hillbilly Whiz" (10/1/57)

LEAVE IT TO BEAVER (S1): "Beaver Gets 'Spelled'" (10/4/57)

LEAVE IT TO BEAVER (S1): "Captain Jack" (10/11/57)

THE DANNY THOMAS SHOW (S5): "Parents Are Pigeons" (11/4/57)

THE GEORGE BURNS AND GRACIE ALLEN SHOW (S8): "An English Tea" (10/21/57)

THE ADVENTURES OF OZZIE AND HARRIET (S6): "Ozzie's Triple Banana Surprise" (11/20/57)

THE PHIL SILVERS SHOW (S3): "Bilko, The Genius" (3/14/58)

## Chapter Eleven

# The Sitcom Drought
### *The Best Television Sitcoms of 1958–1959*

The 1958–1959 season is the height of the sitcom drought, as the genre's dwindling popularity following the demise of popular classics like *I Love Lucy* and the rise in shows that weren't representing the sitcom favorably led to it falling out of favor. At the peak of its visibility in both 1954–1955, when there were close to 40 original sitcoms scheduled in primetime on the three major broadcast networks, and 1955–1956, which narrowed down that number but included the decade's best comedic offerings, eight sitcoms were officially ranked in the annual Nielsen top 30 (including the "modified" *Jack Benny Program* that we have been following).[1] By 1958–1959, those numbers had significantly reduced—approximately 17 sitcoms remained on the big three networks, and only four made the top 30: *The Danny Thomas Show*, *The Real McCoys*, *Father Knows Best*, and newbie *The Ann Sothern Show*.[2] These were the worst stats since before the sitcom boom—a spike caused by *I Love Lucy*—in 1951–1952.[3]

Viewers were turning against the genre due to bad sitcoms, and they had a shortage of good ones to celebrate—indeed, both *The Real McCoys* and *Father Knows Best*, while popular and legitimized by the TV Academy,[4] were nevertheless poor examples of this art form. And yet, when made successful—by a body public perhaps conditioned to find drama nobler than comedy (a bias that goes back to the days of Aristotle)—these bland, character-suppressing family shows inevitably became something of a model. Indeed, at the end of the 1950s, many so-called situation comedies were reacting to this anti-comedy sentiment by either similarly refusing to take risks—refusing to go out on a limb and be ridiculous enough to get laughs—or by pushing *too* hard, thereby extending the cycle of audience aversion that led to the genre's current disrepute.

In that first category are all the benign domestic comedies clogging up the airwaves this year—some straightforward nuclear family sitcoms, others using some kind of "nontraditional" arrangement that nevertheless belies the dull formula underneath. While the fifth season of *Father Knows Best* is especially bad—the quintessential boring family sitcom, led by a super-serious and unerring patriarch who both in the show and behind the scenes was tamping down on humor—perennially mediocre efforts like the aforementioned *Real McCoys* and *Bachelor Father*, both in their second seasons, continued to offer bland, nondescript fare, the former only enlivened by the performance of Walter Brennan and its uniqueness for having a rural setting, and the latter for amping up its usage of Sammee Tong's Peter, a laugh-getting side character and the only Asian regular currently on a television sitcom. Meanwhile, even the best of this subcategory—*Ozzie and Harriet*, in its seventh season, and *Leave It to Beaver*, now in its second year and shifted from CBS to ABC—were not having their finest showcases. On *Ozzie and Harriet*, it was more of the same—a divide between teen shows centered on the boring boys and their real-life career pursuits, and adult shows with an amiable ensemble but less of the so-benign-it's-ridiculous storytelling (centered on Ozzie), which had helped the series stand out in previous seasons.

As for *Leave It to Beaver*, 1958–1959 sees the show at the apex of its morality rut—with Ward Cleaver no longer learning from his children but instead teaching lessons to them and in a manner that often feels so false and treacly that it can counteract the sincerity with which the boys otherwise speak and behave. The next two seasons of *Beaver* will amp up their comedy by focusing more on the title character's exploits, never totally shedding its emotional bent but dialing down some of the syrup and formula that can blunt the series' own unique charms. In terms of good episodes, this year's best is "Price of Fame" (March 26, 1959), which highlights the season's modus operandi with its storytelling, as Beaver errs and gets a lecture, but with plot points that he drives and are themselves more boldly comical, thus making the entry funny and character led.

After letting *Beaver* go to ABC, CBS seemed to have realized that although it was not a popular favorite, the show's appeal to kids was commodifiable in its own right, for in the summer of 1959, the Tiffany Network offered the similarly set up *Peck's Bad Girl*, another nuclear family comedy centered on a child. Although it clearly exhibited some imagination—for instance, the leading character, a 12-year-old girl, talked directly to the audience à la a more famous teen named Dobie Gillis (stay tuned)—the series didn't catch on, with some reviews finding it ultimately derivative.[5] However, as kid-centered shows go and domestic nuclear family shows go, it's remarkably bubbly, with realistic-sounding children *and* believable, multifaceted adults, all of whom display elements of quirk—exhibited in dialogue, if not (yet) in story. To that point, while the characters on *Peck's Bad Girl* are more literally realistic than most in the domestic genre, they're not falsely idealized like those on *Father Knows Best*. They're still funny because of small idiosyncrasies that reveal themselves in the writing (the pilot was penned by Sol Saks)[6] and in the simple storytelling to which they provide a bit of personalization. What's more, as the first sitcom to be shot on videotape, *Peck's Bad Girl* is an interesting footnote in the annals of the medium's technical trajectory—it looks like a kinescope, but it was in fact prerecorded on tape (in Hollywood).[7] As for its textual quality, it's certainly more imaginative than one of this season's other new entries—another iconic but lame suburban 1950s postcard, *The Donna Reed Show*.

Wally (Tony Dow, left) and the Beaver (Jerry Mathers) in *Leave It to Beaver*, "Price of Fame" (1959).

*The Donna Reed Show* is one of those unbearably benign nuclear family efforts, only instead of being led by a bumbling or, in the case of *Father Knows Best*, infallible patriarch, it is anchored by the mom—who apparently knows even better than dad. It could aptly be summed up then as "Mother Knows Best," for it is similarly dull, filled with undefined characters who are not made to be comedic in the slightest, all led by the perfect mama and housewife—a lady only on screen to evangelize the value of family and, in particular, celebrate the matriarch who takes care of the home. Oh, it doesn't quite hit you over the head with its messaging like *Father Knows Best* does, so it is not as immediately didactic, and while it can be similarly sentimental with unearned treacle, it doesn't *as* often veer into straight drama. But this essentially makes it even blander—for it merely remains lightly comic in tone without having actually funny ideas in substance and, most important, without regular characters who have traits that can motivate either stories or laughs. Furthermore, if *Father Knows Best* could once in a while tap into an elevated humanity or sensitivity despite its benignity and idealized depiction of the family, *Donna Reed*—in accordance with its movie star lead—is far too glossy to find such truth. As such, it's not funny, dramatic, or thoughtful in the slightest. Again, you may not have as visceral a reaction to it as *Father Knows Best*, but such forgettable mediocrity is almost worse. And with regard to seasonal quality—there's nothing good here in the first year—it's some of the most unfunny, uninspired stuff of the decade. Like *Father Knows Best*, it is the kind of sitcom that gives 1950s sitcoms—and even 1960s sitcoms—a bad name. The less said about it in this study that considers the sitcom an art form, the better. No wonder the genre was in such dire straits!

Beyond just the season's colorless family sitcoms, perennially subpar efforts like *The Gale Storm Show*, in its third season and still no better for its regular characters, and *December Bride*, now in its fifth and final season, continued to clog up the schedule, displaying the situation comedy not at its best. And in the case of *December Bride*, which had previously been a top 10 show, it was moved out of its cushy Monday at 9:30 p.m. slot, where it had followed *I Love Lucy* and then *The Danny Thomas Show*, riding their coattails to victory. Alone, it proved to have little appeal—even as changes were made to its situation, like funnyman Harry Morgan's Pete becoming a father thanks to the heretofore unseen Gladys (with a baby who would be forgotten about by the time of their 1960 spin-off *Pete and Gladys*), and the official engagement of Lily's sidekick Hilda—played by the aging Verna Felton, who actually suffered a stroke mid-season. Also, although still produced with the multi-camera format, its live audience was dropped[8]—a point noted here only to say that the number of audience-shot shows, pioneered by *Lucy*, had scaled back significantly.

## *Old Favorites: Danny, Bilko, and Bob*

In fact, the only regularly scheduled weekly show produced on film with multiple cameras in front of an audience during 1958–1959 was the Desilu-shot *The Danny Thomas Show*,[9] now in its sixth season and its second costarring Marjorie Lord as Kathy, Danny's second wife. This season is not as smart as its predecessor, for it less often acknowledges last year's "blended family" situation, which was both distinctive to the show and involved all the regulars. Part of this shift is likely due to the departure of Sherry Jackson, who was unhappy on the series following Jean Hagen's exit and left after shooting only one episode for Season Six.[10] With the eldest of Danny's two kids gone, there were naturally fewer story opportunities about the blended format and less of a reminder that Danny, and his show, existed pre–Kathy. Speaking of Kathy, the newlywed gloss was wearing off, so the writers hoped to find a way for her to become more comedically utilizable, leading to several entries that temporarily grant her a daffier depiction than she's ever implied before. In fact, there are several scripts here that were explicitly inspired by old *I Married Joan* entries—namely, "Take a Message" (November 3, 1958) and "Double Dinner" (April 20, 1959), both credited to Arthur Stander and involving comic farces as a result of Kathy's ineptitude or meddling.

However, even though these ideas were not conceived specifically for Kathy and thus indicate a lack of specificity, their funny notions are better applied on a series like *Danny Thomas* than *I Married Joan*, which was big and broad and not well rooted in character. Here, where there's a greater aura of sincerity—thanks to more of a consistency and emotional logic behind the leads' behaviors—we are naturally poised to believe Kathy's actions are motivated, and we more actively seek threads in other episodes that would provide some corroborating continuity. Essentially, we give it more benefit of the doubt because this is a better show.

Unfortunately, future seasons will prove that this depiction of Kathy doesn't stick. In fact, once the blended family part of the situation is removed entirely—and there is no longer a way to use her in plots based on these premised relationships— it slowly becomes clear that she doesn't have much of a characterization at all. She has no broad objective like Lucy Ricardo, and there are no traits that are pinpointably unique to her (in comparison to any other wife on a sitcom where the patriarch stars). We don't quite know this yet in Season Six, though, and for that reason, an episode like "Take a Message," in particular, plays really well, for it feels like it's the start of a possible characterization for Kathy. And with a funny script that again improves on its *I Married Joan* origins by finding a better home inside *Danny Thomas*'s more logical and character-rooted apparatus, it looks like a possibly good example of sitcommery, with laughs coming from mistakes made by a leading character.

This take on Kathy sort of resembles Laura Petrie of the 1960s' *The Dick Van Dyke Show*, a more regular work-plus-home show biz sitcom produced by Danny Thomas's company—and one that this enterprise, *Danny Thomas*, would actively strive to become more like at the very end of its run, seeking to emulate *Dick Van Dyke*'s elevated emotional sincerity and the effortlessness with which creator Carl Reiner married its big comedic ideas to characterizations that were simpler, upheld by even more of an attention to detail and fewer broad strokes. In this regard, "Take a Message" is almost a preview of what *Danny Thomas* would become, and it speaks to one of the things discussed about the series several chapters ago upon its debut— that it exists as a bridge between the great character-driven sitcom of the 1950s, *I Love Lucy* (of which *I Married Joan* was a less intelligent and character-based copy), and the great character-driven sitcom of the 1960s, *The Dick Van Dyke Show*. So it's a rhetorically fascinating entry and the rest of this series is what actually lets it down, with Kathy never reliably maintaining this personality, instead vacillating between overly theatrical and overly dull because of missing continuity in her perspective and attributes. Nevertheless, "Take a Message" is a funny episode from a funny season and indicates one of the major trends during this year of *Danny Thomas*.

Another of this season's big trends is, in the absence of last year's wrinkle, more stories involving Danny's work—specifically, it calls in more guests, including Jack Benny, Bob Hope, Tennessee Ernie Ford, Dinah Shore, and even Lucille Ball and Desi Arnaz as Lucy and Ricky Ricardo, trading crossovers after the *Danny Thomas* cast appeared on one of their hour-long specials. These guest star shows tend to push aside all other leads besides Danny, so they're typically not a good reflection of the situation. Yet these are collectively the best guest star shows of the entire series, in large part due to the overall healthier quality of the writing, which is close enough

Kathy (Marjorie Lord, left) and Danny Williams (Danny Thomas) in *The Danny Thomas Show*, "Take a Message" (1958).

to its fifth season peak that a lot of those strengths remain, including an uptick in its sense of humor, evidenced by bolder comic ideas and more of a willingness to channel them through character.

To wit, one of the other things connecting *Danny Thomas* to *Lucy*, remember, is not just its existence as a Desilu-shot multi-cam domestic sitcom about show biz that uses a lot of autobiographical details, but also that it literally took over its time slot. And in doing so, CBS encouraged it to become more like *Lucy*, which had—at times in its life—plenty of guest stars as well, and a sense of humor even more pronounced than *Danny Thomas*'s. This is the year that probably most matches *Lucy*'s reputation for comedic risks, and for the most part, they pay off—with good ideas inside a setup that offers relatable but funny characters who are not cartoony. Among the season's best is "Uncle Tonoose's Fling" (November 24, 1958), which features the recurring Hans Conried's Tonoose and includes one of Danny Thomas's best ever "spit takes."

If there's any complaint regarding guest stars, it's that the end of the year—well after Sherry Jackson's departure—introduces Annette Funicello in the recurring role of Gina, an Italian foreign exchange student. As a high school teen, Gina essentially functions as a replacement Terry, only now with an immigrant background that jibes with Danny Thomas's comic sensibility as the child of immigrants. But Gina has no emotional history with these characters and her inclusion therefore feels forced. What's more, though charming, Funicello is not a funny enough actress to make us ignore the fact that this feels like a blatant gimmick—a way for this already popular show to stay popular by snagging the teenage Disney audience, which would have been the base of her fans. It's a crass commercial ploy that doesn't really add to the series' situation but in fact almost undermines it, for it is neither especially funny nor believable.

And yet, with all that said, the show is strong enough to sustain her presence and not have it be a drag. This is because it's using its other characters well—especially Danny and the ever-reliable Rusty—and as the only filmed multi-cam of 1958–1959, the show's commitment to audience laughter sets it far apart from the rest of this year's more comedically muted and/or strained output. In this regard, *The Danny Thomas Show* is more enjoyable when compared to its competition, and that helps the way this collection is received.

Another filmed multi-cam also going for laughs this season was *The Phil Silvers Show*, still shot, though, without a live audience—a decision made shortly before creator Nat Hiken departed in Season Two, taking with him the series' most inspired font of ideas and his natural penchant for fast-paced storytelling that, frankly, other scribes have had trouble replicating. This year—the fourth season—includes scripts by great writers such as Arnie Rosen and Neil Simon, who also know how to come up with one-of-a-kind funny setups. Okay, there's still a missing authenticity in the storytelling (whose rhythm is also a key aspect of the series' comic identity), and with a move from a Kansas base to a California base that allows for more "big city" plots and show biz flirtations, the show's typical situation is even less present than before within episodic story. However, as a fundamentally idea-driven sitcom, simply having funny ideas is a big part of the equation, especially when they can be sustained by smart scribes and a well-oiled cast, headed by Phil Silvers, who knows Bilko as well as Hiken did and therefore keeps the show attached to him—or as much as it *can* be in this idea-driven ecosystem.

*Phil Silvers* is no longer at the level of its Season One ingenuity, or even Season Two's, but the quality of its comedy and the intelligence of its scripting relative to the rest of 1958–1959's options guarantee that it remains one of the highlights of the decade, and this otherwise weak TV season in particular. This final collection even boasts several classics, including the metatheatrical finale that also puts Bilko up against Hall—the aforementioned "Weekend Colonel" (June 19, 1959), where the series winks about its identity as a TV show in a story nevertheless straightforward about its characters—along with "Bilko, The Potato Sack King" (October 17, 1958), which has one of the year's funnier schemes; "Bilko's Small Car" (May 8, 1959), where Bilko literally becomes a used car salesman; and "Bilko's Vampire" (October 3, 1958), which has a ridiculous but well-plotted Bilko plan where he labors to make Ritzik think he's slowly turning into a vampire. Though broader, the last is most reminiscent of the comic identity established by Hiken, and it's therefore the year's highlight.

As always, the best entries have the funniest ideas. In fact, *The Phil Silvers Show* has remained elite in that regard—with ideas more comedic and, simply, more unique than any other series of the time. The fact that not even *it* could survive the sitcom drought is telling because this proves what a stifling environment the late 1950s was for TV comedy. But even if the show went out with more of a whimper than a bang, syndication—especially international syndication—proved helpful for cementing *Phil Silvers'* legacy as a classic on par with *I Love Lucy*—a sitcom that would serve as an inspiration to others, particularly Larry David and Jerry Seinfeld, who followed Nat Hiken's idea-driven ethos when scripting their classic *Seinfeld*, offering funny episodic notions—and trademark storytelling patterns—that made both series sublime in comparison to their contemporaries. *Seinfeld*, which was also inspired by the low-concept *Abbott and Costello*, was the success that *Phil Silvers* never truly enjoyed during its first run, and as such, *Seinfeld* became—and remains—an influential reference point, as this genre has increasingly turned (when it *wants* to be funny) to funny ideas, utilizing its leading characters only as a means to this end.

Accordingly, if we see *Seinfeld*'s style rippling through the sitcom as it stands today, then we're seeing *Phil Silvers'* as well, for all of these same attitudes and principles were first displayed in the 1950s, when Nat Hiken presented the first great series in this soon-to-dominate idea-driven category. It may no longer, as of the middle 2020s, be as popular in reruns or on home video as *I Love Lucy*, but its legacy lives on *within* the genre itself.

Meanwhile, even less remembered today is another highlight of the decade that could not survive this sitcom drought. Of course, it also had a far less satisfying final showing, indicating a self-determined decline. I am referring now to the fifth season of *The Bob Cummings Show*, which, in the positive column, continued to amplify its use of the funny Ann B. Davis following her first Emmy win (she'd net another after this season),[11] doing more with Schultzy and her pals, including Kathleen Freeman's Bertha and Rose Marie's Martha (the latter of whom shines in a two-parter guest starring *Burns and Allen*'s Harry Von Zell as himself[12]). Unfortunately, there are more points in the negative column—specifically, an overreliance on guest stars and Grandpa Collins, a self-indulgent gimmick that harms the show's aesthetic realism (which had tended to be more literal), and in stories that don't address the central dramas or core relationships. Ultimately, that's really the problem—this show has previously been so good about using its premised conflict to inform plots, utilizing its ensemble dynamics to support the action. In Season Five, it's almost as if the show wants to move away from that situation. A little girl is even added at the midpoint ... a little girl ... to an adult sitcom like *Bob Cummings*! Now, as you know, I am not fond of kids in sitcoms—Beaver aside, they tend to merely be plot devices to which others react, not actual characters with a communicable decision-making process that suggests a continuity of personality.

The application of this device—a little girl named Tammy—is maybe a little more nuanced, though, for Bob both uses her to attract women and simultaneously finds that she's another obstacle in his pursuit of them—a domestic trap in his way and thus something of a structural replacement for Chuck, who, as Dwayne Hickman inches closer to *Dobie Gillis*, is less present than ever. This makes her a tool to reengage with the series' situation. Additionally, her presence could also allow its lead to indicate growth—that is, bachelor Bob is growing older and now perhaps realizing that he wants his own family after all. Supporting this theory is the fact that there are several signs this year of Bob aging and no longer remaining *as* desirable to the ladies. In other words, there are instances of him striking out. And in fact, this is a seminal concern posed in the season's antepenultimate outing, "Bob, The Last Bachelor" (June 23, 1959), where the lead consciously observes that most of the people around him have given in to the domestic lifestyle he's long been trying to avoid. The question starts to become, for the first time ever, *should* Bob settle down?

This is interesting and suggests a mind for character evolution that we don't see on most 1950s sitcoms, once again affirming Paul Henning's *Bob Cummings* as smarter than so much of the genre's baseline, then and even now. As for Tammy, she's a cloying replacement for Chuck, whose status as a "baby wolf" better enabled premise-related comedy—her episodes are such a drag, and they merely feel like a desperate attempt to breathe new life into the show as it's dying. Unintentional or not, the season ends up looking more like the family series that were poor but popular—*Father Knows Best*, *The Real McCoys*, and heck, the only good one in this bunch, *Danny Thomas*. In this regard, *Bob Cummings* finishes a little bit like *I Love Lucy*, almost giving up on its original premise, turning into something more broadly familiar to the rest of the genre that it used to challenge.

## *More Old Favorites: Ann, George, and Lucy*

Those three family offerings—*Father Knows Best*, *The Real McCoys*, and *The Danny Thomas Show*—all represented the sitcom genre in Nielsen's annual end-of-season top 30 ranking for 1958–1959.[13] The only other show in there was a newbie—the least disappointing freshman of the season. It's *The Ann Sothern Show*, another ensemble workplace comedy led by Ann Sothern, who had ended *Private Secretary* in 1957 following a dispute with producer Jack Chertok. Ready to come back to TV, Sothern enlisted *Lucy* scribes Bob Schiller and Bob Weiskopf, and they came up with an idea for another single-camera filmed sitcom, this time shot by Desilu, that was deliberately far removed from *Private Secretary* (and Chertok's concept). They ended up with something that was indeed different but nevertheless familiar—Sothern would again play another working woman, only not a secretary but an actual manager who *has* a secretary. And instead of a theatrical agency, she'd now work at a hotel. Very different, right?

Well, sort of, for while Schiller and Weiskopf only wrote the pilot,[14] they actually did set up a show that has more narrative avenues for regular story than *Private*

*Secretary*, which, in its own right, claimed some decent workplace opportunities for relationship building between the leading lady and her friends, rivals, and boss. It just too often functioned as a guest or story-of-the-week show, with episodic concerns taking poor Susie away from the other leads and those ensemble dynamics building out the situation. In comparison, *Ann Sothern*'s hotel setting was similarly made to allow for weekly guests, but now she had even more of a principal cast—in addition to Sothern as manager Katy, there'd be her boss (Ernest Truex), a henpecked man beholden to his domineering wife (portrayed with verve by Reta Shaw); a rosy-cheeked bellboy; a French desk clerk; and Katy's quirky secretary Olive, played by her funny-faced sidekick Ann Tyrrell, the only principal carryover from *Private Secretary* (aside from Ann Sothern herself, of course).

So, with more people to engage Katy in story every week, Season One of *The Ann Sothern Show* indeed looks to take better advantage of the elements in its situation than *Private Secretary* did. However, it still cannot help but be more reliant on guests and episodic distractions than it should be. And while the boss and his wife have clear characterizations and Tyrrell remains charmingly odd, there's still a vagueness to all their personalities—particularly Sothern's Katy, who is Susie but with a different name. It keeps the series from being great.

Oh, *Ann Sothern* did well in the ratings because it took *December Bride*'s old spot behind *Danny Thomas*, but viewers apparently longed for *Private Secretary*—specifically, the strong dynamic between Sothern and Don Porter, who had played her boss, Mr. Peter Sands.[15] So, after 23 episodes of *The Ann Sothern Show*, the series was retooled—Treux and Shaw left, and they were replaced by Porter as Mr. James Devery. Slowly, the show became more like *Private Secretary*, with the hotel growing less relevant to the generation of story, and the other regulars outside of Sothern, Tyrrell, and Porter fading into the background. The plots themselves remained equally self-contained and circumstantial in nature, but this time, they consciously made better use of the central relationship: both Katy and Olive's friendship and Katy's flirtatious rapport with Mr. Devery, which would officially become romantic in the series' 1961 finale. But let's not get too far ahead—as far as this first year is concerned, there's only a *little* more texture to these relationships than on *Private Secretary*, and this particular elevation of focus won't really become clear until the following two years, which continue to refine what, frankly, *Private Secretary* built and *Ann Sothern* reconstructed.

And yet, if this weird trajectory for *The Ann Sothern Show* is not clear right away—rejecting its own possibilities to instead correct the prior iteration's own missed opportunities—Season One already shows promise, especially by the standards of the depressed 1958–1959. That's already evident in the season's strongest segment—a likable farce called "The Engagement Ring" (April 6, 1959). Airing after the conceptual and casting retooling that effectively began the process of displaying how *Ann Sothern* could be an improvement on *Private Secretary* by delivering more stories focused on the bond between the core leads—in this case, Katy and Mr. Devery—this entry offers the first indication that the series is intentional about how it will depict their potential romance, already bolder and more relationship-focused than its predecessor. In turn, it's a better form of situation comedy, and while I still can't call it great, I can single it out in this lackluster chapter, especially because at this point in its run, an episode like this is so promising—foretelling better stuff ahead, particularly in the final season (1960–1961), where both Katy's relationship with Devery and Olive's engagement to a dentist played by the funny Louis Nye take center stage, thus tying the show's weekly storytelling to more of a sustaining situation.

Unfortunately, most of the other debuting sitcoms this year were less promising—even those with a strong pedigree, like *The George Burns Show*, the continuation of *Burns and Allen* after Gracie Allen's retirement, with Burns, Harry Von Zell, Bea Benaderet, and Larry Keating, plus Ronnie Burns and Judi Meredith (the woman who played Bonnie Sue, Ronnie's love interest at the end of *Burns and Allen*)—basically everyone but the star. The situation for this new series essentially continues from the original but switches to the workplace, where George is, as before, a TV producer (a mimetic detail), scouting talent and new shows, while Blanche is his secretary, Harry Morton is his business manager/accountant, and Ronnie's own professional career is developing on the side. Now, as we know, these are mostly funny people, so this is a setup that inherently has a lot going for it. But the best thing about *Burns and Allen* was Gracie Allen's well-known comic persona. No one else got to be as comedically developed, for they were merely reacting to her (the only other one with an actively apparent comic personality was Larry Keating's Harry Morton), and since everyone was basically designed as a reactionary satellite to her, or at least made to react off her primarily, her absence is incredibly felt—even with the smart change in scenery, which continued to allow for metatheatrical gags and stunt cameos, including from Bob Cummings and Jack Benny.

Viewers apparently missed Gracie also. The show—now on NBC instead of CBS—did not rate as well,[16] and there was an attempt made to retool the sitcom into a live comedy-variety series, like *The Jack Benny Program*, then in its ninth season and also offering more live broadcasts than filmed entries and less situation comedy overall (in accordance with the genre's declined popularity). Approximately seven *George Burns* variety outings featuring guests galore aired midseason, alternating with some leftover filmed sitcom episodes.[17] But those also failed to spark, and the show ended back as a situation comedy, with 18 sitcom segments airing in total (of 25), none of them recapturing the magic of *Burns and Allen*, a series that worked as a sitcom because it was built around a strong character—the very one missing here. Nothing filled Gracie's void.

Speaking of an unfilled void, Lucille Ball and Desi Arnaz continued to offer five more hour-long broadcasts as the Ricardos in their old *I Love Lucy* format—still with the Mertzes as support but episodic guests as an equal attraction. Now sponsored by Westinghouse and airing as part of the company's anthology show *The Desilu Playhouse*, these five specials were generally less strong than the five from the year before, moving even further away from the situation on which *I Love Lucy* had ended and *really* far away from the character stakes that initially gave the show its engine when it premiered in 1951. Although every offering has at least one memorable comic bit—"Lucy Goes to Alaska" (February 9, 1959) boasts a winning hammock routine, for instance—the segments with Maurice Chevalier ("Lucy Goes to Mexico") and the former stars of *Mr. Adams and Eve*, Howard Duff and Ida Lupino ("Lucy's Summer Vacation"), represent the worst material yet featuring a character called Lucy Ricardo—unfunny and not character rooted.

On the other hand, two winning episodes were produced this season. The first occurred when the cast of *The Danny Thomas Show* (also shot by Desilu) crossed over in "Lucy Makes Room for Danny" (December 1, 1958)—an entry that allowed well-defined characters from both series to shine in several memorable comic centerpieces (most notable a court scene with Gale Gordon playing the judge), indicating the genuine link in textual style between the two, based on the mostly believable display of their leads and a similar interest in using their depictions to propel both story and laughs. It's a lot of fun, and you'll often see it anecdotally cited today by a lot of *Lucy* fans as their favorite of all the *Comedy Hour*s.

The other winning episode is "Lucy Wants a Career" (April 13, 1959), which is a throwback to the series' original dilemma and utilizes her character's initial objective, as its plot finds Lucy scheming to get hired as a "Girl Friday" on an early morning TV news show with Paul Douglas. At last, she's working outside the house—and on TV; she'll be more than the typical housewife and mother! The only problem is, this leaves her little time to see Ricky—as comedically portrayed in a scene where they get a brief passing moment at a train station, allegedly inspired by a real-life incident for the Arnazes.[18] Lucy can't live like this, so she ultimately chooses Ricky, her family, over her career. But not before we're treated to a comic routine where Lucy is forced to do a show while high on sleeping pills. It's hilarious in the classic *Lucy* way and motivated entirely by her original show biz "want"—something barely used in the last few years of the half-hour series. Seeing it invoked again is incredibly satisfying—this *was* the show's situation, and unlike most of these hour-long entries, "Lucy Wants a Career" is more about the leads than the guest. Plus, in returning to the show's intended thematic interests, there's a sense of long-delayed closure. This could be a series finale. It's not. In fact, there'd be more of these segments (syndicated as *The Lucy-Desi Comedy Hour*) in 1959–1960, but never again one as character concerned. It's the last flash of greatness from the decade's most important sitcom.

## *Odds and Ends—Filmed and Otherwise*

As for other debuting programs, the fledgling NTA Film Network sold another sitcom to select stations—*This Is Alice*, a distaff *Leave It to Beaver*, with the same gentle moralizing. The single-camera comedy filmed at Desilu only lasted a year of 39 episodes. It was joined at mid-season by NTA's *Glencannon*, an adventure series shot in Britain and starring movie star Thomas Mitchell as the chief engineer of a freighter called *Inchcliffe Castle*. As an adventure show, its stories tended to be self-contained, less concerned with the exploits of its regular cast.

These two new half hours from NTA were met by the previous year's *How to Marry a Millionaire*, back for a 13-episode second season with breakout star Barbara Eden getting bumped up to top billed in accordance with her prominence. The year also saw an increase in broader comic stories, substituting for plots where the women directly pursue marrying millionaires—the now-diluted situation. It's a trade-off with little distinction, for the character limitations remain the same: only Loco is well defined, Mike is vague, and Lori Nelson's Greta has been replaced by Gwen, played by Lisa Gaye. Gwen works in publicity and is new to the city—a sensible naïf but a naïf primarily. That's a little too close to "ditzy," Loco's persona, and so it's not a great choice for Gwen, especially because it ends up playing as hazy. Once again, the only thing worthwhile here is Barbara Eden. And in the next decade, she'd find a sitcom that showcased her talents far better. These were the only three comedies produced and distributed in 1958–1959 by NTA, whose efforts to become a network never fully materialized, leaving the company to be little more than a glorified syndication service. After their flagship station—WNTA-TV in New York City—abandoned them in 1961, the company hobbled along, distributing shows for syndication until shuttering for good in 1966,[19] never giving the big three networks a true rival.

Also, in first-run syndication this year but shot by Desilu and produced by CBS was a revival of the 1953–1954 season's *Colonel Humphrey Flack*, a high-concept idea-led show about a man who cons the cons. Most of its scripts were direct remakes of the earlier live series—only filmed. Its merits as a situation comedy were thus unchanged—remaining unfortunately slight. And speaking of slight, two more new offerings from 1958 to 1959 came and went even quicker. *The Ed Wynn Show* (not to be confused with his 1949 comedy-variety series of the same name) cast the famous vaudeville comic in a mawkish "nontraditional family" sitcom where he played a grandpa raising his two granddaughters—one a kid, the other a college student. This, of course, set the show up for some of the era's maudlin benignity—it was actually referred to as "Grandfather Knows Best"[20]—and to that moniker, it's just a lighthearted yawner that never quite allowed its star comic to go into the kind of outrageous gaggy shtick for which he was best known. Ultimately, in failing to showcase a known comic entity well, the series disappoints—a sitcom short on comedy, with a situation that itself is hacky and uninspired.

The last new sitcom of the season premiered in May 1959. *Too Young to Go Steady* was another domestic affair, and continuing the trend of *Leave It to Beaver*, *Peck's Bad Girl*, and *This Is Alice*, it centered itself, specifically, on a kid, or rather, a 15-year-old teen—a tried-and-true focus for the genre, ever since the days of *The Aldrich Family*, *A Date with Judy*, *Meet Corliss Archer*, and the like. But this "teen" hook—initially popular—had sort of gotten folded into more generic "nuclear family" shows by the middle of the decade, where often the younger characters rose in prominence, like in

*Ozzie and Harriet*, but seldom at the expense of the adults. *Too Young to Go Steady* is fairly unremarkable, however, and the only thing more interesting than its casting of movie stars Joan Bennett and Donald Cook as the parents is the fact that it was the last *totally live* sitcom of the decade and, more specifically, the last *totally live* sitcom of the decade to come from New York: using the production methods and locale from which the entire medium, and of course the sitcom genre on television, had recently originated.[21] While the shift to film and Hollywood was effectively over by 1956, when Max Liebman nobly tried to make one last big effort with Buddy Hackett and *Stanley*, *Too Young to Go Steady* was the true last gasp for the sitcom as it began in this decade. From now on, liveness could only be a deliberate gimmick—no longer an earnest, regular possibility for the sitcom genre on television.

How fitting that this should end here in 1958–1959, when terrible shows like *Father Knows Best* had helped defame the sitcom and inspire a rash of other bad examples—presenting the false notion that eschewing humor (and all the risks associated with it) was the only way for the genre to exist in a post–*I Love Lucy* world. And as the model that helped usher in way too many domestic, suburban, or family shows that were now indulging formula instead of exploring genuinely unique characters—the elements that actually provide a situation—*Father Knows Best* and its ilk led the sitcom into dire shape. It could not break out of this rut until it vanquished these false ambassadors and replaced them with actually funny offerings—comedies that proved the artistry of the genre, instead of trying to be lesser versions of other forms. This would take a few seasons for this to successfully occur, but 1959–1960 started a several-year offensive by the networks to resurrect the sitcom, and it would prove to be, at the very least, more promising than 1958–1959, the nadir of 1950s sitcommery—technically better than the stuff produced pre–*Lucy* but more aesthetically disappointing, as this was a medium that now should have known better.

## JACKSON'S BEST SITCOMS FROM 1958–59

1. THE PHIL SILVERS SHOW (S4)
2. THE DANNY THOMAS SHOW (S6)
3. THE ANN SOTHERN SHOW (S1)

## EPISODES FROM THE 1958–59 SEASON IN JACKSON'S TOP 50 FROM THE '50s

None this season.

## OTHER NOTABLE EPISODES FROM 1958–59

THE PHIL SILVERS SHOW (S4): "Bilko's Vampire" (10/3/58)
THE DANNY THOMAS SHOW (S6): "Take a Message" (11/3/58)
THE DANNY THOMAS SHOW (S6): "Uncle Tonoose's Fling" (11/24/58)
LEAVE IT TO BEAVER (S2): "Price of Fame" (3/26/59)
THE ANN SOTHERN SHOW (S1): "The Engagement Ring" (4/6/59)
THE PHIL SILVERS SHOW (S4): "Weekend Colonel" (6/19/59)
THE BOB CUMMINGS SHOW (S5): "Bob, The Last Bachelor" (6/23/59)

Chapter Twelve

# Back to Basics
## *The Best Television Sitcoms of 1959–1960*

Reigniting interest in the sitcom genre following its nadir in 1958–1959 would take several seasons. The networks launched major offensives—entire spates of new comedies—in 1959–1960, 1960–1961, and 1961–1962, such that by the end of the 1960–1961 season, there were eight sitcoms in the annual Nielsen top 30 (if you count both the "modified sitcom" *The Jack Benny Program* and the animated *The Flintstones*, which indulged the form's narrative tropes).[1] That number actually increased to 11 the following year,[2] before falling back a bit in 1962–1963,[3] by which time the failed short-lived efforts had faded away and the genre had enough established hits and promising newbies to firmly make it clear that the sitcom was back—and in just a few more years, it would become more popular than ever. So 1959–1960 is the first season where the industry began trying to dig the sitcom out of its 1958 hole via a handful of new programs. Most were unsuccessful, but there *was* some movement— there were more sitcoms on the broadcast networks this year than last year, and five comedies actually made the final annual Nielsen ranking—the same four as last year (*The Danny Thomas Show*, *The Ann Sothern Show*, *Father Knows Best*, and *The Real McCoys*), plus one of the season's new efforts—discussed in this chapter.[4]

The best of the four that maintained their rare popularity during this "bear market" was *The Danny Thomas Show*, whose seventh season would prove to be something of a unique collection, as star Danny Thomas sought to potentially ease himself out of his responsibilities on the series by finding a replacement. After handselecting up-and-coming TV comic Pat Harrington, Thomas conceived an arc in which Pat would play a version of himself and date, become engaged to, and then marry Danny's daughter Terry. The plan then was, by the next season, Danny would hand the reins over to Pat and Terry, who would become the new stars of the show.[5] But since Sherry Jackson refused to return, her role was recast with Penney Parker, a less experienced actress who comes across as less sincere than her predecessor.

What's more, while this arc naturally provides the season with story, not enough care was put into crafting for Pat a characterization, and his blandness, coupled with the relative inferiority of his mate in relation to her predecessor, makes for a season that, although relatable and in validation of the show's sensibilities as a family sitcom (with Danny realistically mourning the maturation of his daughter), still does not quite yield the comedic returns of previous years. Season Seven also has much less of the blended family situation, something that sadly doesn't resurrect on Terry's return and will never come up again. In fact, Terry never makes another appearance on *Danny Thomas* after the sponsor mollified Thomas, rejecting his master plan.[6] Following the young couple's honeymoon, the two disappear entirely, rendering this the last year with Terry—even in this recast, less authentic form.

This wouldn't be the last time that Danny Thomas tried to ease himself out of his own show. In 1962–1963, he would also try to give the series over to Sid Melton and Pat Carroll, the duo who played Charley and Bunny Halper, respectively—Danny's manager, introduced at the end of Season Six, and his wife, introduced in the rejuvenating Season Nine. But the reaction was again unenthusiastic,[7] forcing Danny to return to lead his show for one final season in 1963–1964, where the series more formally embraces some qualities of the now-popular *Dick Van Dyke Show*, which boasted a similar premise to *Danny Thomas* and came from the same company but was funnier and more realistic, thanks to a higher threshold for emotional believability and an even greater attention to detail regarding character. Accepting scripts from many *Dick Van Dyke* writers and striving for a similar comic realism, *Danny Thomas*'s final season ends up being one of its most interesting, especially for Kathy, who's both allowed to be funnier and also more believable than she was in, say, this seventh season, where she's forced to be zany a few times (like last year) but in ideas that now more obviously lack a sustained continuity with the majority of the show's weekly output, thereby rendering her depiction false and strained, not supported by the situation and our expectations of it.

However, if this makes Season Seven sound like a major comedown from Seasons Five and Six, it's not—it's actually the last year with head writer Arthur Stander, so it has a similar tenor as the peak of Season Five. And although the aforementioned Pat and Terry arc does have its shortcomings, it's still fodder for episodic story that centralizes the family and their relationships. Would it be better with Sherry Jackson, who had actual history with Danny and Rusty, inherently reminding us of the blended family part of the situation? Yes. And would it be better if Pat's character had more of a comic personality and wasn't just around for the sole purpose of replacing Danny, with little thought as to his definition? Absolutely. But it's okay, especially in the context of the series as a whole. Plus, with Rusty still being used comedically—as opposed to years ahead—and the affable Sid Melton rising in prominence, *Danny Thomas* still feels like a premier sitcom.

And interestingly, it was the only weekly multi-camera series shooting in front of a live audience this year,[8] carrying on the legacy of *I Love Lucy* and holding out for *Dick Van Dyke*, which Danny Thomas's company would produce beginning in 1961. Speaking of which, this season of *Danny Thomas* also contains a backdoor pilot for what would become *The Andy Griffith Show*, a classic 1960 sitcom that will help revitalize the genre, injecting rural charm into a sweet, "nontraditional family" format (with a workplace component that also includes the stellar Don Knotts, who bolsters the laughs). But that's for a different decade and perhaps a different book. For the record, that entry is "Danny Meets Andy Griffith," which first aired on February 15, 1960.

▶ In the meantime, the funniest episode of this series is from this season. It's **"Danny and the Little Men,"** first broadcast on **December 14, 1959**. Written by **Charles Stewart** and **Jack Elinson** and directed by **Sheldon Leonard**, it comes in at **#43** on my list. In this entry, Kathy and Terry scheme to make Danny and Pat think they are going crazy with overwork.

This hilarious offering uses a variation of the *Gaslight* routine, specifically involving aliens—making it especially reminiscent of a *Phil Silvers Show*, "Bilko and the Flying Saucers" (December 31, 1957). But if that makes the idea seem unoriginal, it works *better* here because it's more rooted in part of this show's original situation—the clash between the work and the home, as Kathy and Terry conspire with Charley to trick Danny and Pat into thinking they're too overworked at the club and in need of a vacation. This logline validates a part of the show's identity that has been undermined since the introduction of Kathy—the tension of Danny's work duties encroaching on his responsibilities to his family at home—and while it would no longer make sense on a week-to-week basis, it's nice to see it back (just as it's nice to see it resurrected more often in the final 1963–1964 season as well), for it gives this low-concept sitcom with some characters who are not as well defined as they need to be (namely, Kathy and Pat) a story template that makes sense and can still allow them to participate comedically. And frankly, in picking one entry to represent the season, I'm glad it includes Pat and Terry, who sort of define Season Seven and what makes it unique—for better and for worse. Also, with big outrageous laughs—the kind *Danny Thomas* only rarely gives us, relative to the other best of this genre (*I Love Lucy*, *The Honeymooners*, *The Phil Silvers Show*), it's much fun—proving that it is indeed competitive.

Also, it's not on my top 50 list, but I would be remiss for not also mentioning a special entry from this season of *Danny Thomas* that guest stars Jack Benny—"That Ol' Devil Jack Benny" (January 11, 1960)—in which Danny believes that he's been losing gigs to Jack, a rival comic, because Jack has made a Faustian deal with the devil (played by Gale Gordon). It breaks the show's typical aesthetic realism and thus can't be celebrated as a great example of this series' situation, but it uses Jack Benny's characterization well, and it's hilariously, memorably fun.

Meanwhile, another one of 1959–1960's popular sitcoms—airing after *Danny Thomas* at 9:30 p.m. on Mondays—was the second season of *The Ann Sothern Show*, which essentially finishes the retooling it began during its first season when Don Porter joined the cast, by phasing out all the remaining regulars from the original format besides Ann Sothern's Katy and Ann Tyrrell's Olive. It also introduces both Ken Berry as a recurring bellhop and adds even more reminders of the old *Private Secretary*: another kid (this time played by Jimmy Fields) and Jesse White as Oscar

Pudney, playing another nuisance at odds with Katy. In essence, it's becoming more and more like *Private Secretary*. These changes are difficult to singularly judge, for the elements that are making the show more reminiscent of the earlier series are not inherently superior to Bob Schiller and Bob Weiskopf's original format for *Ann Sothern*, and they're not themselves more satisfying either. But this year—which also includes a crossover appearance from Lucille Ball as Lucy Ricardo—is better than the previous year, for it actually *is* more relationship driven, more attuned to the romantic possibilities between Sothern's and Porter's characters: the duo whose bond anchored *Private Secretary* and was its main appeal, regardless of how well they were used in story.

Also, this year really starts to make more comedic use of Ann Tyrrell as Olive, and she's delightful, yielding some of the funniest and therefore most worthwhile episodes of the entire series, as Olive's friendship with Sothern's Katy—even more so, again, than on *Private Secretary*—creates more fodder for weekly plot. Thus, this is a better season—not because it's like *Private Secretary* but because it improves on the basics established in *Private Secretary*. The third and final season (1960–1961) will continue this trend, creating a whole engagement arc for Ann Tyrrell's Olive—with Louis Nye playing her bashful dentist beau—that ratchets up the comedy but maintains this relationship focus, ending with Katy and her boss finally romantically paired as well. It's the culmination of two sitcoms' worth of sexual tension.

In this regard, *Ann Sothern* is never a perfect sitcom, but it has more moments than *Private Secretary* at effectively using the tools at its regular disposal. Some of this year's strongest episodes include "Katy Mismanages" (December 28, 1959), which deals with ensemble relationships in the workplace when there's a temporary shift in dynamics; "Slightly Married" (January 11, 1960), a farce predicated on the romantic possibilities of Katy and Mr. Devery; and "Olive's Dream Man" (February 15, 1960), which guest stars Joe E. Brown and makes good use of the hilarious and sensitive Ann Tyrrell. Again, they're not the best of the best sitcom examples, but they are agreeable and solid, especially compared to so much from this fallow period.

That is, it's so much better than the bland domestic fare that continued to overwhelm the airwaves, neither pursuing laughs nor allowing characters to be defined and exist within story in a way that might help earn them. The worst offenders continue to be *Father Knows Best*, which still made the top 30 but mercifully ended this season at Robert Young's behest,[9] and *The Donna Reed Show*, which was actually starting to recycle old *Father Knows Best* scripts, tweaking only subtle details. Both remain far too self-serious, refusing to provide characterizations that are suitable for this genre and its needs. Meanwhile, "nontraditional family" sitcoms like *The Real McCoys*, in its third season, and *Bachelor Father*, also in its third season—its first as a *weekly* series—continue to be overly dull and conflict-free, even as the latter actually counts this year as its most comedic, thanks to the elevated use of Peter, the Asian houseboy. They're just too benign, with little by way of character (e.g., all

*McCoys* continues to have is Walter Brennan). Meanwhile, as for *Ozzie and Harriet*, I hate to be repetitive, but it's more of the same with little variation: boring stories for the boring kids (now with David out of college and working at a law firm) and mildly amusing plots for the mildly amusing adults but most of them without the kind of so-benign-it's-ridiculous storytelling that helped enliven individual episodes in previous seasons, which created a way for this series to genuinely be comedic. In this era, things are mostly blah.

Well, except for on *Leave It to Beaver*, also in its third season and now ready to shake off some of Ward Cleaver's overbearing moralizing for an even greater focus on the kid characters, whose comic exploits enable the show to deliver bolder humor while still showcasing its greatest asset: an ability to write children believably, with perspectives that feel sincere but can also be amusing and existent within relatable stories that are maybe heightened but only a little. Great examples of this include "Larry Hides Out" (January 9, 1960), where Beaver's pal Larry Mondello is at his best (with support from his mom, played by *The Real McCoys*' Madge Blake); "The Spot Removers" (May 14, 1960), where Beaver errs and the rascal Eddie Haskell (the show's funniest character) actually is afforded some dimension; and my pick for the year's best, "Teacher Comes to Dinner" (November 28, 1959), which boasts a unique story told entirely from the point of view of young Beaver, who is both nervous and excited about the prospect of his teacher from school coming over to the house for a dinner with his parents. It's oh so relatable—sweet but without forsaking the comic traits that make Beaver an amusing avatar for rambunctious youth. No prior series has ever written its young leads as well as *Beaver*, here at its comedic peak.

## Comic Strips and Radio Hits

At any rate, while Beaver may not have an equal, he did have a little brother, figuratively at least, after CBS—which allowed ABC to snag *Beaver* after its first season—belatedly decided to try again with another direct appeal to kids. Thus came *Dennis the Menace*, another single-camera family comedy—this one inspired by Hank Ketcham's comic strip of the same name. Serving as the Tiffany Network's attempt to cash in on some of the young audience it lost when ceding *Beaver* to ABC, *Dennis* is a bit of a throwback, like *Blondie*, because of its origins as a comic—coming from a known entity that supplies all the leads with already established personas, just like many of the long-running radio sitcoms that transferred to TV in the early part of the decade, including *Amos 'n Andy* and *Burns and Allen*. This gave *Dennis the Menace* a built-in audience but also more of a formula—with stilted and regressively limited characters, as implied by its source material foundations, which it would need to make flesh.

But it didn't. Specifically, the sitcom version of Dennis (played by Jay North) has a basic persona and a function in story—he's a well-meaning kid who unknowingly causes chaos wherever he goes—but there's not much actually driving him and zero emotional insight or the believability we see in, well, Beaver Cleaver. His comic purpose is clear, but his prospects are limited. And really, no one else is as primed for story except his oft-agitated best friend and neighbor Mr. Wilson, played perfectly by Joseph Kearns, who lasted nearly three of the four seasons before passing away and being replaced by Gale Gordon, another frequently menaced character actor (first by Miss Brooks and soon by Lucy Carmichael). Kearns is the show's saving grace, for the laughs don't actually come from Dennis himself but from the havoc he wreaks and the reactions from those around him—specifically Mr. Wilson. This corroborates my belief that children on sitcoms are seldom characters; they're more like narrative devices—sparking story by allowing for conflict to which adults can then react. Also, without communicable decision-making processes, it's hard to ascribe any psychology and therefore motivation to children on sitcoms, which means we can't infer much of a characterization. And indeed, Dennis here is merely impulsive, and we're supposed to ascribe it to youth. That's buyable, but it's not at all a precise characterization that can inspire plot or provide it some situation-specific nuance in ways either artful or impressive.

That said, it would be foolish to claim that a show anchored by Dennis the Menace doesn't use him as a character. Actually, he *is* active—he is doing a lot, whether there's intention or not—and this centralization within episodic story renders him not like *most* sitcom children. And while I don't think his show depicts him as believably or allows him to make decisions that seem as character suggesting and genuinely reflective of youth as, again, Beaver on *Leave It to Beaver*, Dennis's show is also less earnest and more purely interested in comedy—like a strip. So it's an interesting trade-off: more comedy, less sincerity. In fact, it's ultimately a good introduction for what's to come in the 1960s, where there will be more laughs in the era's sitcoms but less honesty—less emotional logic or aesthetic realism. There will be lots of "character," though, and as always, the best sitcoms are hinged on character. That's why, with comic strips informing the general personas here (for two leads anyway), this feels like a regression—away from nuance, away from attention to detail, away from aesthetic realism predicated on some kind of literal logic.

And yet, *Dennis the Menace* is always amiable—with episodes like "Dennis and the TV Set" (March 13, 1960) and "Alice's Birthday" (April 24, 1960) offering huge laughs based on the ways in which this little kid unknowingly rankles the adults around him. It's thin, but there's a consistency of behavior (at least) that makes it passable situation comedy. And yes, this was the only new sitcom of the season to crack into the top 30, so CBS clearly got what it wanted: not *Beaver* but funnier. It was the first small step in the resurrection of the sitcom genre.

Unfortunately, most of this season's other attempts at revitalizing interest in the sitcom were not as successful, even as a wide variety of tactics was used. For instance, the end of the 1950s turned to a playbook more commonly referenced at the beginning of the decade: recruiting reliable hits from radio—properties with name recognition. Called into action now was *Fibber McGee and Molly*, one of the first "modified" sitcoms ever broadcast, "modified" because of its strong vaudeville roots. Those were surely trimmed for TV—the sitcom had evolved so much from 1935 to 1959—and like filmed adaptations of *Duffy's Tavern* and *The Great Gildersleeve*, a certain authenticity was lost in the process. Without the performers—Jim and Marian Jordan—who made famous these otherwise thin and sketch-like characterizations, there would have to be a lot of extra definition afforded to the leads, just to compensate for that missing comic energy. Sadly, TV's Fibber and Molly remain generic, even when played by funny people like Bob Sweeney and Cathy Lewis, for no unique link is made between them and story, rendering this a trite husband-and-wife domestic sitcom, with episodic support providing narrative stimuli. And it doesn't feel at all like the radio series, which benefited from its vaudevillian sensibilities to fill in the comedic gaps. This is pure mediocrity. Not a worthy postscript for the radio classic.

## *Comedy Dramas and Other Head-Scratchers*

Another tactic used in this era was to downplay the comedy and, like *Father Knows Best*, deliberately offer episodes that feel more like dramas, with a seriousness that often precludes the regular characters from being *allowed* to be funny (and therefore drive story). One of the new shows in this category is *Hennesey*, which was often called a sitcom because it uses a light laugh track. It stars Jackie Cooper (of *The People's Choice*) as a navy doctor at a San Diego base, while others in the cast include his boss, pal, and nurse love interest—the last played by Abby Dalton. Cooper and his scribes prided themselves on offering a "comedy drama," blending the genres evenly (with *Father Knows Best* cited by the star as a chosen comparison, in explicit contrast to *I Love Lucy*).[10]

The result of this, of course, is a show that can not compete comedically with other actual sitcoms—and certainly not by way of character, for again no one here is defined with a mind toward motivating big laughs or comedic story. Well, except for the recurring James Komack as incompetent dentist Harvey Blair—his entries tend to be the funniest because he's allowed to be slightly ridiculous (just like Aristotle prescribed). Otherwise, *Hennesey* might be better referred to as a light drama with a laugh track. After all, this was an era when it wasn't cool to be a sitcom—it was even scheduled at 10:00 p.m. eastern, seldom a slot for expected comedies.

*Hennesey* could thus be considered something of a throwback to the early 1950s, where shows like *The Goldbergs* and even *The Ruggles* were affiliated with the comedic genre but didn't have enough ha-has to cut through their otherwise more muted, serious tones. There will be more shows like this—blending comedy and drama—in the early 1960s (and again in the later part of that decade), even though that era is mostly defined by its laugh-out-loud offerings.

Other shows at least called themselves comedies, like *The Dennis O'Keefe Show*—another single-cam that split its time as a "nontraditional family" effort, with a widower (O'Keefe) raising his son alongside a housekeeper (Hope Emerson), and then as a more procedural, anthology-like career drama, with a parade of different people, places, and things each week in accordance with the lead's career as a newspaper columnist. We've seen that latter type of sitcom before—for instance, with *The Gale Storm Show*, a cruise-set series that often employed one-off stories about certain locales and different guests. Its fourth and final season here in 1959–1960 tries to introduce new recurring people on the ship and even brings in its leading lady's parents, but its overall sensibility remains intact: not enough of the regulars, the situation. The same could be said for the brief run of *The Jeannie Carson Show*, which offered six filmed episodes for first-run syndication following the cancellation of *Hey, Jeannie!* (1956–1957). This new show for Carson was reformatted, casting her now as a flight attendant—another job that could allow for a variety of locales, guests, and stories each week, little of which had to do with the leads. As usual, this yields unsatisfying sitcommery. *Dennis O'Keefe* is a bit better, for O'Keefe is charismatic and Emerson is innately amusing. But its humor is generally muted, and the things that work are seldom foregrounded as they are on finer efforts.

Fortunately, if shows like *Hennesey* and *Dennis O'Keefe* foolishly tried to help the sitcom genre by quieting the comedy, others went out of their way shouting for it—perhaps without noting the importance of having a strong situation, or specifically, strong characters who could earn and uphold it.

In this category, I would put *Love and Marriage*, a filmed multi-cam (though shot without a live audience)[11] from Danny Thomas's stable starring Danny Williams's father-in-law, William Demarest, cast here as the aging owner of a publishing company that's now in trouble due to his disdain for the new popular music: rock and roll. Jeanne Bal is his sensible daughter, who swoops in and becomes his partner—and literally takes him under her roof—with the show's main dramatic tension stemming both from their disagreements in the work and at home, especially since he also clashes with her lawyer husband (Murray Hamilton). Rounding out the ensemble are Stubby Kaye as a song plugger and Kay Armen as a singing secretary.

This cast and premise suggest a decent work-and-home setup—and no surprise, it came from Louis Edelman and Melville Shavelson, two of the guys who helmed *Danny Thomas* back when it was *Make Room for Daddy*. Only, *Love and Marriage* doesn't have the same authentic and detail-providing autobiographical bent, at least not for anyone on screen. And while Danny always sang on his show, *Love and Marriage* seems even more concerned with creating opportunities for music—so much so that very few stories actually take advantage of the way this decent premise establishes relationships, objectives, and characters in contrast. Accordingly, this is a well-designed sitcom that is only lame in execution, not taking advantage of its situation's possibilities, specifically by way of character, who lack the definition to support the premise in a meaningful way.

Another new sitcom with a seemingly smart construction was *The Betty Hutton Show*, also casually known as *Goldie*, which placed Betty Hutton, the wide-mouthed movie star, in an idea-driven format where she would play a manicurist and former showgirl who is suddenly vaulted into enormous wealth when a client dies and gives her his house, staff, and three kids—two teens and a 12-year-old. It's really two separate comic ideas: one about a single woman being thrust into parenthood and another about the classic "rags to riches" arc—the latter of which will become more common fodder for high-concept sitcoms in the 1960s (like *The Beverly Hillbillies* or, in reverse, *The Pruitts of Southampton*). But both ideas are unusual, for theirs is not a traditional "nuclear family," and it's not even about a "nontraditional" widow/widower/uncle taking over. This freshness is exciting—it's a unique situation with different ways to have characters motivate plot! Unfortunately, as with so many inferior sitcoms, *Betty Hutton*'s stories meander around these central ideas, and ultimately, the show is never very funny because it doesn't explore these obvious conflicts—and perhaps more bizarrely, it never lets its central clown ham it up like she's known to do. I think the main issue is there's not enough of a contrast between who Goldie was *before* the high-concept development in the pilot and who she's supposed to be now that her "status quo" has changed. If she was very obviously the non-mothering type and/or more crassly working class, it would be funnier and also more possible to mine story from this tension. As it stands, she's restrained and thus her show is restrained—offering a couple of interesting ideas but neither of them well supported by the characters, who again don't get explored in episodic plots.

Another poorly managed high-concept sitcom premiered in the summer of 1960. It's *Happy*, a filmed single-camera show that takes the talking dog gimmick of *The People's Choice* and applies it to a baby. Unfortunately, this gimmick is really all there is here, for its young parents (including Ronnie Burns), who comanage a Palm Desert hotel with Doris Packer, are bland with generic personalities, and stories can't help but reveal their lack of definition. What's more, the funny Packer is underused, and although she actually gets some laughs chasing Uncle Charley, played by Lloyd Corrigan, this one relational dynamic is not enough to carry a series' worth of story. In essence, *Happy* is an idea-driven but one-joke sitcom, without evidence of conflict in plot, since the baby, like Cleo of *The People's Choice*, only voices his thoughts to the audience, not to any characters in the show, as Mister Ed would when his series premiered in first-run syndication in early 1961. And although *Happy* was brought back as a mid-season replacement in January 1961, it never improved, remaining a mundane affair with a singular gimmick.

## *Dobie Gillis Saves the Sitcom*

However, if the new entries thus far have been mostly disappointing, there was a clear standout. The 1959–1960 season actually did make *some* progress in rehabilitating the situation comedy, and it wasn't via the kiddie popularity of *Dennis the Menace* but rather with an actually well-crafted series in the classic tradition: *The Many Loves of Dobie Gillis*, a filmed single-camera sitcom (with laugh track) based on the popular book (of the same name) by Max Shulman, one of the most well-known humorists of his era—and an auteur on par with Nat Hiken—boasting a unique style evident in all his work. In shepherding the show as its head writer, Shulman was able to naturally infuse TV's *Dobie Gillis* with his own particular voice, providing it a valuable sense of individuality. Also, he made smart choices.

Known for writing about collegiate life, Shulman decided to de-age his beloved character for the small screen, casting *Bob Cummings*'s Dwayne Hickman as the high school Dobie (his hair now dyed platinum blond to make him seen younger and more affiliated with the literary character). This significant change would keep the show in Shulman's trademark campus setting but also hopefully engage a younger, teen demographic, to whom CBS was hoping to directly appeal.[12] Of course, teen sitcoms, as we have seen, were not new—they dated back to radio in the late 1930s and early 1940s with *The Aldrich Family* and *Meet Corliss Archer*, both of which made it to network TV in the early 1950s. And youthful characters had come back into vogue recently, once *Leave It to Beaver* found an audience with children, sparking a rash of imitators (including *Dennis the Menace*).

But both *Dobie Gillis* and the more kid-friendly *Dennis the Menace* are unique in that they represented some of the first blatant attempts by the TV networks at "demo targeting," or a strategy of programming content directly *for* specific subcategories of viewers. This was a fairly new idea. In fact, the first instance of the word "demographic" being used in this context didn't occur in *Variety* until 1960,[13] while the first print reference I have found to the soon-to-be-coveted "18–34 demographic" is in a 1964 edition of *Television Magazine*.[14] These terms speak to one of the primary metrics that networks would soon use when developing all of their shows and, eventually, canceling or renewing them as well. In this regard, *Dobie Gillis*'s conceptual strategy with demographics looks forward to one of the major trends of the 1960s.

However, it wasn't just teens that CBS hoped to court with *Dobie Gillis*; it was adults as well—the same adults who may have been fans of Max Shulman's work in the 1940s, when they were in school. By engaging these adults *and* their teenage children[15]—the first of the baby boomers, a big demographic—CBS's hope was that the show could build a sizable multi-pronged audience and become a hit. This was a correct notion—oh, it would take until its second season to crack the top 30,[16] but it was quickly a competitive property that other networks coveted.[17] How did Shulman manage to cultivate its appeal? Why, with character and comedy, of course—both upheld by an authenticity that could only come from such an individualized voice.

For one, he knew how to write for teens, eschewing sentimentalism and rejecting what he called "togetherness,"[18] the false domestic ideal as portrayed on sanitized, unfunny shows like *Father Knows Best*, where the kids were merely tools for instruction, subordinated to their wise father and far too benign to actually be mimetic. Shulman refused to look down on Dobie and his pals or treat them as narrative devices (as the kids on both *Leave it to Beaver* or *Dennis the Menace* could be). No, his young characters had personalization in dialogue and agency in story—they were treated like the adults on other shows were treated, with humanity. Finally, teens could be *fully realized* sitcom characters, with their humanity forming the foundation that he could then caricature for laughs—and often in ways both wild and wacky.

The wildest and wackiest character on *Dobie Gillis* is Maynard G. Krebs, Dobie's "beatnik" best friend, played with wide-eyed sincerity by future castaway Bob Denver. Maynard has since become the series' most iconic symbol—a mascot for the show's comic sensibilities, spoofing a specific element of late 1950s teen culture. Denver's usage within story grew in prominence throughout the show's run, and some critics have since appraised his presence as ultimately overbearing—too extreme. But the problem with the series' storytelling in those later years has more to do with its diminished ability to play to the situation in plot, rather than anything Maynard himself does. In that regard, his elevation is more a symptom of malaise than a cause.

Frankly, I think Maynard is an asset. He is consistent and clearly defined (exactly what a sitcom needs for laughs and story) and he's thus a credit to this series' character work—so unique compared to all the other leads, like the bookish Zelda Gilroy (played by *Trouble with Father*'s Sheila James); or the fair-haired Thalia Menninger (Tuesday Weld), the materialistic but "creamy" object of Dobie's desire; or the foppish Chatsworth Osborne, Jr. (Steve Franken), the silver-spooned dweeb who lives off mommy (Doris Packer) and serves as a replacement for Dobie's initial rival, Milton, a pretty boy famously played by Warren Beatty in just five early segments. As you can see, these are all distinct, well-communicated characters—a terrific starting point for any situation comedy.

Another thing that made *Dobie Gillis* novel for the time is suggested by the "many loves" in its very title: Dobie is girl-crazy. This basic objective is personified early on by the sensual Tuesday Weld as Thalia, Dobie's central object of desire whom he endeavors to woo. But "many" means *many*, and it soon becomes clear that Dobie's pursuit of the fairer sex is an all-encompassing aspect of his character, and he'll go after *any* "creamy" girl who implies the possibility of amour … well, except the scientifically minded Zelda, who registers as sexless to Dobie despite her strong yen for him. From there, this premised framework—of Dobie the teen lothario—naturally creates strong, clear relationships between the characters, all hinged on something a little realer, more adult, than the typical TV teen "boy likes girl" angst of Henry Aldrich and Corliss Archer. Dobie was, essentially, a junior Bob Collins—and casting an alum of *The Bob Cummings Show*, Dwayne Hickman, only made that link more obvious. This pedigree also sanctioned him as a real *character*—capable of existing in stories as adults would.

Meanwhile, if the kids were attracted to the dynamism of the young leads, the grown-up viewers got the same in Dobie's parents, with Shulman expressly hoping to mine comedy and drama from an exploration of the widening generational gap between adults and teens, who, he believed, weren't communicating.[19] Accordingly, a core part of *Dobie Gillis'* premised design in this first season is the palpable dramatic tension that exists between Dobie and his father Herbert, the crotchety grocer played by Frank Faylen and best remembered for his emblematic catchphrase: "I gotta kill that boy, I just gotta." Their emotional distance is a vital engine for much of the series' early storytelling, with Florida Friebus as Dobie's mother trying to be their neutral mediator, smoothing over their major differences. In this arrangement, neither father or son knows best, and that's not only funnier and more dramatic, but a little closer to real life as well. Together and in juxtaposition, they reveal Shulman's smart step-by-step solution to get the sitcom out of its current rut—eschewing idealized domesticity from dull and infallible bores in favor of more mimetic human tensions via specific, well-defined characters who could maintain their extreme comedic qualities while also boasting identifiable relationships, objectives, and flaws—a mimesis then ripe for benign ridicule in episodic story. You know, *situation comedy*.

Most of this first season is great situation comedy because it's exceptionally character-based. But, as previously indicated, that wouldn't last forever, for Shulman had a natural tendency for comedic extremes, and that can sometimes yield stories that break the show's aesthetic realism, bordering on the surreal. This bubbles up over time but is even evident already in Season One, in episodes like "The Chicken from Outer Space" (March 8, 1960), where an experiment with hormone-injected chickens leads to a giant-sized fowl. It's goofy—another taste of the cartoonish kind of humor that the 1960s was about to usher in, and the ideas that *Dobie Gillis* would become even more comfortable proffering in that decade, as its situation faded from regular view. This installment itself is popular with viewers because it's memorable, but it's not one I would personally cite as a good example of the series beyond this evidenced aspect of Shulman's ethos, for the narrative emphasis is less on the characters and their bonds but rather on the funny, ridiculous idea. This, again, becomes an unfortunate trend for *Dobie Gillis*.

To that point, while I praise the way in which Shulman designed this show and credit him for strategically building an audience and advocating for the sitcom genre unlike any new series had been able to do for several years, the unfortunate truth about *Dobie Gillis* is that its first season is its best season, and it pretty much declines every year thereafter until it's almost unwatchable. That's not just because of the increasingly silly stories (like the example above) but also because of the aforementioned mistake: the dilution of its situation. And it actually does *begin* here, when Tuesday Weld's departure (April 1960) removes the primary inspiration of Dobie's lust and she never gets replaced by anyone who can maintain that same feverish desire and serve as an ambassador in story for his central objective. This minimizes it. Additional changes that hurt the show then come in Season Two—like the purposeful downplaying of Dobie's initial horniness, with the on-screen title literally changing from *The Many Loves of Dobie Gillis* to simply *Dobie Gillis*. This is a shame, for with that title and all that it implied being clipped in story as well, so too goes a lot of the individual adult-like agency that made the characters special.

The other big change for Season Two, and this was even profiled in *TV Guide*, is that "now even his father loves him."[20] That is, out goes the dramatic tension between dad and son—for now, without any motivation (i.e., without any evolution of character as evidenced through believable exploration in story), they just get along better now and suddenly understand each other. That means conflict no longer exists *fundamentally* between them as a regular part of their characters and thus the series' situation, removing a key aspect of the premise that also guaranteed stories based on their contrasting definitions and their relationship. It's likely that Shulman was forced by the network to tone down some of the show's comic raunch and dramatic edge after Season One, but it's still such an obviously bad move—eliminating guaranteed sitcommery without anything worthwhile to fill the void.

Nevertheless, part of the fun of Season Two—which, incidentally, also attempts to make Dwayne Hickman a pop star à la Ricky Nelson (to no avail)—is the rising prominence of Zelda and Maynard, two terrific characters who, with Dobie, form a fun trio and help elevate a great ensemble of players—like Mr. Pomfritt (William Schallert) and the aforementioned Osborns—and they collectively add character dynamics, even as there's less direct conflict between them. There's also an elevation in the show's thoughtfulness—always part of Shulman's work and embodied by Dobie's monologues to the audience in front of "The Thinker" statue. This device—used throughout all four years—is not quite "meta" in the same way that George's "magic TV" allowed him to disrupt that series' internal logic by calling attention to narrative beats and thus the fictional aspects of the storytelling, for Dobie speaks to his audience to explain his feelings and corroborate the plot, not emphasize its artifice. It's similar though. And, again, this is always part of the series' DNA, but the second year really uses his character's introspection to create episodes that validate the situation by being similarly philosophical, such as "The Big Question" (January 24, 1961), where Dobie and Maynard wonder what will happen in their life after graduation from high school.

However, these rising charms are significantly blunted by the series' loss of those bigger aspects of its identity—the generational tension and Dobie's amorous objective—along with the simple fact that the lead, who goes from flaxen to brunette, is forced to grow up. Indeed, midway through Season Two, Dobie and Maynard graduate high school and join the army. Apparently, Shulman was eager for some change in the series' status quo, but these army shows aren't nearly as much fun because they take us away from this recently cultivated ensemble and from the school setting with which his work was best associated. The following year (1961–1962) reverses this, moving the characters—including Zelda—to college, and this restoration of the campus setting begets a seeming renewal of narratives affiliated with the situation. But by that year's midpoint, it's clear *Dobie Gillis* has gone off the rails without its father-and-son drama and any avenue for Dobie to regularly pursue women (as his character was built to do). And as stories continue to become more and more ridiculous, without the kind of help from these premised guardrails—specifically, the characters—the last year and a half (where Zelda only recurs—Sheila James had shot a failed pilot[21]) is dire, far from the excellence of the show's first season.

And yet, for this book, I'm not examining the merits of the final three seasons and their downward trajectory. I only care about the first year—the only season born of the 1950s and the one that finds the show at its best, with classic installments like "Couchville U.S.A." (December 29, 1959), the best entry driven by patriarchal tensions as Herb fears that his son hates him, "Love Is a Fallacy" (March 1, 1960), a very Shulman-esque entry where one of Dobie's "many loves" makes Thalia jealous, and "Soup and Fish" (May 3, 1960), in which the series' teen aspects are well reiterated via character interactions and lots of comedy from Steve Franken's Chatsworth Osborn, Jr. They all represent different but significant aspects of the show's identity.

▶ Three other episodes make my top 50 list. The earliest pops in at **#29**—"**The Best Dressed Man**," which first aired as the series' sophomore outing on **October 6, 1959**. It was written by creator **Max Shulman**, directed by **Rod Amateau**, and finds Dobie turning to clothes to impress Thalia and compete with his rival, Milton—portrayed by the aforementioned Warren Beatty.

This early offering is the best display of the show's initially crafted situation for its teen characters, with Dobie lustily pursuing the sensual Thalia, but finding competition from rich, pretty boy snob Milton. Both Thalia and Milton, who don't even make it to the end of this first season, are wonderful recurring players, for they reinforce the series' premised objective for Dobie (with Dwayne Hickman emphasizing that series' sex-driven tradition through his sheer presence). Although a solid ensemble will arise in Season Two with Sheila James' Zelda, the deliberately platonic way in which Dobie views Zelda ends up robbing him of his key motivation, which serves as a specific engine for stories like this, where Dobie's quest for Thalia's heart (and other body parts) is channeled through a sartorial contest. With this simple but focused framework, all the teen characters are well-defined—Dobie, Thalia, Milton, and Bob Denver's Maynard—and Max Shulman's fresh comedic ethos is guiding.

▶ Said ethos is also well on display in "**Love Is a Science**," which first aired the following week on **October 13, 1959**. It was also directed by **Amateau** and written by **Shulman**, directly based on one of his stories. It comes in at **#39** on my list and is notable because it introduces Zelda Gilroy, the bookish but quirky brunette who loves Dobie and is certain he'll eventually return the favor due to "propinquity," even though he's at the moment smitten with the avaricious Thalia. Zelda was originally supposed to be a one-off character,[22] but the strength of James's chemistry with Hickman eventually turned her into a regular. This was a fortuitous development—she's such a well-defined presence, a testament to Shulman's smart writing.

Foreground, from left: Maynard (Bob Denver), Thalia (Tuesday Weld), and Dobie (Dwayne Hickman) in *The Many Loves of Dobie Gillis*, "The Best Dressed Man" (1959). Also, note Warren Beatty as Milton (corner right behind Hickman).

▶ In addition to those great, formative installments is "**Rock-a-Bye Dobie**," my pick for the best episode from *Dobie*'s first season, first airing as its finale on **July 5, 1960**. It was written by **Ray Allen**, directed by **Rod Amateau**, and features a risqué story about Dobie's parents believing that Dobie has secretly married—and become a father. It's **#23** on my top 50 list.

"Rock-a-Bye Dobie" was held to air until July 1960 (as the season's technical finale) because the network took issue with its plot, where a misunderstanding makes the Gillises think that their babysitting son has actually started a family. In fact, the original title of the episode was the more explicit "Almost a Father."[23] Its narrative concept offers a blend of the show's thematic charms—boasting a sexual undercurrent; a drama stemming from the lack of communication between the generations; and a brilliant display of Shulman the auteur's genius at depicting wacky people believably, which even extends to this entry's guest characters, including Kathleen Freeman and Don Knotts as Dobie's potential in-laws. The half hour was first slated to run in March but a few edits were needed to emphasize the fact that Dobie's parents did *not* think he'd had a kid out of wedlock, but rather that he'd secretly gotten married *and then* had the kid.[24]

Interestingly, a similar plot was used with Ronnie Burns on the final season

(1957–1958) of *Burns and Allen*, but his character was older, and that show had a more mature audience, so the demographic concerns were different. Also, *Dobie*'s version is more tailored to other aspects of its series' situation, which makes it feel more connected to its regular particulars. And indeed, "Rock-a-Bye Dobie" is the funniest example of this series and all the most important elements of its identity, thereby showing a path forward for the sitcom genre: not to shy away from humor but to be clear, consistent, and direct with funny, well-defined characters—the most important component of any situation, whether low concept and character driven like *Dobie* or high concept and idea driven, as so many sitcoms of the 1960s would prove to be.

## *The End of Innocence*

But if 1959–1960 was starting to show the path forward for sitcoms, it was also signaling an end of sorts. The last live episode of *The Jack Benny Program*—now in its tenth season—was broadcast in November.[25] Hereafter, offerings were either filmed or taped. Saying goodbye to total liveness—even through this, a "modified sitcom"— marked the completion of a trend that defined the decade. Jack Benny's TV series would run until 1965, but as a paler and paler imitation of its radio predecessor, as its affiliation to what it once was, along with how it had begun on television, continued to fade as well. This last live episode is symbolic of that trajectory—the evolution of this genre away from radio, away from liveness, away from 1950.

Additionally, 1959–1960 saw the last of Lucy and Ricky Ricardo, the two best sitcom characters of the 1950s, whose half-hour show *I Love Lucy* was a model of character work—the first great ambassador for a character-driven style of writing. As the Arnazes' marriage crumbled amid growing problems with alcohol and infidelity, Desilu chugged on, as did Westinghouse's *Desilu Playhouse*, which managed to offer three final *Lucille Ball–Desi Arnaz Show* specials—one with Milton Berle, another with Bob Cummings, and the last with both Ernie Kovacs and his wife Edie Adams. By this point, the company was no longer shooting these shows in front of a live audience,[26] and while scripts—by the same four scribes from the final season of *I Love Lucy*—still found a way to work in a big comic centerpiece every broadcast (like Lucy and Ethel masquerading as geishas in November 1959's "The Ricardos Go to Japan"), the stories were less affiliated with the characters and their relationships, as Lucy's objective had long faded away and the leads now shared narrative space with big-name guest stars who naturally took focus.

The final segment—"Lucy Meets the Mustache" (April 1, 1960)—is a sad hour, with Ricky feeling depressed about his career, and Lucy appealing to Ernie Kovacs to give her husband a job. Not a job for herself, mind you, but for Ricky, who suddenly and apparently—perhaps after the country move took him out of New York—is no longer in demand. It's a strange deconstruction of the situation. Yes, it was always

**Jack Benny in the last live broadcast of his television series, *The Jack Benny Program*, originally aired November 29, 1959.**

part of Lucy's objective that she wanted the best for Ricky as well because his success would also elevate her stature and take her out of the humdrum of an ordinary existence. (That's a big reason *why* she'd meddle in his affairs so often.) But Ricky was always a working and successful entertainer—he had the thing Lucy wanted. Now she no longer wants it, and he apparently no longer has it. Perhaps one might read into this arrangement for clues about the couple's real-life circumstances, and that would not be entirely unfair, given the autobiographical details once used to inform the show's premise, characters, and relationships, back when it was just *I Love Lucy*. But either way, "Lucy Meets the Mustache" really does seem like the end—the end for these characters, the end for these people.

Contrary to popular belief and the mythology that *Lucy*-philes like to promote, Lucille Ball didn't file for divorce from Desi Arnaz the day after this episode was shot. No, this episode was filmed in January 1960,[27] and she filed in March,[28] once all commitments on their Westinghouse contract for the *Desilu Playhouse* were done.[29] The episode then aired a month later—nearly nine years after the couple first shot the *I Love Lucy* pilot in 1951. It was the last hurrah for the best sitcom characters of the 1950s—and the seminal show of this era. It wouldn't be the end for Lucille Ball, however—she would go on in TV, as would the genre *I Love Lucy* helped define.

## JACKSON'S BEST SITCOMS FROM 1959-60
1. THE MANY LOVES OF DOBIE GILLIS (S1)
2. THE DANNY THOMAS SHOW (S7)
3. LEAVE IT TO BEAVER (S3)

## EPISODES FROM THE 1959-60 SEASON IN JACKSON'S TOP 50 FROM THE '50s
#23. THE MANY LOVES OF DOBIE GILLIS (S1): "Rock-a-Bye Dobie" (7/5/60)
#29. THE MANY LOVES OF DOBIE GILLIS (S1): "The Best Dressed Man" (10/6/59)
#39. THE MANY LOVES OF DOBIE GILLIS (S1): "Love Is a Science" (10/13/59)
#43. THE DANNY THOMAS SHOW (S7): "Danny and the Little Men" (12/14/59)

## OTHER NOTABLE EPISODES FROM 1959-60
LEAVE IT TO BEAVER (S3): "Teacher Comes to Dinner" (11/28/59)
THE MANY LOVES OF DOBIE GILLIS (S1): "Couchville, U.S.A." (12/29/59)
THE DANNY THOMAS SHOW (S7): "That Ol' Devil Jack Benny" (1/11/60)
THE DANNY THOMAS SHOW (S7): "Danny Meets Andy Griffith" (2/15/60)
THE ANN SOTHERN SHOW (S2): "Olive's Dream Man" (2/15/60)
THE MANY LOVES OF DOBIE GILLIS (S1): "Love Is a Fallacy" (3/1/60)
DENNIS THE MENACE (S1): "Dennis and the TV Set" (3/13/60)
THE MANY LOVES OF DOBIE GILLIS (S1): "Soup and Fish" (5/3/60)

# Conclusion.
# The Genre That Doesn't Die
*Television Sitcoms After the 1950s*

Although the 1950s ended with the sitcom genre still trying to fight against a negative standing that led to a reduction of scheduled shows, this decade also saw the TV sitcom develop and evolve alongside the development and evolution of an entire new medium. In 1950, most of the popular sitcoms owed a huge debt to their radio predecessors, and it took time for the medium to fully maximize the benefits (and the limitations) of these new visual opportunities. Furthermore, advancements in technology led to a shift from mostly live broadcasts to preproduced filmed shows—with a corresponding move from New York to Hollywood as a result of these changing standards. Of course, the smash success of *I Love Lucy* accelerated all these trends, with its celebrated excellence inspiring others to mimic it—if not its refined multiple-camera setup, then its simple use of film, which looked so much better than anything else. Beyond its technological advancements, however, *Lucy* also offered a creative model for the sitcom to follow—one that centralized its leading characters, granting them well-defined, believable personalities that could be tied to episodic story using particular traits, like motivating objectives.

As the sitcom then became a popular genre over the next few years—largely *because* of *Lucy*—many great and not-so-great shows made their debuts. The 1954–1955 season was the first peak for the sitcom on television—with more scheduled than any other year this decade—while 1955–1956 saw the emergence of other classics, like *The Honeymooners* and *The Phil Silvers Show*, two gems whose proficiency at offering funny episodic ideas set another template for many future sitcoms to follow, using their leading characters to support specific, identity-validating narrative notions. This idea-driven style of sitcommery, in contrast to *Lucy*'s more character-driven style, would become more popular in the decades after the 1950s, for the last few years of this era were saddled with too many bland domestic shows—sitcoms that refused to allow themselves to present any of the traits, or benign incongruities, necessary for comic story. Accordingly, with fewer great shows to sample the genre's capacity for greatness, the sitcom took a back seat to other formulas—the game show, the variety show, the western. The 1959–1960 season was the first attempted rebound from the absolute nadir of 1958–1959, with *Dobie Gillis* and *Dennis the Menace* elevating the roster of televised sitcoms, but it would take a few more years for a full return to glory.

Indeed, the industry made major efforts in 1960 and 1961, when many new comedies were thrown at the schedule—some hitting, like *The Andy Griffith Show*. But it wouldn't be until 1962 that the sitcom was fully rehabilitated, enlivened by a few big hits that showed the path forward for the genre in this new decade. As *The Dick Van Dyke Show* finally found popularity in its second season—combining a sexy view of suburbia with an expansion of the *Danny Thomas* work-versus-home structure and a focus on detailed, autobiographical consistency for its leads—it emerged as the successor to *I Love Lucy* in practicing character-driven comedy. Not even Lucille Ball's next series—and yes, 1962 also saw *her* return to the sitcom form (with Vivian Vance) in *The Lucy Show*—was as well designed. But the redhead's continued presence in this medium, in which she was a regular participant until 1974, continued to evangelize the comedic strengths of the multi-camera format, which was a helpful counter to what was actually more dominant in the 1960s: emerging single-camera successes, from folks like *The Bob Cummings Show*'s Paul Henning, who offered the high-concept idea-driven mega-hit *The Beverly Hillbillies* in 1962. Its quick ascendance gave rise to the rest of the "Henning trilogy," *Petticoat Junction* and *Green Acres*, and they represented a premise-first brand of sitcommery that was also felt in the new spate of supernatural shows, like *Bewitched*, *I Dream of Jeannie*, *The Munsters*, and *The Addams Family*, where domesticity was spoofed in high-concept packages. With shows like these dominating the schedule in the mid-1960s—1965–1966 offered more sitcoms than ever before—the decade's reputation for sillier, escapist, idea-driven fare was set. Not even attempted forays into low-concept modernity in the latter half of the 1960s could really change that course. And yet, the sitcom was central to TV of that decade, confirming that its brief recession in the late 1950s was just a mere ebb in this overall flow.

In the 1970s, the sitcom proved its adaptability to social trends as high-concept efforts were pushed out in favor of low-concept ensemble comedies from MTM, which produced *The Mary Tyler Moore Show* and all its siblings, and Norman Lear's socially relevant hits, particularly *All in the Family*, which premiered in 1971 and provided the first opportunity for television sitcoms to use characters to vocalize political debates and reflect common issues of the day. These two types of sitcoms, from both MTM and Norman Lear's Tandem—united under a return to the multi-camera format, more literal realism, and situations more concerned with character relationships than any high-concept trappings—nevertheless represented the greatest divide yet between character-driven and idea-driven sitcoms. This gulf would narrow a bit in the second half of the decade, with shows like *Taxi* and *WKRP in Cincinnati* combining qualities of both aesthetics. But then, as the late 1970s and early 1980s sought to be less serious than the early 1970s, the sitcom entered another recession—one that it wasn't fully pulled out of until 1984, with the late-blooming popularity of *Cheers*, the best ensemble workplace comedy the medium had ever seen (utilizing a classic format that went all the way back to *Duffy's Tavern*), and *The Cosby Show*—a family comedy that ushered in a wave of similar but less comedically satisfying examples.

That wave of disappointing family comedies was reminiscent of the late 1950s. Fortunately, though, while it took until the 1960s for high-concept hijinks to help push out the boring family fare of the decade prior, the 1980s responded to this trend much quicker—deflating domestic idealism with a reemergence of rebellious metatheatricality (via the work of Garry Shandling) and anti-family family shows, like the satirical (and thus idea-driven) *Married... With Children*, along with the more crushingly realistic *Roseanne*. This counterculture was aided by the rise of cable and the introduction of the Fox network, beginning an expansion of our media landscape that is still continuing to this day. Although the 1990s remained network focused—with multi-camera hits like *Frasier*, *Friends*, and the highly influential *Seinfeld* shining on top-rated NBC—the slow rise of premium cable's HBO by the turn of the century foretold where the sitcom was heading, with single-camera efforts and a blending of genres.

Despite these lurking changes, the 2000s also clung to past trends with its tiring multi-cams, while emphasizing the emergence of its idea-driven values in single-camera offerings such as *Curb Your Enthusiasm* (HBO's more metatheatrical follow-up to *Seinfeld*) and Fox's short-lived *Arrested Development*, where fast and funny *Bilko*-esque comedic notions thrived. These were then filtered into otherwise more traditional network ensembles like *The Office*, *30 Rock*, and *Parks and Recreation*—classically designed workplace sitcoms that nevertheless embraced the single-camera setup and a more idea-driven predication for narrative comedy. But there was a key difference. In responding to the concurrent rise of reality TV, the sitcom turned now to the "mockumentary"—a satirical documentary format that communicated idea-based interests, as every single joke and story would now be layered with this conceptual gimmick. This was entirely born of viewers' evolving tastes, mining comedy from increased meta-awareness. Although less experimental multi-camera shows (many of them by Chuck Lorre and in the rom-com vein of *Friends*) were still holding on and equally popular—such as *Two and a Half Men* and *The Big Bang Theory*—critics and award givers had a clear affinity for single-cams, deeming them more sophisticated, in large part because of their projected intelligence and capacity for satire.

Accordingly, with the best sitcoms no longer "looking" like what audiences expected—like, frankly, *I Love Lucy*, whose style followed in *The Dick Van Dyke Show* to *The Mary Tyler Moore Show* to *Cheers* to *Seinfeld*—there began cultural murmurs that the sitcom was dead, and these new shows were rather simply "comedies." However, all of those aforementioned examples—from *Curb Your Enthusiasm* to *The Office* and even to *Modern Family* (which thrived in the early 2010s)—very easily meet our definition of what makes a good sitcom, using the elements of their "situation," and particularly their characters, *for* laugh-out-loud comedy. Though idea driven in nature, as we have seen, even idea-driven shows rely on their characters to uphold their conceptual promises. Thus, far from being dead, the sitcom was just adapting to the times—embracing a trendy style indicative of another genre (reality TV) with which it was in competition.

Meanwhile, the continued adoption of traits associated with other genres would continue into the 2010s, when network comedies no longer competed only with cable—basic and premium—but the rapid acceleration of streaming platforms as well, such as Netflix, Amazon Prime, and Hulu. Half-hour shows now marketed as "comedies" that we would traditionally call "sitcoms" began taking on traits of *other* programs—specifically, prestige dramas, a self-congratulatory moniker given to critically adorned serials, which were now laudable in an age where TV had the budget to resemble motion pictures. That is, with all these new platforms providing new opportunities for storytelling, television finally became a respected medium—and perhaps even more so than cinema, with writers and actors now clamoring to work under the new artistic freedom supposedly offered. And yet, with these new attitudes came old prejudices—ones that go back to Aristotle: specifically, the belief that tragedy is a purer form of Drama than comedy.

Okay, there have always been half-hour shows that prided themselves on existing in the gray area between the two aesthetics—in the 1950s, in the 1960s, in the 1970s, and so on. But typically, the funnier the half-hour show, the better it would be received—both by audiences and by critics. And indeed, the goal for half-hour sitcoms was *almost always* to be funny. Now, with auteurs and snobs bringing cinematic ideas to the medium in accordance with its so-called elevation, they not only want to move away from the things that remind of the initial theatricality of sitcommery (like the multi-camera format, the presence of audience laughter, and the associated rhythms) but from actual sitcommery too—shedding, specifically, the comedy.

Shows such as *Louie* and *Atlanta* on FX and *Girls* and *Barry* on HBO resemble dramas visually and are textually selective about when they want to court ha-has versus a more tragic emotional catharsis. While other single-camera sitcoms in the past made it clear that their number-one goal was evoking pleasure by actively making viewers laugh, it's tough to say that this is the number-one goal for these new half hours—all of which *could* be funny (some more than others) but don't seem to always want to be. This, then, complicates our ability to call them sitcoms, for if we can agree they all have "situations," the question then is, are they using them *for* comedy … more than anything else? Certainly, hour-long shows that have snuck into these categorizations (*The Marvelous Mrs. Maisel*) make their non-comedic affiliation clear via structure, and the ones that actively ask to be called a "comedy-drama" or "dramedy" are explicitly ceding that they either don't want to—or *can't*—be amusing with the same consistency that would make them competitive with other full sitcoms. But what does it mean if the most praised half-hour "comedies" are no longer reliably funny—is *that* the sitcom's death knell?

The answer is not yet, for the 2010s' most award-worthy comedies—according to the TV Academy[1]—were *Modern Family* and *Veep*, two half-hour shows with actual laughs as a primary intention. And in the years since then, while several celebrated offerings have been, frankly, not funny (*The Bear*), all the actual comedies stand out more obviously now as a favorable contrast. Indeed, the most-watched half-hour comedies have been, as of late, *The Big Bang Theory*[2] and then its single-camera spin-off *Young Sheldon*,[3] both centralized around one very intense comic character. So comedy is still being prioritized in certain shows and there's still an audience for them, even amidst this overall dramatic, anti-theatrical trend in the industry.

Additionally, traditionalists still have reasons for optimism. No, not because of the many reboots, which exist as a market contrast to the serious shows in the sitcom genre's current orbit. And not even because of the many half-hour animated comedies, which rose as a viable subgenre following *The Simpsons* in the 1990s. But because greatness still exists. And it can still be found in straightforward, traditional setups, like the ensemble workplace comedy of *Abbott Elementary*. Yes, that's a single-camera show and perhaps more idea driven than it should be, but it's primarily about regular characters in relation to one another. And its foremost concern is making viewers laugh—which it regularly does, *because* of its regular characters. So it's a sitcom in the classic tradition—using the tried-and-true school setting of an *Our Miss Brooks* or *Mister Peepers* to host wild, kookily funny leads who inspire laughs and story. It's textbook sitcom.

As long as shows like *Abbott Elementary* exist in this country and are appreciated by even just a few, the sitcom can never die. And all the ones that came before—the *I Love Lucy*s and *The Phil Silvers Show*s—will remain formative texts, even subconsciously. Like the works of Shakespeare and Molière, inspiring dramatists and drama lovers—artists and art lovers—forever.

## APPENDIX A

# Writers of Top 50 1950s Sitcom Episodes

Season is denoted by S followed by a number in parentheses

*ALLEN, RAY*
THE MANY LOVES OF DOBIE GILLIS (S1): "Rock-a-Bye Dobie" (1960)

*ALLEN, WOODY*
STANLEY (S1): "Celia Goes to a TV Show" (1956)

*BALZER, GEORGE*
THE JACK BENNY PROGRAM (S8): "Christmas Shopping Show" (1957)

*BEGGS, RUSSELL*
STANLEY (S1): "Celia Goes to a TV Show" (1956)

*BENSFIELD, DICK*
THE ADVENTURES OF OZZIE AND HARRIET (S6): "Tutti-Frutti Ice Cream" (1957)

*BLITZER, BARRY*
THE PHIL SILVERS SHOW (S1): "Bivouac" (1955)
THE PHIL SILVERS SHOW (S1): "The Twitch" (1955)

*BURNS, WILLIAM*
BURNS AND ALLEN (S8): "Gracie Is Brilliant" (1958)
BURNS AND ALLEN (S8): "Hypnotizing Gracie" (1958)
BURNS AND ALLEN (S8): "A Hole in the Carpet" (1957)
BURNS AND ALLEN (S4): "An Elephant Sits on Gracie's Fender" (1954)
BURNS AND ALLEN (S6): "Mrs. Sohmers Needs a Psychologist" (1956)
BURNS AND ALLEN (S3): "Silky Thompson; Gracie Writes 'My Life with George Burns'" (1952)

*CARROLL, BOB, JR.*
I LOVE LUCY (S2): "Job Switching" (1952)
I LOVE LUCY (S1): "Lucy Does a TV Commercial" (1952)
I LOVE LUCY (S5): "Lucy's Italian Movie" (1956)
I LOVE LUCY (S4): "L.A. at Last!" (1955)
I LOVE LUCY (S4): "Mr. and Mrs. TV Show" (1954)
I LOVE LUCY (S4): "Lucy Gets Into Pictures" (1955)
I LOVE LUCY (S6): "Lucy Does the Tango" (1957)
I LOVE LUCY (S3): "Lucy Tells the Truth" (1953)
I LOVE LUCY (S2): "The Handcuffs" (1952)
I LOVE LUCY (S5): "The Great Train Robbery" (1955)
I LOVE LUCY (S4): "Ethel's Birthday" (1954)
I LOVE LUCY (S3): "The Million Dollar Idea" (1954)
I LOVE LUCY (S4): "The Star Upstairs" (1955)
I LOVE LUCY (S2): "The Operetta" (1952)
I LOVE LUCY (S1): "The Ballet" (1952)
I LOVE LUCY (S4): "Ethel's Home Town" (1955)
I LOVE LUCY (S4): "Harpo Marx" (1955)
I LOVE LUCY (S2): "Lucy's Show Biz Swan Song" (1952)

*CONNELLY, JOE*
THE AMOS 'N ANDY SHOW (S1): "Rare Coin" (1951)

## DORFMAN, SID
BURNS AND ALLEN (S4): "An Elephant Sits on Gracie's Fender" (1954)
BURNS AND ALLEN (S3): "Silky Thompson; Gracie Writes 'My Life with George Burns'" (1952)

## ELINSON, JACK
THE DANNY THOMAS SHOW (S7): "Danny and the Little Men" (1959)

## FINN, HERBERT
THE HONEYMOONERS (S1): "The Golfer" (1955)

## FOWLER, KEITH
BURNS AND ALLEN (S8): "Gracie Is Brilliant" (1958)
BURNS AND ALLEN (S8): "Hypnotizing Gracie" (1958)
BURNS AND ALLEN (S8): "A Hole in the Carpet" (1957)
BURNS AND ALLEN (S4): "An Elephant Sits on Gracie's Fender" (1954)
BURNS AND ALLEN (S6): "Mrs. Sohmers Needs a Psychologist" (1956)

## FRIEDBERG, BILLY
THE PHIL SILVERS SHOW (S2): "Love That Guardhouse" (1957)
THE PHIL SILVERS SHOW (S2): "A Mess Sergeant Can't Win" (1956)
THE PHIL SILVERS SHOW (S2): "Doberman's Sister" (1956)

## FRITZELL, JIM
MISTER PEEPERS (S2): "Nervous Wes" (1953)
MISTER PEEPERS (S2): "The Drive-In Movie" (1952)

## GOLDMAN, HAL
THE JACK BENNY PROGRAM (S8): "Christmas Shopping Show" (1957)

## GOLDSTEIN, JESSE
BURNS AND ALLEN (S3): "Silky Thompson; Gracie Writes 'My Life with George Burns'" (1952)

## GORDON, AL
THE JACK BENNY PROGRAM (S8): "Christmas Shopping Show" (1957)

## GORDON, SHIRL
THE BOB CUMMINGS SHOW (S3): "Double Date" (1956)
THE BOB CUMMINGS SHOW (S3): "Bob Tangles with Ruthie" (1957)

## GRANT, PERRY
THE ADVENTURES OF OZZIE AND HARRIET (S6): "Tutti-Frutti Ice Cream" (1957)

## GREENBAUM, EVERETT
MISTER PEEPERS (S2): "Nervous Wes" (1953)

## HELM, HARVEY
BURNS AND ALLEN (S8): "Gracie Is Brilliant" (1958)
BURNS AND ALLEN (S8): "Hypnotizing Gracie" (1958)
BURNS AND ALLEN (S8): "A Hole in the Carpet" (1957)
BURNS AND ALLEN (S4): "An Elephant Sits on Gracie's Fender" (1954)
BURNS AND ALLEN (S6): "Mrs. Sohmers Needs a Psychologist" (1956)
BURNS AND ALLEN (S3): "Silky Thompson; Gracie Writes 'My Life with George Burns'" (1952)

## HENNING, PAUL
THE BOB CUMMINGS SHOW (S3): "Double Date" (1956)
THE BOB CUMMINGS SHOW (S3): "Bob Tangles with Ruthie" (1957)

## HIKEN, NAT
THE PHIL SILVERS SHOW (S1): "The Court Martial" (1956)
THE PHIL SILVERS SHOW (S2): "Love That Guardhouse" (1957)
THE PHIL SILVERS SHOW (S1): "Empty Store" (1955)
THE PHIL SILVERS SHOW (S2): "A Mess Sergeant Can't Win" (1956)
THE PHIL SILVERS SHOW (S1): "Bivouac" (1955)
THE PHIL SILVERS SHOW (S1): "The Twitch" (1955)
THE PHIL SILVERS SHOW (S2): "Doberman's Sister" (1956)

## JACOBY, COLEMAN
THE PHIL SILVERS SHOW (S1): "The Court Martial" (1956)

THE PHIL SILVERS SHOW (S2): "Love That Guardhouse" (1957)

## KALLEN, LUCILLE
STANLEY (S1): "Celia Goes to a TV Show" (1956)

## LEWIS, AL
OUR MISS BROOKS (S1): "Aunt Mattie Boynton" (1953)
OUR MISS BROOKS (S2): "Second Hand First Aid" (1954)

## MARTIN, AL
TROUBLE WITH FATHER (S1): "TV Comes to the Erwins" (1951)

## MARX, MARVIN
THE HONEYMOONERS (S1): "Better Living Through TV" (1955)

## McGUIRE, BIFF
MISTER PEEPERS (S2): "The Drive-In Movie" (1952)

## MONASTER, NATE
BURNS AND ALLEN (S3): "Silky Thompson; Gracie Writes 'My Life with George Burns'" (1952)

## MOSHER, BOB
THE AMOS 'N ANDY SHOW (S1): "Rare Coin" (1951)

## NELSON, DON
THE ADVENTURES OF OZZIE AND HARRIET (S6): "Tutti-Frutti Ice Cream" (1957)

## NELSON, OZZIE
THE ADVENTURES OF OZZIE AND HARRIET (S6): "Tutti-Frutti Ice Cream" (1957)

## OPPENHEIMER, JESS
I LOVE LUCY (S2): "Job Switching" (1952)
I LOVE LUCY (S1): "Lucy Does a TV Commercial" (1952)
I LOVE LUCY (S5): "Lucy's Italian Movie" (1956)
I LOVE LUCY (S4): "L.A. at Last!" (1955)
I LOVE LUCY (S4): "Mr. and Mrs. TV Show" (1954)
I LOVE LUCY (S4): "Lucy Gets Into Pictures" (1955)
I LOVE LUCY (S3): "Lucy Tells the Truth" (1953)
I LOVE LUCY (S2): "The Handcuffs" (1952)
I LOVE LUCY (S5): "The Great Train Robbery" (1955)
I LOVE LUCY (S4): "Ethel's Birthday" (1954)
I LOVE LUCY (S3): "The Million Dollar Idea" (1954)
I LOVE LUCY (S4): "The Star Upstairs" (1955)
I LOVE LUCY (S2): "The Operetta" (1952)
I LOVE LUCY (S1): "The Ballet" (1952)
I LOVE LUCY (S4): "Ethel's Home Town" (1955)
I LOVE LUCY (S4): "Harpo Marx" (1955)
I LOVE LUCY (S2): "Lucy's Show Biz Swan Song" (1952)

## PAUL, NORMAN
BURNS AND ALLEN (S8): "Gracie Is Brilliant" (1958)
BURNS AND ALLEN (S8): "Hypnotizing Gracie" (1958)
BURNS AND ALLEN (S8): "A Hole in the Carpet" (1957)
BURNS AND ALLEN (S6): "Mrs. Sohmers Needs a Psychologist" (1956)

## PERRIN, SAM
THE JACK BENNY PROGRAM (S8): "Christmas Shopping Show" (1957)

## PUGH, MADELYN (also MARTIN, MADELYN)
I LOVE LUCY (S2): "Job Switching" (1952)
I LOVE LUCY (S1): "Lucy Does a TV Commercial" (1952)
I LOVE LUCY (S5): "Lucy's Italian Movie" (1956)
I LOVE LUCY (S4): "L.A. at Last!" (1955)
I LOVE LUCY (S4): "Mr. and Mrs. TV Show" (1954)
I LOVE LUCY (S4): "Lucy Gets Into Pictures" (1955)
I LOVE LUCY (S6): "Lucy Does the Tango" (1957)
I LOVE LUCY (S3): "Lucy Tells the Truth" (1953)
I LOVE LUCY (S2): "The Handcuffs" (1952)
I LOVE LUCY (S5): "The Great Train Robbery" (1955)
I LOVE LUCY (S4): "Ethel's Birthday" (1954)
I LOVE LUCY (S3): "The Million Dollar Idea" (1954)
I LOVE LUCY (S4): "The Star Upstairs" (1955)

I LOVE LUCY (S2): "The Operetta" (1952)
I LOVE LUCY (S1): "The Ballet" (1952)
I LOVE LUCY (S4): "Ethel's Home Town" (1955)
I LOVE LUCY (S4): "Harpo Marx" (1955)
I LOVE LUCY (S2): "Lucy's Show Biz Swan Song" (1952)

### QUILLAN, JOSEPH
OUR MISS BROOKS (S1): "Aunt Mattie Boynton" (1953)
OUR MISS BROOKS (S2): "Second Hand First Aid" (1954)

### ROSEN, ARNIE
THE PHIL SILVERS SHOW (S1): "The Court Martial" (1956)
THE PHIL SILVERS SHOW (S2): "Love That Guardhouse" (1957)

### ROSS, BOB
THE AMOS 'N ANDY SHOW (S1): "Rare Coin" (1951)

### RUSSELL, A.J.
THE HONEYMOONERS (S1): "The Golfer" (1955)

### RYAN, TERRY
THE PHIL SILVERS SHOW (S1): "Bivouac" (1955)
THE PHIL SILVERS SHOW (S1): "The Twitch" (1955)

### SCHILLER, BOB
I LOVE LUCY (S5): "Lucy's Italian Movie" (1956)
I LOVE LUCY (S6): "Lucy Does the Tango" (1957)
I LOVE LUCY (S5): "The Great Train Robbery" (1955)

### SHUKEN, PHIL
THE BOB CUMMINGS SHOW (S3): "Double Date" (1956)
THE BOB CUMMINGS SHOW (S3): "Bob Tangles with Ruthie" (1957)

### SHULMAN, MAX
THE MANY LOVES OF DOBIE GILLIS (S1): "The Best Dressed Man" (1959)
THE MANY LOVES OF DOBIE GILLIS (S1): "Love Is a Science" (1959)

### SOMMERS, JAY
THE ADVENTURES OF OZZIE AND HARRIET (S6): "Tutti-Frutti Ice Cream" (1957)

### STANDER, ARTHUR
THE DANNY THOMAS SHOW (S5): "Uncle Tonoose Meets Mr. Daly" (1958)

### STERN, LEONARD
THE HONEYMOONERS (S1): "The $99,000 Answer" (1956)
THE PHIL SILVERS SHOW (S2): "A Mess Sergeant Can't Win" (1956)
THE PHIL SILVERS SHOW (S2): "Doberman's Sister" (1956)

### STEWART, CHARLES
THE DANNY THOMAS SHOW (S7): "Danny and the Little Men" (1959)

### STONE, WALTER
THE HONEYMOONERS (S1): "Better Living Through TV" (1955)

### SWIFT, DAVID
MISTER PEEPERS (S2): "The Drive-In Movie" (1952)

### WEBSTER, TONY
THE PHIL SILVERS SHOW (S2): "A Mess Sergeant Can't Win" (1956)
THE PHIL SILVERS SHOW (S2): "Doberman's Sister" (1956)

### WEISKOPF, BOB
I LOVE LUCY (S5): "Lucy's Italian Movie" (1956)
I LOVE LUCY (S6): "Lucy Does the Tango" (1957)
I LOVE LUCY (S5): "The Great Train Robbery" (1955)

### WESSON, DICK
THE BOB CUMMINGS SHOW (S3): "Bob Tangles With Ruthie" (1957)

### ZELINKA, SYDNEY
THE HONEYMOONERS (S1): "The $99,000 Answer" (1956)

# Appendix B

# Shows Officially Released on DVD and/or Streaming

- THE GOLDBERGS (All surviving episodes)
- THE JACK BENNY PROGRAM (A few episodes)
- I LOVE LUCY
- MY LITTLE MARGIE (Season 1)
- MISTER PEEPERS (First half)
- OUR MISS BROOKS (Season 1)
- THE ADVENTURES OF OZZIE AND HARRIET
- THE ABBOTT AND COSTELLO SHOW
- THE DANNY THOMAS SHOW (Seasons 4–11)
- DECEMBER BRIDE (A few episodes)
- FATHER KNOWS BEST
- HEY, MULLIGAN! (Most episodes)
- THE PHIL SILVERS SHOW
- THE HONEYMOONERS
- STANLEY
- BLONDIE
- LEAVE IT TO BEAVER
- THE REAL McCOYS
- HOW TO MARRY A MILLIONAIRE
- THE DONNA REED SHOW (Seasons 1–5)
- DENNIS THE MENACE
- THE MANY LOVES OF DOBIE GILLIS
- LOVE AND MARRIAGE (A few episodes)

NOTE: This list does not account for cheap DVD releases of public domain titles or unofficial YouTube uploads.

# Chapter Notes

## Chapter One

1. Roswitha Fischer, *Lexical Change in Present-Day English: A Corpus-Based Study of the Motivation, Institutionalization, and Productivity of Creative Neologisms* (Tübingen: Gunter Narr Verlag, 1998), 95.
2. Michelle Zerba and David Gorman, eds., *Aristotle Poetics* (New York: Norton, 1982), xiv.
3. Ibid., x.
4. Ibid., 9–11.
5. Ibid., 45–47.
6. Ibid.
7. Ibid., 8.
8. Roland Greene, *The Princeton Encyclopedia of Poetry and Poetics* (Princeton: Princeton University Press, 2012), 282.
9. John Morreall, *Taking Laughter Seriously* (Albany: State University of New York Press, 1983), 15–19.
10. Salvatore Attardo, *Encyclopedia of Humor Studies* (Thousand Oaks: Sage, 2014), 54.
11. Zerba and Gorman, eds., *Aristotle Poetics*, 45.
12. Ibid., 17–18.
13. M.C.G., "New Acts of the Week—The Richardsons," *Variety*, 29 August 1908, 14.
14. "The Photoplay of Tomorrow," *Fresno Morning Republican*, 12 November 1916, 11.
15. Al E. Christine, *The Elements of Situation Comedy* (Los Angeles: Palmer Photoplay Corporation, 1920), 5.
16. "Comedy Must Be Art," *San Francisco Chronicle*, 29 May 1921, 5.
17. Grace Kingsley, "Plans to Make More Comedies," *Los Angeles Times*, 6 December 1925, part 3, 36.
18. "History of Commercial Radio," Federal Communications Commission, updated 17 October 2023, https://www.fcc.gov/media/radio/history-of-commercial-radio#:~:text=November%202%2C%201920,Harding%20and%20James%20Cox.
19. Hugh R. Slotton, *Radio and Television Regulation: Broadcast Technology in the United States, 1920–1960* (Baltimore: Johns Hopkins University Press, 2000), 51.
20. Elizabeth McLeod, *The Original Amos 'n' Andy: Freeman Gosden, Charles Correll and the 1928–1943 Radio Serial* (Jefferson, NC: McFarland, 2005), 27.
21. Ibid., 25.
22. Ibid., 38.
23. Michael Lund, *America's Continuing Story: An Introduction to Serial Fiction, 1850–1900* (Detroit: Wayne State University Press, 1993), 24–25.
24. McLeod, *The Original Amos 'n' Andy*, 45–47.
25. McLeod, *The Original Amos 'n' Andy*.
26. Ibid., 107–126.
27. Ibid., 170.
28. Jim Cox, *American Radio Soap Opera* (Lanham, MD: Scarecrow, 2005), 88.
29. Jim Cox, *The Great Radio Sitcoms* (Jefferson, NC: McFarland, 2007), 264, 266, 269.
30. Elizabeth McLeod, "Development of the Radio Sitcom," *Radio Recall*, February 2010, http://www.mwotrc.com/rr2010_02/sitcom.htm.
31. Ibid.
32. Ibid.
33. Ibid.
34. Frank Cullen with Florence Hackman and Donald McNeilly, *Vaudeville Old & New: An Encyclopedia of Variety Performers in America, Volume 1* (New York: Routledge, 2007), 1235.
35. Cox, *The Great Radio Sitcoms*, 121.
36. Ibid.
37. Ibid., 122.
38. Ibid., 5.
39. Ibid., 135–137.
40. McLeod, *The Original Amos 'n' Andy*, 140–142.
41. Zerba and Gorman, eds., *Aristotle Poetics*, xxii–xxiii.
42. "Your Money or Your Life," *The Jack Benny Program*, NBC Radio, 28 March 1948.
43. "The Longest Laugh," The International Jack Benny Fan Club, https://www.jackbenny.org/biography/other/longest_laugh.htm?fbclid=IwAR31bga-asVwrR-fApngQiW4MNu1k_Op7K7Irac1QYtdoVch0AEVEEsTq_s.

## Chapter Two

1. "Televisor Lets Radio Fans 'Look in' as Well as Listen," *New York Times*, 25 April 1926, section XX, 17.
2. "Experimental Television Stations Authorized in U.S.," *Broadcasting*, 1 November 1938, 29.

3. "Price Ceiling Put on Home Radio Sets," *New York Times*, 31 January 1942, 19.

4. William Hawes, "The Heritage," in *American Television Drama: The Experimental Years* (Tuscaloosa: University of Alabama Press, 1986).

5. "First Sponsored Television," *Daily Variety*, 30 June 1941, 1.

6. "Price Ceiling Put on Home Radio Sets," *New York Times*, 31 January 1942, 19.

7. "Will End Radio 'Freeze,'" *New York Times*, 8 August 1945, 10.

8. "DuMont's H'wood Style Preem in New Studio Builds up to a Big Letdown," *Variety*, 17 April 1946, 38, 46.

9. "First Commercial Television Show Presented Here," *Hollywood Citizen-News*, 23 January 1947, 7.

10. Tim Brooks and Earle Marsh, *The Complete Directory to Prime Time Network and Cable TV Shows, 1946–Present* (New York: , 2007), 862.

11. Ibid.

12. "Mary Kay and Johnny Stearns Interview Part 3 of 4—EMMYTVLEGENDS.org," Television Academy Foundation, 1999, https://www.youtube.com/watch?v=uK8ydDQm4Y0.

13. "Sunday's Television," *Plainfield Courier-News*, 2 October 1948, 11.

14. Brooks and Marsh, *The Complete Directory to Prime Time Network and Cable TV Shows*, 862.

15. "Kinescope Definition and Meaning," *Merriam-Webster*, https://www.merriam webster.com/dictionary/kinescope.

16. "Sales Resistance Definition and Meaning," *Dictionary.com*, https://www.dictionary.com/browse/sales-resistance.

17. Brooks and Marsh, *The Complete Directory to Prime Time Network and Cable TV Shows*, xii.

18. Richard Irvin, *Early Shows: A Reference Guide to Network and Syndicated Primetime Television Series from 1944 to 1949* (Albany, GA: BearManor Media, 2018), 19–20.

19. Ibid., 20–22.

20. Margaret R. Weiss and Barbara Boothe, "The Half-Hour Original: Situation Comedy," in *The TV Writer's Guide* (New York: Pellegrini & Cudahy, 1952).

21. Jack Gould, "First Nights on TV," *New York Times*, 6 March 1949, section x, 11.

22. Larry Wolters, "Infant Video Boomed to Giant in Year," *Chicago Daily Tribune*, 3 January 1949, section 3, 11.

23. "Frantic Bids for Tuesday 8 AM Despite Berle TV," *Variety*, 13 April 1949, 27.

24. Brooks and Marsh, *The Complete Directory to Prime Time Network and Cable TV Shows*, 919.

25. Herm, "Television Reviews—Easy Aces," *Variety*, 21 December 1949, 28.

26. Glenn D. Smith, *"Something on My Own": Gertrude Berg and American Broadcasting, 1929–1956* (Syracuse: Syracuse University Press, 2007), 219.

27. "Radio Mirror Television Awards Winners for 1949," *Radio and Television Mirror*, May 1950, 56–57.

28. "The Goldbergs: The Ultimate Goldbergs—DVD," Shout! Factory, https://www.shoutfactory.com/product/the-goldbergs-the-ultimate-goldbergs?product_id=2483.

29. "TV Radio Mirror Award Winners, 1955–56," *TV Radio Mirror*, May 1956, 31.

30. Mal Boyd, "TV '49ers' L.A. to N.Y.—But Where's All the Gold?" *Variety*, 4 January 1950, 113.

31. "Breakdown of U.S. 2,565,000 TV Sets," *Variety*, 26 October 1949, 39.

32. "Tele-type," *Daily Variety*, 11 January 1950, 6.

33. George Rosen, "1948 Peak Year for Radio," *Daily Variety*, 25 October 1948, 155.

34. Jack O'Brien, "Here's Dope on Kinescope," *Miami Herald*, 10 December 1950, G5.

35. "Telepix Producers Get Cut-Rate Use of Rep Studio," *Daily Variety*, 31 January 1949, 8.

36. "Howard, Gwynne Star in Television Series," *Daily Variety*, 15 July 1947, 10.

37. "NBC Getting Off Hook on 'Prosecutor' Vidfilm Series Via Local Sale," *Variety*, 8 August 1951, 22.

38. Irvin, *Early Shows*, 40–42.

39. Wesley Hyatt, *Emmy Award Winning Nighttime Television Shows, 1948–2004* (Jefferson, NC: McFarland, 2006), 18–19.

40. "Television 'Riley' Matches Success of Radio Show," *Daily Variety*, 29 September 1949, 11.

41. Vincent Terrace, *Encyclopedia of Unaired Television Pilots, 1945–2018* (Jefferson, NC: McFarland, 2018), 133.

42. Hyatt, *Emmy Award Winning Nighttime Television Shows*, 18–19.

43. "Thanks to the Academy of T.A.S. 'The Life of Riley' Best Television (on Film)," *Daily Variety*, 30 January 1950, 10.

44. Erskine Johnson, "Hollywood on TV," *Daily News*, 8 April 1952, 19.

45. Mary Wood, "Wonderful Guy," *Cincinnati Post*, 14 April 1950, 30.

## Chapter Three

1. Cobbett S. Steinberg, *TV Facts* (New York: Facts on File, 1980), 142.

2. Ibid.

3. Ibid.

4. Brooks and Marsh, *The Complete Directory to Prime Time Network and Cable TV Shows*, 1679.

5. Ibid.

6. Ben Gross, "Televiewing," *Daily News*, 31 August 1950, 72.

7. Bril, "Television Reviews—Meet Corliss Archer," *Variety*, 18 July 1951, 30.

8. "'Corliss Archer' Gets CBS-TV Tues. Niche," *Variety*, 20 June 1951, 28.

9. Ibid.

10. Lawrence J. Epstein, *George Burns: An American Life* (Jefferson, NC: McFarland, 2011), 93–95.

11. Anton Rementh, "Paley's Talent Raids for

CBS Have TV Angle," *Chicago Tribune*, 27 February 1949, part 3, 4.

12. Walter Ames, "Gracie Allen, George Burns Move Video Show from N.Y. to Hollywood on Thursday," *Los Angeles Times*, 25 December 1950, 26.

13. George Burns, *Gracie: A Love Story* (New York: Putnam, 1988), 256–257.

14. "Jack Benny Will Head All-Star Cast," *Daily News*, 8 March 1949, part 5, 1.

15. Laura Leff and Martin Gostanian, *39 Forever: Second Edition, Volume 3: Television* (North Charleston, SC: Book Surge, 2006, 2011), 88.

16. Joe Coppola, "Tele-tales," *Newsday* (Suffolk Edition), 13 August 1951, 22.

17. Leff and Gostanian, *39 Forever*, 370–375.

18. Joel Eisner and David Krinsky, *Television Comedy Series: An Episode Guide to 153 TV Sitcoms in Syndication* (Jefferson, NC: McFarland, 1984), 411.

19. Darry Littleton, *Black Comedians on Black Comedy: How African Americans Taught Us to Laugh* (New York: Applause Theatre and Cinema Books, 2006), 53.

20. Leff and Gostanian, *39 Forever*, 88–95.

21. Bert, "Television Review—Beulah," *Variety*, 11 October 1950, 40.

22. Cox, *The Great Radio Sitcoms*, 74.

23. *Ibid.*, 74–75.

24. *Ibid.*, 75.

25. *Ibid.*, 75.

26. "NAACP Okays 'The Beulah Show,'" *Los Angeles Tribune*, 29 November 1947, 1, 13.

27. Carlton Jackson, *Hattie: The Life of Hattie McDaniel* (Lanham: Madison Books, 1989), 122.

28. *The Beulah Show*, CBS Radio broadcast of 30 June 1950.

29. Kay Gardella, "Sunday TV Battle Starts Next Week," *Daily News*, 15 September 1957, section 2, 9.

30. Jack Hellman, "Light and Airy," *Daily Variety*, 24 August 1950, 6.

31. "Bud Harris Tells Chicago Defender Why He Quit 'Beulah,'" *Chicago Defender*, 25 November 1950, 21.

32. "Hattie McDaniel as Video 'Beulah,' Too," *Variety*, 13 June 1951, 31.

33. "P&G Will Film Its 'Beulah' Teleshow; McDaniel in Lead," *Daily Variety*, 13 June 1951, 7.

34. "NAACP Okays 'The Beulah Show,'" 1, 13.

35. Art Cullison, "Hattie McDaniel Seriously Ill," *Akron Beacon Journal*, 25 September 1951, 30.

36. Paul Finkelman, *Encyclopedia of African American History: 1986 to the Present* (Oxford: Oxford University Press, 2009), 160.

37. McLeod, *The Original Amos 'n' Andy*, 128–129.

38. Jack Quigg, "Amos 'n' Andy Team Training TV Heirs," *Roanoke Times*, 17 June 1951, 19.

39. Bob Ellis, "NAACP Meets with CBS, Blatz," *California Eagle*, 19 July 1951, 12.

40. Brooks and Marsh, *The Complete Directory to Prime Time Network and Cable TV Shows*, 1680.

41. "Blatz Beer Cancels TV's 'Amos-Andy,' Also Drops Time," *Variety*, 11 March 1953, 25.

42. Bill Summers, "'My Mother, The Car'—Egad!" *Orlando Evening Star*, 2 March 1966, 20.

43. McLeod, *The Original Amos 'n' Andy*, 148.

44. *Ibid.*

45. James R. Wetzel, "American Families: 75 Years of Change," *Monthly Labor Review*, March 1990, 10.

46. "Mr. Lamont Stays All Night," *Trouble with Father*, ABC-TV, 21 October 1950.

47. "Lucy Puts up a TV Antenna," *The Lucy Show*, CBS-TV, 26 November 1962.

48. *Hog Wild*, MGM, Hal Roach Studios, 1930.

49. *Let Down Your Aerial*, Columbia Pictures, 1949.

50. *Goof on the Roof*, Columbia Pictures, 1953.

51. "Fall Guy," *The Abbott and Costello Show*, Television Corporation of America, 1954.

52. Bril, "Television Reviews—Hank McCune Show," *Variety*, 13 September 1950, 34.

53. "Premiere Thursday Night of 'Buster Keaton Show,'" *Press-Telegram*, 18 December 1949, 15.

54. "Television Chatter," *Variety*, 20 June 1951, 36.

## Chapter Four

1. Paul Anderson, "Checking in with Nifty 50's," *Los Angeles Times*, 16 July 2009, https://www.latimes.com/socal/daily-pilot/news/tn-dpt-xpm-2009-07-16-dpt-checkingin07172009-story.html.

2. Viola Swisher, "Just for Variety," *Daily Variety*, 9 October 1951, 2.

3. Jon Krampner, "Myths and Mysteries Surround Pioneering of 3-Camera TV," *Los Angeles Times*, 29 July 1991, F10.

4. *Ibid.*

5. Mickey Freeman, "Tele-type," *Daily Variety*, 13 December 1950, 8.

6. "Fresnans Cheer Edwards' Zany Radio, TV Show," *Fresno Bee*, 9 February 1951, 16.

7. Coyne Stevens Sanders and Tom Gilbert, *Desilu: The Story of Lucille Ball and Desi Arnaz*, rev. ed. (New York: Dey Street Books, 2011), 26.

8. Jess Oppenheimer and Gregg Oppenheimer, *Laughs, Luck, and Lucy: How I Came to Create the Most Popular Sitcom of All Time* (Syracuse: Syracuse University Press, 1996), 132.

9. *Ibid.*, 133.

10. *Ibid.*, 134.

11. *Ibid.*, 133–134.

12. *Ibid.*, 134.

13. Sanders and Gilbert, *Desilu*, 38.

14. Oppenheimer and Oppenheimer, *Laughs, Luck, and Lucy*, 142.

15. Sanders and Gilbert, *Desilu*, 39–40.

16. *Ibid.*, 42.

17. Ames, "Gracie Allen, George Burns Move Video Show from N.Y. to Hollywood on Thursday."

18. Sanders and Gilbert, *Desilu*, 42–43.

19. *Ibid.*, 43.

20. Oppenheimer and Oppenheimer, *Laughs, Luck, and Lucy*, 157.
21. *Ibid.*, 157–158.
22. *Ibid.*, 114–115.
23. *Ibid.*, 111–113.
24. *Ibid.*, 123–124.
25. *Ibid.*, 124.
26. Sanders and Gilbert, *Desilu*, 33.
27. Oppenheimer and Oppenheimer, 139.
28. "Young Matron League Tryouts" and "Young Matrons' League Play, " *My Favorite Husband*, CBS Radio, 2 October 1948 and 9 October 1948.
29. Oppenheimer and Oppenheimer, 138.
30. Bureau of Labor Statistics, U.S. Department of Labor, "Changes in Women's Labor Force Participation in the 20th Century," *TED: The Economics Daily*, 16 February 2000.
31. "The Ricardos Visit Cuba," *I Love Lucy*, CBS-TV, 3 December 1956.
32. "Be Your Husband's Best Friend," *My Favorite Husband*, CBS Radio, 4 December 1948.
33. *Ibid.*, 180–188.
34. "Liz and George Handcuffed," *My Favorite Husband*, CBS Radio, 30 December 1949.
35. Sanders and Gilbert, *Desilu*, 41.
36. *Ibid.*
37. Oppenheimer and Oppenheimer, 171.
38. "Pioneer Women," *I Love Lucy*, CBS-TV, 31 March 1952.
39. "Bonus Bucks," *I Love Lucy*, CBS-TV, 8 March 1954.
40. "The Fashion Show," *I Love Lucy*, CBS-TV, 28 February 1955.
41. "Lucy Thinks Ricky Is Trying to Murder Her," *I Love Lucy*, CBS-TV, 5 November 1951.
42. "Charity Revue," *My Favorite Husband*, CBS Radio, 11 March 1949.
43. "Liz Writes a Song," *My Favorite Husband*, CBS Radio, 27 January 1950.
44. Walter Winchell, "On Broadway," *Tampa Times*, 23 May 1952, 6.
45. "Be a Pal," *I Love Lucy*, CBS-TV, 22 October 1951.
46. "Ricky Asks for a Raise," *I Love Lucy*, CBS-TV, 9 June 1952.
47. "New Neighbors," *I Love Lucy*, CBS-TV, 3 March 1952.
48. I'm specifically referring here to *The Dick Van Dyke Show* (1961–1966, CBS-TV).
49. Sidney Skolsky, "Hollywood Is My Beat," *Los Angeles Evening Citizen-News*, 2 October 1951, 13.
50. "Gracie Goes to Psychiatrist for Blanche's Dream," *The George Burns and Gracie Allen Show*, CBS-TV, 8 March 1954.
51. "Mrs. Sohmers Needs a Psychologist," *The George Burns and Gracie Allen Show*, CBS-TV, 17 September 1956.
52. Allen Rich, "Listening Post and TV Review," *Valley Times*, 26 June 1952, 10.
53. Cox, *The Great Radio Sitcoms*, 263–264.
54. Rose, "Tele Follow-Up Comment," *Variety*, 13 February 1952, 33.
55. Rose, "Tele Follow-Up Comment," *Variety*, 16 January 1952, 29.
56. Bob Leszczak, *Single Season Sitcoms, 1948–1979: A Complete Guide* (Jefferson, NC: McFarland, 2012), 88.
57. *Ibid.*, 21.
58. David Weinstein, *The Forgotten Network: DuMont and the Birth of American Television* (Philadelphia: Temple University Press, 2004), 96.
59. "The Chess Match," *Mister Peepers*, NBC-TV, 17 July 1952.
60. "The Ventilation System," *Mister Peepers*, NBC-TV, 31 July 1952.
61. "The Janitor Takes Time Off," *Mister Peepers*, NBC-TV, 7 August 1952.
62. "'Peepers' Set to Replace Mayehoff," *Variety*, 15 October 1952, 25.
63. "The Wedding," *Mister Peepers*, NBC-TV, 23 May 1954.
64. David C. Tucker, *Gale Storm: A Biography and Career Record* (Jefferson, NC: McFarland, 2018), 118.

## Chapter Five

1. Brooks and Marsh, *The Complete Directory to Prime Time Network and Cable TV Shows*, 1679.
2. *Ibid.*, 1680–1681.
3. Bart Andrews, *Lucy & Ricky & Fred & Ethel: The Story of "I Love Lucy"* (New York: Dutton, 1976), 79.
4. "Lucille Ball's Baby Arrives; It's a Boy!" *Valley Times*, 19 January 1953, 1.
5. Sanders and Gilbert, *Desilu*, 66.
6. *Ibid.*, 65.
7. Louella Parsons, "Lucille Ball Expecting Stork, Hoping for Boy," *Pittsburgh Sun-Telegraph*, 18 June 1952, 3.
8. Erskine Johnson, "Jones Can't Spike New Novelty Music," *The Courier*, 3 July 1952, 9.
9. Bud Stretch, "Air Waves," *Courier Post*, 13 December 1951, 26.
10. "What's on Tonight," *Ventura Weekly Post and Democrat*, 13 June 1952, 18.
11. "Vacation from Marriage," *I Love Lucy*, CBS-TV, 27 October 1952.
12. "Lucy Becomes a Sculptress," *I Love Lucy*, CBS-TV, 12 January 1953.
13. "The Club Election," *I Love Lucy*, CBS-TV, 16 February 1953.
14. "Women's Rights, Part 2," *My Favorite Husband*, CBS Radio, 12 March 1950.
15. Annie Berke, *Their Own Best Creations: Women Writers in Postwar Television* (Oakland: University of California Press, 2022), 2.
16. Oppenheimer and Oppenheimer, *Laughs, Luck, and Lucy*, 187.
17. Sanders and Gilbert, *Desilu*, 59.
18. David C. Tucker, *Eve Arden: A Chronicle of All Film, Television, Radio and Stage Performances* (Jefferson, NC: McFarland, 2012), 16.
19. Ben Ohmart, *The Bickersons: A Biography of*

*Radio's Wittiest Program* (Albany, GA: BearManor Media, 2004).

20. Martha McHatton, "Indianapolis on the Air," *Indianapolis News*, 18 October 1950, 27.

21. "Radio and Television," *Pasadena Independent*, 7 December 1951, 36.

22. Leszczak, *Single Season Sitcoms*, 13.

23. "Telensing 'Bickersons' at Marcal Theatre," *Daily Variety*, 30 April 1952, 6.

24. "Vidpix Chatter," *Variety*, 9 July 1952, 35.

25. Jack Hellman, "Light and Airy," *Daily Variety*, 20 October 1952, 8.

26. Terrace, *Encyclopedia of Unaired Television Pilots*, 131.

27. Mike McGee, "Joan Davis Starts TV Series of 'I Married Joan' This Week," *Commercial Appeal*, 14 October 1952, 26.

28. "Ballet," *I Married Joan*. NBC-TV, 29 October 1952.

29. "Opera," *I Married Joan*. NBC-TV, 25 February 1953.

30. "The Recipe," *I Married Joan*, NBC-TV, 22 April 1953.

31. Sherwood Schwartz, *Inside Gilligan's Island: A Three-Hour Tour through the Making of a Television Classic* (New York: St. Martin's, 1988), 21.

32. "Memory," *I Married Joan*, NBC-TV, 11 February 1953 and "Take a Message," *The Danny Thomas Show*, CBS-TV, 3 November 1958.

33. "Career," *I Married Joan*, NBC-TV, 22 October 1952 and "Double Dinner," *The Danny Thomas Show*, CBS-TV, 20 April 1959.

34. "Joan's Curiosity," *I Married Joan*, NBC-TV, 3 December 1952 and "The Curious Thing about Women," *The Dick Van Dyke Show*, CBS-TV, 10 January 1962.

35. "The Curious Thing about Women," *The Dick Van Dyke Show*, CBS-TV, 10 January 1962.

36. John Fink, "Bob Cummings Proves a Flop Can Flip Back." *Chicago Sunday Tribune*, 3 March 1957, part 3, 10.

37. John R. Holmes, *The Adventures of Ozzie Nelson: The Life and Career of America's Favorite Pop* (Jefferson, NC: McFarland, 2021), 117.

38. Ibid., 99.

39. Michael Barrett, "'The Adventures of Ozzie and Harriet' and the Nerve-Wracking Nature of Nothingness in 1950s White America," *popmatters*, 28 June 2022, https://www.popmatters.com/ozzie-harriet-nerve-wracking-nothingness/2.

40. Hyatt, *Emmy Award Winning Nighttime Television Shows*, 18–19.

41. "Christmas Show," *The Amos 'n' Andy Show*, CBS-TV, 25 December 1952.

42. Thomas Doherty, *Cold War, Cool Medium: Television, McCarthyism, and American Culture* (New York: Columbia University Press, 2003), 80.

43. Walter Ames, "Ike Talks on Radio, Tonight; Comic Treats Video like a Stage Play," *Los Angeles Times*, 21 September 1953, 30.

44. "Johnny Velvet's Day in Court," *The George Burns and Gracie Allen Show*, CBS-TV, 29 March 1951.

45. "Silky Thompson Moves to Beverly Hills," *The George Burns and Gracie Allen Show*, CBS-TV, 19 July 1951.

46. "Gracie Selling Swamp So Harry Will Buy TV Set," *The George Burns and Gracie Allen Show*, CBS-TV, 4 December 1952.

47. "Buttons Vice 'Luigi' on GF's Agenda?" *Variety*, 24 December 1952, 24.

48. Erskine Johnson, "Telefilm Cowgal Defends Kissin'," *Town Talk*, 27 April 1953, 20.

49. John Dunning, *On the Air: The Encyclopedia of Old-Time Radio* (New York: Oxford University Press, 1998), 234.

50. Ibid.

51. Chan, "Ethel and Albert," *Variety*, 29 April 1953, 33.

52. Hailey Branson-Potts, "Trailblazer Created Early Sitcom," *Los Angeles Times*, 29 July 2015, B7.

53. "'Peepers' Set to Replace Mayehoff," *Variety*, 15 October 1952, 25.

## Chapter Six

1. Helm, "Television Reviews—That's My Boy," *Daily Variety*, 12 April 1954, 11.

2. Rose, "Tele Follow-Up Comment—That's My Boy," *Variety*, 14 April 1954, 27.

3. Brooks and Marsh, *The Complete Directory to Prime Time Network and Cable TV Shows*, 1680–1681.

4. Mary Cremmen, "Holiday Season Brings Fine Show," *Boston Globe*, 28 December 1953, 12.

5. Richard Irvin, *George Burns Television Productions; The Series and Pilots, 1950–1981* (Jefferson, NC: McFarland, 2014), 101.

6. Jose, "Tele Follow-Up Comment—The Duke," *Variety*, 7 July 1954, 27, 36.

7. "Only Truth Is Getting Cuffed as TWA Strike Starts 6th Day," *Daily Variety*, 26 July 1954, 10.

8. Brooks and Marsh, *The Complete Directory to Prime Time Network and Cable TV Shows*, 691.

9. Lindsay Geller, "'Marvelous Mrs. Maisel' Is Based on a Few Real Comedians, according to Its Creators," *Women's Health*, 11 April 2023, https://www.womenshealthmag.com/life/a30125414/is-marvelous-mrs-maisel-based-on-a-real-person/.

10. Gros, "Tele Follow-Up Comment—TAKE IT FROM ME," *Variety*, 11 November 1953, 35.

11. Smith, *Something on My Own*, 161.

12. *The Goldbergs*, DuMont TV, 4 May 1954.

13. *The Goldbergs*, DuMont TV, 31 August 1954.

14. *The Goldbergs*, DuMont TV, 17 August 1954.

15. "Peepers Bests Benny; Sullivan Tops A&C," *Variety*, 26 May 1954, 35.

16. "Tele Follow-Up Comment," *Variety*, 26 May 1954, 39.

17. Allen Rich, "Listening Post and TV Review," *Valley Times*, 23 September 1953, 23.

18. Rose, "Meet Mr. McNutley," *Variety*, 23 September 1953, 32.

19. "The First Aid Course," *Our Miss Brooks*, CBS Radio, 3 June 1951.

20. "'Make Room for Daddy' Truthful," *Wilmington Daily Press Journal*, 13 August 1953, 16.
21. "Garry Marshall Interview Part 2 of 6—EmmyTVlegends.org," *Television Academy Foundation*, 2000, https://www.youtube.com/watch?v=vHPBcCZ0-wo.
22. Hal Humphrey, "If This Be Video Heresy, Hoagy Will Make Best of It," *D.C. Evening Star*, 2 June 1953, B21.
23. "Prep 'Day' on Film," *Variety*, 22 July 1953, 24.
24. "Gracie Goes to Psychiatrist for Blanche's Dream," *The George Burns and Gracie Allen Show*, CBS-TV, 8 March 1954.
25. "Gracie Buys a Toaster Wholesale," *The George Burns and Gracie Allen Show*, CBS-TV, 9 August 1954.
26. Alvin Shuster, "TV Freeze Lifted; 2053 New Stations to Blanket Nation," *New York Times*, 14 April 1952, 1.
27. Betty White, *Here We Go Again* (New York: Scribner, 1995), 30.
28. Wesley Hyatt, *Betty White on TV: From Video Vanguard to Golden Girl* (Orlando: BearManor Media, 2021), chap. 3.
29. "On TV Tonight," *Press Telegram* (Long Beach), 17 May 1952, 3.
30. White, *Here We Go Again*, 75.
31. Bob Thomas, "Churchman, Lucy Win TV Academy Awards," *Press Telegram* (Long Beach), 6 February 1953, 3.
32. "Betty White's Life with Elizabeth: TV May Make Her America's Sweetheart," *TV Guide*, 23–29 April 1954, 15–17.
33. Doherty, *Cold War, Cool Medium*, 80.
34. Sanders and Gilbert, *Desilu*, 76–85.
35. *Ibid.*
36. Brooks and Marsh, *The Complete Directory to Prime Time Network and Cable TV Shows*, 1680.
37. "Fan Magazine Interview," *I Love Lucy*, CBS-TV, 8 February 1954.
38. "The Diner," *I Love Lucy*, CBS-TV, 26 April 1954.
39. "Sentimental Anniversary," *I Love Lucy*, CBS-TV, 1 February 1954.
40. My favorite is the 1941 Paramount film *Nothing but the Truth*, starring Bob Hope and Paulette Goddard.
41. Oppenheimer and Oppenheimer, *Laughs, Luck, and Lucy*, 173–174.

## Chapter Seven

1. Brooks and Marsh, *The Complete Directory to Prime Time Network and Cable TV Shows*, 1679–1680.
2. Geoffrey Mark Fidelman, *The Lucy Book: A Complete Guide to Her Five Decades on Television* (Los Angeles: Renaissance Books, 1999), 81.
3. "Of People and Shows," *The Tablet*, 18 September 1954, 17.
4. "Premiere Set for New Show," *Daily Herald*, 27 June 1955, 7.
5. *Ibid.*
6. "Father Knows Best," Television Academy, https://www.emmys.com/shows/father-knows-best.
7. Wetzel, "American Families," 10.
8. "Poppa Not Blooper King on Young Show," *Orlando Sentinel*, 28 August 1955, E5.
9. Mary R. Desjardins, *Father Knows Best* (Detroit: Wayne State University Press, 2015), 26.
10. Wayne Oliver, "Video Dad 'Feels like a Bigamist,'" *Democrat and Chronicle*, 14 November 1954, C5.
11. "Live My Own Life," *Father Knows Best*, CBS-TV, 31 October 1954.
12. "Typical Father," *Father Knows Best*, CBS-TV, 5 December 1954.
13. "Sparrow in the Window," *Father Knows Best*, CBS-TV, 26 December 1954.
14. Leff and Gostanian, *39 Forever*, 152–193.
15. "Jack Does Christmas Shopping Show," *The Jack Benny Program*, CBS-TV, 12 December 1954.
16. "Preparing for New York Trip," *The Jack Benny Program*, CBS-TV, 17 April 1955.
17. "Jack Takes Beavers to the Fair," *The Jack Benny Program*, CBS-TV, 6 March 1955.
18. "The Robot," *Hey, Mulligan!*, NBC-TV, 7 May 1955.
19. "Private Eye," *Hey, Mulligan!*, NBC-TV, 25 September 1954.
20. "Tiger Mulligan," *Hey, Mulligan!*, NBC-TV, 30 October 1954.
21. "Laugh Track Can Only Hurt," *Los Angeles Mirror*, 18 October 1954, part 2, 5.
22. Janet Kern, "Kingfish Dropped for Father," *Fort Worth Star-Telegram*, 30 December 1954, 7.
23. Summers, "'My Mother, The Car'—Egad!," 20.
24. Leszczak, *Single Season Sitcoms*, 142.
25. "Color Me Slowly: Factor Sales of Color TVs," Ebrain Market Research, https://www.tab.org/public/upload/files/misc/nextgen-consumer-presentation-2021.pdf.
26. "The Wally Cox Story," *Mister Peepers*, NBC-TV, 5 June 1955.
27. Leszczak, *Single Season Sitcoms*, 83.
28. Wesley Hyatt, *Short-Lived Television Series: 1948–1978* (Jefferson, NC: McFarland, 2003), 63.
29. Irvin, *George Burns Television Productions*, 108.
30. Wayne Oliver, "Imogene Coca Show Boasts Hal March," *The Bee*, 7 June 1955, B8.
31. Leszczak, *Single Season Sitcoms*, 172.
32. Jack Hellman, "Light and Airy," *Daily Variety*, 18 July 1955, 10.

## Chapter Eight

1. Brooks and Marsh, *The Complete Directory to Prime Time Network and Cable TV Shows*, 1679–1680.
2. Karen J. Harvey, *Sid Caesar and Your Show of Shows: The Birth of the Television Sketch Comedy*

*Series.* (Jefferson NC: McFarland & Company, 2021), 178, 180.

3. McHatton, "Indianapolis on the Air," 18 October 1950, 27.

4. Peter Crescenti and Bob Columbe, *The Official* Honeymooners *Treasury: To the Moon and Back with Ralph, Norton, Alice, and Trixie* (New York: Perigee Books, 1990), xi.

5. Jack Gaver, "Honeymooners Go on Film," *Detroit Free Press*, 4 September 1955, TV 5.

6. Ibid.

7. Rick DesRochers, *The Comic Offense: From Vaudeville to Contemporary Comedy* (New York: Bloomsbury, 2014), 38.

8. James Kaplan, "Angry Middle-Aged Man," *New Yorker*, 19 January 2004, https://www.newyorker.com/magazine/2004/01/19/angry-middle-aged-man.

9. "Gracie Goes to a Psychiatrist," *The George Burns and Gracie Allen Show*, CBS-TV, 27 September 1951.

10. "Gracie Goes to Psychiatrist for Blanche's Dream," *The George Burns and Gracie Allen Show*, CBS-TV, 8 March 1954.

11. Leff and Gostanian, *39 Forever*, 194–235.

12. "Don Invites Gang to Dinner," *The Jack Benny Program*, CBS-TV, 15 January 1956.

13. Vincent Brook, "The Americanization of Molly: How Mid-Fifties TV Homogenized *The Goldbergs* (and Got 'Berg-larized' in the Process)," *Cinema Journal* 38, no. 4 (1999): 45–67.

14. *Washington Square*, NBC-TV, 27 January 1957 and *The Kate Smith Hour*, ABC-TV, 28 April 1957.

15. "Not Enuf 'Joe & Mabel' Pix in Can; So Show Deferred for a Month," *Variety*, 21 September 1955, 40.

16. Eve Starr, "Sinatra Getting 'Press,' but It's Not All Good," *Democrat and Chronicle*, 20 August 1955, 24.

17. Army Archerd, "Just for Variety," *Daily Variety*, 9 September 1955, 2.

18. Hal Humphrey, "The Second Mr. Gildersleeve," *Los Angeles Mirror*, 13 September 1950, 22.

19. Dunning, *On the Air*, 372.

20. "Not Enuf 'Joe & Mabel' Pix in Can."

## Chapter Nine

1. Steinberg, *TV Facts*, 142.

2. Francis Wood, "TV's Fallen Stars: Where Are They Now?" *Newsday* (Nassau Edition), 25 July 1958, 61.

3. Leff and Gostanian, *39 Forever*, 249, 258, 267, 270.

4. John Anthony Gilvey, *Before the Parade Passes By: Gower Champion and the Glorious American Musical* (New York: St. Martin's, 2005), 71.

5. "Leonard Stern Interview Part 5 of 10—EmmyTVLegends.org," Television Academy Foundation, 2000, https://www.youtube.com/watch?v=9VkbyGnrevE.

6. Marie Torre, "Silvers Outlines Plans—and Bilko's in Them," *Democrat and Chronicle*, 4 September 1957, 15.

7. David Everitt, *King of the Half Hour: Nat Hiken and the Golden Age of TV Comedy* (Syracuse: Syracuse University Press, 2011), 131.

8. Dave Kaufman, "On All Channels," *Daily Variety*, 4 January 1957, 12.

9. "Ricky Nelson Is Set for Disc Career," *Valley Times*, 6 April 1957, 15.

10. "TV Films Now in Production," *Daily Variety*, 22 March 1955, 11. This is the series' last production listing in *Variety*.

11. Hyatt, *Betty White on TV*, 69.

12. United States Council on Environmental Quality, "Part III Environmental Data and Trends," table 1.4, U.S. Department of Commerce, Bureau of the Census, Census of Population and Housing, 1950, 1960, 1970, 1980, and 1990, Number of Inhabitants, U.S. Summary, Washington, DC, and updates by agency.

13. "Barbecue," *Trouble with Father*, ABC-TV, 28 July 1951.

14. Brooks and Marsh, *The Complete Directory to Prime Time Network and Cable TV Shows*, 1681.

15. "Ann Sothern to Scrap 'Secretary' unless TPA Works Out a New Deal," *Variety*, 27 February 1957, 27.

16. John Fink, "TV Series May Lead to Others," *Chicago Tribune*, 29 January 1957, section 2, 7.

## Chapter Ten

1. Sanders and Gilbert, *Desilu*, 130–131.

2. Ibid., 138–140.

3. "'Maverick' Gives S&A a Hotfoot," *Variety*, 13 November 1957, 34.

4. Cynthia Lowry, "TV Viewpoint," *Evening Sun*, 27 April 1962, B5.

5. Brooks and Marsh, *The Complete Directory to Prime Time Network and Cable TV Shows*, 1681–1682.

6. Ibid., 1681–1683.

7. *Abie's Irish Rose* is a classic 1922 Broadway comedy by Anne Nichols about an interfaith marriage between an Irish Catholic woman and a Jewish man—a union to which both fathers object.

8. Charles Witbeck, "Star John Forsythe Is Just Sammee Tong's Straight Man," *The News*, 18 March 1959, 55.

9. Steinberg, *TV Facts*, 142.

10. "Awards Nominees and Winners," Television Academy, https://www.emmys.com/awards/nominees-winners.

11. "Fox Buys into TV Network; Makes 390 Features Available," *Boxoffice*, 3 November 1956, 8.

12. Hal Morris, "NTA Plans More Programs for Fall," *Los Angeles Mirror*, 5 May 1958, part 3, 6.

13. Leff and Gostanian, *39 Forever*, 278–322.

14. Cecil Smith, "Gracie Allen Sets Retirement Date," *Los Angeles Times*, 19 February 1958, part 2, 10.

## Chapter Eleven

1. Brooks and Marsh, *The Complete Directory to Prime Time Network and Cable TV Shows*, 1680–1681.
2. Ibid., 1682.
3. Ibid., 1679.
4. "Awards Nominees and Winners," Television Academy, https://www.emmys.com/awards/nominees-winners.
5. Rose, "Tele Follow-Up Comment—Peck's Bad Girl," *Variety*, 13 May 1959, 39.
6. "Child Actress to Begin TV Series in May," *Buffalo Courier Express*, 12 April 1959, D36.
7. Ibid.
8. Fredrick Tucker, *Verna Felton* (Albany, GA: BearManor Media, 2010), 521.
9. "CBS Still Canning Laughs with No Ban Yet to Prod'rs," *Daily Variety*, 3 November 1959, 4.
10. Mel Neuhaus, "From Baby Sherry to Sherry, Baby: My Memorable Afternoon with Sherry Jackson," *The Examiner*, 21 May 2011.
11. "Schultzy Makes Grade," *Fort Worth Star-Telegram*, 14 June 1959, TV section, 2.
12. "Bob Helps Martha" and "Bob Helps Von Zell," *The Bob Cummings Show*, NBC-TV, 26 May 1959 and 2 June 1959.
13. Brooks and Marsh, *The Complete Directory to Prime Time Network and Cable TV Shows*, 1682.
14. "Bob Schiller and Bob Weiskopf Interview Part 4 of 8—EmmyTVLegends.org," Television Academy Foundation, 2000, https://www.youtube.com/watch?v=xEDI-k9J1FU.
15. David C. Tucker, *The Women Who Made Television Funny: Ten Stars of 1950s Sitcoms* (Jefferson, NC: McFarland, 2007), 134.
16. Eve Starr, "George Burns Show Fades Off," *Columbus Enquirer*, 20 April 1959, 13.
17. Leszczak, *Single Season Sitcoms*, 54.
18. Fidelman, *The Lucy Book*, 131.
19. Hal Erickson, *Syndicated Television: The First Forty Years, 1947–1987* (Jefferson, NC: McFarland, 1989), 17–18.
20. Bob Brooks, "Horse Operas Near Saturation Point," *Los Angeles Mirror*, 23 September 1958, section 3, 6.
21. Leszczak, *Single Season Sitcoms*, 187.

## Chapter Twelve

1. Brooks and Marsh, *The Complete Directory to Prime Time Network and Cable TV Shows*, 1682.
2. Ibid., 1683.
3. Ibid.
4. Ibid., 1682.
5. Marie Torre, "Danny Thomas Eyes TV Production Career," *Roanoke Times*, 4 June 1959, 39.
6. Erskine Johnson, "Danny 'Killed' Wife, Eyes 'Suicide,'" *Orlando Evening Star*, 18 November 1961, C4.
7. Jack Lloyd, "Marjorie Lord Faces Long Stand," *Atlanta Journal*, 22 April 1963, 13.
8. "CBS Still Canning Laughs with No Ban Yet to Prod'rs," *Daily Variety*, 3 November 1959, 4.
9. Cynthia Lowry, "Father, Who Knows Best, Says It's Time to Give Up," *Chicago Sunday Tribune*, 17 April 1960, part 3, section 2, 4.
10. Henry Mitchell, "Television Not Mentioned in Khrushchev 'Trade' Talks," *Commercial Appeal*, 22 September 1959, 22.
11. Forrest Powers, "Cello Plays Theme of Demarest's Life," *Minneapolis Star*, 11 September 1959, 23.
12. Steven Scheuer, "TV Keynotes: New Viewers Expected," *Morning Call*, 12 September 1959, 16.
13. "Sindlinger Profiles a TV Audience in Bid for New Trends in Research," *Variety*, 27 April 1960, 31.
14. Morris J. Gelman, "Forecast 64/65," *Television Magazine*, September 1964, 16.
15. Scheuer, "TV Keynotes," 16.
16. Brooks and Marsh. *The Complete Directory to Prime Time Network and Cable TV Shows*, 1682.
17. Jack Hellman, "Light and Airy," *Daily Variety*, 4 April 1960, 8.
18. Hugh A. Mulligan, "No 'Togetherness' for Dobie," *Fort Lauderdale News*, 26 September 1959, 14.
19. Scheuer, "TV Keynotes," 16.
20. "The Many Changes in Dobie Gillis," *TV Guide*, 15–21 October 1960, 22–23.
21. Jack Allen, "Shulman Says 'Dobie' Still on Wild Side," *Buffalo Courier Express*, 3 October 1962, 37.
22. Michelangelo Signorile, *Queer in America: Sex, the Media, and the Closets of Power* (Madison: University of Wisconsin Press, 2004), 225.
23. Bernie Harrison, "Teen-Ager Dobie 'Spanked' by CBS," *Evening Star*, 16 March 1960, C23.
24. "Risqué 'Dobie' Episode Back from Cleaners for Showing on July 5," *Philadelphia Inquirer*, 14 June 1960, 21.
25. Leff and Gostanian, *39 Forever*, 369–370.
26. Fidelman, *The Lucy Book*, 135.
27. "Kovacs-Adams Guestint," *Daily Variety*, 8 January 1960, 15.
28. Hedda Hopper, "Lucy and Desi Split; Actress Asks Divorce," *Los Angeles Times*, 4 March 1960, part 3, 1.
29. Andrews, *Lucy & Ricky & Fred & Ethel*, 166.

## Conclusion

1. "Awards Nominees and Winners," Television Academy, https://www.emmys.com/awards/nominees-winners.
2. "Ratings: Television and Record Industry History Resources," Timbrooks.net, https://timbrooks.net/ratings/.
3. Matt Webb Mitovich, "What Were the TV Season's Top-Rated and Most-Watched Shows? And Which Cancelled Drama Did the 'Best'?" TVLine, May 31, 2023, https://tvline.com/lists/most-popular-tv-show-rankings-2022-2023-ratings/.

# Bibliography

Andrews, Bart. *Lucy & Ricky & Fred & Ethel: The Story of "I Love Lucy."* New York: Dutton, 1976.

Attardo, Salvatore. *Encyclopedia of Humor Studies.* Thousand Oaks: Sage, 2014.

Berke, Annie. *Their Own Best Creations: Women Writers in Postwar Television.* Oakland: University of California Press, 2022.

Brook, Vincent. "The Americanization of Molly: How Mid-Fifties TV Homogenized *The Goldbergs* (and Got 'Berg-larized' in the Process)." *Cinema Journal* 38, no. 4 (1999): 45–67.

Brooks, Tom, and Earl Marsh. *The Complete Directory to Prime Time Network and Cable TV Shows, 1946–Present.* New York: Ballantine, 2007.

Burns, George. *Gracie: A Love Story.* New York: Putnam, 1988.

Cox, Jim. *American Radio Soap Opera.* Lanham, MD: Scarecrow, 2005.

Cox, Jim. *The Great Radio Sitcoms.* Jefferson, NC: McFarland, 2007.

Crescenti, Peter, and Bob Columbe. *The Official Honeymooners Treasury: To the Moon and Back with Ralph, Norton, Alice, and Trixie.* New York: Perigee Books, 1990.

Cullen, Frank, with Florence Hackman and Donald McNeilly. *Vaudeville Old & New: An Encyclopedia of Variety Performers in America, Volume 1.* New York: Routledge, 2007.

Desjardins, Mary R. *Father Knows Best.* Detroit: Wayne State University Press, 2015.

DesRochers, Rick. *The Comic Offense: From Vaudeville to Contemporary Comedy.* New York: Bloomsbury, 2014.

Doherty, Thomas. *Cold War, Cool Medium: Television, McCarthyism, and American Culture.* New York: Columbia University Press, 2003.

Dunning, John. *On the Air: The Encyclopedia of Old-Time Radio.* New York: Oxford University Press, 1998.

Eisner, Joel, and David Krinsky. *Television Comedy Series: An Episode Guide to 153 TV Sitcoms in Syndication.* Jefferson, NC: McFarland, 1984.

Epstein, Lawrence J. *George Burns: An American Life.* Jefferson, NC: McFarland, 2011.

Erickson, Hal. *Syndicated Television: The First Forty Years, 1947–1987.* Jefferson, NC: McFarland, 1989.

Everitt, David. *King of the Half Hour: Nat Hiken and the Golden Age of TV Comedy.* Syracuse: Syracuse University Press, 2011.

Fidelman, Geoffrey Mark. *The Lucy Book: A Complete Guide to Her Five Decades on Television.* Los Angeles: Renaissance Books, 1999.

Finkelman, Paul. *Encyclopedia of African American History: 1986 to the Present.* Oxford: Oxford University Press, 2009.

Fischer, Roswitha. *Lexical Change in Present-Day English: A Corpus-Based Study of the Motivation, Institutionalization, and Productivity of Creative Neologisms.* Tübingen: Gunter Narr Verlag, 1998.

Gilvey, John Anthony. *Before the Parade Passes By: Gower Champion and the Glorious American Musical.* New York: St. Martin's, 2005.

Greene, Roland. *The Princeton Encyclopedia of Poetry and Poetics.* Princeton: Princeton University Press, 2012.

Harvey, Karen J. *Sid Caesar and Your Show of Shows: The Birth of the Television Sketch Comedy Series.* Jefferson NC: McFarland, 2021.

Hawes, William. "The Heritage." In *American Television Drama: The Experimental Years.* Tuscaloosa: University of Alabama Press, 1986.

Holmes, John R. *The Adventures of Ozzie Nelson: The Life and Career of America's Favorite Pop.* Jefferson, NC: McFarland, 2021.

Hyatt, Wesley. *Betty White on TV: From Video Vanguard to Golden Girl.* Orlando: BearManor Media, 2021.

Hyatt, Wesley. *Emmy Award Winning Nighttime Television Shows, 1948–2004.* Jefferson, NC: McFarland, 2006.

Hyatt, Wesley. *Short-Lived Television Series: 1948–1978.* Jefferson, NC: McFarland, 2003.

Irvin, Richard. *Early Shows: A Reference Guide to Network and Syndicated Primetime Television Series from 1944 to 1949.* Albany, GA: BearManor Media, 2018.

Irvin, Richard. *George Burns Television Productions: The Series and Pilots, 1950–1981.* Jefferson, NC: McFarland, 2014.

Jackson, Carlton. *Hattie: The Life of Hattie McDaniel.* Lanham: Madison Books, 1989.

Krampner, Jon. "Myths and Mysteries Surround Pioneering of 3-Camera TV." *Los Angeles Times*, July 29, 1991.

Krell, David. *Baseball and America in the Time of JFK*. Lincoln: University of Nebraska Press, 2021.

Leff, Laura, and Martin Gostanian. *39 Forever: Second Edition, Volume 3: Television*. North Charleston, SC: Book Surge, 2011.

Leszczak, Bob. *Single Season Sitcoms, 1948–1979: A Complete Guide*. Jefferson, NC: McFarland, 2012.

Littleton, Darry. *Black Comedians on Black Comedy: How African Americans Taught Us to Laugh*. New York: Applause Theatre and Cinema Books, 2006.

Lund, Michael. *America's Continuing Story: An Introduction to Serial Fiction, 1850–1900*. Detroit: Wayne State University Press, 1993.

McLeod, Elizabeth. *The Original Amos 'n' Andy: Freeman Gosden, Charles Correll and the 1928–1943 Radio Serial*. Jefferson, NC: McFarland, 2005.

Morreall, John. *Taking Laughter Seriously*. Albany: State University of New York Press, 1983.

Ohmart, Ben. The Bickersons: *A Biography of Radio's Wittiest Program*. Albany, GA: Bear-Manor Media, 2004.

Oppenheimer, Jess, and Gregg Oppenheimer. *Laughs, Luck, and Lucy: How I Came to Create the Most Popular Sitcom of All Time*. Syracuse: Syracuse University Press, 1996.

Sanders, Coyne Stevens, and Tom Gilbert. *Desilu: The Story of Lucille Ball and Desi Arnaz*. New York: Dey Street Books, 2011.

Schwartz, Sherwood. *Inside* Gilligan's Island: *A Three-Hour Tour through the Making of a Television Classic*. New York: St. Martin's, 1988.

Signorile, Michelangelo. *Queer in America: Sex, the Media, and the Closets of Power*. Madison: University of Wisconsin Press, 2004.

Slotton, Hugh R. *Radio and Television Regulation: Broadcast Technology in the United States, 1920–1960*. Baltimore: Johns Hopkins University Press, 2000.

Smith, Glenn D. *"Something on My Own": Gertrude Berg and American Broadcasting, 1929–1956*. Syracuse: Syracuse University Press, 2007.

Steinberg, Cobbett S. *TV Facts*. New York: Facts on File, 1980.

Terrace, Vincent. *Encyclopedia of Unaired Television Pilots, 1945–2018*. Jefferson, NC: McFarland, 2018.

Tucker, David C. *Eve Arden: A Chronicle of All Film, Television, Radio and Stage Performances*. Jefferson, NC: McFarland, 2012.

Tucker, David C. *Gale Storm: A Biography and Career Record*. Jefferson, NC: McFarland, 2018.

Tucker, David C. *The Women Who Made Television Funny: Ten Stars of 1950s Sitcoms*. Jefferson, NC: McFarland, 2007.

Tucker, Fredrick. *Verna Felton*. Albany, GA: Bear-Manor Media, 2010.

Weinstein, David. *The Forgotten Network: DuMont and the Birth of American Television*. Philadelphia: Temple University Press, 2004.

Weiss, Margaret R., and Barbara Boothe. "The Half-Hour Original: Situation Comedy." In *The TV Writer's Guide*. New York: Pellegrini & Cudahy, 1952.

Wetzel, James R. "American Families: 75 Years of Change." *Monthly Labor Revue*, March 1990, pp. 4–13.

White, Betty. *Here We Go Again*. New York: Scribner, 1995.

Zerba, Michelle, and David Gorman, eds. *Aristotle Poetics*. New York: Norton, 1982.

# Index

**Numbers in *bold italics* indicate pages with illustrations**

Abbott, Bud 38, 56, 101, 173; *see also The Abbott and Costello Show*
*The Abbott and Costello Show* 101–102, 115, 130, 275
*Abbott Elementary* 270
*Actors Hotel* 80
*The Addams Family* 163, 267
*The Adventures of Hiram Holliday* 211–212
*The Adventures of Ozzie and Harriet* 21, 36, 54, ***102–105***, 106, 107, 110, 125, 129, 130, 149–151, 152, 155, 160, 161, 165, 187–188, 192, 203–204, 207, 213, 221, 225, 233, 235, 247, 252, 275; *see also* Nelson, Ozzie
Albert, Eddie 109
Albertson, Mabel 146
Albright, Lola 193
*The Aldrich Family* 21, 29, 30, 37–39, 92, 109, 161, 246, 257, 258
*All in the Family* 168, 267
Allen, Fred 19, 72, 180
Allen, Gracie 19, 39–44, 45, 50, 51, 54, 78–79, 107–108, 127–129, 152, 153, 184–186, 197, 229–232, 244; *see also The George Burns and Gracie Allen Show*
Allen, Ray 262
Allen, Steve 201
Allen, Woody 198–199
Allman, Elvia 90–91, 96, 211
Amateau, Rod 230, 231, 261, 262
Ameche, Don 94
Ames, Florenz 211
*Amos 'n Andy* (radio) ***14–17***, 18, 21, 40, 45, 48–49, 52, 252
*The Amos 'n Andy Show* (television) 36, ***48–53***, 54, 55, 58, 59, 61, 62, 69, 76–80, 85, 87, 107, 110, 115, 121, 132, 160, 171, 220, 224

Amsterdam, Morey 28
Anders, Mike 190, 227
Anderson, Eddie 45
*The Andy Griffith Show* 123, 161, 222, 223, 249–250, 265, 267
*The Ann Sothern Show* 209, 234, 242–244, 247, 248, 250–251, 265; *see also* Sothern, Ann
Arden, Eve 81, 91–92, 99, 121, 123, 226
Aristotle 2, 10–12, 13, 16–18, 22, 29, 234, 254, 269
Armen, Kay 255
Arnaz, Desi 60–62, 65–67, 87, 91, 98, 117, 125, 136, 147, 190, 206–207, 215–217, 238, 244–245, 263–264; *see also I Love Lucy*
Arnaz, Desi, Jr. 87, 133
*Arrested Development* 178, 268
Asher, William 88, 90, 135, 141, 142, 208
*Atlanta* 269

*The Baby Snooks Show* 64, 65, 71, 73
*Bachelor Father* 220, 222, 235, 251
Backus, Jim 97–98
Baer, Parley 187, 203
Bal, Jeanne 255
Ball, Lucille 55, 60–62, 64–66, 68, 69, 71–75, 85, 86–87, 91, 92, 98–100, 116, 117, 125, 133, 135, 143, 147, 148, 206, 208, 215–216, 238, 244, 251, 263–264, 267; *see also I Love Lucy*
Balzer, George 228
Bankhead, Tallulah 216
Banks, Joan 99
*Barry* 269
Barry, Gene 190
Barton, Charles 52
Bavier, Frances 161–162
Beatty, Warren 258, 261–262

Beaumont, Hugh 223
Beavers, Louise 47, 126
Beggs, Russell 199
Benaderet, Bea 40, 41, 65, 68, 108, 127, 231, 244
Bendix, William 32, 105–106, 149
Bennett, Joan 247
Benny, Jack 10, 19, ***23–24***, 28, 40, ***44–45***, 51, 54, 57, 60, 109, 127, 148, 158, 186, 197, 200, ***228–229***, 238, 244, 250, 263–265; *see also The Jack Benny Program*
Benoit, Patricia 82–83, 111–112
Bensfield, Dick 221
Berg, Gertrude 17, 110, 119, 188–189
Berle, Milton 28, 38, 55, 57, 69, 169, 180, 263
Best, Willie 55, 83
*The Betty Hutton Show* (aka *Goldie*) 256
*The Beulah Show* 45–51, 53, 54, 61, 160
*The Beverly Hillbillies* 138, 154–156, 167, 222, 256, 267
*Bewitched* 2, 82, 90, 137, 138, 146, 167, 168, 267
*The Bickersons* 18, 21, 94–95, 164, 170, 171
*The Big Bang Theory* 268, 270
*The Bill Dana Show* 123
Billingsley, Barbara 163, 204, 223
Bishop, Julie 101
Bishop, William 161
Blanc, Mel 228
Blitzer, Barry 181, 182
*Blondie* 21, 102, 210–211, 252, 275
*The Bob Cummings Show* (aka *Love That Bob*) 35, 36, ***153–157***, 164, 165, 192–193, 196, 211, 212–214, 220, 224, 225, 241–242, 247, 257, 258, 267; *see also* Cummings, Bob

# Index

*The Bob Newhart Show* 124
Bolger, Ray 122, 146
*Bonino* 118
Booth, Shirley 91
*Boss Lady* 80–81
*The Brady Bunch* 154
Brecher, Irving 31–32, 192
Brennan, Walter 222, 223, 235, 252
Bretherton, Howard 55
*The Brothers* 205
Brown, David 199
Brown, John 41, 43
Bunce, Alan 111
Burke, Billie 111
Burnett, Carol 198–200
Burns, George 19, 39–44, 78, 107–109, 118, 127–129, 153, 157, 184–186, 192, 197–198, 208, 229–232, 244; see also *The George Burns and Gracie Allen Show*
Burns, Ronnie 153, 185, 197, 230, 244, 256
Burns, William 108, 128, 186, 230, 231
*The Buster Keaton Show* (aka *Life with Buster Keaton*) 57–58, 101
Byington, Spring 147–148

Caesar, Sid 38, 55, 67, 69, 95, 158, 169, 170; see also *Your Show of Shows*
*Caesar's Hour* 170, 198
Cahn, Dann 63
Cantor, Eddie 19, 38
*Car 54, Where Are You?* 180, 181, 183, 203
Card, Kathryn 191
Carney, Art 171–176
Carroll, Bob, Jr. 64, 65, 70, 72, 74, 88–90, 135, 141, 142, 146, 194, 195, 208, 271
Carroll, Leo G. 137
Carroll, Pat 159, 249
Carson, Jeannie 210, 255
Cartwright, Angela 217
Caulfield, Joan 116, 226
*Cavalcade of Stars* 95, 164, 170–173
Chapin, Lauren 152
Chaplin, Charlie 15, 90
*The Charlie Farrell Show* 191
*Cheers* 3, 268
Chertok, Jack 99, 209, 243
Chevillat, Dick 161
Childress, Alvin 49, 52
Clark, Fred 41, 108
Coca, Imogene 38, 158, 170
*The Colgate Comedy Hour* 38, 163
Collins, Ray 160

Collyer, June 54
Colman, Ronald 160
*Colonel Humphrey Flack* (aka *Colonel Humphrey J. Flack*) 136–139, 246
"The Commuters" 170
Connelly, Joe 52, 121, 224
Conried, Hans 125, 187, 213, 218, 219, 239
Coogan, Jackie 163
Cook, Donald 247
Cooper, Jackie 192, 254
Corcoran, Noreen 220
Correll, Charles 14–15, 48
*The Cosby Show* 268
Costello, Lou 38, 56, 101, 173; see also *The Abbott and Costello Show*
Cox, Wally 81–83, 111–114, 120, 163, 211
Crenna, Richard 92, 222
Croft, Mary Jane 92, 94, 123, 192, 203, 204, 207, 211
Cronyn, Hume 118
Cross, James 227
Cummings, Bob 101, 153–157, 212, 225, 241, 244, 263; see also *The Bob Cummings Show*
*Curb Your Enthusiasm* 178, 268

Dalton, Abby 254
D'Andrea, Tom 163, 188
Dandridge, Ruby 47
Daniels, Marc 72, 74, 89–90, 96
*The Danny Thomas Show* (aka *Make Room for Daddy*) 35, 36, 98, **122–126**, 139, 146, 186–187, 190–191, 196, 204–205, 210, 213, 214, **217–220**, 224, 226, 232–234, 237–240, 242–243, 245, 247–250, 255, 265, 267, 275; see also Thomas, Danny
*A Date with Judy* 81, 111, 246
*Date with the Angels* 205–206, 226
David, Larry 178, 180, 241
Davis, Ann B. 154, 225, 241
Davis, Joan 96–100
Day, Dennis 45, 79, 80, 127, 148
Deacon, Richard 191, 206
*Dear Phoebe* 159
DeCamp, Rosemary 153
De Caprio, Al 181, 182, 201–203
*December Bride* 147–148, 190, 196, 205, 227, 237, 243, 275
De Cordova, Frederick 128, 186
DeFore, Don 187, 203
Demarest, William 218, 219, 255
Denning, Richard 60, 65
*The Dennis Day Show* 79, 80, 109, 148

*The Dennis O'Keefe Show* 255
*Dennis the Menace* 111, 227, 252–253, 257, 258, 265, 267, 275
Denver, Bob 258, 261, 262
Desilu 62–63, 86, 91–95, 99, 114, 122–123, 125, 127, 140, 146–148, 153, 163, 172, 189, 190, 205–206, 215–217, 226, 237, 239, 242, 244–246, 263–264
DeWilde, Brandon 118
*Dick and the Duchess* 227
*The Dick Van Dyke Show* 98, 99, 123–126, 146, 167, 191, 218, 238, 249, 267, 268
*Doc Corkle* 82, 111
Donahue, Elinor 152
*The Donald O'Connor Show* (aka *Here Comes Donald*) 158
*The Donna Reed Show* 102, 104, 152, 235–237, 251, 275
Donovan, King 154, 157
Dorfman, Sid 108, 128
Dow, Tony 223, 236
Duff, Howard 212, 226, 245
*Duffy's Tavern* 21, 130–131, 147, 160, 191, 254, 268
*The Duke* 118
Dulo, Jane 210
Dunn, James 161, 162

*Easy Aces* 18, 29
*The Ed Wynn Show* 246
Eden, Barbara 227–228, 246
Elinson, Jack 250
Ellis, Robert 161
Emerson, Hope 255
Erwin, Stu 54–57, 76–77, 102, 105, 106, 151
*Ethel and Albert* 21, 110–111, 118, 132, 163, 164, 170, 189
*The Eve Arden Show* 226

Fabray, Nanette 170
Fairbanks, Jerry 31, 60
Farrell, Charlie 84, 117, 191
*Father Knows Best* 21, 77, 102, 104, 106, 130, **151–153**, 154–157, 161, 164, 188, 195, 196, 203, 207, 213, 220, 223, 224, 232, 234–237, 242, 246–248, 251, 254, 257–258
Faye, Herbie 183
Faylen, Frank 259
Fedderson, Don 131, 206
Felton, Verna 148, 190, 237
*Fibber McGee and Molly* 19–21, 23, 28, 45, 159, 169, 191, 254
Filmcraft 94
Filmtone 31
Finn, Herbert 175
Fisher, Bob 192

## Index

*The Flintstones* 248
Ford, Paul 182, 183
Forman, Joey 159
Forsythe, John 220
Fowler, Keith 128, 186, 230, 231
Foxx, Redd 51
Franken, Steve 258, 261
*Frasier* 3, 268
Frawley, William 69
Freeman, Kathleen 137, 193, 241, 262
Freund, Karl 62
Friebus, Florida 259
Friedberg, Billy 201–203
*Friends* 167, 268
Fritzell, Jim 113
Funicello, Annette 239–240

*The Gale Storm Show* (aka *Oh, Susanna!*) 209–210, 226, 237, 255
Gardner, Ed 130
Gaye, Lisa 246
Gelbart, Larry 163
*The George Burns and Gracie Allen Show* 19, 21, 35, 36, 38, **39–44**, 45, 46, 50, 51, 54, 58, 59, 61, 63, 66, 69, 76–81, 85, 97, **107–109**, 115, 127–129, 139, 152, 153, 155, 157, 158, 163, 165, **184–186**, 196, **197–198**, 199, 201, 212–214, **229–232**, 233, 241, 244, 252, 262–263
*The George Burns Show* 231, 244
Gibbs, Marla 51
*Girls* 269
Gleason, Jackie 32–33, 95, 105, 170–177, 200
*Glencannon* 245–246
*The Goldbergs* 17, 19, **29–30**, 33, 37, 38, 61, 67, 80, 81, 109, 119, 120, **188–189**, 254, 275
*The Golden Girls* 3, 167
Goldman, Hal 228
Goldstein, Jesse 108
Goodwin, Bill 40, 41
Gordon, Al 228
Gordon, Gale 65, 68–69, 92, 123, 205, 227, 245, 250, 253
Gordon, Shirl 213
Gosden, Freeman 14–15, 48
Gosfield, Maurice 183, 201–202
Grant, Perry 221
Gray, Billy 152
*The Great Gildersleeve* 21, 45, 191, 254
*Green Acres* 84, 104, 109, 138, 155, 156, 160, 222, 267
Greenbaum, Everett 113
Grey, Virginia 94
*The Growing Paynes* 28

Hackett, Buddy 198, 200, 247
Hagen, Jean 123, 126, 186–187, 204, 237
*The Halls of Ivy* 159–160
Halop, Florence 109
Hamer, Rusty 126, 206, 217
*The Hank McCune Show* 57
*Happy* 256
Harrington, Pat 248–249
Harris, Percy "Bud" 46
Harris, Phil 21, 45, 161
*The Hartmans* 28
Havoc, June 147
Hayden, Don 85
Helm, Harvey 108, 128, 185, 230, 231
Henderson, Marcia 159
*Hennesey* 254, 255
Henning, Paul 40, 155–156, 193, 212, 213, 222, 223, 225, 242, 267
*Hey, Jeannie!* (aka *The Jeannie Carson Show*) 210, 255
*Hey, Mulligan!* (aka *The Mickey Rooney Show*) 159, 275
The Hickenloopers 95, 170–171
Hickman, Dwayne 153, 156, 213, 225, 242, 257, 258, 260–262
Hiken, Nat 177, 180–184, 200–203, 229, 240, 241, 257
*His Honor, Homer Bell* 160–161
Hoffmann, Gertrude 84
Holloway, Sterling 147, 188
Holm, Celeste 163
*Honestly, Celeste!* 163
*The Honeymooners* 32, 33, 35, 36, 95, 105, 151, 163–164, 166, 169, **170–177**, 200, 201, 212, 250, 266, 275
Hope, Bob 238
*How to Marry a Millionaire* 227–228, 246
Hume, Benita 160
Hurt, Marlin 45–46
Hutton, Betty 256

*I Dream of Jeannie* 137, 227, 267
*I Love Lucy* 2, 10, 26–27, 35, 36, **59–76**, 77–80, 82–85, **86–91**, 92–93, 95–98, 99, 102, 106–110, 113–117, 120, 122, **123–126**, 127, 132–136, 138–139, **140–145**, 146–149, 151–153, 155, 157–160, 162, 164–166, 168, 169, 171–174, 176–179, 181, 182, 184, 185, 190–197, 205, **206–209**, 210, 214, **215–217**, 218–220, 231–234, 237–239, 241–242, 244–245, 247, 249–251, 253, 254, 263–268, 270
*I Married Joan* 96–99, 107, 115, 117, 122, 133, 142, 148–149, 237–238
*The Imogene Coca Show* 158
*It's a Business* 80
*It's a Great Life* 161–162, 191
*It's Always Jan* 190–191

*The Jack Benny Program* 10, 19, **23–24**, 28, 35, 38, 40, **44–45**, 51, 54, 57, 61, 79, 99, 109, 120, 127, 148, 158, 160, 169, 186, 197, 199–200, 220, **228–229**, 231, 233, 234, 244, 248, 263, 264, 275
*The Jackie Gleason Show* 95, 164, 170–172, 200; see also Benny, Jack
Jackson, Sherry 126, 217, 237, 239, 248, 249
*Jackson and Jill* 31
Jacoby, Coleman 182, 203
James, Sheila 54, 77, 149, 258, 261
*Jamie* 118
Janis, Conrad 118
Jarvis, Al 131
*The Jean Carroll Show* (aka *Take It from Me*) 118–119
Jeffreys, Anne 137, 226
Jenkins, Allen 210
*Joe and Mabel* 189, 191
*The Joey Bishop Show* 123, 126
Johnson, Arte 190, 227
Johnson, Georgann 112
Jordan, Jim 19–20, 254
Jordan, Marian 19–20, 254
*Julia* 160

Kallen, Lucille 198, 199
*The Kate Smith Hour* 110, 170
Kaye, Stubby 255
Kearns, Joseph 227, 253
Keating, Larry 41, 127–128, 184, 185, 244
Keaton, Buster 57–58, 101
Keith, Hal 113
Kelton, Pert 170–172
Kern, James V. 194–195
Knotts, Don 223, 225, 250, 262
Komack, James 254
Kovacs, Ernie 263
Kulp, Nancy 154, 190, 193

Lake, Arthur 210
Lane, Charles 159
Langford, Frances 94
Lansing, Joi 154
Laurel & Hardy 16, 54, 56, 173
Lawford, Peter 159
Lawrence, Mary 193, 212
*The Laytons* 28
Lear, Norman 163, 167, 168, 267

*Leave It to Beaver* 102, 104, 121, 130, 151–152, 163, 223–225, 233, 235, 236, 241, 245–247, 252–253, 257, 258, 265, 275
*Leave It to Larry* 109
Lee, Johnny 49
Lembeck, Harvey 183
Lemmon, Jack 33
Leonard, Sheldon 108, 123, 146, 190, 219, 250
Levy, Parke 147
Levy, Ralph 108, 227
Lewis, Al 93, 122
Lewis, Cathy 254
Lewis, Jerry 38, 116
Liebman, Max 199–200, 247
*The Life of Riley* (1949) 21, 29, **31–33**, 37, 46, 105
*The Life of Riley* (1953) 54, 55, 67, 103, 105–106, 125, 129–130, 149, 152, 163, 171, 188, 192, 203, 207, 220
*Life with Elizabeth* 131–132
*Life with Father* 117–118, 120, 153
*Life with Luigi* 61, 67, 109–110
Lipscott, Alan 192
Livingstone, Mary 44–45
Loeb, Philip 119
Lord, Marjorie 123, 204, 217–219, 237, 239
Lorne, Marion 82, 111, 112, 120, 226
Lorre, Chuck 268
*Louie* 269
*Love That Jill* 226
*The Lucille Ball-Desi Arnaz Show* (aka *The Lucy-Desi Comedy Hour*) 215–217, 244–245, 263–264; see also *I Love Lucy*
*The Lucy Show* 55–56, 69, 267
*Luke and Mirandy* 19
*Lum and Abner* 18
Lupino, Ida 212, 226, 245
Lynch, Peg 110–111, 132, 163
Lynde, Paul 198

*The Magnificent Montague* 180
*Mama* 29–30, 37–38, 117–119
*The Many Loves of Dobie Gillis* 35, 36, 54, 156, 161, 213, 235, 242, **256–263**, 265, 267, 275
March, Hal 40, 41, 163
*The Marge and Gower Champion Show* 199–200
Marie, Rose 225, 241
*The Marriage* 118, 120
*Married… with Children* 268
Marshall, Garry 126
Martin, Dean 38
*The Marvelous Mrs. Maisel* 269
Marx, Harpo 143

Marx, Marvin 174, 176
*Mary Kay and Johnny* 26–28, 87, 197
*The Mary Tyler Moore Show* 2, 100, 124, 267, 268
*M\*A\*S\*H* 3
Mathers, Jerry 223, 236
Maxey, Paul 192
Mayehoff, Eddie 111, 116
*Mayor of the Town* 161
McCadden 118, 127, 152, 154, 157, 163, 192, 213
McDaniel, Hattie 46–48
McDevitt, Ruth 112
McGuire, Biff 113
McLeod, Elizabeth 16–18, 48
McMillan, Gloria 92
McQueen, Butterfly 46
Meadows, Audrey 171–172
*Meet Corliss Archer* 38, 39, 161, 165, 246, 257, 258
*Meet Millie* 109, 116, 121, 163, 189, 191, 200
*Meet Mr. McNutley* (aka *The Ray Milland Show*) 121, 149
Melton, Sid 190, 249
Melvin, Allan 183
Meredith, Judi 244
Milland, Ray 121
*Mr. Adams and Eve* 212, 226, 245
*Mr. and Mrs.* 18–20
*Mister Ed* 41, 127, 256
*Mister Peepers* 35–36, **81–83**, 85, 93, 101, **111–114**, 115, 119–121, 139, 162–163, 189, 198, 211, 226, 270, 275
Mitchell, Shirley 96
*Modern Family* 268, 270
Monaster, Nate 108
Moore, Alvy 84–85
Moore, Del 131
Moore, Mary Tyler 124, 167; see also *The Mary Tyler Moore Show*; MTM
Moore, Tim 49, 52
Morgan, Harry 148, 190
Morgan, Jane 92
Mosher, Bob 52, 120, 224
Mowbray, Alan 136
MTM 124, 167, 267; see also *The Mary Tyler Moore Show*; Moore, Mary Tyler
*The Munsters* 121, 181, 267
Mustin, Burt 206
*My Favorite Martian* 137
*My Favorite Husband* (radio) 60–63, 66–68, 70–72, 90, 116, 135
*My Favorite Husband* (television) 116–117, 163, 189, 206, 226
*My Friend Irma* 79–80, 109, 116, 147, 189

*My Hero* 100, 107, 153
*My Little Margie* 83–85, 107, 117, 148–149, 191, 209–210, 275
*My Son Jeep* 111
*My Three Sons* 131

Naish, J. Carroll 110
Nelson, David 102, 187, 252
Nelson, Don 221
Nelson, Frank 186, 194, 207, 228
Nelson, Harriet 102–104, 106, 150, 204, 221
Nelson, Lori 227, 246
Nelson, Barry 116
Nelson, Ozzie 102–106, 110, 150–151, 153, 187–188, 203–204, 221, 235; see also *The Adventures of Ozzie and Harriet*
Nelson, Ricky 102, 104, 152, 187, 203–204, 221, 260
Nolan, Kathleen 222
*Norby* 162
North, Jay 252
*Nothing But the Truth* 135
Nye, Louis 244, 251

O'Connor, Donald 158
O'Demus, Nick 49
*The Office* 181, 268
O'Keefe, Dennis 255
Oppenheimer, Jess 64–67, 70, 72, 74, 75, 88–90, 135, 141, 142, 194, 195, 206
O'Shea, Michael 161–162
Osmond, Ken 224
*Our Gang* (aka *The Little Rascals*) 16, 31
*Our Miss Brooks* 35, 36, 69, 81, **91–94**, 95, 99, 100, 106, 109, 112, 114, **121–123**, 138, 139, 146, 152, 159, 190, 205, 222, 226, 253, 270, 275

Packer, Doris 185–186, 256, 258
Paige, Janis 190
Paley, Bill 40
Paris, Jerry 146, 205
Parker, Penney 248–249
*Parks and Recreation* 268
Patrick, Lee 137
Paul, Norman 185, 230, 231
Peary, Harold 21, 45, 147, 191, 211
*Peck's Bad Girl* 235, 246
*The People's Choice* 192, 196, 211, 226, 254, 256
Perrin, Sam 228
*Pete and Gladys* 148, 237
*Petticoat Junction* 155, 222, 267
*The Phil Harris-Alice Faye Show* 21, 161
*The Phil Silvers Show* (aka *You'll Never Get Rich*) 35, 36, 151, 164, 166, 169, 173, **177–184**,

## Index

189, 193, 195, 196, **200–203**, 212, 214, 229, 232–233, 240–241, 247, 250, 266, 270, 275; see also Silvers, Phil
Pinza, Ezio 118
Pitts, ZaSu 210
*Pleasantville* 151–152
Pons, Beatrice 202
Porter, Don 99, 243, 250
Prickett, Maudie 206
*The Pride of the Family* 129–130
*Private Secretary* (aka *Susie*) **99–101**, 107, 109, 117, 120, 127, 148–149, 158, 159, 192, 209, 216, 242–243, 250–251
*Professional Father* 163
*The Pruitts of Southampton* 256
*Public Prosecutor* 31, 60
Pugh, Madelyn (aka Martin, Madelyn) 64, 65, 70, 72, 74, 88–90, 135, 141–142, 146, 194, 195, 208

Quillan, Joseph 93, 122

Rae, Charlotte 181–182
Randall, Tony 82, 111–114, 120, 124
Randolph, Amanda 28, 49, 79, 126
Randolph, Isabel 190
Randolph, Joyce 171
Rapp, Phil 94–95, 211
Raye, Martha 180
*The Real McCoys* 222–223, 232, 234–235, 242, 248, 251–252, 275
*The Red Buttons Show* 158
Reed, Roland 46, 53, 83
Reiner Carl 38, 124, 238
Roach, Hal 31, 46–48, 53–55, 58, 62, 83, 101, 191, 209, 210
Roberts, Roy 210
Rockwell, Robert 92
Rooney, Mickey 159
*Roseanne* 268
Rosen, Arnie 182, 203, 240
Ross, Bob 52
Ross, Joe E. 183, 202
*The Ruggles* 30, 80, 254
Ruggles, Charlie 30
Russell, A.J. 175
Russell, Evelyn 156
Ryan, Terry 181–182

Saks, Sol 235
*Sally* 226–227
*Sam 'n' Henry* 14–15, 18
Sands, Billy 183
Satenstein, Frank 173–175
Schallert, William 260
Schiller, Bob 194–195, 208, 242, 251

*The School House* 81
Scotti, Vito 110
*Seinfeld* 119, 167, 168, 178–179, 181, 241, 268; see also Seinfeld, Jerry
Seinfeld, Jerry 11, 168, 241; see also *Seinfeld*
Shaw, Reta 112, 243
Shuken, Phil 213
Shulman, Max 257–262
Silvers, Phil 177, 180, 183, 202, 240; see also *The Phil Silvers Show*
Simon, Al 60, 62, 96
Simon, Danny 198
Simon, Neil 180, 198, 240
Singer, Ray 161
Singleton, Doris 96, 136, 143
Skelton, Red 69, 72
*Smackout* 19–20
*So This Is Hollywood* 158–159
*The Soldiers* 163–164, 170, 188
Sommers, Jay 104, 105, 160, 221
Sondheim, Stephen 139
Sothern, Ann 99–101, 117, 148, 209, 216, 242–243, 250, 251
Stander, Arthur 98, 190, 219, 237, 249
*Stanley* 35, 198–201, 214, 247, 275
*Star Time* 94, 170
Stearns, Johnny 26; see also *Mary Kay and Johnny*
Stearns, Mary Kay 26; see also *Mary Kay and Johnny*
Sterling, Robert 137, 226
Stern, Leonard 173, 180, 201, 202, 212
Stevens, Rusty 223
Stewart, Charles 250
Stone, Walter 174, 176
Storm, Gale 84–85, 117, 209–210
Stritch, Elaine 28, 171
Sweeney, Bob 190, 205, 254
Swift, David 81, 113, 162

Talbot, Lyle 154, 191, 193, 203
Talbot, Nita 191
Tandy, Jessica 118
Tarloff, Frank 98
*Taxi* 267
*Texaco Star Theater* 28, 38
*That Girl* 100
*That Wonderful Guy* 33
*That's My Boy* 116, 153
Thibodeaux, Keith 206
*30 Rock* 268
*This Is Alice* 245, 246
Thomas, Danny 122–126, 146, 217–220, 222, 237–240, 248–250, 255
*Those Whiting Girls* 146–147, 205
Three Stooges 16, 56

Tibbles, George 131
Todd, Ann 54
Tokar, Norman 213
Tong, Sammee 220, 235
*The Tony Randall Show* 124
*Too Young to Go Steady* 246–247
*Topper* 137–139, 149, 166, 168, 211, 226
Treen, Mary 147
*Trouble with Father* (aka *The Stu Erwin Show*) 35, 49, **53–57**, 58, 62, 67, 69, 76–77, 83–85, 87, 102–103, 105–106, 125, 129, 130, 149, 151, 207, 258
Truex, Ernest 243
*Truth or Consequences* 60, 62–63
*Two and a Half Men* 268
Tyrrell, Ann 99, 243, 250–251

Vance, Vivian 69, 73, 91, 142, 143, 267
Van Dyke, Dick 229; see also *The Dick Van Dyke Show*
*Vic and Sade* 18
Von Zell, Harry 41, 108, 186, 229, 241, 244

Wade, Ernestine 49
Waterman, Willard 191
Waters, Ethel 46–48
Wayne, John 193–194, 196
Webster, Tony 201
Weiskopf, Bob 80, 194, 195, 208, 242, 251
Weld, Tuesday 258, 259, 262
Wesson, Dick 211, 213
*Where's Raymond?* (aka *The Ray Bolger Show*) 122, 146
White, Betty 131, 205–206
White, Jesse 99, 126, 250
Whiting, Margaret 146
Whitman, Ernest 47
Wickes, Mary 118, 160, 204
Williams, Spencer, Jr. 49, 52
*Willy* 147
Wilson, Don 44
Wilson, Dooley 46
Winninger, Charles 191
*WKRP In Cincinnati* 267
Wyatt, Jane 251
Wynn, Ed 18, 246

Yorkin, Bud 163
Young, Alan 158
Young, Robert 151–152, 188, 251
*Young Mr. Bobbin* 80
*Young Sheldon* 270
*Your Show of Shows* 38, 95, 170, 198

Zelinka, Sydney 173

www.ingramcontent.com/pod-product-compliance
Lightning Source LLC
Chambersburg PA
CBHW060337010526
44117CB00017B/2857